Family and Population in
East Asian History

This book is based on a conference sponsored by the joint committees on Chinese Studies and Japanese Studies of the American Council of Learned Societies and the Social Science Research Council. The joint committees are supported by the National Endowment for the Humanities and the Ford Foundation.

Family and Population in East Asian History

Edited by Susan B. Hanley and Arthur P. Wolf

STANFORD UNIVERSITY PRESS
Stanford, California 1985

Stanford University Press
Stanford, California

© 1985 by the Board of Trustees of the
Leland Stanford Junior University

Printed in the United States of America

Library of Congress Cataloging in Publication Data
Main entry under title:

Family and population in East Asian history.

   "Based on a conference sponsored by the joint
committees on Chinese Studies and Japanese Studies of the
American Council of Learned Societies and the Social
Science Research Council."—Half t.p.
   Includes index.
   1. China—Population—History—Congresses. 2. Japan—
Population—History—Congresses. 3. Family—China—His-
tory—Congresses. 4. Family—Japan—History—Congresses.
5. Fertility, Human—China—History—Congresses. 6. Fertil-
ity, Human—Japan—History—Congresses. 7. Marriage age—
China—History—Congresses. 8. Marriage age—Japan—His-
tory—Congresses. I. Hanley, Susan B., 1939–   . II. Wolf,
Arthur P., 1932–   . III. Joint Committee on Chinese Studies
(U.S.) IV. Joint Committee on Japanese Studies.
HB3654.A3F34 1985   304.6'0951   83-40283
ISBN 0-8047-1232-8

Preface

With the exception of the contributions by Arthur P. Wolf and Ansley J. Coale, the papers published here were prepared for a conference convened August 20-25, 1978, at Wadham College, Oxford. The conference was jointly sponsored by several committees of the American Council of Learned Societies and the Social Science Research Council: the Committee on Studies of Chinese Civilization and the Joint Committee on Contemporary China (which merged in 1982 to form the Joint Committee on Chinese Studies), and the Joint Committee on Japanese Studies. In addition to the authors of the papers presented in this volume, the participants included Keith Brown, Michel Cartier, Peter Laslett, Gilbert Rozman, Nariko Saso, Daniel Scott Smith, Kurumi Sugita, Richard Wall, and E. A. Wrigley.

The editors owe a debt of gratitude to their sponsors, who not only financed and helped organize the conference but also contributed to the costs of publication; to Wadham College for the use of its facilities and for its hospitality; to Peter Laslett, Daniel Scott Smith, and E. A. Wrigley, who served as discussants and gave the conference a comparative perspective; to the writers of the papers, who waited patiently to see their conceptions delivered; and to Muriel Bell and J. G. Bell, whose editing of this volume has made our ideas clearer and their expression more attractive.

S.B.H.
A.P.W.

Contents

1. Introduction   1
   Arthur P. Wolf and Susan B. Hanley

2. The Demography of Two Chinese Clans in Hsiao-shan,
   Chekiang, 1650-1850   13
   Ts'ui-jung Liu

3. Samurai Income and Demographic Change: The
   Genealogies of Tokugawa Bannermen   62
   Kozo Yamamura

4. The Rich Get Children: Segmentation, Stratification, and
   Population in Three Chekiang Lineages, 1550-1850   81
   Stevan Harrell

5. Rural Migration and Fertility in Tokugawa Japan: The
   Village of Nishijo, 1773-1868   110
   Akira Hayami

6. Urban Migration and Fertility in Tokugawa Japan: The
   City of Takayama, 1773-1871   133
   Yōichirō Sasaki

7. Fertility in Prerevolutionary Rural China   154
   Arthur P. Wolf

8. Fertility in Rural China: A Reconfirmation of the
   Barclay Reassessment   186
   Ansley J. Coale

9. Family and Fertility in Four Tokugawa Villages   196
   Susan B. Hanley

10. Fertility and Mortality in an Outcaste Village in Japan,
    1750-1869   229
    Dana Morris and Thomas C. Smith

11. Transformations of Commoner Households in Tennōji-
        mura, 1757-1858   247
        Robert J. Smith

12. Marriage among the Taiwanese of Pre-1945 Taipei   277
        Sophie Sa

13. On the Causes and Demographic Consequences of
        Uxorilocal Marriage in China   309
        Burton Pasternak

Notes   337

Index   357

Tables

2. Liu: Two Chekiang Clans

2.1. Number of Members of Various Statuses Recorded in the
Shen Genealogy (1893) and the Hsü Genealogy (1911)   14

2.2. Degree-Holders in the Shen and Hsü Genealogies   19

2.3. Estimated Duration Between First and Second Marriages of
Males in the Shen and Hsü Genealogies   22

2.4. Proportion Single at Each Age Group and Singulate Mean
Age at Marriage for Selected Cohorts of Hsü Clan
Males, 1700-1844   24

2.5. Difference in Age Between Husband and First Wife, Selected
Cohorts of Shen and Hsü Clans, 1650-1804   26

2.6. Number and Proportion of Widows among First Wives in
the Shen and Hsü Clans, 1700-1839   27

2.7. Data Used to Estimate Age-Specific Marital Fertility among
First Wives of the Shen Clan   30

2.8. Marital Age-Specific Fertility and Total Fertility of First
Wives by Cohort, Shen and Hsü Clans, 1680-1829   34

2.9. Marital Age-Specific Fertility and Total Fertility of First
Wives by Period, Shen and Hsü Clans, 1725-1844   37

2.10. Male Age-Specific Fertility Rates for Sons and Gross
Reproductive Rate (GRR) by Cohort, Shen and Hsü
Clans, 1680-1829   40

2.11. Male Age-Specific Fertility Rates for Sons and Gross
Reproductive Rate (GRR) by Period, 1725-1844   42

2.12. Observed Number of Deaths in the Shen Clan by Age and
Cohort   44

2.13. Probability of Dying (q_x) for Females by Age Group and
Cohort, Shen and Hsü Clans, 1680-1829   46

2.14. Probability of Dying (q_x) for Females by Age Group and
Period, Shen and Hsü Clans, 1725-1844   48

2.15. Probability of Dying (q_x) for Males by Age Group and
Cohort, Shen and Hsü Clans, 1680-1829   50

2.16. Probability of Dying (q_x) for Males by Age Group and
      Period, Shen and Hsü Clans, 1725-1844   52
2.17. Life Table Survivorship (l_x) Values for the Shen and Hsü
      Clans for Selected Cohorts and Periods   59
2.18. Intrinsic Rate of Increase (r), Mean Age at Childbearing
      ($\bar{m}$), and Gross Reproductive Rate (GRR) for Selected
      Cohorts and Periods, Shen and Hsü Clans, 1695-1844   60

3. Yamamura: Tokugawa Bannermen

3.1. Stipend Changes of 4,956 Sample Bannermen, 1641-1798   66
3.2. Number of Bannermen and Selected Data on Their Children
     by Cohort Group of Bannermen, 1500-1798   67
3.3. Relative Frequency of Family Sizes by Cohort Group of
     Bannermen, 1500-1798   68
3.4. Relative Frequency of Numbers of Wives by Cohort Group
     of Bannermen, 1500-1798   69
3.5. Number and Percentage of Unmarried Bannermen by
     Stipend Class, 1641-1798   70
3.6. Relative Frequency of Family Sizes of Sample Bannermen by
     Stipend Class, 1641-1798   70
3.7. Number of Children of Selected Bannermen by Stipend
     Class, 1641-1798   71
3.8. Successors of Sample Bannermen by Relationship to Person
     Succeeded, 1641-1798   72
3.9. Yōshi Successors of Sample Bannermen by Stipend Class,
     1641-1798   73
3.10. Zekke by Stipend Class of Sample Bannermen, 1641-1798   74
3.11. Zekke Owing to Misconduct, by Cohort Group of
      Bannermen, 1500-1798   75
3.12. Relative Frequency of Ages at Death by Cohort Group of
      Bannermen, 1500-1798   78
3.13. Age Distribution of Sample Bannermen in 1650, 1695,
      1725, and 1755   79

4. Harrell: Three Chekiang Lineages

4.1. Basic Data Contained in the Ho, Lin, and Wu Genealogies   85
4.2. Ho Lineage: Male Population Index and Holdings by Fang,
     1850   87
4.3. Male Population Index and Its Growth Rate in the Ho, Lin,
     and Wu Lineages, 1550-1850   93
4.4. Ho Lineage: Male Population Index by Fang for Fifty-Year
     Intervals, 1550-1850   94
4.5. Ho Lineage: Annual Growth Rate of Male Population Index
     by Fang, 1550-1850   95
4.6. Lin Lineage: Male Population Index and Its Growth Rate by
     Fang, 1650-1850   96

4.7. Wu Lineage: Male Population Index by Fang for Fifty-Year
Intervals, 1600-1850   96

4.8. Wu Lineage: Annual Growth of Male Population Index by
Fang, 1600-1850   97

4.9. Ho Lineage: Percentage of Degree-Holders by Fang and Age
Cohort, 1500-1850   98

4.10. Spearman Rank-Order Correlations Between Percentage
of Degree-Holders in a Given Fang Born During a
Particular Fifty-Year Period and Various Demographic
Factors   99

4.11 Lin Lineage: Percentage of Degree- and Office-Holders by
Fang and Age Cohort, 1601-1850   100

4.12. Wu Lineage: Percentage of Degree- and Office-Holders by
Fang and Age Cohort, 1601-1850   100

4.13. Ho Lineage: Age of Father at Birth of First Surviving Son by
Fang and Father's Age Cohort, 1551-1850   102

4.14. Lin Lineage: Age of Father at Birth of First Surviving Son by
Fang and Father's Age Cohort, 1601-1850   102

4.15. Wu Lineage: Age of Father at Birth of First Surviving Son by
Fang and Father's Age Cohort, 1601-1850   103

4.16. Lin Lineage: Age of Mother at Birth of First Surviving Son
by Fang and Father's Age Cohort, 1601-1850   104

4.17. Wu Lineage: Age of Mother at Birth of First Surviving Son
by Fang and Men's Age Cohort, 1601-1850   104

4.18. Ho Lineage: Number of Women per Man Brought In to
Reproduce, by Fang and Men's Age Cohort, 1501-1850   105

4.19. Lin Lineage: Number of Women per Man Brought In to
Reproduce, by Fang and Men's Age Cohort, 1601-1850   105

4.20. Wu Lineage: Number of Women per Man Brought In to
Reproduce, by Fang and Men's Age Cohort, 1601-1850   106

4.21. Ho Lineage: Number of Sons per Woman by Fang and
Men's Age Cohort, 1501-1850   107

4.22. Lin Lineage: Number of Sons per Woman by Fang and
Men's Age Cohort, 1601-1850   107

4.23. Wu Lineage: Number of Sons per Woman by Fang and
Men's Age Cohort, 1601-1850   108

5. Hayami: The Village of Nishijo

5.1. Birth and Death Rates for Nishijo by Decade, 1773-1868   112

5.2. Dekasegi Rates by Sex and Landholding Status of
Household, 1773-1869   115

5.3. Percentage of Households Whose Members Went Out on
Dekasegi, 1780, 1820, and 1860   116

5.4. Age at First Dekasegi by Sex, Landholding Status, and
Destination   117

5.5. Distribution of Dekasegi by Sex, Time Period, and
      Destination   117
5.6. Distribution of Urban Dekasegi by Sex, Time Period, and
      Urban Area   120
5.7. Reasons for Terminating Dekasegi   121
5.8. Age at Marriage of Men and Women According to Whether
      Subject Ever Worked Away from Nishijo, 1773-1800
      and 1801-1825 Cohorts   124
5.9. Age-Specific Marital Fertility Rates   124
5.10. Average Number of Births in Completed Families by
      Woman's Age at Marriage   125
5.11. Average Age at Marriage by Landholding Status, 1773-1835
      Cohort   125
5.12. Age-Specific Marital Fertility by Landholding Status   125
5.13. Presence of Heirs by Landholding Status   126
5.14. Distribution of Households by Landholding Status,
      Selected Years, 1780-1869   126

6. Sasaki: The City of Takayama

6.1. Birth, Death, Immigration, and Emigration Data for
      Takayama, 1773-1871   134
6.2. Major Population Indices for Takayama   137
6.3. General and Marital Fertility and Proportions Married in
      Takayama and Two Villages, 1773-1871   139
6.4. Number of Births to Takayama Mothers Aged 15-49 by
      Mother's Place of Birth   141
6.5. Values of m and M for Takayama and Two Villages   144
6.6. General and Marital Fertility and Proportions Married in
      Takayama by Mother's Place of Origin   146
6.7. Data on Owning, Renting, and Migration in Old and New
      Sections of Takayama   148
6.8. Death and Emigration by Sex and Age for Residents of
      Takayama Born in the City Between 1773 and 1796   148
6.9. Immigration to Takayama by Age and Purpose   148
6.10. Reproduction Rates for Takayama by Mother's Age   150
6.11. Birth and Death Rates for Takayama   152

7. Wolf: Fertility in Rural China

7.1. Chinese Farm Survey, 1929-1931: Number of Women by
      Age and Age-Specific Fertility Rates Based on Reported
      Number of Children Born in Year Preceding Survey   157
7.2. Chinese Farm Survey, 1929-1931: Number of Married
      Women by Age and Age-Specific Marital Fertility Rates
      Based on Reported Number of Children Born in Year
      Preceding Survey   158
7.3. Chinese Farm Survey, 1929-1931: Average Number of
      Children Ever Born by Age of Mother   159

7.4. Chinese Farm Survey, 1929-1931: General and Marital
    Fertility Rates of Areas Selected for Analysis by
    Notestein Compared with Rates of All Areas Surveyed   164
7.5. Age-Specific Fertility Rates Estimated by Princeton Group
    on the Basis of the Chinese Farm Survey   165
7.6. Age-Specific Fertility Rates for Hai-shan, Taiwan,
    1906-1945   168
7.7. Age-Specific Marital Fertility Rates for Hai-shan, Taiwan,
    1906-1945   169
7.8. Age-Specific Marital Fertility Rates for Hai-shan, Taiwan,
    by Form of Marriage, 1906-1945   170
7.9. Age-Specific Fertility Rates Based on Retrospective Reports
    by Women Born Between 1896 and 1927 and
    Interviewed in China in 1980-1981   173
7.10. Age-Specific Marital Fertility Rates Based on Retrospective
    Reports by Women Born Between 1896 and 1927 and
    Interviewed in China in 1980-1981   174
7.11. Age-Specific General and Marital Fertility Rates for Chiang-
    yin County, Kiangsu, 1931-1935   176
7.12. Age-Specific Marital Fertility Rates for Hai-shan, Taiwan,
    by Form of Marriage and Number of Surviving Sons,
    1906-1945   178
7.13. Various Chinese Age-Specific Marital Fertility Rates
    Compared with Louis Henry's Natural Fertility Rate   179
7.14. Age-Specific Marital Fertility Rates for Hai-shan, Taiwan,
    by Amount of Land Tax, 1906-1945   182
7.15. Age-Specific Marital Fertility Rates for Hai-shan, Taiwan,
    by Form of Marriage and Amount of Land Tax,
    1906-1945   184

8. Coale: The Barclay Reassessment

8.1. Fertility Rates from Farm Survey Data as Calculated by
    Barclay et al. and from "Natural" Fertility and
    Proportion Married   189

9. Hanley: Four Tokugawa Villages

9.1. Population and Average Household Size in Fujito,
    1775-1863   203
9.2. Population and Average Household Size in Nishikata,
    Numa, and Fukiage for Selected Years, 1683-1871   204
9.3. Frequency Table of Households Headed by Males (Females)
    by Size of Family in Fujito for Selected Years, 1775-1847   205
9.4. Coefficient of Variation for Changes in Family Size over
    Time by Household in Fujito, 1775-1863   206
9.5. Relative Frequency of Households by Family Type in Fujito
    for Selected Years, 1775-1863   209

9.6. Relative Frequency of Persons by Family Type in Fujito for Selected Years, 1775-1863   209

9.7. Percentage of Persons Classified as Elementary and Stem Family Members in Fujito for Selected Years, 1775-1863   210

9.8. Categories of Kinsmen in Fujito for Selected Years, 1775-1863, in Declining Order of Frequency Seen in 1775   211

9.9. Crude Birth and Death Rate Averages for Four Japanese Villages in Selected Periods, 1693-1871   212

9.10. Percentage of Population Composed of Wives of Persons Not in Main Line of Descent for Four Japanese Villages in Selected Years, 1683-1871   213

9.11. Average Number of Households Containing Married Women of Childbearing Age in Four Japanese Villages in Selected Years, 1683-1871   214

9.12. Percentage of Women Married by Age Group for Four Japanese Villages in Selected Years, 1683-1871   215

9.13. Distribution of Completed Family Size in Fujito for Selected Cohort Groups of Families with Children   218

9.14. Distribution of Family Size in Fukiage and Numa at Various Dates, 1773-1871   219

9.15. Sex Ratios of Last-Born Children for Four Japanese Villages in Various Periods, 1693-1871   220

9.16. Average Ages at First and Last Births in Fujito by Cohort Group and Kokudaka Class   221

9.17. Incidence of Adoption Compared to Marriage in Four Japanese Villages for Selected Periods, 1693-1871   222

9.18. Average Number of Children in the Completed Family in Fujito by Cohort Group and Kokudaka Class   224

9.19. Sex Ratios of Children Born in Fujito by Cohort Group and Kokudaka Class of Mother   224

9.20. Incidence of Infant and Child Mortality in Fujito by Kokudaka Class   225

10. Morris and Smith: A Japanese Outcaste Village

10.1. Unexplained Exits and Entries Between Years of Consecutive Registers in Minami Ōji, 1830-1837   233

10.2. Discrepancies in Recorded Ages of Villagers Between 1830 and 1869   233

10.3. Discrepancies in Recorded Ages of Landholding Family Members in 1830   233

10.4. Crude Birth Rates, 1750-1869; and Crude Death Rates, 1830-1869, for Minami Ōji   236

10.5. Rates of Natural and Actual Increase in the Population of Minami Ōji, 1829-1869   236

10.6. Minami Ōji Life Table, 1830-1869   238

10.7. Life Expectancy at Age 0 and Age 10 in Minami Ōji and
       Selected European Parishes   239
10.8. Life Expectancy at Age 1 in Selected Japanese Villages,
       1711-1869   239
10.9. Percentage of Women in Minami Ōji Currently Married at
       Selected Ages, 1830-1869   241
10.10. Age-Specific Marital Fertility in Minami Ōji, 1746-1868   241
10.11. Age-Specific Marital Fertility in Selected Japanese
       Communities During the Tokugawa Period   242
10.12. Age-Specific Marital Fertility in Minami Ōji and Selected
       European Parishes   243

11. Smith: Commoners in Tennōji-mura

11.1. Summary of All Occurrences of Family Form in Tennōji by
       Ward and Household Status for Various Years,
       1757-1858   254
11.2. Summary of All Occurrences of Family Types in Tennōji by
       Ward and Household Status for Various Years,
       1757-1858   255
11.3. Relative Importance of Family Form among Owners'
       Families in Tennōji in Selected Years, 1757-1858   256
11.4. Relative Importance of Family Form among Tenants'
       Families in Tennōji in Selected Years, 1757-1858   257
11.5. Relative Importance of Family Form among All Families in
       Tennōji in Selected Years, 1757-1858   258
11.6. Age of Family Head by Family Form in Tennōji   259
11.7. Ages of Senior and Junior Family Heads of Stem Family
       Forms in Tennōji   260
11.8. Sex of Family Head by Family Form in Tennōji   260
11.9. Family Form by Sex and Marital Status of Family Head in
       Tennōji   262
11.10. Average Size of Household by Family Form in Tennōji   263
11.11. Number of Tennōji Households Having at Least One
       Kinsman or Other Resident of Various Types, by Family
       Form   264
11.12. Categories of Kinsmen in Tennōji Households in Declining
       Order of Frequency   265
11.13. Duration of Family Forms in Tennōji   266
11.14. Number of Independent Occurrences and Duration of
       Family Forms in Tennōji   267
11.15. Transformations of Family Forms in Tennōji: Owners   268
11.16. Transformations of Family Forms in Tennōji: Tenants   270
11.17. Transformations of Family Forms in Tennōji: Owners and
       Tenants   271
11.18. Transformations and Disappearances of Family Forms in
       Tennōji   272

11.19. Recurrences of Family Form Without Transformation in
      Tennōji   274
11.20. Family Form at First Appearance of Family in the Tennōji
      Registers   274

12. Sa: Marriage in Taipei

12.1. Frequency of Household Sizes by Household Status in
      Taipei, January 1, 1906   288
12.2. Frequency of Household Types by Household Status in
      Taipei, January 1, 1906   288
12.3. Frequency of Household Depths in Generations by
      Household Status in Taipei, January 1, 1906   288
12.4. Sex Ratio of the Population of Taipei City, 1896 and
      1905-1946   291
12.5. Frequency of Premarital Pregnancy by Status among Women
      Born 1886-1925 Marrying in Minor Fashion in Taipei   294
12.6. Surname Styles of First-Born Sons of Uxorilocal Marriages
      by Household Status, Taipei Sample, 1906-1945   295
12.7. Proportions of Taiwanese Ever Married by Age and Sex,
      1905-1935   297
12.8. Age Differences Between Husbands and Wives by
      Household Status in Taipei Sample's Major
      Marriages, 1896-1925   298
12.9. Age at Marriage by Household Status for Men in Taipei
      Sample Born 1876-1905   298
12.10. Frequency of Marriage Forms by Husband's Household
      Status and Date of Birth for Men Born or Adopted into
      Sample Taipei Households, 1906-1945   300
12.11. Forms of First Marriage by Household Status for Women
      Born 1886-1925 Who Were Born or Adopted into
      Taipei Sample Households   302
12.12. Sibling Set at Marriage by Household Status for Women
      Born 1876-1925 in Taipei Sample Who Married
      Uxorilocally   302
12.13. Frequency of Marriage Forms by Receiving Household
      Status for Taipei Sample, 1896-1945   304
12.14. Males in Taipei Sample Born 1896-1925 Who Were
      Matched with Foster Sisters, by Household Status   305
12.15. Incidence of Death among Girls in Taipei Sample Matched
      to Boys Born 1896-1925 by Household Status and
      Intended Husband's Year of Birth   306
12.16. Completion Rate of Minor Marriages by Household Status
      for Matched Boys in Taipei Sample Born 1896-1925   307
12.17. Probability of Adoption by Age 15 of Girls in Taipei Sample
      Born 1906-1935 by Household Status and Composition
      of Sibling Set at Birth   307

13. Pasternak: Uxorilocal Marriage in China

13.1. Form of First Marriage by Sex and Birth Cohort in Three
Taiwan Localities   315

13.2. Form of First Marriage in Lung-tu by Sex and Birth Cohort   316

13.3. Uxorilocal Marriages as Mean Percent of All Marriages in
Three Regions of Taiwan, 1908-1919   317

13.4. Form of First Marriage by Sex and Marriage Cohort of
Persons Born 1886-1930 and Raised in Chung-she   318

13.5. First Marriages by Composition of Receiving Family at
Time of Marriage and Form of Marriage of Persons
Born 1886-1930 and Raised in Chung-she   320

13.6. Comparison of Family at Marriage for Major and
Uxorilocal First Marriages of Persons Born 1886-1930
and Raised in Chung-she   320

13.7. Frequency of Widow Remarriage in Chung-she, Hai-shan,
and Lung-tu among Women Born 1856-1920 Whose
Husbands Died Before 1940   322

13.8. Likelihood of Widow Remarriage in Chung-she, 1901-1920
and 1921-1940, for Women Born 1856-1920 Whose
Husbands Died Before 1940 and Who Lived at Least
Three Years After Husband's Death   322

13.9. Frequency of Widower Remarriages in Chung-she and Hai-
shan among Men Born 1856-1920 Whose Wives Died
Before 1940   322

13.10. Form of Marriage by Amount of Land Owned for Chung-
she Villagers Born 1886-1930   323

13.11. Percent of First Marriages Contracted 1901-1940 Ending in
Divorce, by Form of Marriage, in Chung-she, Hai-shan,
and Lung-tu   325

13.12. Frequency of Major and Uxorilocal Intravillage Marriage
among Chung-she Women, All Marriages Initiated
1877-1945   325

13.13. Frequency of Premarital Conception in Major and
Uxorilocal First Marriages of Women Born in Chung-
she 1891-1920   326

13.14. Median Age at First Marriage by Form of Marriage in
Chung-she, Hai-shan, and Lung-tu   326

13.15. Age-Specific Fertility by Form of First Marriage in Lung-tu,
Chung-she, and Hai-shan, ca. 1900-1945   327

13.16. General and Total First Marital Fertility Rates by Form of
First Marriage in Lung-tu, Chung-she, and Hai-shan,
ca. 1900-1945   328

13.17. Frequency of Families with at Least One Adopted Daughter
in Selected Communities in Taiwan and South China in
the 1930's   330

13.18. Percent of Population in Status of Adopted Daughter of Head of Household in Selected Communities in Taiwan and South China in the 1930's — 330

13.19. Number of Adopted Daughters per 100 Unmarried Daughters in Selected Communities in Taiwan and South China — 330

13.20. Probability of Adoption by Sex of Legitimate Children Born in Chung-she and Hai-shan, 1906-1935 — 332

13.21. Death Rates of Children Age 0-4 in Tai-pei Chou and Tai-nan Chou, 1921 — 332

Maps and Figures

Maps

7.1. Eight Regions of China Covered by Buck's Surveys 161
7.2. Hai-shan and Vicinity, Showing Location of the Thirteen
    Districts Included in the Present Study 166
13.1. The Chia-nan Irrigation System 312

Figures

2.1. Total Fertility of First Wives by Cohorts and Periods,
    1690-1840 31
2.2. Age-Specific Marital Fertility Rates of First Wives for Selected
    Cohorts and Periods, 1695-1829 32
2.3. Adjusted Male Age-Specific Fertility Rates in Terms of Sons
    for Selected Cohorts and Periods, 1695-1844 33
2.4. Mortality Curves (q_x) for 1695-1709 Cohorts 53
2.5. Mortality Curves (q_x) for the Period 1830-1844 54
2.6. Excess Male Mortality $(q_x$ Male $/ q_x$ Female), for Selected
    Cohorts and Periods, 1710-1829 55
2.7. Survivorship at Each Age Group (l_x) for Selected Cohorts,
    1695-1829 56
2.8. Life Expectancy at Age 15 (e_{15}) for Selected Cohorts and
    Periods, 1660-1840 57
4.1. The Origin of the Eight Fang of the Ho Lineage 88
4.2. The Ping 6 Fang of the Ho Lineage, Tenth to Fifteenth
    Generations 89
4.3. The Fang of the Lin Lineage 90
4.4. The Fang of the Wu Lineage 91
5.1. Trends of Population and Household Size 111
5.2. Rural Dekasegi by Direction and Distance from Nishijo 118
5.3. Dekasegi from Nishijo by Sex and Destination 119
5.4. Age-Specific Mortality by Dekasegi Experience 122
5.5. Distribution of Age at Marriage for Women Born in Nishijo,
    1773-1840 123

5.6. The Balance of In- and Out-Migration in Three Villages   128
5.7. Dekasegi Destinations for Migrants from Three Villages   129
6.1. The Population of Ichi-no-machi and Ni-no-machi,
        1773-1871   135
6.2. Age Composition of Ichi-no-machi and Ni-no-machi,
        1773-1871   136
6.3. Infant (Age 0) Death Rate in Takayama, 1773-1870   138
6.4. Age-Specific General Fertility, Marital Fertility, and
        Proportions Married for Takayama   140
6.5. Marital Fertility in Takayama and Two Villages   143
6.6. Values of *m* for Takayama and Two Villages   144
6.7. General and Marital Fertility and Proportions Married in
        Takayama by Mother's Place of Origin   147
6.8. Age at Marriage for Females in Takayama and Two Villages   149
6.9. Simulated Population Trends for Takayama under Closed
        Conditions   151
7.1. Premodern Chinese Fertility Rates Compared with Natural
        Fertility Rates   180
8.1. Age-Specific Fertility Rates of Chinese Farmers Compared to
        Rates in Hai-shan and in Preindustrial Europe   190
8.2. Age-Specific Fertility of Chinese Farmers Compared to
        Retrospective Fertility of Wolf's Older Respondents   191
9.1. Population Growth in Four Japanese Villages, Various
        Periods, 1680-1870   199
9.2. Cohort Groups and Kokudaka Classes for Fujito, 1775-1863   208
10.1. The Population of Minami Ōji, 1750-1870   234
10.2. Crude Birth and Death Rates for Minami Ōji   237
11.1. Family Forms and Types   253
12.1. The Wang Family of Bankha   283
12.2. The Li Family of Bankha   284
12.3. The Li Family of Toatotia: 285
13.1. First Uxorilocal Marriages as Percent of All First Marriages
        of Persons Born 1886 and Later and Brought Up in
        Chung-she, by Year of Marriage   319
13.2. Births per Thousand Woman Years, by Form of Marriage,
        Lung-tu (1906-1945), Chung-she (1906-1945), and Hai-
        shan (Women Born 1881-1915)   329

Contributors

Ansley J. Coale, Professor of Economics and Public Affairs, and Associate Director, Office of Population Research, Princeton University.

Susan B. Hanley, Associate Professor of Japanese Studies and History, University of Washington.

Stevan Harrell, Associate Professor of Anthropology, University of Washington.

Akira Hayami, Professor of Economic History, Keio University.

Ts'ui-jung Liu, Fellow of the Institute of American Culture, Academia Sinica.

Dana Morris, Ph.D. in Japanese History, University of California, Berkeley.

Burton Pasternak, Professor of Anthropology, Hunter College of the City University of New York.

Sophie Sa, Executive Director, Matsushita Foundation.

Yōichirō Sasaki, Professor of Economics, Chiba University.

Robert J. Smith, Goldwin Smith Professor of Anthropology, Cornell University.

Thomas C. Smith, Professor of History, University of California, Berkeley.

Arthur P. Wolf, Professor of Anthropology, Stanford University.

Kozo Yamamura, Professor of East Asian Studies and Economics, University of Washington.

Family and Population in
East Asian History

ONE

Introduction

Arthur P. Wolf and Susan B. Hanley

In 1965 John Hajnal set Europe apart from the rest of the world by demonstrating that its pattern of marriage "for at least two centuries up to 1940 was . . . unique or almost unique."[1] The distinctive features of what Hajnal termed "the European pattern" were a high age at marriage and a high proportion of people who never married at all. To the west of a line running roughly from Leningrad to Trieste, many women failed to marry and in some countries the average age for those who did marry was as high as 25 to 27; to the east of this line (and, in Hajnal's view, in the rest of the world), marriage was universal for women and the average age was commonly as low as 17 or 18.

Was Europe (by which Hajnal means Western Europe) really unique in the strong sense of being the single representative of a type of society? Or did it merely occupy an extreme position on a graduated scale? And if it was in fact only an extreme case of a condition that varied by degrees, where did China and Japan stand on the scale? Were there significant differences between them? And if so, what do these differences suggest about the causes and consequences of Hajnal's "European pattern"? Though most of the papers collected in this volume focus on some aspect of a particular Chinese or Japanese community, it is with respect to such general questions as these that they ought to be read. Taken together, they argue that as much is to be learned by a comparison of China and Japan as by a comparison of Western and Eastern Europe. Malthus was rarely so entirely wrong as when he argued that "the state of Japan resembles in so many respects that of China, that a particular consideration of it would lead into many repetitions."[2]

Though Hajnal made age at marriage and proportions marrying the central characteristics of his two demographic regimes, he suggested that they might be linked with other aspects of family life. In Western Europe people could not marry until they had established an income adequate to

support an independent family, which often meant that the marriages of
the junior generation had to wait on the death or retirement of the senior
generation. In Eastern Europe and elsewhere newly married couples joined
established domestic units, and thus there was no need to delay marriage
for economic reasons. Consequently, "a system of large estates with large
households as in Eastern Europe might be conducive to a non-European
marriage pattern, while small holdings occupied by a single family and
passed on to a single heir would result in the European pattern."[3]

Hajnal foresaw the possibility that departures from the European marriage pattern might be found "not only as one proceeds eastward but on
the southern edge of Europe as well,"[4] and in fact there is now evidence
that women in Tuscany, Malta, Sicily, and Iberia usually married before
age 20.[5] But with the exception of these forays against an admittedly weak
southern flank, Hajnal's line has stood strong against an onslaught of new
evidence. A mass of reconstitution studies from England, France, Belgium,
Germany, and Scandinavia have only served to solidify his position, and he
has gained important new support from historical research in Greater Russia and the Baltic provinces. Where the mean age at marriage for women in
1780-1820 was 27.9 in Belgium, 24.2 in England, 26.7 in France, 27.5
in Germany, and 29.8 in Scandinavia,[6] the singulate mean age at marriage
among women on the Mishino estate in Central Russia never rose above
19.0 in the years 1782-1858 and fell to 17.6 in 1782 and 16.6 in 1858.[7]

There is also increasingly impressive evidence of a relationship between
age at marriage and family organization, but this only becomes apparent
when Hajnal's comments are reformulated to take account of the discovery
that inheritance patterns and family complexity are not linked. Impartible
inheritance is generally associated with stem families (as LePlay's definition suggested), but partible inheritance does not create a characteristic
form of the family. In Greater Russia and the Balkans partible inheritance
was associated with a high frequency of joint families, whereas in Lower
Saxony it favored an unusually high frequency of elementary families.[8] We
will therefore ignore inheritance and define what we call family systems
with respect to composition alone. In what we term the stem family system
one child and one child only remains at home after marriage; in the alternative grand family system two or more children remain after marriage,
creating a joint family or what we prefer to call a grand family. Under the
first regime the most complex family form to emerge in the course of the
developmental cycle consists of an elderly couple and their married son
and his wife and children; under the second, a family can achieve a membership of twenty to thirty people if the senior couple manages to raise
three or four sons and see them all marry. However, it is important to note
that a high frequency of such complex forms is not necessary for a system

to qualify as grand. All we require is that when people manage to raise a number of children, two or more of the children marry and remain with their parents for a few years. The actual frequency of grand families in a grand family system varies widely depending on fertility, mortality, age at marriage, and timing of family division.

Though this is not the place to review the evidence (and we are not the people to do it), it appears that Western Europe was dominated by a stem family system and Eastern Europe by a grand family system. With the notable exception of tenant farmers in the Nivernais,[9] there is no evidence of grand families west of the Hajnal line since medieval times. The debate that has added spice to family history in Western Europe has been concerned, not with the frequency of grand families, but with the frequency of stem families, which appear large and complex in the Western European context.[10] Scholars whose interests fall east of the Hajnal line show little interest in the frequency of stem families. For them the question is whether or not such grand family specimens as the *zadruga* and the *dvor* were as large and as common as traditionalists would like to believe.[11] Though the evidence brought to light in recent years says they were not, it also says that the grand family system was the family system of most of Eastern Europe. The most striking evidence comes from Russia, where the reality appears to have fallen only a little short of the myth. Peter Czap shows that "in 1811, 68 percent of all households [on the Mishino estate] contained married brothers living together with a parent, coresident brothers without the parent living (*frereches*), or coresident brothers living as nephews of the head."[12]

Thus it may not have been the appeal of alliteration alone that led Hajnal to take Belgium/Bulgaria and Sweden/Serbia as prototypical of the contrast between European and non-European marriage patterns.[13] Belgium and Sweden are in the north of Europe, where grand families were completely unknown; in the region of Bulgaria and Serbia the grand family system has held sway since at least the fourteenth century. In other words, we are suggesting that Hajnal's comparison of marriage patterns is part of a larger contrast of family systems. In the west of Europe and particularly in the northwest, marriage was late, celibacy was common, and the family system was stem; in the east of Europe and perhaps also in the southwest, marriage was early, celibacy was rare, and the family system was grand.

We make this point here because taken together the papers collected in this volume suggest that the contrast between Western and Eastern Europe may have an East Asian parallel. From the global perspective necessary to see such broad patterns, it appears that China is to Japan as Eastern is to Western Europe. Consider first the Chinese and Japanese family systems. Although Hanley's paper shows that grand families were not un-

known in Japan, it is clear that the Japanese family system was a stem system of the Western European type. Looking for a comparison to help
elucidate the Japanese system, Robert Smith turns not to the Chinese or
the Koreans but to the Basques. For both the Japanese and the Basques the
paradigmatic domestic group is "three-generational with a senior married
couple, a junior married couple, and the unmarried offspring of both. In
any generation siblings of the heir who fail to marry retain a right to continued residence. . . . Siblings who marry are required to leave the domestic group." [14]

Although the size and complexity of the Chinese family has been de-
bated for nearly forty years, no one has ever seriously suggested that the
system was other than a grand system. Those who argue that grand families were rare among Chinese peasants give demographic reasons. [15] Everyone seems agreed that under favorable demographic conditions, the Chinese family system produces large, complex families that closely resemble
the Serbian *zadruga* and the Russian *dvor*. A sinologist reading Peter
Czap's account of family structure on the Mishino estate is not amazed to
discover that 128 families included 50 sisters-in-law of the head and 110
daughters-in-law. [16] Yuzuru Okada's 1936 survey of 148 farm families in
northern Taiwan lists 31 sisters-in-law and 150 daughters-in-law. [17] The
system that seems foreign to the sinologist is the Japanese. In his paper in
this volume Robert Smith examines the composition of the 5,214 households that appear in the annual registers of an administrative unit called
Tennōji-mura. He finds only 263 daughters-in-law and no sisters-in-law.

The difference between the Chinese and Japanese marriage patterns is
not as marked as the East/West contrast in Europe, but it is substantial and
stands in the same relation to the two family systems. In her paper in this
volume Ts'ui-jung Liu analyzes two Chinese genealogies covering the years
1650 to 1850. Her calculations place women's mean age at first marriage
somewhere between 16.1 and 16.8. As she notes, this is somewhat lower
than the estimates given by John Lossing Buck's 1929-31 survey of 46,601
farm families. A recent reanalysis of the Buck data yields a singulate mean
age at marriage of 18.3 for the Lower Yangtze region, 17.5 for the North
China Plain, 17.8 for 30 localities scattered across South China, and 17.2
for seven localities in Shensi and Shansi in the northwest. [18] Since by 1930
many young women in the Lower Yangtze were delaying marriage to work
in factories in Shanghai and Wu-hsi, the estimate from this region can be
set aside as the product of a new regime. Thus Liu's estimates and those
based on the farm survey are not far apart and suggest a premodern mean
age at marriage of approximately 17.0.

Noting that in 1920, 31 percent of all Japanese women aged 20-24 remained unmarried, Hajnal comments: "If we had statistics going further

back in time (e.g. for nineteenth-century Japan) the contrast with Europe might well be greater." [19] In fact, the evidence collected by our authors suggests that Japanese women have always married at a relatively late age. The seven communities described in this volume are representative of the situation in Japan in the seventeenth and eighteenth centuries. They are Fujito, a farming village in Okayama that became involved in the cotton industry at an early date; Fukiage, a fishing village on the Inland Sea; Numa, a landlocked farming village with little opportunity for economic expansion; Nishikata, a farming village on an important road near Mikawa Bay; Nishijo, a farming village near Nagoya in an area in which the textile industry was well-developed; Takayama, a small city in Hida province; and Minami Ōji, an outcaste village near the port of Kishiwaka on Ōsaka Bay. Our authors tell us that the mean age at first marriage in these communities was 23.3 in Fujito, 23.4 in Fukiage, 25.5 in Numa, 23.4 in Nishikata, 24.0 in Nishijo, 21.8 for natives of Takayama and 26.3 for the immigrants who made up 62.7 percent of the population, and 17.6 in Minami Ōji. Thus it was only in the outcaste village, a village with a number of other special characteristics, that age at marriage was below 20.

Since "a non-European pattern implies that the mean age for marriage of single women is below 21 [and] according to the European pattern the mean age for the marriages of single women must be above 23," [20] China is non-European but Japan is European. The difference between the Chinese and the Japanese is not as great as that between Russian serfs and Irish farmers, but it is in the range of five to six years, which is not insignificant. There is, however, more to the contrast than is evident in these estimates of age at marriage. Although female infanticide was common in some parts of China in difficult times, there is no evidence that the Chinese ever tried to limit the number of sons they raised and hence the size of the household. On the contrary, the Chinese attitude was always the more sons the better. Arthur Wolf shows that even if they had five surviving sons, farmers on Taiwan did not attempt to limit their fertility.

In Japan, in sharp contrast, infanticide and abortion were commonplace, not only as a response to natural and social catastrophes, but as "a kind of family planning with long-range objectives." [21] This is evident in the small size of completed families, the early age at which women bore their last child, the concave trajectory of age-specific fertility, parity-specific sex ratios, and the comments of contemporary observers. Of the seven Japanese communities that figure in our authors' analyses of fertility, only Minami Ōji, the outcaste village studied by Dana Morris and Thomas C. Smith, fails to show evidence of deliberate birth control, and it was "socially as deviant a community as we are likely to find." For most of the Tokugawa communities studied to date, there is good evidence that family

planning, including both abortion and infanticide, was widely practiced
and even accepted as a way of life.[22] This was true not only in farming villages but also in small cities like Takayama, and not only among farmers
and fishermen but also among the bannermen who were the mainstay of
the Japanese bureaucracy, as Kozo Yamamura shows.

As Ruth Dixon's comparison of 57 countries demonstrates, Japan and
the Ryukyu Islands share an unusual marriage pattern.[23] Almost everyone
marries, but, compared with other countries with nearly universal marriage, people marry late. The reason for this is that the Japanese (and, de-
rivatively, the Ryukyuans) have a long and well-established tradition of re-
sponding to changed economic circumstances by varying their age at
marriage as well as by terminating unwanted pregnancies. In her study of
four villages undergoing different kinds of economic change, Susan Hanley
shows that age at first marriage falls when times are good and rises when
times are bad.[24] Her work and that of others indicates that Japanese farmers made whatever adjustments were necessary to preserve the family farm
and promote the family's status.[25] It was only in villages like Minami Ōji,
in which the primary source of income was wage labor, that demographic
behavior was not tightly constrained by economic and social calculations.

In sum, it appears that where Western European families limited their
fertility by a combination of late marriage and celibacy, the Japanese accomplished the same end by a combination of late marriage and deliberate
birth control. Thus if the comparison is cast in terms of "preventative
checks" rather than marriage customs, we can say that the Japanese have
long conformed to Hajnal's European pattern while the Chinese have remained resolutely non-European. Though it remains to be shown how this
difference relates to the parallel differences in family systems, it is surely no
accident that the stem family system ruled in Western Europe and Japan,
the grand family system in Eastern Europe and China. Our best guess is
that the critical link is parental authority. Where parents can command the
labor of most of their adult children, they adopt a strongly pronatalist policy that encourages early marriage and high fertility; where they cannot
control their children or can control only the one child who inherits, they
adopt a more conservative policy that aims at preserving resources rather
than expanding their labor force.

Whatever the merits of our Asian version of the Hajnal hypothesis, one
aspect of the argument is beyond doubt: China and Japan were very different countries. The evidence presented here shows that they differed not
only as regards age at marriage and family composition, but also as regards the relationship between fertility and social status. Taken together,
the papers by Yamamura, Hanley, Hayami, Sasaki, and Morris and Smith
show that in Japan the relationship between status and fertility was negative, the bannermen at the top of the system having fewer children (despite

multiple wives) than the outcastes at the bottom of the system. But if in Japan (as in the West) the poor got children, the opposite was true in China, as the papers by Stevan Harrell and Arthur Wolf demonstrate. Whether the comparison is in terms of the amount of land tax paid, the size of lineage estates, or success in the examination system, the relationship between fertility and social status is always positive: people with land and prestige produced more children than their landless, nameless neighbors.

The Japanese demographic regime appears to make sense. Marriage was universal but relatively late, and fertility was controlled by the most fecund portion of the population. Consequently, population growth was kept within tolerable bounds. But what of the Chinese regime? Why didn't the combination of early and universal marriage and a strongly pronatalist attitude among all classes stimulate rapid growth and eventually demographic disaster? In a paper reporting a careful reassessment of John Lossing Buck's farm survey data, Ansley J. Coale and his Princeton colleagues (hereafter the Princeton group) suggest that it is characteristic of systems like the Chinese to exhibit low marital fertility. As the Princeton group put it, "There is reason to expect long established traditions of early and universal marriage to exert a moderating influence on marital fertility. The alternative would be a growth of population so rapid that it could not be indefinitely sustained." [26] Thus we have the element of marital fertility added to Hajnal's oppositions. Late marriage and a high celibacy rate allow high marital fertility, whereas early marriage and a low celibacy rate enforce low marital fertility.

Although the Princeton group suggests that poor health, poor nutrition, and prolonged breastfeeding may have kept marital fertility to a low level in China, they do not show how these conditions were related to early and universal marriage. Their argument rests entirely on the fact that the Buck data indicate a low level of fertility. But are the Buck data reliable? Was Chinese marital fertility really only half that of the Hutterites? This is where the papers in this volume enter the debate. In an important methodological contribution as well as a provocative analysis of Ch'ing demography, Ts'ui-jung Liu uses data drawn from two genealogies to evaluate the Princeton group's claims. Her conclusion is that "the population of late traditional China was characterized by high (and probably increasing) mortality, nearly universal marriage, and surprisingly low marital fertility." [27] Wolf disagrees. He rejects the view that Chinese marital fertility was "very low" as implausible and unfounded. It is implausible, he argues, because the Chinese wanted many children and made no effort to control fertility, and unfounded because the estimates from the Buck study are much lower than those provided by more reliable sources.

Ansley Coale's paper was written in response to Wolf's critique of the

Princeton's group's use of the Farm Survey data. Coale clarifies the procedures employed in extracting fertility estimates from the Buck data and
then elaborates on the reasons why moderate fertility is to be expected in a
population with early and nearly universal marriage. Where Wolf argues
that Chinese customs were motivated by the desire to produce as many
children as possible, Coale holds that Chinese customs were selected to
keep fertility at a moderate level. The difference between the two views is
most strikingly evident in the authors' interpretation of the relationship
between fertility and minor marriages on Taiwan. In reply to Wolf's argument that the low fertility of minor marriages was an unintended and unwanted consequence of raising a son's wife, Coale suggests that this form
of marriage represented a class of customs whose primary purpose was to
check fertility. Thus the disagreement about the level of fertility in premodern China appears to reflect a more fundamental disagreement about
the origins of customs that affect fertility. Wolf expects high fertility in
China because he assumes that customs are responsive to the goals of individual actors; Coale expects moderate fertility because he assumes that
customs serve the aggregate good.

One of the major problems scholars face in resolving issues like this is
the great diversity they find in China. The horizontal divisions that create
distinctive social layers are cross-cut by vertical divisions that reflect regional differences in culture and environment. The significance of this
source of variation is noted by all the papers in this volume, but the problem is addressed directly only in Burton Pasternak's study of uxorilocal
marriage in China. Comparing three forms of marriage across three Taiwanese communities, Pasternak shows that the interaction between marriage, local tradition, and demography is intricately complex. Not only
does fertility vary by form of marriage and the frequency of the three
forms of marriage by locality, but more than this, the effects of the three
forms of marriage are not the same in all three localities. This is not to
deny the influence of such general features of the Chinese kinship system as
its tendency to form grand families, but it does warn against taking the
demography of a locality as representative of anything more than the
forces operating in that locality. There is a China, but it is a China that
displays many facets.

The point is underlined and another level of complexity added by Sophie
Sa's analysis of marriage and adoption customs in Taipei City. Sa compares
the marriage choices made by representatives of three distinct social strata:
the educated elite, shopkeepers and petty merchants, and the urban pro-
letariat. No one will be surprised to learn that the choices made by these
three strata differed, and that the differences are largely attributable to the
costs and prestige of the options. The surprise is that Sa finds less variation

between social strata in one locality than other researchers find between localities. A wealthy merchant in Taipei was less likely to choose to raise his son's wife than a shopkeeper or a coolie, but he was far more likely to choose this form of marriage than a tenant farmer in southern Taiwan. This suggests that the vertical divisions in Chinese society cut deeper than the horizontal divisions. It follows that treating people as primarily motivated by personal advantage may help explain variation within a local tradition but does not help explain variation across local traditions.

Sa's paper also helps us to see the significance of rural as against urban conditions. Her comparison of the types of households formed by the three social strata included in the study shows that grand families were common among the elite and rare among the middle and lower classes. Taken at face value, this appears to affirm the widely held view that there were two versions of the Chinese family, a "poor version," in which the developmental cycle alternated between elementary and stem phases, and a "rich version," in which a grand phase was dominant.[28] But this simple dichotomy is confounded when we compare Sa's Taipei study with the results of Wolf's research in nine farming villages in Hai-shan, a few miles southwest of Taipei. Though more than half of these villagers were tenant farmers, farm laborers, or odd-jobbers, grand families were far more common in Hai-shan than they were among Sa's middle- and lower-status urbanites. In 1906, grand families accounted for 23.3 percent of all families in Hai-shan as compared with 3.7 percent among Sa's lower-status families, 9.3 percent of her middle-status families, and 42.0 percent of her high-status families.[29] One does not want to minimize the significance of social class in a complex society like China, but it must be understood that class divisions were cross-cut by other cleavages that were as deep and as abiding. The situation of a poor man in a village in one region cannot be directly compared to that of a poor man in a nearby city or a poor man in another village in another region.

Comparison is easier for Tokugawa Japan because it was smaller and more nearly uniform than China, but it was nonetheless a complex society in which vital rates varied by social class and from country to city. Thus one of the primary goals of the Japanese papers in this volume is to discover how movement across these social barriers affected the behavior of the people on either side. The stimulating analyses offered by Akira Hayami and Yōichirō Sasaki converge on one essential point: migration from the country to the city reduced the rate of natural increase in both areas. Regardless of whether migrants returned home or remained in the city, their mortality was higher than that of people who stayed in the country; and the fertility of both migrants and urbanites was lower than that of rural residents, in part because of reduced marital fertility and in part because of delayed marriage and a strikingly higher divorce rate. With the demand for labor in developing cities like Takayama creating conditions that served to break and then reduce the rate of natural increase, economic development in central Japan in the eighteenth and early nineteenth centuries was accompanied not by population growth but by stagnation.

The effects of migration are also clearly evident in Robert J. Smith's analysis of the developmental cycle of commoner households in Tennōji-mura. Although the cycle followed by both owner and tenant families can be roughly characterized by an oscillation between elementary and stem types, Tennōji-mura's families were unusually small and included a surprisingly large number of solitaries—17.5 percent of the 5,214 families that appear in the annual registers. This is almost certainly due at least in part to the fact that Tennōji had for centuries been a satellite of Ōsaka. Its families were small and fragmented because its population was composed largely of migrants who came individually or in nuclear families and did not remain in the village very long. "Only 13 of the 1,095 separate households that resided in these wards between 1757 and 1858 were present for the entire period."

The effects of movement are also central to Kozo Yamamura's analysis of the genealogies of Tokugawa bannermen, but Yamamura is concerned with social rather than geographical mobility. His paper establishes and then explains the fact that during the years 1500-1740, the fertility of bannermen declined steadily and to a surprisingly low level. This was partly because more and more of the bannermen's constant income was spent on an increasing supply of consumer goods, but it was also a result of dwindling opportunities for social mobility. By the early seventeenth century, there was little chance of a younger son's being appointed a bannerman himself and hence little chance of his adding appreciably to the family income. Thus the bannerman who raised a large family had to choose between supporting his younger sons himself and scrambling to arrange their adoption by families of acceptable rank. Worse yet, since the limitation on appointments created a highly competitive marriage market, he had either to provide handsome dowries for his daughters or to marry them to men of lesser rank.

All these analyses remind us of European parallels that renew confidence in the argument while raising questions about how widely the assumptions apply. Yamamura's analysis of declining fertility among the Tokagawa bannermen has a clear parallel in Louis Henry's pioneering study of the Genevan bourgeoisie.[30] Both groups experienced a fertility decline that appears to be the result of deliberate birth control, and in both cases this decline was accompanied by shrinking economic opportunities that made it difficult to raise many children and provide them all with the means of maintaining high status. Yet if changed economic circumstances motivated the fertility decline in these cases, why did similar circumstances not have the same effect on the Chinese elite? Studies conducted as late as the 1930's show that well-educated couples in China had as many or more children than couples with little or no education.[31] Did the Chinese elite somehow avoid the hard choices faced by the Tokugawa bannermen and the Genevan bourgeoisie? Or did they choose differently because the family system put a higher value on children? This is one of the questions that must be addressed.

Another concerns the relationship between urban conditions, economic development, and population growth. Sasaki's discovery that the city of Takayama could not have maintained itself without rural recruits has many European parallels. Indeed, it has been claimed that "West European cities went through much or all of their evolution with a negative replacement rate."[32] Thus evidence from the opposite ends of the Eurasian continent appears to confirm the view that cities were population sinks draining away the growth stimulated by economic development.[33] But we must be cautious. Not only were European travelers who knew from experience the condition of Europe's cities impressed with the quality of life in such Chinese metropolises as Hangchow, Soochow, and Nanking, but there is also evidence that Kyoto and Edo were more spacious, were better drained, and enjoyed better sanitation than their European counterparts. Thus it could be that Takayama is only representative of Japanese centers of a certain size and condition: i.e., that it cannot be taken as representative of Japanese cities in general, let alone Chinese cities. The very fact that Hangchow and Edo were far larger than European cities of their day suggests that urban life in Asia was less hazardous than it was in Europe.

We have introduced the papers published here by striking broad comparisons between Asia and Europe because we would like to see them read as contributions to historical demography. The Asian field lags far behind the European field and has much to learn from it, but we believe that in time the Asian field will repay its debt by providing a fresh perspective on European developments. Though the premises that support them are largely speculative, the questions that appear the most interesting at present concern the causes and consequences of grand and stem family systems. Suppose for the moment that grand and stem family systems are shown to give rise to what might be termed pro- and anti-natalist strategies. The next question will be why we find stem family systems in Western Europe and Japan and grand family systems in Eastern Europe and China. We have suggested that the key to the problem is the ability of parents to control their adult offspring, but why should parental authority vary among agrarian societies? Recalling Marcel Granet's suggestion that "parental authority" is derived from "lordly authority,"[34] we hazard the guess that the critical institutions were the European manor and the Chinese state. The European lord supported parents because it was in his interest as well as theirs to discourage family division; Chinese law supported parents because Confucian thought made parental authority the basis of all authority.

The question of the consequences of stem and grand family systems takes us back where we began, to John Hajnal. After arguing that late marriage may allow for the accumulation of savings and thereby stimulate a demand for goods other than those needed for immediate survival, he continues:

In this respect delayed marriage may be similar to income inequality in stimulating the diversion of resources to ends other than those of minimum subsistence; but when later marriage is the norm the total volume of demand generated might be much larger than that which can be caused by a small class of wealthy families in a population at subsistence level. Could this effect, which was uniquely European, help to explain how the ground-work was laid for the uniquely European "take-off" into modern economic growth?[35]

Having seen that the European marriage pattern is not unique, we are led to wonder about the source of Japan's economic "take-off." Could it be that similar marriage patterns explain why northwestern Europe and Japan led their regions in economic development? And if this is so, might it not be that one of the preconditions for modern economic development is a stem family system?

TWO

The Demography of Two Chinese Clans in Hsiao-shan, Chekiang, 1650-1850

Ts'ui-jung Liu

In a previous study of genealogies from Taiwan, I found that despite certain defects Chinese genealogies can be made to yield data valuable to historical demography.[1] In this paper I shall investigate two genealogies from Hsiao-shan county in Chekiang on the China mainland with a view to seeing, among other things, how well they fit the Princeton group's controversial reinterpretation of John Lossing Buck's famous 1929-33 survey of Chinese farm families. In the Princeton group's view, "The demographic picture that emerges is of a population with high mortality, low marital fertility, and a rate of increase little different from zero, characteristics that were of sufficient persistence to have generated a stable age distribution."[2] Do the data from Chinese genealogies support this picture of the demography of premodern China?

Sources

The genealogies I employ are the *Hsiao-shan Ch'ang-hsiang Shen-shih tsung-p'u*, published in 1893 by the Shen clan of Hsiao-shan, and the *Hsiao-shan T'ang-wan Ching-t'ing Hsü-shih tsung-p'u*, published in 1911 by the Hsü clan of Hsiao-shan. Both genealogies had been revised several times before these editions were published. The Shen genealogy was compiled in 1408 and revised in 1526, 1673, and 1841; the original Hsü genealogy covers eleven generations and was updated in 1789 by a member of the thirteenth generation. The information concerning later generations was probably added when new prefaces were appended in 1805, 1820, 1836, 1859, and 1911. The attention the two clans devoted to their genealogies suggests that they are exemplary products of the rules governing their genre. To exploit them the demographer must discover what these rules were and how best to translate the data they provide.

The rules governing the treatment of males who died young are particularly important. In general, boys who died before reaching seven *sui* were

TABLE 2.1

Number of Members of Various Statuses Recorded in the Shen Genealogy (1893) and the Hsü Genealogy (1911)

SHEN

Generation	Male (1)	Marr. male & 1st wife (2)	Second wife (3)	Third wife (4)	Fourth wife (5)	Concubine (6)	No. of sons (7)	No. of daughters (8)	Male d. young (9)	Unmarried male d. −50 (10)	Unmarried male d. 50+ (11)	Marital status unknown (12)
18	8	8	1	1			26	11	1			
19	27	25	10	1		3	63	31	4			1
20	61	54	13	3		2	119	45	6			3
21	124	89	13	1		2	165	64				29
22	63	41	6	1	1		91	2				22
23	85	57	7	3	1	2	80	2	1			27
24	102	95	20	4	3	11	157	12		1	1	6
25	162	128	29	5	3	20	208	11	4	3	1	28
26	274	225	32	4	0	22	418	21		3	2	44
27	452	366	39	12	1	26	686	49	8	7		75
28	702	547	78	10	2	29	978	126	18	14	3	127
29	962	673	111	11	2	30	1,195	256	51	18	9	215
30	1,206	895	147	7	1	44	1,583	476	70	53	8	215
31	1,583	1,019	130	4	0	28	1,659	610	127	75	7	377
32	1,668	968	113	7	2	17	1,603	616	145	58	13	467
33	1,461	640	62	1			739	364	70	16	5	688
34	749	153	12				144	63	48	7		532
35	124	28	1				12	14	6			83
36	8	1										7
TOTAL	9,821	6,012	824	75	16	236	9,926	2,773	559	255	49	2,946

1	1						?					
2	1						2					
3	2	1					5					
4	5	2	3	1			10					1
5	10	4	2	1			34					1
6	39	9	6	3			83					
7	77	38	12	2			152	1				6
8	129	70	10	5		1	209	9	1			8
9	186	115	20	1		3	310	44	1	1		14
10	300	164	28	3		3	491	136	6	21		20
11	478	271	59	5		6	641	249	8	60		21
12	602	403	71	11	1	7	773	380	18	80	15	8
13	738	480	87	5	3	15	815	365	25	92	29	68
14	789	562	58	1	1	12	749	239	10	55	18	135
15	740	532	34	1		2	597	108	20	25	10	273
16	577	426	22			4	305	44	18	5	4	294
17	302	255	8			5	90	3	1	3	2	215
18	89	82					5					75
19	5	11										5
TOTAL	5,070	3,425	420	40	5	58	5,271	1,578	116	342	78	1,143

neglected entirely, whereas those aged eight to 19 sui were entered in the
genealogy classified as *hsia-shang*, *chung-shang*, or *chang-shang*. In fact,
however, these particular genealogies do not always follow these rules. The
Shen genealogy says that in the earlier generations males who died young
were commonly thrown together under the label *tsao-shih* ("died young")
because the old records precluded greater precision, and the Hsü genealogy tells us that boys who died before reaching 15 sui were not entered at
all unless they were married.[3] All we can be certain of is that males who
died as infants and small children were not given a place in their clan genealogy, and are therefore lost to the demographer as well as to the clan.

To estimate the fertility of the Shen and Hsü clans I have applied the
family reconstitution procedures used in the analysis of parish records
in western Europe. Since this method requires linking children to their
mothers, it is important to note that despite frequent male adoption and
polygyny among the wealthy, Chinese genealogies do identify the mothers
of most male (but not female) children. Instances of adoption are clearly
noted because of the strong interest in descent, and the male offspring of
polygynous families are usually linked with their own mothers.[4] Problems
arise only when the first of two or more wives fails to bear a male child.
Under these conditions the male offspring of a concubine may be listed as
the son of the first wife. Since concubines are only noted in a clan genealogy if they produce male descendants, the appearance of a concubine who
has not borne a son may be taken as evidence of such a transfer. The
woman has had to surrender her son to the fist wife but has not lost her
status as the mother of a clansman.

The format of the Shen and Hsü genealogies is simple. The names of the
male members are listed generation by generation, and for each member
the genealogy notes his birth and death dates and, if relevant, the names
and dates of his wives, the number of sons borne by each wife, and the
sons' names. The number of daughters is sometimes noted but not consistently, and daughters' names are never given. Unfortunately, many birth
and death dates are missing because they were not known to the compilers,
but we must not allow this to discourage us from exploiting these sources.
Whatever their defects (and they are many), genealogies like those compiled by the Shens and Hsüs are almost the only source we have for reconstructing China's demographic history.

Table 2.1 describes the populations recorded in the Shen and Hsü genealogies. Both contain nineteen generations, the Shen compilation beginning
with the eighteenth generation of the Shen descent line and the Hsü with
the founding generation of that line. The earliest birth noted in the Shen
genealogy is that of an eighteenth-generation member born in 1380; the

earliest birth recorded in the Hsü genealogy is that of a fourth-generation member born in 1458. Columns 1 through 12 list by generation the number of males born, their wives and concubines (with wives classified by the order of the husband's marriage), their sons and daughters, and the number of men who died young or unmarried or whose marital status is unknown. These are the major segments of the population that is the subject of the following analysis.

Though it might be rewarding to compare the demography of the component parts of the Shen and Hsü clans (that is, the lineages and their branches), I have not attempted such a comparison in this paper. Moreover, the small numbers and inadequate data have forced me to confine my analysis to persons born between 1650 and 1849 for whom a birth date is given: 4,115 males and 2,380 females from the Shen clan, and 2,965 males and 2,047 females from the Hsü clan. This amounts to approximately half the men and women named in the two genealogies. In the analysis that follows these people are organized into 40 five-year birth cohorts. I present the data in terms of birth cohorts rather than in terms of genealogical generations because generations overlap and thus distort temporal change.

Social Context

The Shen and Hsü clans have lived for centuries in Hsiao-shan, a county located southeast of Hangchow along the bank of the Ch'ien-t'ang River. It was during the Northern Sung dynasty that the first member of the Shen clan, a man named Heng, settled in Hsiao-shan. Heng was a native of Ch'ang-hsiang-li, a place near Soochow, and no doubt for that reason named the community he founded Ch'ang-hsiang-li. Though poverty was a common motive for migration in traditional China, Heng and his descendants in Hsiao-shan were not impoverished refugees. On the contrary, the Hsiao-shan branch of the Shen clan was long known as a "prominent lineage" (*wang-tsu*). Heng, a member of the fourth generation, earned his *chin-shih* degree in 1034, and one of his descendants, a member of the fifth generation, earned another degree in 1073.[5] After the sixth generation, however, the fortunes of the clan declined, and it is said that they devoted themselves to farming. There is no further evidence of success in the examination stalls until the early Ch'ing period, six hundred years later.

The Hsü clan traces its descent to a man named Hsü Shih, a chin-shih of 1012, but the Hsiao-shan branch of the clan was founded by a man named Pen-i, said to be a fifteenth-generation descendant of Hsü Shih. It is not clear when Pen-i was born, but it was recorded that during the early Ming period he moved to Hsiao-shan from his native Shan-yin to avoid a population census ordered by the founding emperor. Unlike Shen Heng, who

came to Hsiao-shan as the holder of a prestigious chin-shih degree, Hsü
Pen-i came as a kind of male bride. The records tell us that he married
uxorilocally into a family surnamed Wen.[6]

Despite the great differences in the social circumstances attending their
move to Hsiao-shan, the social gap between the Shens and the Hsüs appears to have largely disappeared by the beginning of the Ch'ing period.
By then the Shens had regained something of their former eminence, and
the Hsüs had overcome their lowly origin and established themselves as a
prominent lineage. Table 2.2 compares the two clans in terms of number
and kind of degrees held by clan members. The proportion of degree-
holders was larger among the Shens than among the Hsüs, but the difference was not great and should not be seen as evidence of their belonging to
different social strata. The two clans were equally successful at the highest
levels of the examination system, each earning four chin-shih degrees, the
Shens in 1685, 1733, 1772, and 1868 and the Hsüs in 1793, 1825, 1850,
and 1876. (Three earlier military chin-shih of the Shen clan are excluded
from the reckoning.) Moreover, the slight advantage the Shens gained
in the traditional examination systems was probably offset by the fact that
the first graduates of the few modern schools established before the end
of the Ch'ing period included several members of the Hsü clan.

Since some descent groups were more powerful and more prestigious
than others, one can usefully compare the social status of lineages and
clans. However, it is important to remember that the most prominent descent groups included many people who were poor and politically impo-
tent. The Shen and Hsü genealogies only note the occupations of their
members when they achieve official rank, but remarks contained in a few
of the biographies give us a glimpse of the diversity characteristic of all
Chinese descent groups. The Shen genealogy mentions several men who
became rich through trade, several others who were famed for their skill in
medicine, even some who appear to have earned their living as fortunetellers. And the Hsü genealogy tells us that several of the clan's members
supported themselves as shopkeepers, running such establishments as a
copper shop, a grain and salt shop, a carpentry shop, a lantern shop, and a
noodle shop. Though this evidence does not allow us to determine the social status of more than a handful of the people listed in the two genealogies, it does serve to remind us that Chinese descent groups belonged to a
complex society and reflected that complexity. What follows should not be
compared with T. H. Hollingsworth's study of the English peerage.[7] The
people whose success in the examination took them to the top of Chinese
society may have dominated the Shen and Hsü clans, but they were out-
numbered 1,000 to one by merchants, shopkeepers, farmers, and farm
laborers.

TABLE 2.2
Degree-Holders in the Shen and Hsü Genealogies

Generation	Chin-shih[a]	Chü-jen	Kung-sheng	Sheng-yüan	Kuo-hsüeh-sheng	Total	Pct. of all adult males
			SHEN				
18		1				1	12.5%
19		1	2			3	11.1
20		1	1	1		3	4.8
21		3	1	5		9	7.3
22					1	1	1.6
23			1	3	1	5	5.9
24	1			2		3	2.9
25		1		2	1	4	2.5
26	2	1[b]		7	4	14	5.1
27	1	1	1	13	10	26	5.8
28	1	3	3	23	21	51	7.3
29	1	3	2	25	30	61	6.3
30		1	2	13	25	41	3.4
31		1	1	9	23	34	2.1
32	1	3	1	2	23	30	1.8
33		1	3	8	15	27	1.8
34			1	2	2	5	0.7
TOTAL	7	21	19	109	156	318	
			HSÜ				
1							
2							
3							
4							
5							
6							
7				3	2	5	6.49%
8				1		1	0.78
9				1	1	2	1.08
10				1	3	4	1.33
11			3	3	2	8	1.67
12				3	6	9	1.50
13	1	1	2	0	13	17	2.30
14	2		2	3	15	22	2.79
15		2		4	11	17	2.30
16	1		1	3	6	11	1.91
17			1	3	8	12	3.97
TOTAL	4	3	9	25	67	108	

[a] The three chin-shih in the 24th and 26th generations of the Shen clan were military chin-shih.
[b] Military chü-jen.

20   TS'UI-JUNG LIU

Marriage

Though our genealogies do not provide marriage dates for either men or women, they do yield information that reveals a good deal about marriage practices. Probably because a woman's rights and duties with respect to her husband and his kinsmen varied with the form of her marriage, a number of terms were employed to distinguish the status of in-marrying women. A first wife was termed *p'ei*; a second wife (that is, a woman marrying a man who had lost his first wife), *chi*; a third wife, *yu-chi*; a fourth wife, *san-chi*. A woman who had herself married previously was dubbed *ch'ü* regardless of whether or not she was her husband's first wife, and concubines were termed *ts'e* or *fu*. The proportion of all Shen and Hsü wives occupying each of these statuses is shown in Table 2.1. These data enable us to estimate the incidence of polygynous unions, the frequency of remarriage, and the rapidity with which widows and widowers married a second or third time.

Consider first the incidence of polygynous unions. Of a total of 7,163 women marrying into the Shen clan, 236 came as concubines; and of 3,948 women taken as wives by members of the Hsü clan, 58 entered as concubines. Concubines accordingly account for 3.3 percent of the Shen wives and 1.5 percent of the Hsü wives. Since concubines were not recorded if they did not bear a son, and since some women who came as concubines were later elevated to the status of second or third wife,[8] these figures say that whereas monogamy was the rule, polygyny was completely acceptable and was probably very common among the elite. The fact that the Shen men took twice as many concubines as the Hsü men presumably reflects their having achieved prominence earlier and in somewhat greater numbers.

Lumping together the generations displayed in Table 2.1, we find that 6,012 of the men named in the Shen genealogy married at least once and that 824 of these men took a second wife. In other words, of all the men who married once, 13.7 percent married a second time. And in this case we find almost no difference between the two clans. The Hsü genealogy names 3,425 men who married at least once, 12.3 percent of whom married a second time. Given that the Shens were somewhat wealthier than the Hsüs and took almost twice as many concubines, this suggests that a concubine was a luxury, a wife a necessity. This is also evident in the relative frequency of third marriages. Of all the Shen men who married twice, 9.1 percent married a third time, and of the Hsü men who took a second wife, 9.5 percent took a third wife.

What then of remarriage by women? Though traditional ideology discouraged widow remarriage by elevating the celibate widow to the level of a minor cultural hero, both the Shen and the Hsü genealogies indicate that widows did remarry and not infrequently. We find 120 women listed under the label *ch'ü* in the Shen genealogy and another 51 in the Hsü genealogy. And there is also evidence that women who married into these two clans sometimes married out again after their husband died. Twenty-eight boys (nine Shens and 19 Hsüs) are listed as *sui-mu-ch'u*, that is, as having accompanied their mothers when they married out of the clan. Though these figures indicate that second marriages were far less common among women than among men, it is likely that some second marriages were passed off as first marriages. The most we can conclude with confidence is that the cult of the celibate widow did not succeed in entirely suppressing second marriages by widows.

We do not have the evidence necessary to discover how quickly widows remarried, but we can estimate how long it took widowers to remarry by calculating the interval between the first wife's death and the birth of her replacement's eldest son. The results are shown in Table 2.3. Needless to say, they are not precise since they depend not only upon the accuracy of our records but also on what assumptions we make about the length of the mourning period and the birth interval. Since mourning would not have exceeded nine months,[9] I have allowed three years for mourning and the birth interval. The means, medians, and standard deviations for the distributions shown there are (in years) 6.75, 5.27, and 4.80 for the Shen clan and 7.86, 6.83, and 4.94 for the Hsü clan. If we subtract three years from either the means or the medians, we find that the Shen and Hsü clan males remarried within three or four years. Perhaps the most interesting thing about these figures is that the behavior of the two clans is so similar. Whatever the true interval between marriages, it was the same for the Shens and the Hsüs and thus arguably characteristic of Hsiao-shan in general.

As we have seen, the founder of the Hsiao-shan branch of the Hsü clan married into his wife's family. There is other evidence of uxorilocal marriage to be found in the two genealogies. A fifteenth-generation member of the Hsü clan is listed as having married out of his family, and the genealogy also notes two men who married into the Hsü descent group. The Shen genealogy contains no evidence of men marrying into the clan, but it does mention four men who married out. Though these few cases may represent only a tiny fraction of all uxorilocal unions, they are interesting as evidence that both clans contained some impoverished families. Only a man too poor to acquire a wife any other way would agree to marry into his wife's family.

The traditional view of Chinese marriage practices says that marriage was nearly universal and that it occurred at an early age. Was this so? Let us see what our genealogies tell us. Columns 10-12 of Table 2.1 list all adult men who might possibly be considered as never marrying. To calcu-

TABLE 2.3

Estimated Duration Between First and Second Marriages of Males
in the Shen and Hsü Genealogies

No. of years between marriages	Number of males		No. of years between marriages	Number of males	
	Shen	Hsü		Shen	Hsü
1	12	5	16	3	1
2	25	9	17	1	1
3	14	7	18	1	4
4	13	9	19	2	0
5	17	10	20	0	1
6	15	12	21	2	1
7	16	6	22	0	1
8	8	10	23	1	0
9	8	5	24	1	0
10	10	7	TOTAL	170	111
11	7	5			
12	6	2	Mean (yrs.)	6.75	7.86
13	4	5	Median (yrs.)	5.27	6.83
14	2	8	Standard		
15	2	2	deviation (yrs.)	4.80	4.94
			Coef. of variation	.71	.63

late the proportion of men never marrying we must decide which of these men died unmarried and beyond the possibility of marriage. The men enumerated in Column 11 obviously qualify, but what of those in Columns 10 and 12? Since there is no clear answer, let us set both groups aside and count only those men whom we know to have died unmarried after age 50. Thus we assume that the men in Column 10 would have married if they had lived, and that those in Column 12 either were in fact married or might have married if they had lived longer. This leaves us with 49 Shens and 78 Hsüs who never married. Since these calculations involve several questionable assumptions, it is encouraging to see that the results agree with what we know about the relative affluence of the Shen and Hsü clans. The proportion of Shens failing to marry was only 0.5 percent compared to 1.5 percent among the Hsüs.

Since Chinese genealogies do not report age at marriage for either males or females, we have no choice but to resort to indirect methods of estimating the value of this important variable. The most appropriate procedure for men is to estimate the proportions single at given ages and then to apply John Hajnal's method of calculating what he terms the "singulate mean age at marriage" (SMAM).[10] The problem is to decide what assumptions to apply in estimating the proportion of single men in the critical age categories 15-19 and 20-24. One possibility is to assume that all men who did not have sons were single. Another is to assume that the only single men were those who died single. Since the two sets of assumptions produce very different results, I have calculated two sets of figures, one under the high-age-at-marriage assumption and the other under the low-age-at-marriage assumption. Our best estimate of men's age at marriage is probably an average of these two sets of figures.

Table 2.4 reports the results of my calculations for selected cohorts of the Hsü clan. Under the high-age-at-marriage assumption the average age at marriage for these fifteen cohorts was 25.02 years; under the low-age-at-marriage assumption it was 17.58 years; on the average it is 21.3 years, which is strikingly close to the Princeton group's estimate of 21.39 years for South China in the 1930's.[11] Though this could be nothing more than a happy coincidence, I prefer to view it as support for my assumptions and as evidence that a low age at marriage has been characteristic of China for several centuries.

With no way of estimating the proportion of women single at different ages, we cannot apply the Hajnal procedure to solve the problem of estimating age at marriage for women. However, since we know the birth dates of most husbands and wives, we can calculate the average difference in their ages and thus use the husband's age at marriage to estimate the wife's age at marriage. Table 2.5 says that on the average the men born into the Shen and Hsü clans in 1650-1804 were 5.2 years older than their wives.[12] If the average age at marriage of men born into the two clans was 21.3 years, the average age at marriage of their wives was approximately 16.1 years. This is considerably lower than the 17.78 years obtained by the Princeton group for South China,[13] but well within the range of possibility in a society in which marriages were arranged by the elderly and in which grandchildren and great-grandchildren were looked on as signs of prosperity and good fortune.

The figures in the last column of Table 2.5 indicate that a surprisingly large percentage of all wives were older than their husbands. The average for all cohorts is 14 percent (18 percent in the Shen clan and 10 percent in the Hsü clan), with some cohorts exceeding 30 percent. These figures confirm a tendency noted by Michel Cartier in his analysis of Ming biographies,[14] and suggest that a preference for matches in which the wife is younger than the husband is a relatively recent phenomenon.

We can obtain another estimate of women's age at marriage in the Hsiao-shan area by examining the biographies included in the *Hsiao-shan hsien-chih kao* (Draft Gazetteer of Hsiao-shan). Age at marriage is noted for 94 of the 546 women mentioned in the biographies.[15] The mean of these 94 reports is 17.83 sui, or approximately 16.83 years, a figure com-

TABLE 2.4

Proportion Single at Each Age Group and Singulate Mean Age at Marriage (SMAM) for Selected Cohorts of Hsü Clan Males, 1700-1844

Cohort	Age								SMAM	
	15-19	20-24	25-29	30-34	35-39	40-44	45-49	50-54	High-age assumption	Low-age assumption
1700-1704	25/26 .9615 .0769	20/26 .7692 .0769	1/25 .0400	1/25 .0400	1/24 .0417	1/23 .0435	1/20 .0500	0/19 –	24.08	15.99
1710-1714	23/24 .9583 .0417	18/24 .7500 .0417	1/23 .0435	1/22 .0455	1/22 .0455	0/21 –	0/18 –	0/16 –	24.21	16.09
1720-1724	36/40 .9000 .0750	26/39 .6667 .0526	2/38 .0526	2/38 .0526	1/37 .0270	1/34 .0294	0/31 –	0/27 –	23.64	16.44
1730-1734	31/32 .9688 .0625	27/32 .8438 0.625	2/32 .0625	2/31 .0323	2/30 .0666	1/29 .0345	1/26 .0385	1/22 –	24.75	16.15
1740-1744	62/65 .9692 .0932	54/64 .8438 .0781	4/63 .0635	3/61 .0492	1/58 .0172	0/55 –	0/54 –	0/46 –	24.71	16.50
1750-1754	41/42 .9762 .0714	39/42 .9286 .0714	3/42 .0714	3/42 .0714	2/40 .0500	1/36 .0278	0/33 –	0/30 –	25.63	16.81
1760-1764	50/50 1.0000 .1800	43/47 .9149 .1277	5/46 .1087	4/45 .0889	4/45 .0889	2/41 .0488	1/38 .0263	1/32 .0313	25.68	17.41

1770-1774	55/55 1.0000 *.1818*	45/54 .8333 *.1667*	8/53 .1509	8/52 .1538	8/51 .1569	6/48 .1250	5/45 .0178	2/34 .0588	26.27	18.56
1780-1784	67/68 .9853 *.3235*	53/66 .8030 *.3030*	15/60 .2500	10/54 .1852	9/51 .1765	7/47 .1489	4/39 .1026	2/28 .0714	26.18	19.82
1790-1794	68/74 .9189 *.2077*	50/71 .7042 *.1569*	8/68 .1176	7/67 .1045	4/61 .0656	4/57 .0702	2/49 .0408	2/40 .0500	23.93	17.30
1800-1804	64/67 .9552 *.2835*	54/65 .8308 *.2615*	13/61 .2131	11/57 .1929	8/51 .1569	4/41 .0976	4/31 .1290	1/23 .0435	25.79	18.99
1810-1814	65/71 .9155 *.1972*	51/59 .7391 *.1739*	7/58 .1207	4/49 .0816	3/48 .0625	3/41 .0732	2/28 .0714	0/11 –	24.42	17.75
1820-1824	55/57 .9649 *.3333*	42/54 .7778 *.2963*	13/49 .2653	8/41 .1851	5/28 .1786	1/18 .0556	0/15 –	0/13 –	27.19	21.62
1830-1834	52/54 .9630 *.2963*	40/49 .8163 *.2245*	5/42 .1190	0/33 –	0/31 –	0/23 –	0/20 –	0/16 –	24.49	18.20
1840-1844	45/47 .9574 *.1489*	37/42 .8809 *.0476*	1/39 .0256	0/35 –	0/32 –	0/31 –	0/24 –	0/13 –	24.32	16.11
AVERAGE									25.02	17.58

NOTE: The first cell reads as follows: Out of 26 males in the cohort, 25 (96.15%) were single in the 15-19 age group on the high-age-of-marriage assumption. On the low-age-of-marriage assumption, only 7.69% were single. Italic figures throughout are low-age assumptions.

25

TABLE 2.5

Difference in Age Between Husband and First Wife, Selected Cohorts of Shen and Hsü Clans, 1650-1804

| | | Difference in years between the ages of husband and wife | | | | | | | | | | |
| | | Wife older | | | | Husband older | | | | | | |
Cohort	Clan	10+	6-10	1-5	0	1-5	6-10	11-15	16-20	20+	Mean[a]	Pct. of marriages where wife is older
1650-	S				1	2		1	1		7.4	0%
1654	H					2		1	1		6.3	0
1660-	S			4		7	1		1		2.3	33
1664	H				1	1	4				5.5	0
1670-	S			3	1	5		1	1		4.6	20
1674	H				1	2				1	7.0	0
1680-	S			1	4	1	2	1			1.9	14
1684	H	1	1	1	0	5	2	1			3.3	20
1690-	S			4	4	4	2	2			1.1	31
1694	H					6			1		5.5	0
1700-	S			1	1	5	3	2	1		4.1	11
1704	H		2	4	0	12	1	1			4.7	27
1710-	S		2	1	1	7	5	1			3.0	17
1714	H			5	1	7	4	2	1	1	3.1	26
1720-	S			7	3	10	10	5	2	1	3.9	28
1724	H			4	2	5	2	2	0	1	6.5	12
1730-	S			2	2	7	2	5			5.2	14
1734	H			3	2	12	2	7			4.9	16
1740-	S		1	3	1	17	5	6	1		5.6	13
1744	H			2	3	10	10	3	0		5.9	5
1750-	S		1	3	3	4	8	7	1	1	4.8	14
1754	H	1		1	2	13	8	3	1		7.9	4
1760-	S		2	9	2	8	6	13	1	1	2.9	32
1764	H				2	12	12	9	5		9.5	0
1770-	S		1	9	1	13	12	11	2	1	5.6	19
1774	H			2	6	21	21	14	2	2	7.2	4
1780-	S			6	3	14	15	11	4		6.5	9
1784	H			3	3	27	14	8	2	1	7.1	6
1790-	S			11	3	15	18	4			5.4	15
1794	H			5	3	23	15	9	1		5.8	11
1800-	S		1	15	7	11	16	10	1		3.9	22
1804	H			7	6	11	15	10	1	1	5.6	14
AVERAGE[b]											5.2	14%

[a] The mean age of the husbands is in every case higher than the mean age of the wives.
[b] Cohorts 1810-14, 1820-24, 1830-34, 1840-44 are not included in the table but are counted in the average.

TABLE 2.6

Number and Proportion of Widows among First Wives in the Shen and Hsü Clans, 1700-1839

Cohort	Shen					Hsü				
		Age 20-44		Age 45+			Age 20-44		Age 45+	
	N	No. of widows	Percent widowed	No. of widows	Percent widowed	N	No. of widows	Percent widowed	No. of widows	Percent widowed
1700-1704	9	3	33%	3	33%	15	3	20%	6	40%
1705-1709	14	7	50	4	29	12	1	08	7	58
1710-1714	18	4	22	5	28	19	5	26	6	32
1715-1719	12	1	08	4	33	28	6	21	11	39
1720-1724	24	5	21	8	33	34	7	21	12	35
1725-1729	22	7	32	6	27	20	6	30	6	30
1730-1734	26	9	35	10	39	19	5	26	5	26
1735-1739	22	9	41	5	23	25	10	40	8	32
1740-1744	29	2	07	15	52	38	12	32	14	37
1745-1749	32	10	31	15	47	42	12	29	13	31
1750-1754	25	7	28	9	36	23	4	17	10	44
1755-1759	44	12	27	10	23	27	9	33	7	26
1760-1764	30	4	13	14	47	38	12	32	10	26
1765-1769	39	9	23	16	41	40	11	28	18	45
1770-1774	34	6	18	19	56	41	8	20	16	39
1775-1779	42	8	19	12	29	35	8	23	19	53
1780-1784	42	12	29	13	31	43	10	23	15	35
1785-1789	41	6	15	19	46	44	13	30	19	43
1790-1794	46	13	28	15	33	31	10	32	8	26
1795-1799	27	6	22	13	48	22	4	18	5	23
1800-1804	52	7	14	28	54	21	5	24	5	24
1805-1809	52	16	31	22	42	27	5	19	9	33
1810-1814	56	11	20	21	38	22	6	27	8	36
1815-1819	51	18	35	13	26	26	11	42	3	12
1820-1824	41	15	37	12	29	18	9	50	4	22
1825-1829	32	10	31	9	28	18	4	22	7	39
1830-1834	21	8	38	6	29	15	6	40	2	13
1835-1839	16	6	38	2	13	11	4	36	5	46
Mean			.266		.353			.275		.337
Standard deviation			.101		.104			.086		.105
Coef. of variation			.380		.295			.313		.312

fortingly close to our 16.1 years. I am therefore satisfied that the fertility estimates reported in the following section are not far from the truth in taking 17 years as the mean age at marriage for women in Hsiao-shan.

One last point about marriage as such before we turn to the question of fertility. We have seen that despite the ideal of the celibate widow, many widows did remarry. We must now ask how many women were widowed during their reproductive years, since the proportion of young widows in a population can have a significant effect on fertility and might account for some of the results reported below.

Table 2.6 lists the number of marriages under observation (N) and then reports the number of widows and the percent of women widowed for each of two broad age classes. The analysis is limited to the years 1700-1839 because the data for women born before 1700 and after 1840 are incomplete. The results indicate that a large proportion of all women were widowed, and that this was true of both clans. The average for women aged 20-44 was .266 in the Shen clan and .275 in the Hsü clan; for women aged 45 and above, the average was .353 among the Shens and .337 among the Hsüs. The fact that more than one-fourth of all women were widowed during the reproductive period should be borne in mind when we attempt to explain the relatively low fertility reported in the next section.

Fertility

The information provided by the Shen and Hsü genealogies allows us to estimate both male and female fertility rates. There are, however, limitations imposed by the data. First, the lack of information on unmarried women (who are not even mentioned in the genealogies) means that our female rates must be limited to marital fertility. Second, the failure to record all second wives and concubines, together with the difficulty of determining their age at marriage, forces us to confine the female rates to the fertility of first wives; as a result, the children of second wives and concubines are reflected in the male rates but not the female rates. Third, the obvious neglect of many female births and the failure to record the dates of those births in the genealogies leaves us no choice but to estimate fertility on the basis of male births. Were we to accept at face value the data presented in Columns 7 and 8 of Table 2.1, we would be forced to the absurd conclusion that Chinese women bore three times as many sons as daughters. One of the most important unanswered questions about Chinese genealogies is why some female births were noted but not others. Neither the Shen nor the Hsü genealogy offers any clue to a rule or convention in this regard.

A crude estimate of fertility can be obtained directly from Table 2.1 by calculating the son/mother ratio or the son/father ratio by generation or cohort. A more laborious but ultimately more fruitful approach is to apply family reconstitution techniques to estimate age-specific fertility and total fertility, and this is the procedure I have followed. After designating a family reconstitution sheet for each male who survived to adulthood, I recorded on that sheet his vital dates and those of his wives and sons. Gaps in the data (and fortunately there were very few of these) were filled by applying the conventions that I developed in analyzing the two Taiwanese genealogies.[16] If the birth date of one of several sons, let us say the first-born, was missing, I subtracted three years from the birth date of the second-born son. The birth date of a last-born son was obtained by adding three years to the birth date of the next-to-last born, and a missing date for a boy born in the middle of a series was estimated by taking the midpoint of the interval bounded by the births of the next-oldest and next-youngest sons. Parental dates were complete for the great majority of all people born before 1820, but there were gaps in the record for those born after that date. In the case of a missing death date (the most common problem), childbearing was traced to the birth of the last son but that birth was not counted.

My next step was to calculate, first, the age of the parents at the birth of each son, and, second, the date at which each period of observation terminated. For women in their first marriages (the basis of my female fertility rate) the termination date was the date of their husband's death, the date of their own death, or their fiftieth birthday, whichever came first; for adult men (the basis of my male fertility rate) it was simply their sixtieth birthday. I then organized my two samples (married women and adult men) into birth cohorts and estimated the two fertility rates by dividing the number of sons born to each cohort by the number of person-years experienced by the members of that cohort. An example of the results obtained is presented in Table 2.7. The data for the cohorts listed at the left of the table are read horizontally; those for the periods listed at the right of the table are read obliquely. To save space and deemphasize random fluctuation, the rates presented below are the average of three cohorts or three periods.[17]

A refined estimate of age-specific fertility was obtained by means of the "children-ever-born" technique, or what might better be termed the "sons-ever-born" technique given the limitations of my data. Taking parity (P) to equal the number of sons born to each cohort by the end of each age interval, I calculated cumulative fertility (F) by the formula $F_i = \phi_i + 3f_i$ (where f_i is the age-specific fertility rate and ϕ_i is the cumulated fertility up to the lower boundary of the ith age interval), and then used the P/F ratios to adjust the age-specific fertility rates.[18] The results obtained for the adult males are reported as the male fertility rate, but the results for married females were divided by 1.06 (the assumed sex ratio at birth) to obtain esti-

TABLE 2.7

Data Used to Estimate Age-Specific Marital Fertility among First Wives of the Shen Clan

Cohort	15-19	20-24	25-29	30-34	35-39	40-44	45-49	Period
				Age				
1650-1654	1/ 25	4/ 25	1/ 25	3/ 25	0/ 25	0/ 25	0/ 25	1695-1699
1655-1659	2/ 40	2/ 40	2/ 25.32	3/ 25	0/ 25	1/ 25	0/ 25	1700-1704
1660-1664	4/ 65	6/ 65	5/ 60.79	4/ 55	2/ 53.28	1/ 44.30	3/ 34.79	1705-1709
1665-1669	2/ 35	8/ 35	4/ 32.67	6/ 30	0/ 30	1/ 30	0/ 27.21	1710-1714
1670-1674	1/ 75	6/ 75	11/ 75	8/ 71.02	6/ 64.44	4/ 57.82	0/ 49.13	1715-1719
1675-1679	4/ 45	5/ 45	2/ 45	5/ 45	6/ 37.31	0/ 34.97	0/ 30	1720-1724
1680-1684	1/ 35	4/ 35	5/ 30.96	7/ 30	1/ 30	0/ 27.36	0/ 15.62	1725-1729
1685-1689	2/ 40	3/ 38.41	4/ 35	3/ 25.07	1/ 25	0/ 17.66	0/ 15	1730-1734
1690-1694	1/ 80	4/ 80	7/ 78.03	9/ 67.88	3/ 60.77	2/ 54.93	1/ 45.85	1735-1739
1695-1699	0/ 90	9/ 90	11/ 85.34	9/ 85.34	3/ 83.55	4/ 75	0/ 67.52	1740-1744
1700-1704	2/ 45	9/ 45	8/ 45	4/ 45	5/ 45	1/ 32.14	0/ 20	1745-1749
1705-1709	3/ 70	9/ 67.76	11/ 61.93	4/ 46.28	4/ 30.19	1/ 26.55	0/ 12.97	1750-1754
1710-1714	4/ 90	5/ 83.61	10/ 80	8/ 80	6/ 79.04	2/ 73.19	1/ 60.13	1755-1759
1715-1719	1/ 65	5/ 62.5	13/ 58.88	5/ 54.37	4/ 47.91	1/ 37.94	0/ 34.63	1760-1764
1720-1724	4/125	14/122.48	8/115	13/110.64	10/ 96.73	7/ 77.41	1/ 67	1765-1769
1725-1729	1/110	10/100.75	14/100.68	7/100	6/ 95.3	2/ 74.06	1/ 70	1770-1774
1730-1734	3/135	11/135	13/134.11	18/122.98	7/109.25	2/ 69.72	0/ 60.04	1775-1779
1735-1739	1/115	13/114.97	13/100.15	13/ 98.24	4/ 82.56	3/ 63.49	0/ 43.18	1780-1784
1740-1744	10/155	17/150	22/140	17/133.81	10/121.68	5/110.27	0/ 94.08	1785-1789
1745-1749	10/170	15/165.37	21/155.5	15/144.41	15/124.13	4/109.89	0/ 82.66	1790-1794
1750-1754	5/135	17/132.26	15/125.88	9/125	15/122.81	5/ 92.62	1/ 75.22	1795-1799
1755-1759	8/225	23/215.53	23/207.18	21/173.61	14/139.98	1/108.54	0/ 87.02	1800-1804
1760-1764	9/190	14/185.79	27/172.5	14/144.13	10/119.44	6/102.58	1/ 83.4	1805-1809
1765-1769	10/245	22/223.94	16/210	15/189.23	21/160.21	8/129.64	1/ 97.47	1810-1814
1770-1774	10/255	30/249.37	24/225.16	24/185.76	15/166.49	6/139.89	2/119.22	1815-1819
1775-1779	11/315	32/310.19	41/298.52	26/249.76	24/184.22	9/144.88	1/113.3	1820-1824
1780-1784	22/330	36/301.32	36/272.67	25/219.32	23/161	4/108.85	0/ 90.46	1825-1829
1785-1789	14/320	39/307.97	36/271.18	36/205.12	15/162.31	9/138.45	1/101.34	1830-1834
1790-1794	15/360	35/340.97	47/311.31	29/235.71	18/165.91	3/122.03	0/103.76	1835-1839
1795-1799	6/285	33/275.96	31/248.21	27/205.82	7/158.68	5/110.74	0/ 86.8	1840-1844
1800-1804	14/395	37/367.33	45/321.27	40/283.39	24/216.84	9/187.53	1/196.16	1845-1849
1805-1809	20/460	56/425.22	50/355.56	39/235.15	15/187.5	5/153.85	2/115.03	1850-1854
1810-1814	19/465	47/456.28	58/366.57	37/287.13	12/226.21	9/189.53	2/128.64	1855-1859
1815-1819	17/440	62/403.89	39/326.99	35/275.92	17/203.87	2/141.88	0/ 81.13	1860-1864
1820-1824	18/400	54/363.27	44/302.42	23/225.26	14/174.95	4/ 96.55	0/106.41	1865-1869
1825-1829	21/410	45/378.03	50/330.97	24/232.21	14/131.55	2/ 91.06	1/ 52.58	1870-1874

NOTE: The numerators are the number of sons born, the denominators the number of woman-years or years of observation.

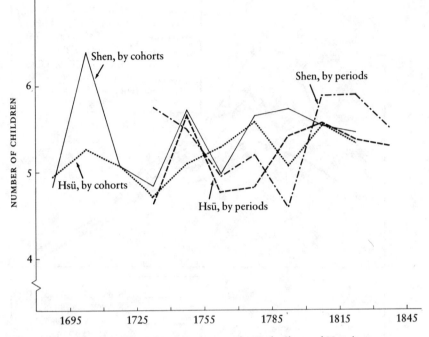

NUMBER OF CHILDREN

Fig. 2.1. Total fertility of first wives by cohorts and periods, Shen and Hsü clans, 1690-1840

mates of the number of daughters born and hence rates that reflect both male and female births. Total fertility was also calculated for married females by multiplying the sum of the age-specific fertility rates by five.

The results of these procedures are summarized in visual form in Figures 2.1-3 and are reported in detail in Tables 2.8-11. Note that the *P/F* ratio in Table 2.8 is about 1.00 for the first age group of most cohorts and that it declines steadily as the cohort ages. Clearly we cannot be far from the truth in taking 17 as the average age at marriage, and in lowering our estimates of age-specific fertility among the older age groups.

One conclusion to be drawn from Tables 2.8-11 is that the fertility of the Shen and Hsü clans was quite similar and conformed closely to the age pattern found in human populations in general. Not only does this give us confidence in our sources, but our estimate of marital fertility is remarkably close to that obtained by the Princeton group. Like the wives of the Chinese farmers included in Buck's surveys, the women taken as first wives by the Shen and Hsü clans bore an average of five children.[19] Taken together with the stability displayed by both male and female fertility rates, this finding argues that Chinese reproductive behavior did not change

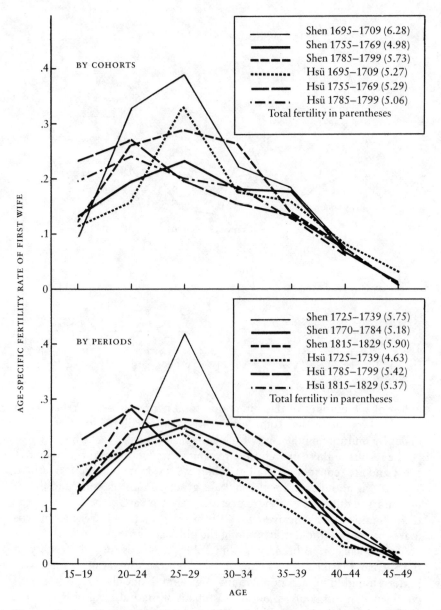

Fig. 2.2. Age-specific marital fertility rates of first wives for selected cohorts and periods, Shen and Hsü clans, 1695-1829

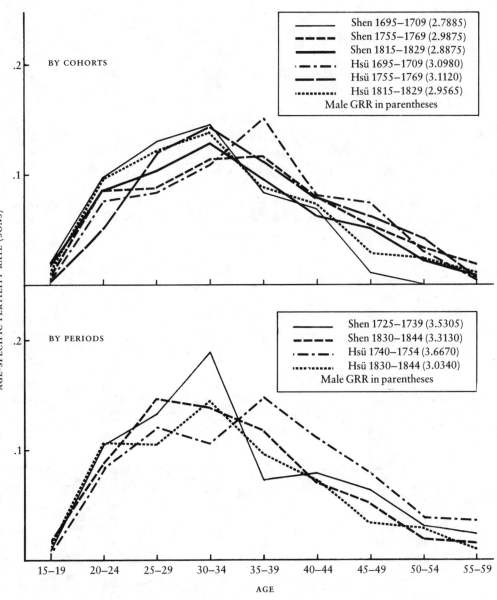

Fig. 2.3. Adjusted male age-specific fertility rates in terms of sons for selected cohorts and periods, Shen and Hsü clans, 1695-1844

TABLE 2.8

Marital Age-Specific Fertility and Total Fertility of First Wives by Cohort, Shen and Hsü Clans, 1680-1829

Cohort	Measure	Age							Total
		15-19	20-24	25-29	30-34	35-39	40-44	45-49	
		SHEN							
1680-1694	Observed fs	.0506	.0808	.1218	.1618	.0409	.0310	.0073	
	P/F	1.0000	1.1114	1.0771	.9975	.8450	.8354	.8154	
	Adj. fs	.0506	.0898	.1312	.1614	.0346	.0259	.0060	2.4975
	SR = 1.06, fd	.0477	.0847	.1238	.1523	.0326	.0244	.0057	2.3560
	Both sexes	.0983	.1745	.2550	.3139	.0672	.0503	.0117	4.8535
1695-1709	Observed fs	.0485	.1143	.1592	.1010	.0932	.0407	–	
	P/F	1.0000	1.4687	1.2556	1.0814	1.0043	.9396	–	
	Adj. fs	.0485	.1679	.1999	.1092	.0936	.0382	–	3.2865
	SR = 1.06, fd	.0458	.1584	.1886	.1030	.0883	.0360	–	3.1005
	Both sexes	.0943	.3263	.3885	.2122	.1819	.0742	–	6.3870
1710-1724	Observed fs	.0510	.0835	.1367	.1032	.0876	.0480	.0055	
	P/F	1.0000	1.1088	1.0952	.9819	.9286	.8714	.8404	
	Adj. fs	.0510	.0926	.1497	.1013	.0813	.0418	.0046	2.6115
	SR = 1.06, fd	.0481	.0874	.1412	.0956	.0767	.0394	.0043	2.4635
	Both sexes	.0991	.1800	.2909	.1969	.1580	.0812	.0089	5.0750
1725-1739	Observed fs	.0222	.0955	.1219	.1162	.0585	.0238	.0048	
	P/F	1.0015	1.3645	1.1564	1.0475	.9493	.9118	.8930	
	Adj. fs	.0237	.1303	.1410	.1217	.0555	.0217	.0043	2.4910
	SR = 1.06, fd	.0224	.1229	.1330	.1148	.0524	.0205	.0041	2.3505
	Both sexes	.0461	.2532	.2740	.2365	.1079	.0422	.0084	4.8415
1740-1754	Observed fs	.0891	.1108	.1371	.1010	.1084	.0453	.0044	
	P/F	1.0135	1.0499	1.0293	.9554	.9314	.8714	.8451	
	Adj. fs.	.0903	.1163	.1411	.0965	.1010	.0395	.0037	2.9420
	SR = 1.06, fd	.0852	.1097	.1331	.0910	.0953	.0373	.0035	2.7755
	Both sexes	.1755	.2260	.2742	.1875	.1965	.0768	.0072	5.7175
1755-1769	Observed fs	.0687	.0934	.1146	.0991	.1049	.0431	.0074	
	P/F	1.0005	1.0734	1.0329	.9398	.8724	.8008	.7739	
	Adj. fs	.0687	.1003	.1184	.0931	.0915	.0345	.0057	2.5610
	SR = 1.06, fd	.0648	.0946	.1117	.0878	.0863	.0325	.0054	2.4155
	Both sexes	.1335	.1949	.2301	.1809	.1778	.0670	.0111	4.9765

1770–1784	Observed fs	.0782	.1143	.1253	.1157	.1210	.0472	.0085	
	P/F	1.0004	1.0811	1.0080	.9268	.8522	.7808	.7560	
	Adj. fs	.0782	.1236	.1263	.1072	.1031	.0369	.0064	2.9085
	SR = 1.06, fd	.0738	.1166	.1192	.1011	.0973	.0348	.0060	2.7440
	Both sexes	.1520	.2402	.2455	.2083	.2004	.0717	.0124	5.6525
1785–1799	Observed fs	.0591	.1162	.1362	.1405	.0817	.0449	.0033	
	P/F	1.0598	1.1674	1.0851	.9579	.8600	.8069	.7810	
	Adj. fs	.0626	.1357	.1478	.1346	.0703	.0362	.0026	2.9490
	SR = 1.06, fd	.0591	.1280	.1394	.1270	.0663	.0342	.0025	2.7825
	Both sexes	.1217	.2637	.2872	.2616	.1366	.0704	.0051	5.7315
1800–1814	Observed fs	.0666	.0996	.1463	.1453	.0812	.0426	.0127	
	P/F	1.0205	1.0996	1.0093	.8763	.7754	.7307	.7069	
	Adj. fs	.0680	.1229	.1477	.1273	.0630	.0311	.0090	2.8450
	SR = 1.06, fd	.0642	.1159	.1393	.1201	.0594	.0293	.0085	2.6835
	Both sexes	.1322	.2388	.2870	.2474	.1224	.0604	.0175	5.5285
1815–1829	Observed fs	.0749	.1404	.1386	.1108	.0899	.0258	.0063	
	P/F	1.0187	1.1299	.9737	.8675	.7926	.7425	.7257	
	Adj. fs	.0763	.1586	.1350	.0961	.0713	.0192	.0046	2.8055
	SR = 1.06, fd	.0720	.1496	.1274	.0907	.0673	.0181	.0043	2.6470
	Both sexes	.1483	.3082	.2624	.1868	.1386	.0373	.0089	5.4525

HSÜ

1680–1694	Observed fs	.0409	.1154	.1344	.0950	.0551	.0228	.0166	
	P/F	.9992	1.2539	1.0903	.9738	.9108	.8749	.8597	
	Adj. fs	.0409	.1447	.1465	.0925	.0502	.0199	.0143	2.5450
	SR = 1.06, fd	.0386	.1365	.1382	.0873	.0474	.0188	.0135	2.4015
	Both sexes	.0795	.2812	.2847	.1798	.0976	.0387	.0278	4.9465
1695–1709	Observed fs	.0590	.0777	.1531	.0918	.0873	.0478	.0204	
	P/F	.9994	1.0536	1.1080	.9789	.9378	.8855	.8532	
	Adj. fs	.0590	.0819	.1696	.0899	.0819	.0423	.0174	2.7100
	SR = 1.06, fd	.0557	.0773	.1600	.0848	.0773	.0399	.0164	2.5570
	Both sexes	.1147	.1592	.3296	.1747	.1592	.0822	.0338	5.2670
1710–1724	Observed fs	.0914	.1118	.1143	.1100	.0626	.0396	—	
	P/F	.9996	1.0497	1.0099	.9655	.9080	.8739	—	
	Adj. fs	.0914	.1174	.1154	.1062	.0568	.0346	—	2.6090
	SR = 1.06, fd	.0862	.1108	.1089	.1002	.0536	.0326		2.4615
	Both sexes	.1776	.2282	.2243	.2064	.1104	.0672		5.0705

TABLE 2.8 (cont.)

Cohort	Measure	15-19	20-24	25-29	30-34	35-39	40-44	45-49	Total
1725-1739	Observed fs	.0550	.0987	.1017	.0832	.0878	.0543	—	—
	P/F	1.0000	1.1289	1.0444	.9824	.9525	.8791	—	
	Adj. fs	.0550	.1114	.1062	.0817	.0836	.0477	—	2.4280
	SR = 1.06, fd	.0519	.1051	.1002	.0771	.0789	.0450	—	2.2910
	Both sexes	.1069	.2165	.2064	.1588	.1625	.0927	—	4.7190
1740-1754	Observed fs	.0708	.0949	.1163	.0934	.1012	.0495	—	—
	P/F	1.0000	1.0673	1.0509	.9778	.9433	.8773	—	
	Adj. fs	.0708	.1013	.1222	.0913	.0955	.0434	—	2.6225
	SR = 1.06, fd	.0668	.0956	.1153	.0861	.0901	.0409	—	2.4740
	Both sexes	.1376	.1969	.2375	.1774	.1856	.0843	—	5.0965
1755-1769	Observed fs	.1186	.1380	.1080	.0890	.0787	.0447	—	—
	P/F	.9997	1.0113	.9389	.8996	.8661	.8181	—	
	Adj. fs	.1186	.1396	.1014	.0801	.0682	.0366	—	2.7225
	SR = 1.06, fd	.1119	.1317	.0957	.0756	.0643	.0345	—	2.5685
	Both sexes	.2305	.2713	.1971	.1557	.1325	.0711	—	5.2910
1770-1784	Observed fs	.1146	.1315	.1211	.1073	.0848	.0278	.0031	2.8335
	P/F	1.0003	1.0183	.9819	.9315	.8724	.8252	.8094	
	Adj. fs	.1146	.1339	.1189	.0999	.0740	.0229	.0025	2.7510
	SR = 1.06, fd	.1081	.1419	.1122	.0942	.0698	.0216	.0024	5.5845
	Both sexes	.2227	.2758	.2311	.1941	.1438	.0445	.0049	
1785-1799	Observed fs	.1013	.1213	.1097	.1042	.0768	.0390	—	—
	P/F	.9997	1.0205	.9476	.9077	.8545	.8063	—	
	Adj. fs	.1013	.1238	.1040	.0946	.0656	.0314	—	2.6035
	SR = 1.06, fd	.0956	.1168	.0981	.0892	.0619	.0296	—	2.4560
	Both sexes	.1969	.2406	.2021	.1838	.1275	.0610	—	5.0595
1800-1814	Observed fs	.0716	.1250	.1195	.1271	.0999	.0650	—	—
	P/F	1.0000	1.1314	1.0067	.8878	.7762	.7100	—	
	Adj. fs	.0716	.1414	.1203	.1128	.0775	.0462	—	2.8490
	SR = 1.06, fd	.0675	.1334	.1135	.1064	.0731	.0436	—	2.6875
	Both sexes	.1391	.2748	.2338	.2192	.1506	.0898	—	5.5365
1815-1829	Observed fs	.0933	.1286	.1379	.1275	.0924	.0186	.0064	—
	P/F	.9996	1.0321	.9446	.8285	.7449	.6983	.6873	
	Adj. fs	.0933	.1327	.1303	.1056	.0688	.0130	.0044	2.7405
	SR = 1.06, fd	.0880	.1252	.1229	.0996	.0649	.0123	.0042	2.5855
	Both sexes	.1813	.2579	.2532	.2052	.1337	.0253	.0086	5.3260

NOTE: The fd figures in the Total column represent Gross Reproductive Rate (GRR).

TABLE 2.9

Marital Age-Specific Fertility and Total Fertility of First Wives by Period, Shen and Hsü Clans, 1725-1844

Period	Measure	Age							Total
		15-19	20-24	25-29	30-34	35-39	40-44	45-49	
				SHEN					
1725-1739	Observed fs	.0510	.0897	.1583	.1010	.0655	.0488	.0073	
	P/F	1.0000	1.1566	1.3605	1.1506	.9864	.7742	.7723	
	Adj. fs	.0510	.1037	.2154	.1162	.0646	.0353	.0056	2.9590
	SR = 1.06, fd	.0481	.0978	.2032	.1096	.0609	.0333	.0053	2.7910
	Both sexes	.0991	.2015	.4186	.2258	.1255	.0686	.0109	5.7500
1740-1754	Observed fs	.0222	.0959	.1432	.1032	.0973	.0320	—	
	P/F	1.0015	1.4535	1.1887	1.0119	.9776	1.0483	—	
	Adj. fs	.0222	.1394	.1702	.1044	.0951	.0335	—	2.8240
	SR = 1.06, fd	.0209	.1315	.1606	.0985	.0897	.0316	—	2.6640
	Both sexes	.0431	.2709	.3308	.2029	.1848	.0651	—	5.4885
1755-1769	Observed fs	.0891	.1057	.1279	.1162	.0768	.0479	.0055	
	P/F	1.0135	.9809	.9347	.8257	.7716	.7701	.7609	
	Adj. fs	.0903	.1037	.1195	.0959	.0593	.0369	.0042	2.5490
	SR = 1.06, fd	.0852	.0978	.1127	.0905	.0559	.0348	.0040	2.4045
	Both sexes	.1755	.2015	.2322	.1864	.1152	.0717	.0082	4.9535
1770-1784	Observed fs	.0687	.1035	.1217	.1010	.0838	.0299	.0048	
	P/F	1.0005	1.0749	1.0666	1.0715	1.0006	.9050	.7699	
	Adj. fs	.0687	.1113	.1298	.1082	.0839	.0271	.0037	2.6635
	SR = 1.06, fd	.0648	.1050	.1225	.1021	.0792	.0256	.0035	2.5135
	Both sexes	.1335	.2163	.2523	.2103	.1631	.0527	.0072	5.1770
1785-1799	Observed fs	.1011	.1072	.1131	.0991	.1019	.0332	.0044	
	P/F	.7738	.8870	.8815	.8295	.8560	.8356	.8998	
	Adj. fs	.0782	.0951	.0997	.0822	.0872	.0277	.0040	2.3705
	SR = 1.06, fd	.0738	.0897	.0941	.0775	.0823	.0261	.0038	2.2365
	Both sexes	.1520	.1848	.1938	.1597	.1695	.0538	.0078	4.6070
1800-1814	Observed fs	.0591	.1162	.1340	.1157	.1171	.0544	.0074	
	P/F	1.0598	1.2577	1.0896	.9476	.8196	.7331	.6802	
	Adj. fs	.0626	.1461	.1460	.1096	.0960	.0399	.0050	3.0260
	SR = 1.06, fd	.0591	.1378	.1377	.1034	.0906	.0376	.0047	2.8545
	Both sexes	.1217	.2839	.2837	.2130	.1866	.0775	.0097	5.8805

TABLE 2.9 (*cont.*)

Period	Measure	15-19	20-24	25-29	30-34	35-39	40-44	45-49	Total
1815-1829	Observed fs	.0666	.1173	.1386	.1405	.1147	.0546	.0085	
	P/F	1.0205	1.0778	.9770	.9320	.8416	.7744	.7197	
	Adj. fs	.0680	.1264	.1354	.1309	.0965	.0437	.0061	3.0350
	SR = 1.06, fd	.0642	.1192	.1277	.1235	.0910	.0412	.0058	2.8630
	Both sexes	.1322	.2456	.2631	.2544	.1875	.0849	.0119	5.8980
1830-1844	Observed fs	.0749	.1350	.1393	.1453	.0783	.0392	.0033	
	P/F	1.0187	1.0971	.9563	.8271	.7464	.7254	.7385	
	Adj. fs	.0763	.1481	.1332	.1202	.0584	.0284	.0024	2.8350
	SR = 1.06, fd	.0720	.1397	.1257	.1134	.0551	.0268	.0023	2.6750
	Both sexes	.1483	.2878	.2589	.2336	.1135	.0552	.0047	5.5100
				HSÜ					
1725-1739	Observed fs	.0914	.1110	.1349	.0918	.0588	.0217	.0166	
	P/F	.9996	.9556	.8969	.8604	.8350	.7827	.7836	
	Adj. fs	.0914	.1061	.1210	.0790	.0491	.0170	.0130	2.3830
	SR = 1.06, fd	.0862	.1001	.1142	.0745	.0463	.0160	.0123	2.2480
	Both sexes	.1776	.2062	.2352	.1535	.0954	.0330	.0253	4.6310
1740-1754	Observed fs	.0550	.0936	.1177	.1100	.0620	.0613	.0204	
	P/F	1.0000	1.2753	1.2328	1.1143	1.0369	.9391	.8817	
	Adj. fs	.0550	.1194	.1451	.1226	.0643	.0576	.0180	2.9100
	SR = 1.06, fd	.0519	.1126	.1369	.1157	.0607	.0543	.0170	2.7455
	Both sexes	.1069	.2320	.2820	.2383	.1250	.1119	.0350	5.6555
1755-1769	Observed fs	.0708	.1056	.0951	.0832	.1051	.0329	—	
	P/F	1.0000	1.0720	.9411	.9332	1.0178	.9852	—	
	Adj. fs	.0708	.1132	.0895	.0776	.1070	.0324	—	2.4525
	SR = 1.06, fd	.0668	.1068	.0844	.0732	.1009	.0306	—	2.3135
	Both sexes	.1376	.2200	.1739	.1508	.2079	.0630	—	4.7660
1770-1784	Observed fs	.1186	.1126	.1208	.0934	.0640	.0547	—	
	P/F	.9997	.9414	.8884	.8101	.7727	.7205	—	
	Adj. fs	.1186	.1060	.1073	.0757	.0495	.0394	—	2.4825
	SR = 1.06, fd	.1119	.1000	.1012	.0714	.0467	.0372	—	2.3420
	Both sexes	.2305	.2060	.2085	.1471	.0962	.0766	—	4.8245

Period									Total
1785-1799	Observed fs	.1146	.1435	.1020	.0890	.0965	.0533	—	
	P/F	1.0003	1.0085	.9390	.9094	.8296	.7854	—	
	Adj. fs	.1146	.1447	.0958	.0809	.0801	.0419	—	2.7900
	SR = 1.06, fd	.1081	.1365	.0904	.0763	.0756	.0395	—	2.6320
	Both sexes	.2227	.2812	.1862	.1572	.1557	.0814	—	5.4220
1800-1814	Observed fs	.1013	.1276	.1228	.1073	.0849	.0429	—	
	P/F	.9997	1.0245	1.0143	.9662	.9094	.7898	—	
	Adj. fs	.1013	.1307	.1246	.1037	.0772	.0339	—	2.8570
	SR = 1.06, fd	.0956	.1233	.1175	.0978	.0728	.0320	—	2.6950
	Both sexes	.1969	.2540	.2421	.2015	.1500	.0659	—	5.5520
1815-1829	Observed fs	.0716	.1199	.1180	.1042	.0839	.0230	.0031	
	P/F	1.0000	1.2338	1.0882	.9633	.9444	.9625	.9124	
	Adj. fs	.0675	.1479	.1284	.1004	.0792	.0221	.0030	2.7630
	SR = 1.06, fd	.1391	.1395	.1211	.0947	.0747	.0208	.0028	2.6055
	Both sexes	.0933	.2874	.2495	.1951	.1539	.0429	.0058	5.3685
1830-1844	Observed fs	.0933	.1340	.1205	.1271	.0859	.0608	—	
	P/F	.9996	1.0043	.8809	.8214	.7515	.7004	—	
	Adj. fs	.0933	.1346	.1061	.1044	.0646	.0426	—	2.7280
	SR = 1.06, fd	.0880	.1270	.1001	.0985	.0609	.0402	—	2.5735
	Both sexes	.1813	.2616	.2062	.2029	.1255	.0828	—	5.3015

NOTE: The fd figures in the Total column represent Gross Reproductive Rate (GRR).

TABLE 2.10

Male Age-Specific Fertility Rates for Sons and Gross Reproductive Rate (GRR) by Cohort, Shen and Hsü Clans, 1680-1829

Cohort	Measure	Age									GRR
		15-19	20-24	25-29	30-34	35-39	40-44	45-49	50-54	55-59	
		SHEN									
1680-1694	Obs. fs	.0086	.0483	.0787	.1086	.0844	.0775	.0403	.0177	.0183	
	P/F	–	1.788	1.396	1.267	1.131	1.075	1.017	.988	.972	
	Adj. fs	.0086	.0863	.1098	.1376	.0954	.0834	.0410	.0175	.0178	2.9870
1695-1709	Obs. fs	.0201	.0977	.1038	.1240	.0754	.0654	.0102	–	–	
	P/F	–	1.023	1.255	1.176	1.100	1.047	.994	–	–	
	Adj. fs	.0201	.0999	.1303	.1458	.0830	.0685	.0101	–	–	2.7885
1710-1724	Obs. fs	.0098	.0406	.0819	.0993	.0991	.0639	.0388	.0251	.0202	
	P/F	–	1.617	1.417	1.250	1.157	1.068	1.015	.985	.961	
	Adj. fs	.0098	.0657	.1161	.1241	.1146	.0682	.0394	.0247	.0194	2.9100
1725-1739	Obs. fs	.0048	.0380	.0859	.0980	.1095	.0734	.0492	.0395	.0139	
	P/F	–	2.009	1.417	1.260	1.168	1.065	1.012	.978	.951	
	Adj. fs	.0048	.0763	.1217	.1235	.1279	.0782	.0498	.0386	.0132	3.1700
1740-1754	Obs. fs	.0063	.0467	.0623	.0971	.0912	.0651	.0415	.0458	.0181	
	P/F	–	1.962	1.360	1.271	1.152	1.068	.960	.913	.882	
	Adj. fs	.0063	.0916	.0847	.1234	.1051	.0695	.0398	.0418	.0160	2.8910
1755-1769	Obs. fs	.0065	.0545	.0681	.0953	.1039	.0778	.0559	.0357	.0199	
	P/F	–	1.592	1.285	1.202	1.115	1.030	.975	.936	.918	
	Adj. fs	.0065	.0868	.0875	.1146	.1158	.0801	.0545	.0334	.0183	2.9875
1770-1784	Obs. fs	.0083	.0464	.0865	.0899	.1042	.0908	.0788	.0320	.0247	
	P/F	–	1.595	1.373	1.190	1.110	1.024	.948	.888	.867	
	Adj. fs	.0083	.0740	.1188	.1070	.1157	.0930	.0747	.0248	.0214	3.1885
1785-1799	Obs. fs	.0090	.0402	.0847	.1101	.1047	.0874	.0632	.0223	.0135	
	P/F	–	1.630	1.421	1.240	1.111	1.003	.926	.875	.857	
	Adj. fs	.0090	.0655	.1204	.1365	.1163	.0877	.0585	.0195	.0116	3.1250
1800-1814	Obs. fs	.0119	.0525	.1114	.1174	.1047	.0618	.0298	.0231	.0099	
	P/F	–	1.653	1.411	1.184	1.047	.957	.681	.885	.867	
	Adj. fs	.0119	.0868	.1572	.1390	.1096	.0591	.0203	.0204	.0086	3.0645
1815-1829	Obs. fs	.0175	.0545	.0765	.1060	.0882	.0631	.0580	.0255	.0113	
	P/F	–	1.593	1.346	1.215	1.080	.988	.895	.876	.852	
	Adj. fs	.0175	.0868	.1030	.1288	.0953	.0623	.0519	.0223	.0096	2.8875

Period		C1	C2	C3	C4	C5	C6	C7	C8	C9	Total
1680–1694	Obs. fs	.0188	.0465	.0633	.0680	.0773	.0694	.0526	.0252	.0350	
	P/F	–	1.413	1.252	1.165	1.120	1.061	1.006	.961	.949	2.5675
	Adj. fs	.0188	.0657	.0793	.0792	.0866	.0736	.0529	.0242	.0332	
1695–1709	Obs. fs	.0067	.0475	.0647	.0902	.1287	.0763	.0736	.0335	.0052	
	P/F	–	1.605	1.302	1.213	1.177	1.065	1.014	.961	.943	3.0980
	Adj. fs	.0067	.0762	.0842	.1094	.1515	.0812	.0746	.0309	.0049	
1710–1724	Obs. fs	.0149	.0556	.0796	.0686	.1095	.0633	.0372	.0117	.0172	
	P/F	–	1.734	1.426	1.253	1.232	1.113	1.062	1.028	1.018	2.9260
	Adj. fs	.0149	.0964	.1135	.0860	.1349	.0705	.0395	.0120	.0175	
1725–1739	Obs. fs	.0044	.0269	.0534	.0736	.0889	.0769	.0413	.0248	.0145	
	P/F	–	1.828	1.615	1.480	1.388	1.301	1.208	1.165	1.138	2.8370
	Adj. fs	.0044	.0492	.0862	.1089	.1234	.1000	.0499	.0289	.0165	
1740–1754	Obs. fs	.0050	.0242	.0415	.0926	.0918	.0851	.0415	.0304	.0090	
	P/F	–	1.803	1.549	1.503	1.291	1.187	1.095	1.060	1.030	2.7925
	Adj. fs	.0050	.0436	.0643	.1392	.1185	.1010	.0454	.0322	.0093	
1755–1769	Obs. fs	–	.0239	.0674	.0924	.0859	.0620	.0512	.0368	.0050	
	P/F	–	2.158	1.790	1.541	1.383	1.273	1.211	1.156	1.118	3.1120
	Adj. fs	.0040	.0516	.1206	.1424	.1188	.0789	.0620	.0425	.0056	
1770–1784	Obs. fs	.0040	.0420	.0774	.0883	.0837	.0450	.0401	.0228	.0103	
	P/F	–	2.297	1.830	1.582	1.442	1.321	1.271	1.219	1.184	3.2645
	Adj. fs	.0040	.0965	.1416	.1397	.1207	.0594	.0510	.0278	.0122	
1785–1799	Obs. fs	.0141	.0415	.0651	.0945	.0733	.0632	.0347	.0365	.0058	
	P/F	–	2.026	1.661	1.486	1.308	1.208	1.125	1.094	1.041	3.0200
	Adj. fs	.0141	.0841	.1081	.1404	.0959	.0764	.0391	.0399	.0060	
1800–1814	Obs. fs	.0120	.0396	.0628	.1027	.1017	.0767	.0524	.0194	.0055	
	P/F	–	1.837	1.556	1.362	1.175	1.044	.956	.902	.886	2.9720
	Adj. fs	.0120	.0727	.0977	.1399	.1195	.0801	.0501	.0175	.0049	
1815–1829	Obs. fs	.0122	.0523	.0800	.1091	.0839	.0788	.0354	.0275	.0105	
	P/F	–	1.904	1.528	1.257	1.049	.918	.837	.802	.779	2.9565
	Adj. fs	.0122	.0996	.1222	.1371	.0880	.0723	.0296	.0221	.0082	

TABLE 2.II

Male Age-Specific Fertility Rates for Sons and Gross Reproductive Rate (GRR) by Period, 1725-1844

Period	Measure	15-19	20-24	25-29	30-34	35-39	40-44	45-49	50-54	55-59	GRR
						SHEN					
1725-1739	Obs. fs	.0098	.0603	.0844	.1240	.0598	.0739	.0657	.0335	.0265	
	P/F	—	1.747	1.569	1.521	1.219	1.073	.969	.933	.864	
	Adj. fs	.0098	.1053	.1324	.1886	.0729	.0793	.0636	.0313	.0229	3.5305
1740-1754	Obs. fs	.0048	.0390	.0909	.0993	.0968	.0759	.0102	.0106	.0183	
	P/F	—	1.440	1.545	1.234	1.190	1.229	1.186	1.140	1.054	
	Adj. fs	.0048	.0561	.1404	.1226	.1152	.0933	.0121	.0121	.0193	2.8795
1755-1769	Obs. fs	.0063	.0426	.0733	.0980	.1104	.0582	.0388	.0201	.0035	
	P/F	—	1.657	1.306	1.306	1.133	1.112	1.034	.997	1.089	
	Adj. fs	.0063	.0706	.0957	.1280	.1250	.0647	.0401	.0200	.0038	2.7710
1770-1784	Obs. fs	.0065	.0549	.0669	.0971	.1025	.0792	.0495	.0296	.0243	
	P/F	—	1.850	1.266	1.182	1.151	1.060	1.018	.940	.942	
	Adj. fs	.0065	.1016	.0847	.1148	.1180	.0840	.0504	.0278	.0229	3.0535
1785-1799	Obs. fs	.0083	.0478	.0788	.0953	.0955	.0602	.0415	.0501	.0101	
	P/F	—	1.558	1.317	1.166	1.094	.971	.971	1.013	1.000	
	Adj. fs	.0083	.0745	.1038	.1111	.1044	.0584	.0403	.0508	.0101	2.8085
1800-1814	Obs. fs	.0090	.0478	.0826	.0899	.1096	.0972	.0559	.0270	.0218	
	P/F	—	1.633	1.435	1.201	1.129	1.028	.913	.846	.776	
	Adj. fs	.0090	.0781	.1185	.1080	.1238	.0999	.0510	.0228	.0169	3.1400
1815-1829	Obs. fs	.0352	.0432	.0858	.1101	.0968	.0794	.0788	.0414	.0213	
	P/F	—	1.014	1.066	1.077	1.020	.958	.902	.855	.846	
	Adj. fs	.0352	.0438	.0915	.1185	.0987	.0761	.0711	.0354	.0180	2.9415
1830-1844	Obs. fs	.0175	.0564	.1047	.1174	.1227	.0838	.0632	.0231	.0196	
	P/F	—	1.560	1.402	1.171	.955	.840	.812	.802	.786	
	Adj. fs	.0175	.0880	.1468	.1375	.1172	.0704	.0513	.0185	.0154	3.3130

1725–1739	Obs. fs	.0177	.0614	.0773	.0902	.1151	.0298	.0526	.0091	–	
	P/F	–	1.472	1.168	.998	1.034	.804	.891	.949	.965	2.4345
	Adj. fs	.0177	.0904	.0903	.0901	.1190	.0239	.0469	.0086	–	
1740–1754	Obs. fs	.0044	.0413	.0670	.0686	.1091	.0910	.0730	.0412	.0470	
	P/F		2.040	1.814	1.558	1.365	1.223	1.093	.941	.795	3.6670
	Adj. fs	.0044	.0843	.1216	.1069	.1489	.1113	.0798	.0388	.0374	
1755–1769	Obs. fs	.0050	.0265	.0519	.0736	.0990	.0694	.0372	.0128	.0224	
	P/F	–	1.767	1.509	1.495	1.504	1.480	1.264	1.249	1.283	2.9175
	Adj. fs	.0050	.0468	.0783	.1101	.1489	.1027	.0470	.0160	.0287	
1770–1784	Obs. fs	–	.0169	.0480	.0926	.0770	.0763	.0413	.0228	.0040	
	P/F		2.270	2.031	1.576	1.309	1.231	1.256	1.198	1.298	2.8045
	Adj. fs	–	.0384	.0975	.1459	.1008	.0939	.0512	.0273	.0052	
1785–1799	Obs. fs	.0040	.0369	.0701	.0924	.0883	.0748	.0415	.0248	.0139	
	P/F	–	2.178	1.488	1.358	1.192	1.107	1.021	1.007	.955	2.9150
	Adj. fs	.0040	.0804	.1043	.1255	.1053	.0828	.0424	.0250	.0133	
1800–1814	Obs. fs	.0141	.0495	.0786	.0883	.0846	.0588	.0512	.0481	.0057	
	P/F		1.766	1.636	1.429	1.312	1.137	1.040	.994	.939	3.2030
	Adj. fs	.0141	.0874	.1286	.1262	.1110	.0668	.0533	.0478	.0054	
1815–1829	Obs. fs	.0120	.0283	.0544	.0945	.0827	.0454	.0401	.0210	.0074	
	P/F	–	2.115	1.294	1.741	1.528	1.432	1.357	1.310	1.240	2.9465
	Adj. fs	.0120	.0599	.0704	.1645	.1264	.0650	.0544	.0275	.0092	
1830–1844	Obs. fs	.0122	.0554	.0739	.1027	.0927	.0686	.0347	.0296	.0103	
	P/F		1.907	1.428	1.180	1.039	1.014	.983	1.012	1.001	3.0340
	Adj. fs	.0122	.1057	.1055	.1431	.0964	.0696	.0341	.0299	.0103	

TABLE 2.12

Observed Number of Deaths in the Shen Clan by Age and Cohort

markedly until the introduction of family planning in the 1950's. Considering the massive and often violent social changes that shook Chinese society in the eighteenth and nineteenth centuries, one expects to find sharp fluctuations in fertility. What one finds in fact is impressive continuity.

Mortality

As we have seen, patrilineal descent did not ensure a person a place in his or her father's genealogy. Sons were certain of notice only if they survived to age 15, and daughters were normally excluded no matter how long they lived. Thus we have no choice but to base our estimates of male mortality on the experience of those men who survived to age 15, and our estimates of female mortality on the experience of the only women regularly noted in the genealogies, their wives.

To estimate mortality with these data I first organized my population into five-year birth cohorts and then assigned all deaths to one of 14 five-year age groups (15-19 to 80 and above). There were, of course, a number of persons whose exact age at death could not be determined. Under what I term the low-mortality condition, they were assigned to the age groups 60-64 and above, with the undated deaths distributed across the age classes in the same proportions as the dated deaths. Under the alternative high-mortality condition, the undated deaths were assigned to the age groups under 60, and again the distribution of the undated deaths followed that of the dated deaths.[20] Where the number of undated deaths is small, as it is for the cohorts born before 1760, I have based my final calculations on dated deaths only. Where the number of undated deaths is larger, I have taken the average of the values obtained under the high and low mortality conditions. This has the effect of modifying an otherwise unbelievably sharp increase in mortality in the late eighteenth and early nineteenth centuries.

Having assigned all the people in my sample to birth cohorts and their deaths to age groups, I then proceeded to construct life tables for the males and females in each of the clans. The actual numbers employed in calculating the q_x (probability of dying) values of the Shen males are given in Table 2.12 by way of illustration.[21] The figures shown in each parallelogram are the number of persons surviving to that age and the number of deaths occurring during the age interval. Though life tables based on the q_x values of each cohort might have revealed interesting temporal trends, I did not prepare such refined figures for this paper. Instead, I bunched cohorts and periods in groups of three and took the average value. This had the advantage of smoothing the mortality schedules, but further graduation was required before I could proceed. This was accomplished by applying the polynomial function $\log q_x = a + bx + bx^2$.[22]

TABLE 2.13

Probability of Dying (q_x) for Females by Age Group and Cohort, Shen and Hsü Clans, 1680–1829

	Cohort									
					SHEN					
Age	1680-1694	1695-1709	1710-1724	1725-1739	1740-1754	1755-1769	1770-1784	1785-1799	1800-1814	1815-1829
0-1	.1218	.1525	.1770	.1051	.1093	.1041	.1650	.1829	.1992	.1064
1-4	.0802	.1003	.1145	.0680	.0707	.0695	.1117	.1252	.1330	.0728
5-9	.0231	.0288	.0331	.0197	.0205	.0199	.0318	.0355	.0381	.0207
10-14	.0180	.0225	.0259	.0153	.0161	.0155	.0248	.0278	.0297	.0161
15-19	.0239	.0303	.0345	.0205	.0213	.0205	.0327	.0364	.0393	.0212
20-24	.0301	.0346	.0359	.0259	.0259	.0258	.0390	.0438	.0494	.0265
25-29	.0339	.0402	.0385	.0292	.0318	.0343	.0468	.0530	.0555	.0382
30-34	.0436	.0476	.0428	.0330	.0396	.0454	.0568	.0646	.0627	.0543
35-39	.0565	.0573	.0492	.0457	.0499	.0599	.0693	.0794	.0692	.0760
40-44	.0738	.0702	.0585	.0628	.0637	.0787	.0855	.0981	.0752	.1048
45-49	.0971	.0875	.0719	.0857	.0822	.1030	.1063	.1224	.0956	.1425
50-54	.1286	.1110	.0914	.1164	.1074	.1343	.1333	.1536	.1234	.1909
55-59	.1718	.1432	.1202	.1572	.1419	.1746	.1684	.1943	.1618	.2520
60-64	.2310	.1880	.1636	.2109	.1897	.2260	.2148	.2478	.2154	.3282
65-69	.3131	.2513	.2301	.2813	.2569	.2917	.2760	.3182	.2914	.4206
70-74	.4278	.3416	.3348	.3726	.3516	.3749	.3580	.4114	.4005	.5321
75-79	.5891	.4723	.5040	.4911	.4872	.4799	.4681	.5357	.5587	.6623
80+	1.0000	1.0000	1.0000	1.0000	1.0000	1.0000	1.0000	1.0000	1.0000	1.0000
Model West levels	9-10	9-10	9-10	9-10	9-10	8-9	7-8	6-7	8-9	6-7

H S Ü

	8-9	8-9	8-9	7-8	6-7	8-9	8-9	4-5	3-4	4-5
0-1	.1253	.1269	.1213	.1322	.2304	.1293	.1045	.2540	.2835	.1886
1-4	.0837	.0848	.0810	.0894	.1577	.0864	.0698	.1772	.1995	.1316
5-9	.0239	.0243	.0232	.0255	.0448	.0247	.0200	.0500	.0561	.0371
10-14	.0187	.0189	.0181	.0199	.0350	.0193	.0156	.0390	.0438	.0290
15-19	.0247	.0250	.0239	.0261	.0459	.0255	.0206	.0509	.0570	.0378
20-24	.0310	.0314	.0301	.0328	.0574	.0314	.0259	.0635	.0660	.0464
25-29	.0348	.0353	.0338	.0420	.0593	.0390	.0344	.0687	.0768	.0572
30-34	.0393	.0399	.0382	.0538	.0633	.0486	.0456	.0763	.0899	.0707
35-39	.0434	.0441	.0421	.0690	.0697	.0611	.0606	.0868	.1061	.0879
40-44	.0472	.0689	.0553	.0885	.0794	.0773	.0805	.1014	.1259	.1097
45-49	.0614	.1043	.0733	.1136	.0932	.0983	.1070	.1217	.1503	.1373
50-54	.0824	.1527	.0982	.1460	.1132	.1259	.1424	.1497	.1805	.1727
55-59	.1145	.2163	.1329	.1876	.1419	.1621	.1895	.1890	.2180	.2182
60-64	.1643	.2967	.1815	.2413	.1839	.2103	.2523	.2446	.2650	.2769
65-69	.2436	.3937	.2505	.3105	.2461	.2744	.3362	.3253	.3243	.3523
70-74	.3734	.5056	.3495	.3998	.3399	.3605	.4479	.4435	.3989	.4511
75-79	.5915	.6287	.4926	.5152	.4852	.4761	.5975	.6202	.4941	.5792
80+	1.0000	1.0000	1.0000	1.0000	1.0000	1.0000	1.0000	1.0000	1.0000	1.0000
Model West levels	8-9	8-9	8-9	7-8	6-7	8-9	8-9	4-5	3-4	4-5

TABLE 2.14

Probability of Dying (q_x) for Females by Age Group and Period, Shen and Hsü Clans, 1725-1844

Age	Period							
	1725-1739	1740-1754	1755-1769	1770-1784	1785-1799	1800-1814	1815-1829	1830-1844
				SHEN				
0-1	.1489	.1270	.1221	.1102	.1660	.1922	.1603	.1448
1-4	.0980	.0806	.0790	.0713	.1123	.1284	.1070	.0980
5-9	.0282	.0231	.0229	.0206	.0320	.0367	.0306	.0279
10-14	.0220	.0180	.0178	.0161	.0250	.0287	.0239	.0218
15-19	.0292	.0238	.0238	.0215	.0329	.0379	.0316	.0287
20-24	.0339	.0299	.0275	.0272	.0383	.0421	.0374	.0360
25-29	.0400	.0336	.0325	.0306	.0451	.0477	.0446	.0453
30-34	.0478	.0380	.0392	.0375	.0540	.0550	.0538	.0570
35-39	.0581	.0539	.0482	.0467	.0656	.0646	.0657	.0720
40-44	.0716	.0754	.0604	.0589	.0809	.0774	.0809	.0911
45-49	.0897	.1042	.0773	.0754	.1012	.0946	.1007	.1155
50-54	.1141	.1423	.1009	.0979	.1286	.1176	.1268	.1466
55-59	.1472	.1919	.1341	.1289	.1658	.1491	.1612	.1863
60-64	.1928	.2554	.1820	.1722	.2167	.1928	.2072	.2371
65-69	.2564	.3355	.3518	.2331	.2879	.2538	.2690	.3024
70-74	.3461	.4356	.3556	.3204	.3882	.3406	.3527	.3863
75-79	.4743	.5582	.5122	.4466	.5309	.4657	.4676	.4046
80+	1.0000	1.0000	1.0000	1.0000	1.0000	1.0000	1.0000	1.0000
Model West levels	9-10	9-10	9-10	9-10	7-8	8-9	8-9	7-8
				HSÜ				
0-1	.1444	.1444	.1512	.1817	.1521	.2690	.2246	.2352
1-4	.0964	.0964	.1010	.1229	.1016	.1604	.1537	.1626
5-9	.0276	.0276	.0289	.0350	.0291	.0426	.0436	.0460
10-14	.0215	.0215	.0225	.0274	.0227	.0307	.0341	.0359
15-19	.0285	.0285	.0298	.0360	.0299	.0429	.0447	.0470
20-24	.0358	.0358	.0342	.0424	.0377	.0593	.0494	.0587
25-29	.0402	.0402	.0401	.0504	.0423	.0662	.0556	.0661
30-34	.0454	.0454	.0477	.0608	.0478	.0700	.0638	.0755
35-39	.0501	.0501	.0578	.0741	.0527	.0766	.0746	.0874
40-44	.0545	.0545	.0714	.0917	.0643	.0868	.0889	.1025
45-49	.0728	.0719	.0896	.1148	.0800	.1017	.1079	.1219
50-54	.0978	.0963	.1145	.1455	.1016	.1235	.1334	.1470
55-59	.1319	.1309	.1489	.1869	.1317	.1552	.1683	.1796
60-64	.1790	.1806	.1970	.2429	.1741	.2018	.2163	.2222
65-69	.2438	.2530	.2653	.3201	.2345	.2717	.2830	.2788
70-74	.3338	.3598	.3637	.4265	.3227	.3787	.3775	.3545
75-79	.4597	.5194	.5074	.5763	.4524	.5466	.5137	.4570
80+	1.0000	1.0000	1.0000	1.0000	1.0000	1.0000	1.0000	1.0000
Model West levels	8-9	8-9	8-9	7-8	8-9	5-6	6-7	5-6

When these procedures produced what appear to be regular and plausible adult mortality estimates for both the Shen and Hsü clans, I was encouraged to try to estimate child mortality by extrapolating backward from the adult q_x values. I first selected from the Coale and Demeny series two model life tables for each set of adult q_x values, and then estimated childhood values on the basis of the observed values of the adults.[23] In most cases I accepted the observed values for persons over 15 and extrapolated the values of those under 15, but in a few cases the observed values for persons aged 15-19 and 20-24 appeared too low, probably because people who died unmarried at these young ages were never recorded. In these cases I took age 30 as my empirical base and estimated the q_x values for all persons under 30.

The results obtained for the Shen and Hsü clans are presented in full detail in Tables 2.13-16, but the reader who is not adept at visualizing the shape of q_x curves should look first at Figures 2.4 and 2.5. These figures compare the observed values of one cohort and one period with the corresponding life table values. Generally speaking, the two curves are very similar, but note that the observed values usually rise above the life table values after age 45. This could be an artifact introduced by the polynomial chosen to smooth the mortality schedules; but there is also the possibility that as the population of China grew and pressed on available resources, the elderly were the first to suffer the consequences.[24] I hope to explore this hypothesis in my future research.[25]

Figure 2.6 compares male and female mortality for selected cohorts and periods. Whether the comparison is made in terms of cohorts or periods, the data say that adult males had far lower chances of surviving to the next age interval than adult females. But for children the situation is less clear. With the striking exception of the Hsü clan in the years 1725-39, the period comparisons say that male mortality exceeded female mortality at most ages up to about 18, but the cohort comparisons argue for the opposite conclusion. Why this difference exists is not clear. All I can do at present is remind the reader that whereas the adult comparisons are based on observed values, the child comparisons are based on extrapolations from model life tables. The dilemma could probably be resolved by obtaining better estimates of childhood mortality.

The general trend of mortality during the period covered by the Shen and Hsü genealogies is best described as one of stability followed by a fairly sharp rise in mortality in the late eighteenth and early nineteenth centuries. This is evident in the q_x values reported in Tables 2.13-16, the l_x (survivorship) curves displayed in Figure 2.7, and the e_x (life expectancy) levels shown in Figure 2.8. There are, however, several interesting (and somewhat puzzling) departures from this general trend. Whereas the Hsü

TABLE 2.15

Probability of Dying (q_x) for Males by Age Group and Cohort, Shen and Hsü Clans, 1680-1829

Age		1680-1694	1695-1709	1710-1724	1725-1739	1740-1754	1755-1769	1770-1784	1785-1799	1800-1814	1815-1829
						Cohort					
						SHEN					
0-1		.1495	.1274	.1914	.1644	.1253	.1569	.1782	.2026	.2284	.2065
1-4		.0830	.0708	.1063	.0930	.0709	.0887	.1038	.1195	.1347	.1244
5-9		.0229	.0195	.0294	.0254	.0194	.0243	.0279	.0319	.0360	.0328
10-14		.0166	.0142	.0213	.0184	.0140	.0176	.0201	.0230	.0259	.0236
15-19		.0234	.0199	.0299	.0257	.0196	.0245	.0278	.0316	.0256	.0321
20-24		.0331	.0282	.0344	.0364	.0278	.0347	.0394	.0447	.0504	.0455
25-29		.0365	.0312	.0403	.0403	.0307	.0384	.0438	.0498	.0561	.0509
30-34		.0420	.0358	.0481	.0463	.0353	.0442	.0504	.0574	.0647	.0587
35-39		.0568	.0563	.0583	.0624	.0561	.0630	.0739	.0831	.0861	.0928
40-44		.0766	.0851	.0721	.0837	.0864	.0885	.1055	.1175	.1138	.1400
45-49		.1035	.1241	.0908	.1121	.1286	.1227	.1464	.1623	.1497	.2018
50-54		.1394	.1744	.1162	.1495	.1852	.1676	.1978	.2191	.1957	.2777
55-59		.1878	.2364	.1516	.1988	.2582	.2253	.2602	.2890	.2346	.3645
60-64		.2528	.3091	.2012	.2639	.3481	.2990	.3332	.3723	.3292	.4570
65-69		.3399	.3890	.2719	.3488	.4542	.3906	.4256	.4690	.4235	.5471
70-74		.4570	.4723	.3741	.4602	.5729	.5035	.5045	.5775	.5417	.6250
75-79		.6132	.5532	.5241	.6053	.6997	.6395	.5963	.6941	.6893	.6818
80+		1.0000	1.0000	1.0000	1.0000	1.0000	1.0000	1.0000	1.0000	1.0000	1.0000
Model West levels		9-10	9-10	9-10	9-10	9-10	9-10	7-8	6-7	6-7	6-7

HSÜ

	9-10	9-10	8-9	7-8	7-8	8-9	4-5	3-4	3-4	3-4
0-1	.1093	.1253	.1233	.1602	.1280	.1577	.2192	.1888	.3215	.3281
1-4	.0619	.0696	.0708	.0933	.0746	.0906	.1320	.1147	.1985	.1994
5-9	.0169	.0192	.0192	.0251	.0200	.0246	.0349	.0301	.0517	.0524
10-14	.0123	.0139	.0139	.0181	.0145	.0178	.0251	.0217	.0371	.0376
15-19	.0171	.0196	.0192	.0250	.0199	.0246	.0341	.0293	.0499	.0510
20-24	.0239	.0277	.0272	.0354	.0283	.0320	.0453	.0416	.0708	.0723
25-29	.0338	.0306	.0302	.0393	.0314	.0416	.0598	.0596	.0899	.0834
30-34	.0389	.0352	.0348	.0453	.0362	.0543	.0785	.0835	.1130	.0972
35-39	.0458	.0515	.0566	.0673	.0602	.0709	.1025	.1148	.1402	.1145
40-44	.0559	.0740	.0886	.0975	.0949	.0928	.1331	.1544	.1722	.1361
45-49	.0857	.1044	.1334	.1380	.1427	.1217	.1722	.2037	.2088	.1634
50-54	.1266	.1448	.1932	.1905	.2039	.1599	.2215	.2631	.2505	.1982
55-59	.1797	.1973	.2692	.2569	.2772	.2105	.2833	.3328	.2967	.2426
60-64	.2453	.2642	.3609	.3379	.3584	.2777	.3605	.4127	.3478	.3002
65-69	.3220	.3474	.4657	.4338	.4413	.3671	.4565	.5010	.4029	.3753
70-74	.4065	.4488	.5786	.5433	.5163	.4867	.5757	.5963	.4611	.4733
75-79	.4936	.5700	.6914	.6649	.5752	.6459	.7210	.6948	.5215	.6035
80+	1.0000	1.0000	1.0000	1.0000	1.0000	1.0000	1.0000	1.0000	1.0000	1.0000
Model West levels	9-10	9-10	8-9	7-8	7-8	8-9	4-5	3-4	3-4	3-4

TABLE 2.16
Probability of Dying (q$_x$) for Males by Age Group and Period, Shen and Hsü Clans, 1725-1844

Age	Period							
	1725-1739	1740-1754	1755-1769	1770-1784	1785-1799	1800-1814	1815-1829	1830-1844
				SHEN				
0-1	.1975	.1498	.1335	.1097	.1651	.1711	.2379	.1881
1-4	.1135	.0847	.0741	.0620	.0934	.0983	.1403	.1110
5-9	.0307	.0232	.0205	.0170	.0255	.0266	.0375	.0296
10-14	.0222	.0168	.0149	.0123	.0185	.0193	.0270	.0214
15-19	.0308	.0234	.0209	.0171	.0258	.0267	.0371	.0293
20-24	.0373	.0331	.0295	.0243	.0365	.0378	.0525	.0415
25-29	.0457	.0367	.0326	.0269	.0404	.0420	.0585	.0462
30-34	.0566	.0422	.0375	.0309	.0465	.0483	.0674	.0533
35-39	.0707	.0607	.0549	.0425	.0672	.0674	.0891	.0809
40-44	.0892	.0856	.0787	.0584	.0934	.0928	.1171	.1183
45-49	.1138	.1185	.1104	.0802	.1286	.1261	.1532	.1666
50-54	.1464	.1610	.1519	.1102	.1734	.1696	.1992	.2258
55-59	.1905	.2145	.2045	.1513	.2294	.2253	.2574	.2949
60-64	.2500	.2805	.2698	.2076	.2976	.2958	.3312	.3708
65-69	.3315	.3595	.3488	.2850	.3787	.3836	.4231	.4488
70-74	.4439	.4524	.4413	.3910	.4728	.4911	.5384	.5236
75-79	.5998	.5582	.5471	.5357	.5781	.6218	.6804	.5886
80+	1.0000	1.0000	1.0000	1.0000	1.0000	1.0000	1.0000	1.0000
Model West levels	8-9	9-10	9-10	9-10	8-9	8-9	6-7	6-7
				HSÜ				
0-1	.1368	.1662	.1158	.1337	.1745	.1891	.2799	.2897
1-4	.0786	.0968	.0666	.0788	.1017	.1127	.1686	.1775
5-9	.0213	.0260	.0180	.0211	.0273	.0299	.0445	.0464
10-14	.0154	.0188	.0130	.0152	.0197	.0216	.0320	.0333
15-19	.0213	.0259	.0181	.0208	.0272	.0294	.0435	.0450
20-24	.0302	.0367	.0256	.0295	.0345	.0417	.0617	.0638
25-29	.0335	.0408	.0284	.0412	.0440	.0537	.0736	.0804
30-34	.0386	.0470	.0327	.0570	.0565	.0690	.0882	.1009
35-39	.0444	.0653	.0507	.0780	.0730	.0886	.1063	.1261
40-44	.0680	.0895	.0765	.1055	.0948	.1137	.1289	.1570
45-49	.1012	.1209	.1118	.1409	.1239	.1457	.1572	.1947
50-54	.1460	.1613	.1585	.1863	.1630	.1867	.1928	.2405
55-59	.2043	.2122	.2180	.2436	.2158	.2390	.2376	.2958
60-64	.2774	.2752	.2911	.3150	.2873	.3057	.2946	.3624
65-69	.3656	.3520	.3771	.4025	.3848	.3906	.3671	.4421
70-74	.4676	.4444	.4737	.5086	.5189	.4985	.4602	.5379
75-79	.5798	.5537	.5775	.6357	.7039	.6363	.5804	.6511
80+	1.0000	1.0000	1.0000	1.0000	1.0000	1.0000	1.0000	1.0000
Model West levels	8-9	7-8	8-9	6-7	7-8	5-6	4-5	2-3

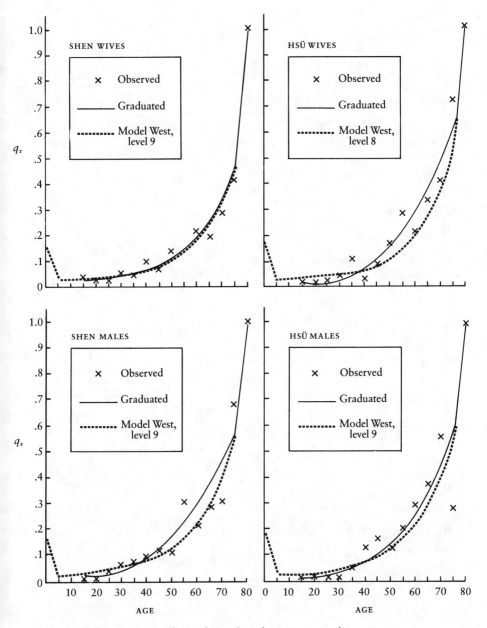

Fig. 2.4. Mortality curves (q_x), Shen and Hsü clans, for 1695-1709 cohorts

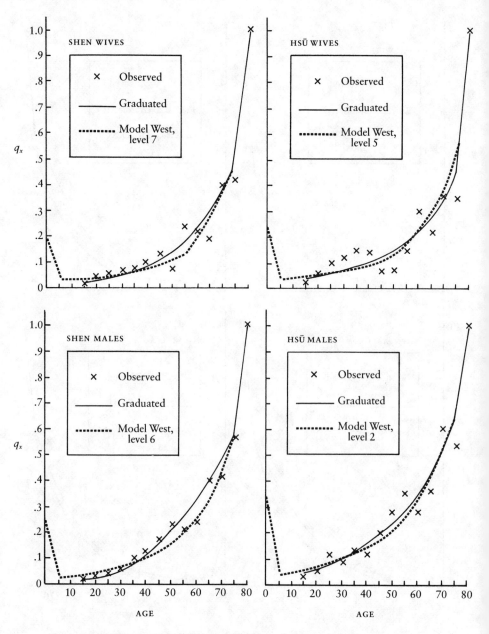

Fig. 2.5. Mortality curves (q_x), Shen and Hsü clans, for the period 1830-1844

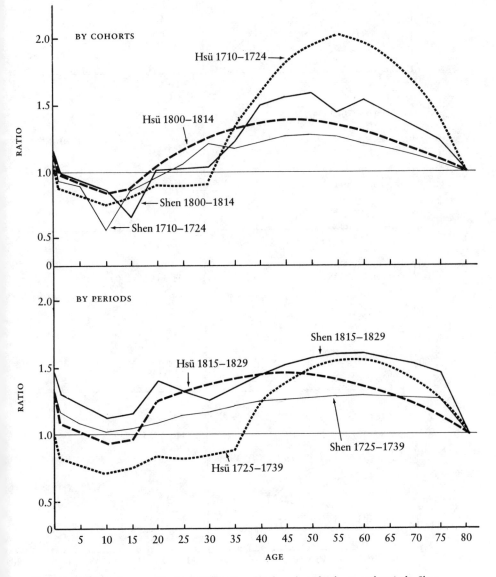

Fig. 2.6. Excess male mortality (q_x Male/q_x Female), for selected cohorts and periods, Shen and Hsü clans, 1710-1829

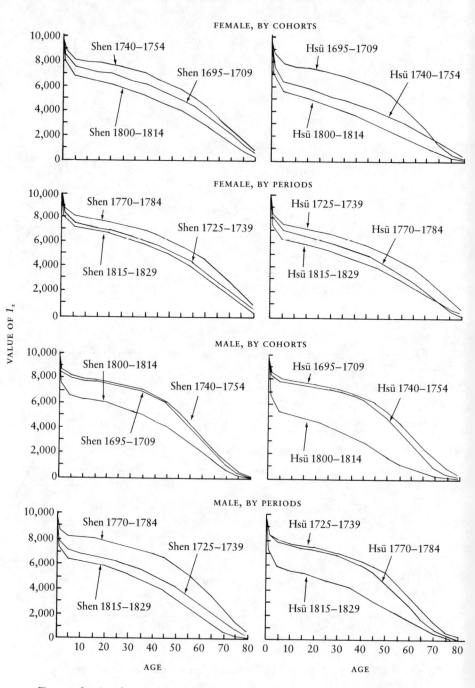

FEMALE, BY COHORTS

Shen 1740–1754
Shen 1695–1709
Shen 1800–1814

Hsü 1695–1709
Hsü 1740–1754
Hsü 1800–1814

FEMALE, BY PERIODS

Shen 1770–1784
Shen 1725–1739
Shen 1815–1829

Hsü 1725–1739
Hsü 1770–1784
Hsü 1815–1829

MALE, BY COHORTS

Shen 1800–1814
Shen 1740–1754
Shen 1695–1709

Hsü 1695–1709
Hsü 1740–1754
Hsü 1800–1814

MALE, BY PERIODS

Shen 1770–1784
Shen 1725–1739
Shen 1815–1829

Hsü 1725–1739
Hsü 1770–1784
Hsü 1815–1829

VALUE OF l_x

AGE

AGE

Fig. 2.7. Survivorship at each age group (l_x) for selected cohorts, Shen and Hsü clans, 1695-1829

56

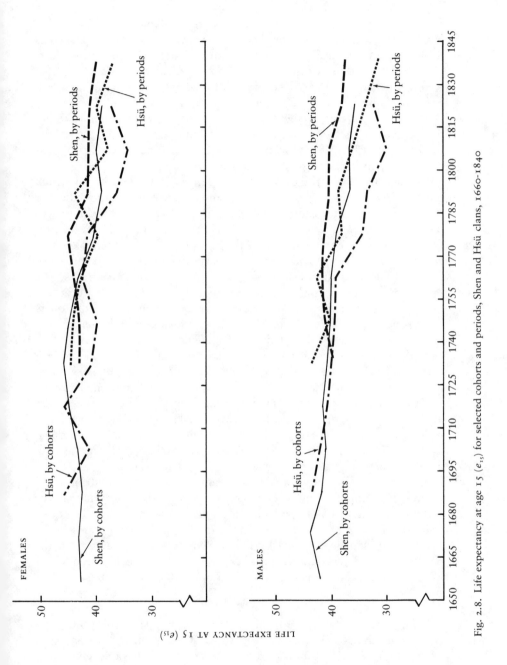

Fig. 2.8. Life expectancy at age 15 (e_{15}) for selected cohorts and periods, Shen and Hsü clans, 1660–1840

57

l_x curves, whether male or female, show a steady pattern of increasing mortality over time, none of the Shen curves show this pattern. And whereas the e_{15} values for the Shen clan change over time but display little short-term variation, those of the Hsü clan, and particularly those of the Hsü wives, fluctuate markedly. The shapes of the curves shown in Figure 2.8 seem to point to a natural disaster in the early 1770's.

Though it is premature (and perhaps even foolhardy) to attempt to explain all the shifts in mortality evident in Figures 2.7 and 2.8, some of the more striking changes are clearly the result of historical events. The general decline in life expectancy among cohorts born after 1785 is at least partly attributable to the ravages of the Taiping Rebellion, which struck the Hsiao-shan area in force in 1860-61 and is frequently mentioned in the two genealogies as the cause of a clan member's death. And the differences between the Shen and Hsü clans were partly if not wholly caused by a disastrous flood in 1770, which the Hsü genealogy repeatedly invokes as a cause of death but the Shen genealogy never mentions.[26] Why, one wonders, did the flood affect Hsü females so much more than Hsü males? For some reason peculiar to this particular situation? Or did natural disasters usually kill more females than males? A satisfactory answer to this question is essential to understanding long-term population trends in a country in which natural disasters struck with frightening regularity.

At the end of the seventeenth century the mortality of the Shen and Hsü clans was at about Level 9 in the Model West life tables (female e_o = 40, male e_o = 37.3). By the end of the eighteenth century it had risen markedly, and more among the Hsüs than among the Shens. The life chances of the Shens declined to Level 6 in the Model West tables (female e_o = 32.5, male e_o = 30), those of the Hsüs to Level 5 (female e_o = 30, male e_o = 27.6). Yet if the mortality of the Shen and Hsü clans was high, it was not as high as that estimated by the Princeton group for Chinese farmers in the 1930's.[27] Does this mean that mortality was generally lower in the seventeenth and eighteenth centuries than in the twentieth? Obviously we cannot say for certain, but the available evidence all points in that direction. The mortality of the Shen and Hsü clans is very similar to that found among the Kwangtung clan investigated by I-chin Yüan.[28] The estimates from the Kwangtung and Chekiang genealogies diverge only in the nineteenth century, when Chekiang was struck by the Taiping Rebellion.

Plausibility of the Findings

We have shown that it is possible to derive estimates of fertility and mortality from Chinese genealogies. Now we must ask whether these estimates are plausible. Do they produce growth rates that are believable, given conditions in late traditional China? These questions are best addressed by

TABLE 2.17

Life Table Survivorship (l_x) Values for the Shen and Hsü Clans for Selected Cohorts and Periods

	Cohort				Period			
	1695-1709		1785-1799		1725-1739		1830-1844	
Age	Shen	Hsü	Shen	Hsü	Shen	Hsü	Shen	Hsü
				FEMALES				
15-19	35643	37773	32900	27308	35953	36255	36153	28758
20-24	34488	36710	31583	25750	34820	35090	34983	27243
25-29	33200	35488	30058	24050	33468	33758	33563	25548
30-34	31745	34155	28295	22310	31933	32315	31850	23743
35-39	30083	32723	26265	20495	30245	30775	29803	21813
40-44	28170	30883	23920	18573	28290	29168	27383	19748
45-49	25958	28228	21273	16510	26018	27318	24570	17543
				MALES				
15-19	38795	38970	32680	33575	33195	37918	33768	26320
20-24	37863	38050	31438	32388	32065	36943	32575	24895
25-29	36738	36940	29955	30755	30738	35765	31148	23108
30-34	35508	35725	28353	28565	29170	34478	29600	21023
35-39	33878	34183	26373	25753	27320	33050	27625	18650
40-44	31495	32048	23748	22318	25145	31203	24895	16030
45-49	28228	29208	20458	18368	22605	28583	21388	13238
50-54	24063	25603	16608	14143	19685	25085	17250	10390
55-59	19193	21278	12460	10003	16405	20750	12835	7643

calculating the intrinsic rate of growth and then comparing the results with those obtained from an appropriate model of a stable population.[29] I have selected for this test the cohorts born in the years 1695-1709 and 1785-99 and the periods spanning the years 1725-39 and 1830-44. The data used in calculating the intrinsic rates of growth are shown in Tables 2.8-11 and Table 2.17.

Table 2.18 compares our selected cohorts and periods with the Model West stable population, reporting the intrinsic rate of increase (r), the gross reproduction rate (GRR), and the mean age at childbearing ($\bar{m}$). Four points should be noted. First, all the r values derived from the genealogies decline steadily as we approach the middle of the nineteenth century, but the change is much greater among the Hsüs than among the Shens. This confirms our discovery of an ever-increasing difference in the mortality of the two clans. Second, the Chinese GRRs appear to be somewhat lower than those of the model populations (note the ratios). This could mean that our adjusted fertility rates underestimate the extent to which births went unrecorded, but it could also mean that low marital fertility was characteristic of the Chinese. Third, although the Chinese GRRs are lower than those of the stable populations, they remain stable through

TABLE 2.18

Intrinsic Rate of Increase (r̄), Mean Age at Childbearing (m̄), and Gross Reproductive Rate (GRR) for Selected Cohorts and Periods, Shen and Hsü Clans, 1695-1844

Cohort or period	Clan	Observed			Mortality level	Model West			Observed GRR ÷ Model GRR
		r	GRR	m̄		r	GRR	m̄	
				FEMALE					
Cohort	Shen	.0255	3.1005	28.61	9	.025	3.339	29	.93
1695-1709	Hsü	.0199	2.5570	29.81	9	.020	2.910	29	.88
Cohort	Shen	.0179	2.7825	28.63	6	.020	3.484	29	.80
1785-1799	Hsü	.0062	2.4560	27.44	5	.010	2.704	27	.91
Period	Shen	.0216	2.7910	28.92	9	.020	2.910	29	.96
1725-1739	Hsü	.0156	2.2480	27.41	9	.020	2.745	27	.82
Period	Shen	.0214	2.6750	27.78	7	.020	3.066	27	.87
1830-1844	Hsü	.0098	2.5735	27.87	5	.010	2.704	27	.95
				MALE					
Cohort	Shen	.0225	2.7885	31.24	9	.020	3.201	31	.87
1695-1709	Hsü	.0212	3.0980	35.96	9	.020	3.418	33	.91
Cohort	Shen	.0153	3.1250	35.10	6	.015	3.570	33	.88
1785-1799	Hsü	.0147	3.0200	34.46	5	.015	3.871	33	.78
Period	Shen	.0209	3.5305	34.55	9	.020	3.418	33	1.03
1725-1739	Hsü	.0161	2.4345	32.68	9	.015	2.915	33	.84
Period	Shen	.0196	3.3130	33.92	7	.020	3.886	33	.85
1830-1844	Hsü	.0063	3.0340	33.78	5	.005	2.815	33	1.07

time. Obviously, the decline in the intrinsic rate of increase is almost entirely a result of deteriorating life chances. Fourth—and most important—the intrinsic growth rates calculated from the genealogies and those provided by the model populations are in close agreement. This does not prove that the estimates based on the genealogies are accurate, but it does argue that they are plausible.

Given a declining growth rate as a result of increasing mortality, the age structure of the Chinese population could not have remained stable. To this extent the conclusions drawn by the Princeton group from Buck's survey of Chinese farmers may have to be modified. Otherwise, the genealogies tend to bear out the Princeton group's findings. The population of late traditional China was characterized by high (and probably increasing) mortality, nearly universal marriage, and surprisingly low marital fertility. This conclusion is important not only for what it says about the history of the eighteenth and nineteenth centuries, but also for what it implies about the role genealogical research has to play in reconstructing that history.

Comparing the genealogy populations with model populations shows that the estimates obtained from the genealogies are plausible; comparing these estimates with those obtained from a very different source suggests that they are also reasonably complete and accurate. In a word, Chinese demographic history is possible.

THREE

Samurai Income and Demographic Change: The Genealogies of Tokugawa Bannermen

Kozo Yamamura

Villages in Tokugawa Japan have been actively analyzed by demographers for several decades, but the samurai class has been largely ignored for lack of comparable data. Although samurai are estimated at only about 5 to 6 percent of the total Tokugawa population of nearly 35 million, their significance makes them worth a demographer's attention. There exist for the samurai class neither the religious investigation registers nor the Bakufu surveys from which our data for commoners are obtained. We do have, however, a set of official genealogies of *hatamoto*, or bannermen, a class of about 6,000 men who formed the mainstay of the Bakufu's bureaucracy and standing army. The equivalent of today's bureaucrats and military officers in the central government, the bannermen were an important part of the ruling class of Tokugawa Japan.

An analysis of the bannermen is interesting for several reasons. For one thing, if we know how the average family size of the bannerman changed over time, we can estimate changes in the per capita income of members of the bannerman class. Such knowledge might also suggest possible causal relationships between family size and stipend level or family size and real income level. In short, examining certain of the bannerman's demographic characteristics may help us gain a better understanding of his changing economic status.

A demographic study leads to broader questions. We know that the samurai's real income gradually declined, but we do not know why. Why did the political leaders of Tokugawa Japan permit their own relative income to fall? Is it possible that their political power was not so great as we have thought? Is there perhaps some causal relationship between declining samurai income and the fall of the shogunate? A historian can easily compile a long list of such questions. And as for the possible causal relationships between family size and stipend level or family size and real income level, they have implications for analyzing and interpreting growth trends of other classes of Japanese society.

The Kansei Revised Samurai Genealogies as a Source for Demographic Data

My data source is the *Kansei chōshū shokafu* (Kansei Revised Samurai Genealogies) compiled by the Bakufu. Using the genealogies compiled in 1641 as a base, about fifty bannermen in 1799 set out to compile genealogies for all persons who became either daimyo or bannermen after 1641. Lineages that ceased to exist prior to 1798, the last date of inclusion in the compilation, were included. The tasks of collection, evaluation, and rewriting took nearly 14 years, and the compilation, in 1,530 folios, was completed in 1812. The actual source I have used is a revised version, with obvious inaccuracies and inconsistencies corrected, which was published between 1963 and 1966 in 22 volumes by a group of Japanese historians.[1]

The information listed for a given person in the genealogies may include:

A brief description of corrections made in adopting the 1641 genealogy, if applicable.

The family name and the first name of the subject.

Any other names the subject used as an infant or during his boyhood, and any earlier names used after attaining adulthood. During and before the Tokugawa period, it was common to change names on important occasions.

The name of the father of the subject's mother.

The date of the first audience the subject had with the shogun or the date when the subject first came into service of the shogunate.

Military or administrative accomplishments, if any. The length of this description is nearly proportional to the rank (and the stipend) of the subject.

Any noteworthy events, deeds, or incidents in the subject's life, including descriptions of rewards, promotions, demotions, crimes, and punishments, along with a brief explanation of the nature and causes of the events described.

Any changes in stipend or in fief.

Date and age of retirement.

Date and age at death.

The name of the temple at which the subject was buried.

The names of daughters with the names of their husbands, and the names of sons and of their adoptive fathers where applicable.

Although not many entries contain all the above information, a majority include most of the items. Still, these genealogies are far from being an ideal source of information for a thorough demographic analysis. Their concern is with heads of households, and information on other family members is limited to name and relationship to the head of the household. Unfortunately, we are given no demographic information on bannermen's wives; indeed, they frequently appear without names, listed only as "wife" or "woman." Still another weakness is that the compilation does not cover the last seventy years of the Tokugawa period. Nonetheless, if examined with proper care the genealogies can tell us a lot about the bannerman class during this period. But before going on, let us consider the background and characteristics of this class.

Who Were the Bannermen?

After the battle of Sekigahara in 1600, Tokugawa Ieyasu commanded sufficient military and political strength to unite the war-torn nation. Ieyasu rewarded his allies with fiefs and punished his former foes by confiscating or reducing their territory. He aggrandized his landholdings until he held nearly a quarter of Japan's arable land as measured in *koku* units of rice. He put his capital at Edo in the Kantō plain and there established the Tokugawa Bakufu, which functioned both as his house government and as the central government of the nation. His administration was staffed by his direct vassals: a minority of daimyo (*fudai*), who served on the highest councils to set national policy; and a much larger number of hatamoto or bannermen and *gokenin* (housemen), who constituted the Bakufu's general staff. By the mid-seventeenth century, the newly unified nation had established a working bureaucracy for carrying out national policy and for administering the lands directly held by the Bakufu.

Most of the bannermen continued to live in Edo in order to perform the military, administrative, ceremonial, and housekeeping functions of the Tokugawa shogunate. Though they were warriors in origin and in theory, the continued peace gradually converted them into bureaucrats and underemployed peacetime soldiers. The bannermen ranked just below the daimyo, whose stipend in fief yielded 10,000 or more koku of rice per year, but above the housemen, the lowest-ranked samurai group.

The distinction between daimyo and bannerman was clear, but that between bannerman and houseman was not. A standard definition of a bannerman was someone with a stipend exceeding 100 koku but less than 10,000 koku (in reality 9,500), and who had had an audience (*omemie*) with the shogun and had the right to an audience in the future.[2] However, a few hundred housemen had stipends as high as 200 koku and some bannermen received less than 100. Also, an audience could be granted to a houseman who had a long record of service to the Tokugawa house, a close or favored relationship to a daimyo or a high-ranking bannerman, or a more or less hereditary job yielding over 100 koku in stipend.[3] Some Japanese scholars add the supposed distinction that a bannerman's stipend nominally came in the form of a fief (*chigyō*) rather than in rice itself;[4] but this, too, is of little help, since in practice many bannermen received their stipend in rice. Despite these difficulties, bannermen were a distinct group of shogunal retainers, and were seen as such during the Tokugawa era.

Because of the incompleteness of the existing records, it is difficult to ascertain the exact number of bannermen. An early count based on *Records of the Status of Direct Vassals (Gokenin bungechō)* gives a figure (dating from 1705) of 2,354 persons receiving a stipend in the form of a fief and 3,688 receiving a stipend of at least 100 koku of rice.[5] Of the former, 19 are known to have been housemen; of the latter, approximately 1,000 were housemen. This means that there were about 5,000 bannermen at the beginning of the eighteenth century—an estimate supported by a 1722 count of 5,205 bannermen who had a right to the shogunal audience. Of this total, 2,670 received a fief yielding at least 100 koku, and 2,535 received a rice stipend of at least 100 koku.[6]

The *Kansei Revised Samurai Genealogies* are, however, a more reliable source for the Kansei period (1789-1800). This source lists about 6,000 bannermen who had at least 100 koku in stipend along with the right to a shogunal audience. Thus we can consider the number of bannermen to have been about 5,000 at the beginning of the eighteenth century and to have increased by about 1,000 during the century. Bannermen could be created by dividing the fief of a daimyo or bannerman among several sons, by promoting a houseman, or even by employing a *rōnin*. We should note in passing that the total number of housemen was about 17,500 in 1705 and about 20,000 at the beginning of the nineteenth century. Thus, the ratio of bannermen to housemen was about 1 to 3.5.[7]

In between the daimyo, who held some sixty of the most important positions, and the housemen, who functioned as bureaucratic and military underlings of the shogunate, stood the bannermen, who held a wide range of positions analogous to those held by college graduates in today's Japanese ministries and army. These several thousand bannermen were the mainstay of both the Bakufu's bureaucracy and the standing army, whose structures and functions were well established by the 1660's.[8]

Economic and Social Background of the Bannermen

First, this study will show that bannermen's social and economic mobility was limited, and that even this limited mobility declined over the first two centuries of the Tokugawa regime. Since all evidence seems to indicate that the bannermen's social and economic mobility continued to decline during the last two generations of the Tokugawa period, we are forced to

TABLE 3.1

Stipend Changes of 4,956 Sample Bannermen, 1641-1798

Pattern	Number	Percent of sample
Unchanged throughout life and same as father's	3,291	66.4%
Increased for merit or other reasons	441	8.9
Decreased owing to division of stipends	154	3.1
Decreased because of demerit or as punishment	108	2.2
Received stipend lower than father's, which thereafter remained unchanged	23	0.5
Received part of another's stipend, which thereafter remained unchanged	205	4.1
Increased because increases exceeded loss due to division of stipends	8	0.2
Decreased because increases were less than loss due to division of stipends	2	0.0
Received a part of another's stipend and later increases	9	0.2
Initial stipends unknown or incomplete stipend information	715	14.4

conclude that the Bakufu persistently failed to reward the mainstay of its bureaucracy, mainly owing to its fiscal inability to do so, and partly owing to a lack of concern.

Second, we shall see that the income of the bannerman class was relatively stable over time, thanks in large part to the Bakufu's efforts to keep real income stable by controlling the way samurai stipends were paid. From a sample of 4,956 bannermen randomly selected from the genealogies, the stipends of 3,519 remained constant during their lifetimes; the stipends of only 458 rose, and those of 264 declined (see Table 3.1). This means that the incomes of 76.3 percent remained constant or declined. This evidence is not sufficient to argue that bannermen were growing poorer in terms of real income. But given the economic growth in Tokugawa times and the tremendous increase in the availability of consumer goods, especially in cities, where the samurai were concentrated, it seems clear that bannermen were not able to participate fully in the new urban culture, nor were they able to purchase all the new goods that continually appeared on the market.

In the absence of much more reliable data on household consumption patterns, on the actual burden of debt, on the rates of growth of agricultural productivity for rice and for other products, and on changes in the effective tax rates by region and by period, the findings here can only be termed tentative. But if we accept the hypothesis that the bannermen's real income was relatively stationary during the Tokugawa period, all the existing narratives and descriptions seem to fall into place: that is, they support the argument that bannermen's increasing anxiety about income was caused by increasing wants.

Demographic Characteristics of the Bannermen as a Class

The demographic findings presented here are based on 34,471 entries of bannermen, which is 2,511 fewer than the total number contained in the source. Most of those excluded were pre-Tokugawa ancestors of bannermen who traced their genealogies for a few centuries preceding 1600; and of the 2,511, entries for nearly 2,400 consisted only of names. Table 3.2 presents data on the children of bannermen by cohort group of bannermen. Though ten cohort groups were formed for this study, group VII, comprising bannermen born between 1711 and 1740, is the last that can be included in the table since bannermen in later cohort groups could not be considered to have had by 1798 all the children they were to have during their lifetime.

As we examine the number of male and female children (rows 2 and 3) and the sex ratio of male to female (row 5), we see that some female children must have been omitted from the genealogies, with omissions being more flagrant for earlier cohort groups. The statistics on the number of children per bannerman (row 7) therefore cannot be considered reliable. To adjust for this obviously unrealistic sex ratio, I assumed that the sex ratio was unity for all cohort groups and that all male children were in-

TABLE 3.2

Number of Bannermen and Selected Data on Their Children
by Cohort Group of Bannermen, 1500-1798

	Cohort group						
	I	II	III	IV	V	VI	VII
	1500-	1561-	1591-	1621-	1651-	1681-	1711-
Measure	1560	1590	1620	1650	1680	1710	1740
Number of bannermen	1,908	1,792	2,149	2,927	4,471	5,375	6,169
Male children	4,052	3,648	4,309	5,237	7,153	9,073	10,241
Female children	1,662	2,078	2,795	3,560	5,429	7,456	9,099
Total children	5,714	5,726	7,104	8,797	12,582	16,529	19,340
Sex ratio of children (male to female)	2.44	1.76	1.54	1.47	1.32	1.22	1.13
Adopted children	308	370	583	1,252	2,376	2,544	3,480
Children per bannerman	3.00	3.31	3.31	3.01	2.81	3.08	3.14
Ratio of adopted to natural children	.054	.065	.082	.142	.189	.154	.180
Total children, adjusted	8,104	7,296	8,618	10,574	14,306	18,146	20,482
Children per banner-man, adjusted	4.24	4.07	4.01	3.61	3.20	3.38	3.32

TABLE 3.3

Relative Frequency of Family Sizes by Cohort Group of Bannermen, 1500-1798

	Cohort group						
Family size	I 1500- 1560	II 1561- 1590	III 1591- 1620	IV 1621- 1650	V 1651- 1680	VI 1681- 1710	VII 1711- 1740
1	0.94%	1.73%	1.91%	1.81%	1.90%	3.33%	2.92%
2	2.57	3.57	5.17	5.36	6.31	7.14	7.15
3	33.18	24.16	16.33	15.44	15.72	12.63	11.43
4	15.04	16.57	14.80	16.02	17.22	14.88	13.39
5	12.74	14.23	15.96	16.67	17.22	15.39	14.14
6	9.28	10.04	12.80	13.26	12.97	14.25	12.97
7	7.08	8.37	10.24	11.17	10.15	9.19	11.74
8	5.14	6.53	7.86	6.63	6.06	8.19	8.38
9	4.72	3.85	5.03	5.02	3.94	4.73	5.98
10	2.67	3.63	3.26	2.53	2.91	3.33	4.33

NOTE: Columns do not add up to 100% because families numbering over ten are not included.

cluded in the source. The second assumption, I believe, is justified since the source is extremely detailed in regard to male children, even to the point of including last-born male children who died in infancy.[9]

Thus the number of male children was doubled to obtain the total number of children (row 9), and the result was divided by the number of bannermen in each cohort group to obtain the mean number of children per bannerman (row 10). What the last row indicates is extremely significant; during the first two centuries of the Tokugawa period, there was a visible decline in the mean number of adopted children per bannerman. Another important fact is that the number of adopted children (row 6) and the ratio of adopted to natural children (row 8) increased rapidly.

Table 3.3, presenting the relative frequency of family sizes by cohort group, is also useful in showing the decreasing number of children per bannerman over time. In this table a family includes parents and all children listed, including whose who died in infancy and adopted children; no corrections have been made for the underreporting of female children. In interpreting this table, if we assume as before that the sex ratio was unity for cohort group I, we find that about 2,390 female children must have been unreported, which comes to slightly more than one child per bannerman for the 1,908 bannermen in this group. This suggests that the modal frequency for this cohort group was probably somewhere between four and five persons per family, instead of three as shown in Table 3.3.[10] By the time of group VII, which has an improved sex ratio, indicating that much less underreporting of female children was taking place, the modal class was that of families with five persons. The relative frequency of families

TABLE 3.4

Relative Frequency of Numbers of Wives by Cohort Group of Bannermen,
1500-1798

Number of wives	Cohort group						
	I 1500- 1560	II 1561- 1590	III 1591- 1620	IV 1621- 1650	V 1651- 1680	VI 1681- 1710	VII 1711- 1740
Unmarried	3.51%	4.91%	6.75%	7.31%	8.10%	10.18%	9.99%
One wife	77.83	71.37	67.15	65.12	66.88	63.39	58.16
Two wives	16.14	20.31	21.73	22.89	20.87	20.93	24.85
Three wives	1.89	2.57	3.30	3.52	3.20	4.00	5.41
Four wives	0.42	0.50	0.56	0.85	0.60	0.86	1.12
Five wives	0.05	0.06	0.23	0.17	0.20	0.20	0.24
More than five wives	0.16	0.28	0.28	0.14	0.16	0.45	0.23

NOTE: See note 14 for explanations concerning bannermen who had multiple wives concurrently and over time. Out of the randomly selected sample of 4,956 bannermen for whom socioeconomic information was coded, we were able to obtain necessary information on the wives of 4,884. When bannermen were under 45 years of age at the last entry date of the source, the information pertaining to their wives was considered incomplete.

with fewer than five members also increased significantly over time. It follows that the decreasing average number of children per bannerman over time must be explained not by a change in the modal class by family size, but by increases in the proportions of childless bannermen and bannermen having fewer than three children (see also Tables 3.6 and 3.7).

Another finding, consistent with the preceding, is that the proportion of unmarried bannermen increased over time (Table 3.4). Whereas only 3.51 percent of the bannermen in group I were unmarried, this proportion gradually increased to around 10 percent by the time of the last two cohort groups. Because of the possible omission of wives of bannermen in earlier cohort groups, those farthest removed in time from the date of compilation, the proportion of unmarried bannermen in the earlier cohort groups could have been even lower.

Table 3.5 shows the proportion of unmarried bannermen by stipend class for a sample of 4,884. If we ignore the 7,000-koku class, whose high percentage is due to the small sample, it is evident that the lower stipend classes have higher proportions of unmarried men and that the proportion decreases as the stipend rises.[11] Because proportion of unmarried men and stipend level are correlated, and because the men at the higher stipend levels tended to marry more than one woman,[12] bannermen in the higher stipend classes tended to have significantly more children (see Tables 3.6 and 3.7).

TABLE 3.5

Number and Percentage of Unmarried Bannermen by Stipend Class, 1641-1798

Stipend class (koku)	Number of bannermen	Percent unmarried	Stipend class (koku)	Number of bannermen	Percent unmarried
Under 100	71	14.1%	1,000-1,999	435	10.8%
100-199	874	14.3	2,000-2,999	183	7.1
200-299	1,046	10.7	3,000-3,999	107	5.6
300-399	507	15.4	4,000-4,999	83	1.2
400-499	392	7.4	5,000-5,999	22	0
500-599	212	6.6	6,000-6,999	30	0.7
600-699	167	10.2	7,000-7,999	7	28.6
700-799	102	7.8	8,000-8,999	2	0
800-899	52	7.7	9,000-9,999	43	2.3
900-999	181	11.0	10,000+	368	7.6

NOTE: The total sample for this table is 4,884 bannermen because of the exclusion of those bannermen aged 20 or less in 1798 and those bannermen in the earlier cohort groups whose marital status could not be established.

TABLE 3.6

Relative Frequency of Family Sizes of Sample Bannermen by Stipend Class, 1641-1798

Stipend class (koku)	Bannermen with fewer than 3 children		Bannermen with 3 to 5 children		Bannermen with 6 or more children		Mean number of children for each stipend class
	Number	Percent	Number	Percent	Number	Percent	
Under 100	44	61.1%	24	33.2%	4	5.6%	2.39
100-199	556	63.3	259	29.5	64	7.3	2.23
200-299	627	59.5	330	31.4	96	9.2	2.44
300-399	335	65.7	108	21.1	67	13.3	2.44
400-499	202	51.4	148	37.5	44	11.0	2.87
500-599	94	44.0	91	42.5	29	13.5	2.89
600-699	76	45.0	61	36.1	32	18.9	3.20
700-799	56	54.4	30	29.1	17	16.6	2.86
800-899	35	66.1	14	26.3	4	7.6	2.28
900-999	92	50.0	68	37.0	24	13.0	2.97
1,000-1,999	199	45.4	175	39.9	64	14.6	3.01
2,000-2,999	66	35.6	72	39.0	47	25.4	4.04
3,000-3,999	36	32.4	58	52.2	17	15.3	3.43
4,000-4,999	34	40.0	24	28.3	27	31.9	4.00
5,000-5,999	9	39.1	10	43.5	4	17.4	3.74
6,000-6,999	11	36.7	10	33.4	9	29.9	3.73
7,000-7,999	3	42.9	2	28.6	2	28.6	4.14
8,000-8,999	1	50.0	–	–	1	50.0	4.00
9,000-9,999	8	18.6	14	32.6	21	48.8	5.81
10,000+	149	40.3	77	20.7	144	38.8	4.71
Unknown	18	58.1	10	32.3	3	9.6	2.42

NOTE: The sample size for this table is 4,956.

TABLE 3.7

Number of Children of Selected Bannermen by Stipend Class, *1641-1798*

Stipend class (koku)	Number of children											
	0	1	2	3	4	5	6	7	8	9	10	More than 10
Under 100	10	24	10	5	14	5	—	—	4	—	—	—
100-199	187	191	178	110	91	58	35	13	13	3	—	—
200-299	204	210	213	139	107	84	47	20	22	2	5	6
300-399	113	119	103	42	39	27	33	11	11	3	3	6
400-499	66	66	70	60	52	36	10	12	8	4	6	4
500-599	35	28	31	50	26	15	15	4	6	2	2	2
600-699	34	13	29	27	21	13	11	9	8	2	2	2
700-799	15	22	19	10	10	10	10	5	—	—	2	—
800-899	10	19	6	4	6	4	—	2	—	—	—	—
900-999	28	32	32	25	27	16	7	7	5	2	2	3
1,000-1,999	85	44	70	85	56	34	25	14	13	2	5	5
2,000-2,999	25	18	23	18	38	16	16	8	5	5	3	10
3,000-3,999	17	5	14	21	21	16	10	2	—	3	2	—
4,000-4,999	13	9	12	10	6	8	9	6	5	2	2	3
5,000-5,999	5	2	2	—	—	10	2	—	—	2	—	—
6,000-6,999	5	3	3	5	3	2	3	3	1	1	1	1
7,000-7,999	—	2	1	2	—	—	1	—	—	—	—	1
8,000-8,999	—	1	—	—	—	—	—	1	—	—	—	—
9,000-9,999	3	1	4	4	6	4	4	4	4	1	4	4
10,000+	73	38	38	36	22	19	29	29	19	14	12	41
Unknown	4	11	3	4	6	—	1	1	—	1	—	—

Adoption and Lineage Dissolution

Along with mobility, another often-discussed social aspect of the bannerman's life is the question of succession. Because official position, stipend, and family status could be continued only through inheritance, succession was one of the prime concerns of bannermen. As Table 3.8 shows, primogeniture was practiced by only slightly over half the sample. Yōshi successions (the succession of adopted sons) ranked second with 1,124 cases (or 23 percent), 907 of them due to no male issue and 121 due to the death of the only son. In 17 cases yōshi were adopted to replace bannermen's own sons who had become yōshi of others, and in another 17 cases the eldest son or only son was disqualified from succession because of incompetence, misconduct, or ill health.[13]

Table 3.9, showing the incidence of yōshi succession by income class, indicates that the middle and lower stipend classes tended to have proportionately more yōshi than the higher stipend classes. Bannermen in the higher stipend classes were seemingly better able to reduce the necessity of adoption not only by often taking two or more wives, but by having a larger number of children per wife than bannermen with lower stipends.

It is interesting to compare the social and economic performance of yōshi with that of the sample as a whole. Of the 1,124 yōshi, 1,002 received throughout their lives the same stipend as their adoptive fathers; 80 at some time received a higher stipend than their adoptive fathers; and 30 saw their stipends decreased, 25 by way of punishment for crime or misconduct and the other five because the stipend was divided between the yōshi and a relative of the adoptive father. Only two yōshi received smaller stipends than their adoptive fathers from the outset and remained at that income throughout their lives. In class terms, of the 1,124 yōshi in the

TABLE 3.8

Successors of Sample Bannermen by Relationship to Person Succeeded, 1641-1798

Relationship	Number of successors	Relationship	Number of successors
First son	2,553	First younger brother	159
Second son	506	Second younger brother	63
Third son	215	Third younger brother	17
Fourth son	98	Fourth younger brother	9
Fifth son	40	Fifth younger brother	3
Sixth son	18	Sixth younger brother	3
Seventh son	7	Nephew	34
Eighth son	2	Uncle	10
Yōshi	1,124	Unknown	8
Grandson	87		

TABLE 3.9

Yōshi Successors of Sample Bannermen by Stipend Class, 1641-1798

Stipend class (koku)	Number of sample bannermen	Number of yōshi successors	Percentage of yōshi successions
Under 100	72	11	15.3%
100-199	879	210	23.9
200-299	1,053	276	26.2
300-399	510	98	19.2
400-499	394	116	29.4
500-599	214	46	21.5
600-699	169	42	24.5
700-799	103	18	17.5
800-899	53	24	45.3
900-999	184	23	12.5
1,000-1,999	438	104	23.7
2,000-2,999	185	47	25.4
3,000-3,999	111	23	20.7
4,000-4,999	85	15	17.6
5,000-5,999	23	3	13.0
6,000-6,999	30	4	13.3
7,000-7,999	7	1	14.3
8,000-8,999	2	0	0.0
9,000-9,999	43	2	4.7
10,000+	370	58	15.7
Unknown	31	3	9.7

sample, 782 (about 70 percent) remained within the same class as their adoptive fathers; 261 were promoted, of whom 79 received bona fide promotions that could not have been anticipated from their adoptive fathers' positions; and 42 were demoted.[14]

Increases in stipends were given to 7 percent of yōshi (80 out of 1,124) as compared with 8.9 percent of the entire sample, and decreases were experienced by 2.6 percent of yōshi as against 5.3 percent of the entire sample. Punitive decreases came to 2.2 percent for both yōshi and the entire sample. These findings seem to indicate that yōshi were not significantly different from nonadopted heirs in their social and economic prospects.[15]

Finally, out of 998 genealogies some 40 *zekke* (termination of a lineage) resulted from failure to adopt a yōshi.[16] Such zekke, as distinguished from zekke owing to crime or misconduct, could occur under any of the following circumstances: (1) a bannerman died in youth before he married; (2) an heirless bannerman died suddenly before a yōshi could be adopted; (3) a bannerman's son or yōshi died suddenly and the bannerman died before a new heir could be adopted; and (4) the Bakufu denied official recognition to a yōshi for political or other reasons. The first two circumstances were most common, and the fourth was rare: there are only three cases of it in our sample, one for a daimyo, perhaps for political reasons,[17] and two

TABLE 3.10
Zekke by Stipend Class of Sample Bannermen,
1641-1798

Stipend class (koku)	Number of zekke	
	Owing to lack of heir	Owing to misconduct
Under 300	5	29
300-499	3	13
500-999	7	9
1,000-4,999	15	6
5,000-9,999	3	0
10,000+ (daimyo)	7	6
TOTAL	40	63

for bannermen in the 5,000-9,999-koku class. Table 3.10 enumerates the two types of zekke by stipend class. Although zekke owing to misconduct were roughly proportional to the number of bannermen in each stipend class, zekke owing to lack of heir were not: there was an unusually high incidence in the 5,000-9,999-koku class. Though no specific reason can be found for this in the *Kansei Revised Samurai Genealogies,* the fact that many of the bannermen in this stipend class were younger sons of daimyo may be a clue. Since the Bakufu had many more samurai than positions in which to place them, it is likely that the Bakufu wanted to prevent further increases in the bannerman ranks. Also, the family lines of the younger sons of daimyo were continued by their older brothers.

Zekke was the ultimate form of downward mobility. As Table 3.10 shows, there were 63 zekke for misconduct in our sample of 998 genealogies. The offenses involved differed by stipend class. For the six cases of daimyo zekke, the causes were: disrespectful attitudes in front of a Buddhist statue, "madness," drawing a sword in Edo Castle,[18] administrative ineptitude resulting in political difficulties within the daimyo's domain (*oiesōdō*), "excessive indulgence in women," and a sword fight involving the daimyo's homosexual partner.[19]

For the stipend classes under 300 koku, the offenses that resulted in zekke were, in order of frequency: immoral behavior, excessive debts, habitual and excessive drinking, gambling, embezzlement, bribe-taking, fighting, lack of interest in and neglect of duties, "madness," feigned illness, and a crime committed by the subject's father. The first three offenses were committed by many bannermen, the last two by one each. Seven bannermen incurred zekke because of their disappearance for reasons ranging from bankruptcy to "disgrace."

As we have seen, zekke owing to misconduct were not significantly more frequent for one stipend class than for another. An analysis by cohort

TABLE 3.11

Zekke Owing to Misconduct, by Cohort group of Bannermen, 1500-1798

Cohort group	Number of zekke	Cohort group	Number of zekke
1500-1560	1	1681-1710	16
1561-1590	1	1711-1740	8
1591-1620	7	1741-1770	2
1621-1650	11	1771-1800	3
1651-1680	14		

group (Table 3.11) yields a more interesting pattern: a disproportionately high frequency for bannermen born in the hundred years beginning about 1620. Since the total number of bannermen changed only gradually over time, it seems clear that the proportion punished by zekke was unusually high for those who lived in the period of political and cultural transition during which, as Kitajima has shown, the Bakufu took unusually harsh measures against bannermen.[20]

When the 40 zekke owing to the lack of an heir are added to the 63 zekke owing to misconduct, we find that over 10 percent of the sample, 103 out of 998 genealogies, suffered zekke. Zekke therefore was by no means an insignificant factor in holding down the number of bannermen during the first two centuries of the Tokugawa period.

Analysis and Conclusions

Limited by the data as these demographic observations are, they argue forcefully that the mean size of bannermen families decreased over time as a result of increasing economic difficulties and decreasing intraclass mobility.

Before 1600, the samurai who were to become Tokugawa bannermen lived not in Edo but in rural areas. Their real income may have been no higher than it was to be after 1600; but they had not yet been exposed to the urban life of Edo, which was to stimulate their demand for goods and services. The children of those in cohort group I and some in group II were born before the bannermen settled in Edo and became a part of the structured hierarchy of the shogunate.

But the economic and social life of some bannermen in cohort group II, and of all in group III, was considerably different from that of their fathers and grandfathers. The men in these groups lived in a decidedly urban society, as did the shogun, the daimyo and their retainers (who had to live in Edo in alternate years), and the wealthier merchants. The Bakufu's constant warnings notwithstanding, the men who had fought under the Tokugawa banner and who had previously lived in villages were gradually transformed into city dwellers who wished to emulate the consumption patterns of their more prosperous neighbors. Most of the bannermen in cohort group II who had received newly awarded stipends, increases in stipends, and Bakufu loans were able to satisfy their increasing demand for goods and services in Edo. But to some of them, and to all in group III, it became increasingly obvious that the chance of receiving either promotion to a higher income level or an increased stipend had grown small indeed. It also became painfully evident that the Tokugawa hierarchy, well established by the time of cohort group III,[21] was not eager to create positions for new bannermen. Not only had the chance of promotion dwindled, but so had the possibility of having one's younger son raised to bannerman status.

Real income failed to rise and intraclass mobility remained at a low level for bannermen in cohort groups IV and V, while prospering Edo made more and more goods and services available to those who could afford them.[22] Bannermen's debts began to increase, and new tastes acquired during the Genroku years (1688-1703) served only to increase their financial burden. To judge from such contemporary materials as we have, bannermen were by this time acutely aware of their weakening economic position—relative not only to merchants and artisans, who benefited from the increasing commerce, but even to peasants, whose living standard appears to have been rising.

Though not written by a bannerman, the diary of a low-class samurai of the Owari *han* in Nagoya during the Genroku period suggests how many a bannerman of that period must have felt. This extremely rare source was written by a *tatami bugyō* (a magistrate in charge of matters pertaining to straw mats) with a stipend of 100 koku. Living in a large castle town, he had become familiar with the various new theatrical entertainments that blossomed during this period. Although he wrote of these amusements admiringly and made references to merchants and some peasants who attended them, his own attendance was limited for lack of money. In his numerous entries on samurai borrowing, rising prices, a new tax levied on "even those earning less than 30 koku," higher fees charged by rice-jobbers, and persons of his acquaintance who fled to avoid paying debts, he clearly laments his financial status.[23] Many a bannerman in Edo must have felt the same way.

The life of those in cohort group VI may have been slightly better, since this group enjoyed (mostly through accidents of nature) more than their share of high rice prices and relatively slow rises in commodity prices. In the years 1726, 1731-32, 1738, 1742-43, and 1745-50 bannermen's real income was at least 10 percent higher than in the Genroku years. Some in cohort group VII also benefited from these good years, but thanks to the many worse-than-average years after 1750, this group was generally no better off than group III.

If the foregoing observations are accurate, many of the data presented earlier can be plausibly explained. The average number of children per bannerman (Table 3.2), which was found to be highly correlated with stipend level (Tables 3.6 and 3.7), declined from a high of 4.24 for cohort group I to a low of 3.20 by the time of cohort group V, and then rose slightly for cohort groups VI and VII, perhaps reflecting the apparent rise in real income from 1726 to 1750. The proportion of unmarried bannermen followed a similar pattern; as shown in Table 3.5, stipend level, and thus real income, was inversely correlated with the proportion of unmarried bannermen in each stipend class. The increasing number of adopted children (Table 3.2) reflected bannermen's increasing efforts to reduce the cost of rearing children but still secure an heir.

In short, the evidence suggests that bannermen attempted to minimize their financial difficulties by reducing the size of their family. Partly this was a matter of their increasing inability to make ends meet; partly it was a matter of diminished prospects for their younger sons. When upward mobility, which could bring a large enough stipend to be divided among sons, lessened, having more than one son became a burden to a father: he had either to support his younger sons as long as he lived or to compete with others like him to find families of acceptable rank and stipend who would adopt them as yōshi. Fathers understandably tended to be unwilling to raise sons whose future was precarious both economically and socially.

Daughters' prospects were also unfavorable. In a society that stressed narrow distinctions between socioeconomic classes and even socioeconomic differences within a class, many bannermen's daughters had increasing difficulty finding desirable husbands. To marry younger sons of bannermen[24] or daimyo retainers[25] was, in most cases, to marry downward socially and economically. As Table 3.4 shows, many daughters of bannermen instead chose to be a bannerman's second or third wife.[26] Reinforcing this practice was the Tokugawa policy of strongly encouraging strict endogamy.[27] Even so, the supply of bannermen's daughters may well have outrun the demand for wives. And since in addition daughters were expensive, particularly at the time of marriage, bannermen had added incentive for limiting the number of their children.

Though our genealogies end in 1798, we may be justified in extending our hypothesis to cover the entire Tokugawa period and expanding it to include the samurai class in general. What sources we have argue that the economic condition of the samurai class deteriorated even further during the nineteenth century and that intraclass mobility, if it changed at all, declined still further.[28] Even at the comparatively affluent daimyo level the

TABLE 3.12

Relative Frequency of Ages at Death by Cohort Group of Bannermen,
1500-1798

Age at death	Cohort group						
	I 1500- 1560	II 1561- 1590	III 1591- 1620	IV 1621- 1650	V 1651- 1680	VI 1681- 1710	VII 1711- 1740
0-5	11.85%	16.96%	15.96%	11.37%	8.58%	5.30%	2.87%
6-10	0.05	0.00	0.23	0.14	0.13	0.28	0.18
11-15	0.00	0.06	0.09	0.10	0.22	0.37	0.11
16-20	0.16	0.22	0.47	0.41	0.65	1.06	1.62
21-25	1.62	1.12	1.16	1.23	1.30	2.46	2.97
26-30	1.05	2.18	2.84	1.64	2.15	3.44	4.26
31-35	1.62	3.52	3.49	1.71	1.99	4.86	4.98
36-40	2.25	4.41	3.68	3.11	3.53	5.36	6.21
41-45	4.56	5.13	5.21	4.00	4.25	6.08	6.95
46-50	3.35	5.41	4.89	4.82	6.17	6.79	6.81
51-55	5.08	7.14	6.84	6.76	7.05	8.86	8.87
56-60	5.03	8.43	6.98	7.72	9.53	9.38	9.92
61-65	8.54	8.76	8.28	9.77	10.71	9.99	9.14
66-70	7.70	6.98	8.56	10.56	11.83	9.84	7.20
71 and over	27.31	18.92	26.24	30.95	25.41	20.84	8.61
Unknown	19.81	10.77	5.07	5.71	6.49	5.10	19.31
Mean age at death	44.4	42.3	47.8	52.6	51.7	51.3	40.3 [a]

[a]Figures for this last group are incomplete, since some of its members were still alive in 1798.

problems were serious; thus we read frequently of a daimyo's "borrowing" from retainers, which was in effect a reduction in stipends.[29] Contemporary accounts of life in the capitals of daimyo domains describe effects on the daimyo's retainers similar to those of Edo on the bannermen;[30] and numerous case studies of domain bureaucracies show clearly that, except in a few domains, intraclass mobility for daimyo retainers declined steadily.[31]

How was family size limited? Almost surely by abortion and infanticide, according to Sekiyama Naotaro[32] and Nishijima Minoru.[33] In the tatami bugyō's diary to which I have already referred, a number of entries refer not only to abortions (e.g., by his maid, whom he had impregnated, and by a wife of the Owari daimyo) but to homosexuality, typically in the form of matter-of-fact references to the homosexuality of his fellow samurai.[34] One must, however, be cautious in applying this hypothesis to lower-class daimyo retainers and especially to low-stipend samurai, who supplemented their income with by-employments and whose life styles and demographic patterns may well have been more akin to those of commoners than to those of higher-stipend bannermen.[35]

Finally, a few by-products of our study merit a brief discussion. Table 3.12 shows the relative frequency of ages at death for bannermen in each

TABLE 3.13

Age Distribution of Sample Bannermen in 1650, 1695, 1725, and 1755

	1650		1695		1725		1755	
Age	Number	Percent	Number	Percent	Number	Percent	Number	Percent
1-5	0	0.00%	1	0.02%	0	0.00%	2	0.07%
6-10	2	0.04	3	0.06	3	0.06	–	–
11-15	1	0.02	6	0.15	5	0.10	2	0.06
16-20	9	0.20	24	0.58	61	1.13	55	1.85
21-25	31	0.76	73	1.74	148	2.75	132	4.45
26-30	47	1.16	116	2.76	257	4.77	246	8.30
31-35	64	1.59	158	3.75	310	5.75	313	10.57
36-40	118	2.92	229	5.44	353	6.56	369	12.47
41-45	163	4.02	259	6.15	402	7.47	427	14.42
46-50	213	5.26	336	7.98	434	8.05	338	11.42
51-55	326	8.04	413	9.82	535	9.94	366	12.36
56-60	374	9.23	441	10.48	600	11.14	308	10.41
61-65	476	11.75	517	12.28	583	10.82	252	8.50
66-70	537	13.25	534	12.68	599	11.12	114	3.86
71-75	625	15.44	452	10.74	528	9.81	25	0.84
76-80	484	11.95	331	7.86	345	6.41	4	0.13
81-85	355	8.76	203	4.82	155	2.89	2	0.16
86-90	165	4.07	89	2.11	52	0.97	–	–
91-95	39	0.96	20	0.47	7	0.14	1	0.30
96-100	13	0.32	3	0.07	0	0.00	–	–
Over 100	9	0.22	1	0.02	8	0.15	4	0.14
Mean	65.1		59.0		55.4		45.0	
Median	68		61		57		45	

cohort group. Because of the relatively large proportion of unknowns and the impossibility of identifying the exact age at death for persons said to have "died in infancy" (included in the 0-5 category in Table 3.12), no detailed demographic analysis of this table is warranted. (Note also that the category "71 and over" in the table undoubtedly includes, especially for earlier cohort groups, exaggerated claims to advanced age.) But we do learn from this table that life expectancy improved for all age groups over time and that the mean age at death also rose over time. This is consistent with what we know of Tokugawa advances in the areas of medicine and sanitation.[36]

Another by-product is of special interest for students of Japanese social history. Although the mean age at death was rising, Table 3.13 shows that both the mean and median ages of bannermen holding office decreased during the period the data cover, 1650 to 1755. We know that most bannermen under 15 either held their positions in name only or waited for appointments. But the rest of the bannermen accounted for in this table, save for just over 20 percent who were unemployed at any given time, were the regime's officeholders. In short, the average age of the bannermen who manned the Tokugawa bureaucracy became much lower during the century; from a modal age of 71-75 in 1650 to a modal age of 41-45 in 1755. One important cause of this change must have been increasing pressure on fathers to retire early in favor of their sons, since by the mid-eighteenth century there was little probability that sons would be appointed to positions of their own. But clearly the causes and consequences of such a change call for an in-depth analysis by social historians.

In conclusion, it should be stressed that since demographic changes are products of numerous complex factors, the socioeconomic factors we have examined cannot fully account for the observed changes. The most that can be said is that increasing "poverty" and limited social mobility were important, and possibly dominant, factors in the process of change. In the aggregate, as we have seen, the changes were dramatic: during the first two centuries of the Tokugawa period, the bannerman class (including families) increased by only a few thousand members, chiefly because of reductions in family size; its social mobility dwindled; and its economic position relative to that of its social inferiors deteriorated. Since bannermen were the elite of the Tokugawa ruling class and the mainstay of the shogunal bureaucracy and military power, what the quantitative evidence suggests about the cause of their decline is significant to our understanding of social, economic, and political changes in Tokugawa Japan.

FOUR

The Rich Get Children: Segmentation, Stratification, and Population in Three Chekiang Lineages, 1550-1850

Stevan Harrell

This paper attempts to demonstrate, on a very small scale, the connection between two important social processes in late Ming and Ch'ing society: the growth and segmentation of patrilineages and the growth of population. These two processes were closely connected because the upper classes produced more children. Thus wealthy branches of lineages became numerically dominant as well until they grew so large that they became differentiated internally and themselves segmented into wealthy and poor branches, and the cycle repeated itself.[1] In this paper I illustrate the connection between segmentation, stratification, and population in the Ho, Lin, and Wu lineages of Hsiao-shan hsien, Chekiang, between 1550 and 1850.

The Basic Processes

Segmentation and stratification. In the 1940's and 1950's, it became clear from the pioneering work of Hu[2] and the more systematic accounts of Freedman[3] that the Chinese patrilineage was an internally stratified body, that the alienability and partible inheritance of property made it possible for the same lineage to contain both wealthy and poor families. And since wealth was the primary factor enabling boys to study for the civil-service examinations, which conferred elite status, a single lineage could encompass families from nearly the full range of social strata, from titled bureaucrats down to landless peasants. Studies by C. K. Yang, H. D. R. Baker, and Jack Potter amply demonstrate the range of wealth and social status within lineages.[4]

But this is only half the story. It is also clear that wealth and high status were not distributed randomly throughout the lineage, but were concentrated in certain segments. Freedman showed that the characteristically Chinese process of asymmetrical segmentation came about when families who had acquired wealth set aside part of that wealth as a corporate estate, to be held undivided in perpetuity by the descendants of that family.[5] Such corporate estates, in turn, helped preserve the identity of the genealogical segment that held them by funding the worship of the ancestors of that segment and by paying for such activities as schooling and examination expenses for the members. Such wealthy corporate segments would often come to dominate an entire lineage economically, politically, and occasionally demographically.[6]

Stratification and population. We know that the population of Ming China, which was about 80 million in 1368, increased to approximately 200 million by 1600;[7] and that after a reduction to 150 million during the turmoil accompanying the Ming-Ch'ing transition, it rose again to about 400-450 million in 1850, on the eve of the demographically destructive Taiping Rebellion. It is clear, however, that this growth was neither randomly nor uniformly distributed across the Chinese population, but was great at certain times, in certain places, and among certain social classes. For example, the Lower Yangtze macroregion, of which northern Chekiang is a part, experienced relatively little demographic disruption during the Ming-Ch'ing interregnum,[8] whereas other areas, such as Szechwan and parts of the North China Plain, were devastated demographically as well as economically. And because the balance between population and resources differed greatly from region to region, the population growth curve over the centuries differed greatly from one region (or even one village) to another. Of the three lineages discussed here, for example, one showed consistent demographic growth from 1550 to 1850; another grew from 1600 to 1750, declined in the next fifty years, and then grew again; and a third grew from 1600 to 1750 and declined somewhat thereafter.

But more central to the purposes of this analysis than spatial and temporal variation is variation across social class. Many anthropologists have commented that wealthy families tend to be larger and more complex than poor ones. Although some of this variation can be accounted for by differences in the timing of family division,[9] it also seems almost certain that wealthy families had more children in the first place, thus making larger families possible. There are several reasons why this may have been so. Freedman, for example, states that "poverty postponed marriage,"[10] meaning that the poor had a shorter potentially reproductive period during their lifetimes. It is also clear that a wealthy man had an easier time acquiring a second wife if his first wife died, or a concubine if she did not. In addition, the wealthy were probably more likely to have children once born grow to maturity, since they had the wherewithal to keep their children alive in times of famine.

Segmentation, stratification, and population. Thus we see that certain segments within a given patrilineage tended to be wealthy and influential, others poor and powerless. At the same time, we have reasons to expect the wealthy and influential to produce considerably more children than the poor, and thus to display higher rates of population growth. Putting these two considerations together, we can deduce that wealthy and influential branches of lineages will grow faster than poorer branches. But wealth and influence do not last forever; and in an expanding population that practices partible inheritance, certain subsegments within a wealthy segment will eventually become poor and cease to expand. When this happens, the cycle of wealth and segmentation may begin again, with the wealthy subsegments reproducing themselves at a greater rate than those subsegments that were once wealthy but have since become poor.

The Nature of the Data

The genealogies. The data I have used to demonstrate the process outlined above come from three genealogical books: *The Genealogical Records of the Ho Lineage of Ch'in-i, Hsiao-shan* (Hsiao-shan Ch'in-i Ho-shih tsung-p'u), *The Genealogical Records of the Lin Lineage of the Eastern Gate, Hsiao-shan* (Hsiao-shan Tung-men Lin-shih tsung-p'u), and the *Genealogical Records of the Wu Lineage of Hsiao-shan* (Hsiao-shan Wu-shih tsung-p'u). These three genealogies, all compiled during the late Kuang-hsu period (1893-1904), all document lineages residing in the northern part of Hsiao-shan hsien, Shao-hsing fu, Chekiang, just across Hangchow Bay from the provincial capital of Hangchow. The Lins can presumably be located just outside the Eastern Gate of Hsiao-shan city; I cannot find the exact locations of the other two lineages on any map of Hsiao-shan.

The main resource in each genealogy is the genealogical table (*shih-hsi t'u*), which lists certain information about each male member of the lineage who reached adulthood, with certain exceptions noted below. Such data are provided for 3,078 members of the Ho lineage, 438 members of the Lin lineage, and 1,082 members of the Wu lineage. The data listed for each lineage member are not as complete as a demographer would like to have, but they do provide a reasonable basis for the kind of analysis attempted in this paper. A complete entry in the Ho genealogy lists the man's name or names; his birth order within his generation in his own segment of the lineage; his father's name and his own same-sex sibling order (e.g., third son of Shao-wu); any imperial titles, degrees, offices, or other honors he might have held; the surnames of his wife or wives, in the order he married them, and of any concubines who bore him sons; the names of his sons, listed by mother if the man had children by more than one woman; the number of daughters by each woman, and the surnames of the men they married; and the man's birth date, death date, and place of burial. In addition, complete entries in the Lin and Wu genealogies give birth and death dates for wives and concubines as well.

Not all entries in any of the genealogies are complete; many are lacking death dates, and a few lack birth dates as well. In addition, the ratios of sons to daughters suggest severe and probably systematic underreporting of daughters, so that any analysis involving daughters would have to proceed with extreme caution. Not only are some entries incomplete, but certain categories of men are not given entries in any of the genealogies. According to genealogy prefaces, the following categories are not recorded systematically: men who neither reached the age of 19 *sui* (17-18 years) in the Ho and Lin lineages—or 16 sui in the Wu lineage—nor married, illegitimate sons of lineage women, adopted sons of other surnames, men who became monks, and men who married out uxorilocally and never returned. Some entries for such men do, however, exist. Table 4.1 lists the particulars of the genealogies: date of compilation, period of time covered, number of entries, and completeness of entries.

Limitations and usefulness of the data. These data are obviously of limited usefulness for conventional demographic analysis. In particular, they record nothing whatsoever about birth or childhood mortality, since they do not list people who did not live to adulthood. Thus no birth rates or fertility rates of any sort can be obtained from them. Though we can record mortality after the age of eighteen, we cannot do so for women who married into the Ho lineage, whose birth and death dates are not listed. And we can say nothing directly about age of marriage, though we can derive age at the birth of the first son for men of all three lineages and for women who married into the Lin and Wu lineages.

But despite these severe limitations, the data are still useful for an analysis of population growth. Since we cannot measure fertility, and have only limited measures of mortality, we have to approach the problem of population growth rather unconventionally. First, we must remember that each lineage is an exogamous patrilineal isolate. This means that the growth of population from one generation to the next will be equal to the ratio of sons to fathers; daughters are irrelevant to the analysis, since they will marry virilocally and reproduce for some other lineage. So in order to measure population growth, what we have to do in effect is measure the population of males on a particular date and compare it with the population of males at some other date. We can do that by constructing a particular kind of male population index (MPI). This index is basically a sum of probabilities that particular men were alive on the date in question (the *date*). It is computed as follows.

First, take all the men who were demonstrably alive on the *date*. This will include men whose birth and death dates are listed in the genealogy, and for whom the *date* falls between them. It will also include men born before the *date* who had sons born after the *date*, as well as men with no sons who were born within eighteen years of the *date*, and who would not

TABLE 4.1
Basic Data Contained in the Ho, Lin, and Wu Genealogies

Lineage	Date of compilation	Period of time covered	Number of entries	Number of entries with both birth and death dates
Ho	1893	1240-1893	3,078	1,311
Lin	1897	1462-1897	438	240
Wu	1904	1550-1904	1,082	674

have been listed in the genealogy had they not lived to be eighteen, that is until or beyond the *date*. Each of these men is assigned a probability of one. Then construct a life table for all men born during the century during which the men alive at the *date* were born. This table will give the probability, given survival to any age eighteen or greater, of survival to any older age. For example, if we know a man lived to 36, because he had a son born at that age, then we can compute the probability that that man lived to 60. For any man whose death date is not given in the genealogy, but whose birth date is less than 80 but more than eighteen years before the *date*, use the life table to compute the probability that he was alive at the *date*. Add all the probabilities obtained in this way to the probabilities (each measuring one) for the men who can be demonstrated to have been alive at the *date*. Finally, for men whose birth dates are not given, estimate a birth date (birth-order numbers, birth dates of fathers and sons, etc., help with such estimates) and figure the probability that he was alive at the *date* in the same way as was done for the men whose birth dates but not death dates were known. (Fortunately, the number of men for whom birth dates have to be estimated is very small; among other things, many such men are eliminated from consideration by indications that they migrated from Hsiaoshan.) The sum of all the probabilities figured in this way constitutes the MPI for the *date*.

It is clear that the MPI tells us nothing about the actual population figure. It does not include women, or boys who died before reaching age eighteen. Even if it were expanded to include wives, which would be possible for the Lin and Wu lineages, it would tell us nothing about daughters. It is merely a probabilistic estimate of the population, at a particular date, of adult men plus boys who will grow to be adults. In addition, it is based on a probably false uniformitarian assumption that the life-table probabilities for men whose death dates are not recorded can be figured from those of men whose death dates *are* recorded. There is obviously a reason (usually lack of descendants) why certain men's death dates are not recorded; and this surely has something to do, in some cases at least, with early mortality, or perhaps migration out.

Nevertheless, the MPI remains a useful tool if we make one other uniformitarian assumption, which I believe to be considerably more justified. This is that the accuracy and the systematic biases in the data are approximately the same across time and across branches within a lineage. If this is true, the systematic bias in one MPI figure will be the same as the systematic bias in others, and we will be able to compare one figure with another in order to estimate rates of growth. I have no proof that this assumption is justified; but since it is both necessary to a valid comparison and clearly plausible, I will make it.

Having computed the MPI's for various dates, we can compare them to compute rates of population growth or decline in lineages and branches for particular periods. If we want to explain the differences in growth rates between branches or between time periods, the genealogies provide us with other data that can be used for this purpose. From the *shih-hsi t'u* itself we can derive measures of generational span, of marriage rates of men, and of reproduction rates of men and women, as well as the all-important measure of degree- and office-holding, which is as close as we can get to a measure of social status. From other parts of the genealogies we can obtain some confirmation of the stratification measures by examining the numbers of corporate estates held by particular branches. Correlating the stratification measures with the demographic measures, we can test the hypothesis of association between segmentation, stratification, and population.

The Structure and Segmentation of the Three Lineages

Before proceeding to demonstrate the correlations between segmentation, stratification, and population, we first need to describe the segmentation patterns of the three lineages. From Table 4.2 we can see that the Ho lineage, at the time of the compilation of its genealogy in 1893, was divided into 8 great *fang*, or segments, and that these segments varied greatly both in population (as reflected in the MPI for 1850) and in the number and extent of collectively owned estates owned by their subsegments. In particular, the Lun 21 fang had almost half the total population and well over half the corporately owned estates. How did this unequal division come about, and what was the relationship of the eight great fang to one another?

We can see this relationship more clearly from Figures 4.1 and 4.2. Figure 4.1 shows the early history of the lineage, from the founder through the sixth generation. The founder, Tsung-chü, who came to Hsiao-shan in the late thirteenth century, had but one son, Cheng, who had two sons. The grandsons of the younger of these, Hua, all moved away, meaning that all members of the lineage in later centuries were descended from Cheng's

TABLE 4.2

Ho Lineage: Male Population Index and Holdings by Fang, 1850

Fang	Male population index, 1850	Number of estates	Total area of estates (*mu*)
Ping 1	7.27	0	0
Lun 13	200.92	11	82
Lun 14	27.24	0	0
Lun 21	280.29	41	594
Lun 21/2	37.25	3	42
Lun 21/3	243.04	37	509
Ping 7	10.45	0	0
Chen 8	98.16	4	24
Chen 20	36.26	3	21
K'un 12	71.20	6	45

elder son, Jung. Similarly, the seventh and eighth generation descendants[11] of Jung's younger son all moved away as well, leaving the whole lineage descended from a single great-grandson of the founder, a man named Mou. Mou had two sons, Ching-yüan and Ching-shen, both of whose descendants remained in the nineteenth century. Ching-yüan had two sons, Yung and Shan, and by the tenth generation the fang descended from these two brothers were separate enough to give their members different birth-order number series. So all the tenth-generation descendants of Yung were assigned a birth-order number preceded by the character *ping*, and all the tenth-generation descendants of Shan were assigned a birth-order number preceded by the character *chen*. The descendants of Mou's younger son, Ching-shen, were not so differentiated among themselves in the tenth generation, so all his descendants in that generation bore a birth-order number preceded by the character *k'un*.

The descendants of a man, insofar as they constituted a corporate segment, were referred to in this lineage by the birth-order number of their apical ancestor. Two of the eight fang in Table 4.2 (Ping 1 and Ping 7) have as their apical ancestors tenth-generation descendants of Yung; two more fang (Chen 8 and Chen 20) have as their apical ancestors tenth-generation descendants of Shan. The three fang designated Lun 13, Lun 14, and Lun 21, however, were originally part of a larger fang designated Ping 6. But because the Ping 6 fang, whose demographic success was spectacular in the sixteenth and early seventeenth centuries (see below), got so unwieldy, it was divided, both for administrative purposes and for purposes of genealogy compilation, into four fang descended from the four sons (eleventh generation) of the founder of the Ping 6 fang (see Figure 4.2). Since eleventh-generation descendants of Yung bore birth-order numbers preceded by the character *lun*, these fang, called Lun 11 (which died out in the early

GENERATION

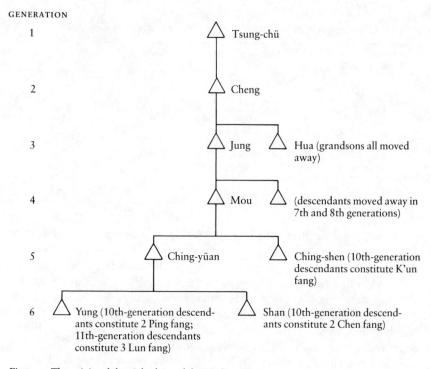

Fig. 4.1. The origin of the eight fang of the Ho lineage

nineteenth century), Lun 13, Lun 14, and Lun 21, became recognized as equivalents of the other five great fang, each of which had as its apical ancestor a man of the tenth generation.

The division into eight great fang was not, however, the whole picture of segmentation in the Ho lineage in the nineteenth century. As can be seen from Figure 4.2, there were many corporate-property-holding segments within the great fang, particularly within the larger and wealthier segments. Thus, for example, the descendants of Ju-chiao (twelfth generation, Lun 21 fang) are grouped together in the genealogy as the second fang of the Lun 21 fang. And although fang at levels of segmentation lower than this are not explicitly recognized in the structure of the genealogy or the formal political structure of the lineage, they were still important units, some of them, and the genealogy makes reference to certain of them occasionally. In particular, for the purposes of this analysis, I have singled out the Yü 64 fang, a segment consisting of all the descendants of the fifteenth-generation ancestor Hsüan, whose birth-order number was Yü 64. In the

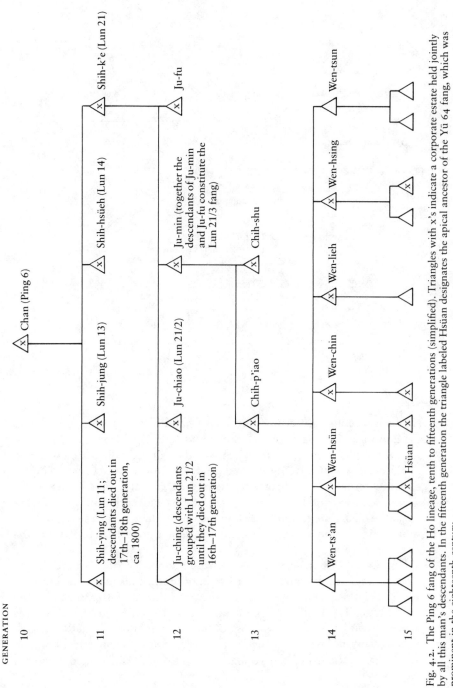

GENERATION

10

11

12

13

14

15

Chan (Ping 6)

Shih-ying (Lun 11; descendants died out in 17th–18th generation, ca. 1800)

Shih-jung (Lun 13)

Shih-hsüeh (Lun 14)

Shih-k'e (Lun 21)

Ju-ching (descendants grouped with Lun 21/2 until they died out in 16th–17th generation)

Ju-chiao (Lun 21/2)

Ju-min (together the descendants of Ju-min and Ju-fu constitute the Lun 21/3 fang)

Ju-fu

Chih-p'iao

Chih-shu

Wen-ts'an

Wen-hsün

Wen-chin

Wen-lieh

Wen-hsing

Wen-tsun

Hsüan

Fig. 4.2. The Ping 6 fang of the Ho lineage, tenth to fifteenth generations (simplified). Triangles with x's indicate a corporate estate held jointly by all this man's descendants. In the fifteenth generation the triangle labeled Hsüan designates the apical ancestor of the Yü 64 fang, which was prominent in the eighteenth century.

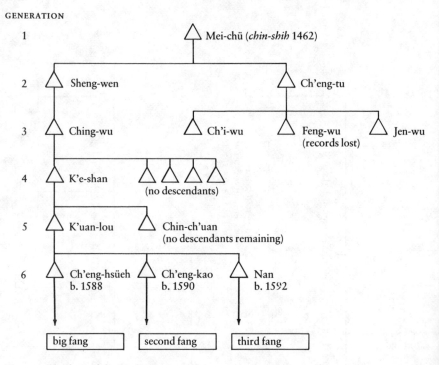

GENERATION

Fig. 4.3. The fang of the Lin lineage

eighteenth century, after the Ping 6 fang had differentiated internally and
the Lun 21 and to a lesser extent the Lun 13 fang had become predominant
within the Ping 6 fang, at the expense of the Lun 11, which died out, and
the Lun 14, which stayed small and poor, the Lun 21 itself began to differentiate internally. All evidence points to the fact that a notable increase in
wealth, honors, and population began in the eighteenth century to distinguish the Yü 64 fang from the rest of the Lun 21 fang, which seems to have
sunk, economically and in terms of demographic growth, to the level of the
rest of the lineage.

For the other two lineages, we have no such clear data on corporate
landholding, but we can trace the origin of the various fang. The Lin lineage (see Figure 4.3) was younger, smaller, and simpler in structure than the
Ho lineage. The first member of this lineage to settle in Hsiao-shan was
Yung-Pien (1353-1433), who established a temporary abode there with
his son Chih-hsiu. Both of them later returned to their ancestral home in
Fu-ch'ing, Fukien, but the youngest son of Chih-hsiu, named Mei-chü,

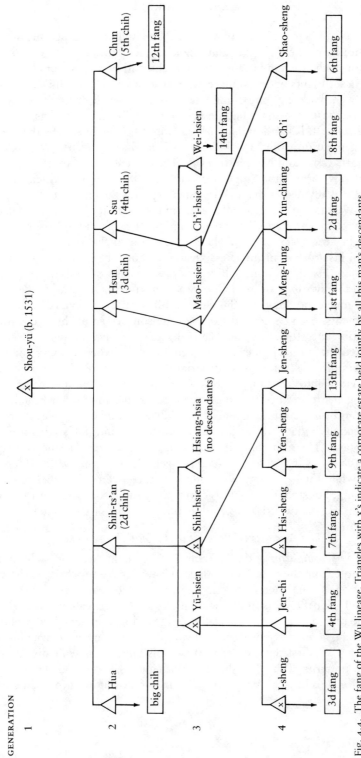

Fig. 4-4. The fang of the Wu lineage. Triangles with x's indicate a corporate estate held jointly by all this man's descendants.

changed his home registration to Hsiao-shan and in 1462 became a *chin-shih* (holder of the highest examination degree). He is considered the first ancestor of the Lins in Hsiao-shan. Mei-chü had two sons, but all records of the descendants of the younger, Ch'eng-tu, are lost. Mei-chü's elder son, Sheng-wen, had one son, Ching-wu, who in turn had five sons. Only the eldest of these, K'e-shan, had descendants; and of his two sons, in turn, only the eldest, K'uan-lou, had descendants who remained. His three sons (sixth generation from Mei-chü) were Ch'eng-hsüeh, born 1588; Ch'eng-kao, born 1590; and Nan, born 1592. The descendants of these three men respectively formed the "big," second, and third fang into which the Lin lineage was divided at the time its genealogy was compiled in 1897.

The Wu lineage, though more recent in residence at Hsiao-shan than the Lins, nevertheless started to expand in population at about the same time, as can be seen in Figure 4.4. The first ancestor of the Wus, Shou-yü, arrived in Hsiao-shan in the late sixteenth century; he had five sons, Hua, Shih-ts'an, Hsün, Ssu, and Chün. The descendants of each of these sons formed the five *chih*, or branches, into which the lineage was divided. But by the nineteenth century, the chih had in turn been divided into fang, or segments, each descended from a grandson of one of the five second-generation ancestors. The "big" chih, descended from Shou-yü's eldest son Hua, became extinct in the late eighteenth century, when its two remaining members in the seventh generation failed to reproduce. The second chih was divided into five fang, each with the birth-order number of its focal fourth-generation ancestor: these were called the third, fourth, seventh, ninth, and thirteenth fang. The third chih was similarly divided into the first, second, and eighth fang, and the fourth chih into the sixth and fourteenth fang. The fifth chih, like the first, became extinct in the late eighteenth century; it is referred to in the genealogy as the twelfth fang. In 1904, when the genealogy was compiled, there were altogether ten fang remaining; but since this analysis covers the period from 1600 to 1850, the big chih and the twelfth fang, both extinct by 1850, are included.[12]

The Analysis of Population Growth by Segments

Rates of population growth. Table 4.3 shows the MPI for each lineage as a whole from the time statistics become available until 1850, along with the average annual increase in the MPI for each 50-year interval. (To compile MPI's for the years of publication of the three genealogies would distort the record of growth, since all three genealogies include in their latest editions boys recently born, some of whom were to die before reaching age eighteen.) The first thing to notice from this table is the wide disparity in growth patterns of the three lineages during the same period. The Ho lineage, already a large group when we begin to follow it in 1550, grew stead-

TABLE 4.3

Male Population Index and Its Growth Rate in the Ho, Lin, and
Wu Lineages, 1550-1850

Year	Male population index			Annual growth rate over past 50 years (percent)		
	Ho	Lin	Wu	Ho	Lin	Wu
1550	91.88	5				
1600	130.69	5	5.8	0.71%	0%	
1650	189.06	16	35.46	0.74	2.35	3.69%
1700	365.21	45	130.63	1.33	2.09	2.64
1750	488.32	54.3	289.34	0.58	0.38	1.60
1800	576.13	47.9	281.83	0.33	−0.25	−0.05
1850	732.52	106.1	202.03	0.48	1.60	−0.66

ily at rather modest rates throughout the 300-year period in question; only in the interval 1650-1700, a time of prosperity at the beginning of the Ch'ing dynasty, was the rate of growth substantially larger. The Lins, on the other hand, showed rapid rates of growth when they were still few in number, from 1600 to 1700, but their growth rate diminished in the first half of the eighteenth century and they actually lost population between 1750 and 1800. In the nineteenth century, however, the lineage again showed a rather spectacular population gain. The Wus show a third pattern. Their rapid growth in the seventeenth century slowed down in the eighteenth, when the lineage had gotten larger, and from 1750 to 1850 the Wus consistently lost population.[13]

These variations in growth patterns are at first sight puzzling. The very high rates of growth for the Lin and Wu lineages during their respective first centuries of existence could be explained simply as a demographic accident; we might argue that if the first few generations of Lins and Wus had not expanded in this way, there would have been no genealogies for us to read. This may be true, but I submit that there was a reason for this rapid growth, a kind of growth that is reflected again and again in the history not of any of the lineages as a whole but of individual segments within the lineages. Similarly, we can throw more light on some of the demographically less successful periods by examining less successful segments within each of the lineages.

We begin by examining the segmentary growth patterns of the Ho lineage. The MPI figures for this lineage at 50-year intervals are set out in Table 4.4; the annual percentage growth rates for each interval are given in Table 4.5. Please note that indented rows are subordinate to unindented rows above them; thus all the Lun fang are part of Ping 6 and included in the figure given for Ping 6 during the interval 1650-1700; Yü 64 and "rest

TABLE 4.4

Ho Lineage: Male Population Index by Fang for Fifty-Year Intervals, 1550-1850

Fang	1550	1600	1650	1700	1750	1800	1850
Ping 1	8.95	9.77	9.24	14.96	15.27	14.62	7.27
Ping 6	5	24	86.45	239.95			
Lun 11			3	10.72	6.17	5.17	extinct
Lun 13			44.53	123.88	155.68	159.96	200.92
Lun 14			10.93	22.06	19.86	24.19	27.24
Lun 21/2			7	17.66	44.81	51.84	37.25
Lun 21/3			20.99	65.43	108.90	162.87	243.04
Yü 64				3	13	49.18	72.02
Ping 7	5.31	16.27	15.89	11.80	18.16	8.03	10.45
Chen 8	4	19.33	20.56	36.43	58.07	85.42	98.16
Chen 20	4	10	14.59	29.24	25.26	23.33	36.26
K'un 12		3	3	3	8	30.98	98.16
Others, extinct	63.62	48.32	39.33	30.03	28.14	9.72	(.73)
TOTAL	91.88	130.69	189.06	365.21	488.32	576.13	732.52

NOTE: The figures for Lun 11-21/3 are components of the Ping 6 figures for 1650 and 1700; the figures for Yü 64 are components of the Lun 21/3 figures.

of Lun 21/3" are part of and included in the figures for Lun 21/3. Extraordinarily high figures of population growth are circled in the table for easy reference.

We can see from these tables that from 1550 through 1700 the Ping 6 fang showed a consistently high yearly rate of population growth, over 2 percent per year for the entire 150-year period. After 1700, the Ping 6 fang became differentiated internally with regard to population growth; the Lun 11 fang declined in population for the next hundred years and finally died out shortly after 1800; the Lun 14 fang showed either decline or only slight growth through to 1850; and the Lun 13, as well as the Lun 21/2 and the Lun 21/3 taken as an aggregate, showed only modest growth for the remainder of the period. The Yü 64 fang, on the other hand, showed extremely rapid growth during the eighteenth century; although the rate of increase from 1700 to 1750 may be dismissed as not unusual given the small base from which it started, the continuation of this high rate into the second half of the eighteenth century suggests that the Yü 64 fang was growing not just because of some fluke of individual reproductive success, but because of a general trend. Finally, we find very interesting figures for the K'un 12 fang. This decidedly minor branch had gone along throughout the entire seventeenth century with approximately three adult male members; but this figure increased to eight in 1750, about 31 in 1800, and nearly 100 in 1850, exhibiting the very high growth rates circled in Table 4.5. Particularly noteworthy is the fact that K'un 12 was the only one of the great fang that showed an annual growth rate of over 1 percent for 1800-1850.

TABLE 4.5

Ho Lineage: Annual Growth Rate of Male Population Index by Fang,
1550-1850

Fang	1600	1650	1700	1750	1800	1850
Ping 1	0.17%	−0.11%	0.97%	0.04%	−0.09%	−1.39%
Ping 6	3.19	2.60	2.06			
Lun 11			2.58	−1.10	−0.35	
Lun 13			2.07	0.46	0.05	0.46
Lun 14			1.41	−0.21	0.40	0.24
Lun 21/2			1.87	1.88	0.29	−0.66
Lun 21/3			2.30	1.02	0.81	0.80
Yü 64				2.98	2.70	0.77
Rest of Lun 21/3				0.86	0.34	0.83
Ping 7	2.26	−0.05	−0.59	0.87	−1.62	0.53
Chen 8	3.20	0.12	1.15	0.94	0.77	0.28
Chen 20	1.85	0.76	1.40	−0.29	−0.16	0.89
K'un 12		0	0	1.98	2.74	1.86
Others, extinct	−0.55	−0.41	−0.54	−0.13	−2.10	
TOTAL	0.71%	0.76%	1.33%	0.58%	0.33%	0.48%

NOTE: Figures represent annual growth rate over the preceding 50 years. The figures for Lun 11-21/3 are components of the Ping 6 figures for 1650; the figures for Yü 64 and "rest of Lun 21/3" are components of the Lun 21/3 figures.

The population growth patterns for the Lin lineage (see Table 4.6) show similar disparities by fang. The big fang grew rapidly in its early years, lost members during the eighteenth century, and grew again after 1800. The second fang, which grew until 1750, declined thereafter. And the third fang, which showed rather moderate growth rates during the eighteenth century, experienced a real spurt between 1800 and 1850, almost quadrupling its population during this period.

The patterns for the Wu lineage, shown in Tables 4.7 and 4.8, are rather different, but still illustrate differentials between fang. Between 1650 and 1700, when all the fang were just coming into existence, they nearly all showed positive growth rates, and some of them grew quite rapidly. Between 1700 and 1750, two fang that were later to become extinct, the big chih and the twelfth fang, began to lose population, while all the other fang continued to gain. During the next fifty years, several fang began to lose population: in addition to the two that became extinct, the third, ninth, first, sixth, and fourteenth fang all showed negative growth rates. At this time, the negative growth rates of these fang just about balanced the positive rates of the others, and the population of the lineage as a whole declined only insignificantly. In the first half of the nineteenth century, however, the entire lineage lost population, and nine of the eleven fang re-

TABLE 4.6

Lin Lineage: Male Population Index and Its Growth Rate by Fang, 1650-1850

Measure	1650	1700	1750	1800	1850
Big fang					
Male population index	9	26	24.5	22.1	40.4
Annual growth rate					
over past 50 years		2.14%	−0.12%	−0.24%	1.21%
Second fang					
Male population index	6	9	17.8	10.6	6
Annual growth rate					
over past 50 years		0.81%	1.37%	−1.03%	−1.13%
Third fang					
Male population index	1	10	12	15.2	59.7
Annual growth rate					
over past 50 years		4.71%	0.37%	0.47%	2.77%

TABLE 4.7

Wu Lineage: Male Population Index by Fang for Fifty-Year Intervals, 1600-1850

Fang	1600	1650	1700	1750	1800	1850
Big Chih	2.8	2.1	2.8	2.7	0.8	extinct
Second Chih						
3		6	24	44.4	37	21.9
4		2	19	21.28	24.66	21.25
7		2	11	37	55.84	32.19
9		4	22	54.03	19.22	7.82
13		1	8	21	60.76	53.06
Third Chih						
1		3.36	6.13	8.72	4.37	3.61
2		2	2	3	4	extinct
8		4	6	9	27	35.48
Fourth Chih						
6	1	3	13	61.83	38.93	22.09
14		3	10.7	22.9	9.25	4.63
Fifth Chih						
12	2	3	6	3.48	extinct	

maining in 1800 lost population. Nevertheless, even at this time one fang, the eighth, showed modest gains in population.

Social stratification and population growth. How do we account for these separate patterns of segmentation and population growth? If the hypothesis set out in the first part of this paper is correct, we should be able to demonstrate that wealthy fang grew faster than poor fang, and that those fang that showed high rates of population growth were those with the most wealth or highest social status. Unfortunately, we have no direct way of measuring wealth either of individual families or of fang as aggre-

TABLE 4.8

Wu Lineage: Annual Growth of Male Population Index by Fang, 1600-1850

Fang	1650	1700	1750	1800	1850
Big Chih	−0.57%	0.57%	−0.07%	−2.40%	extinct
Second Chih					
3		2.81	1.24	−0.36	−1.04%
4		4.61	0.23	0.30	−0.30
7		3.47	2.46	0.83	−1.10
9		3.47	1.81	−2.05	−1.78
13		4.25	1.95	2.15	−0.27
Third Chih					
1		1.21	0.71	−1.37	−0.38
2		0	0.81	0.58	extinct
8		0.81	0.81	2.22	0.55
Fourth Chih					
6	2.22	2.98	3.17	−0.92	−1.13
14		2.58	1.53	−1.80	−1.37
Fifth Chih					
12	0.81	1.40	−1.08	extinct	

gates; none of the genealogies provide data on private landholdings. We can, however, come close to measuring social status, and even determine some very rough indicators of wealth itself. Fortunately for us, all the genealogies list all imperial degrees, offices, or honors held by each man in the genealogical tables. And when we tabulate these honors, we find that they are not randomly distributed throughout the population of the lineages, but tend to concentrate in certain fang. Table 4.9 gives degree-holders as percentages of the total number of men born in each fang of the Ho lineage during each 50-year interval from 1500 through 1850. We notice immediately that the number of degree-holders in the lineage as a whole is very high compared with the number in the general population. Chang Chung-li, for example, has estimated that gentry families, that is those holding degrees of any kind, amounted to between 1 and 2 percent of the population of Chekiang in the nineteenth century.[14] By contrast, 7 percent of the members of the Ho lineage who were born during the first half of the nineteenth century held degrees, and this 7 percent figure represents a precipitous decline from the figures for preceding periods, which range from 13 to 25 percent. The Ho lineage had a school for lineage members (i-hsüeh) and also reserved the income from certain plots of corporately owned land to pay the expenses of examination degree candidates. So it is abundantly clear that members of most of the great fang of the lineage had access to the kind of schooling that allowed them to achieve degree-holder status. In addition, a large number of men in many of the great fang purchased the degree of chien-sheng, which was ordinarily available only to those with considerable money.

TABLE 4.9

Ho Lineage: Percentage of Degree-Holders by Fang and Age Cohort, 1500-1850

Fang	Men born:						
	1501-1550	1551-1600	1601-1650	1651-1700	1701-1750	1751-1800	1801-1850
Ping 1	14%	22%	11%	0%	0%	0%	0%
Ping 6	60	91	34	26			
Lun 11				0	0	0	
Lun 13				22	10	10	3
Lun 14				13	5	0	0
Lun 21/2				72	29	24	23
Lun 21/3				25	21	22	11
Yü 64					65	54	16
Ping 7	25	0	0	0	0	0	0
Chen 8	50	21	5	12	10	10	6
Chen 20	3	0	8	9	12	36	8
K'un 12		0	3	0	0	23	3
Others, extinct	5	0	3	4	5	0	
TOTAL	20%	25%	19%	18%	13%	15%	7%

NOTE: The figures for Lun 11-21/3 are components of the Ping 6 figure for 1651-1700; the figures for Yü 64 are components of the Lun 21/3 figures.

But, as we might expect from our general discussion of the relationship between segmentation and stratification in Chinese lineages, examination success and the purchase of degrees were not evenly distributed through the branches of the Ho lineage. Table 4.9 shows that the pattern of degree-holding is remarkably similar to the pattern of demographic growth indicated in Tables 4.2 and 4.3. We find that the Ping 6 fang, from 1500 on, was extraordinarily successful in gaining imperial degrees. An astounding 21 of 23 members born in the last half of the sixteenth century gained some sort of degree, and the percentage remained high throughout the seventeenth century. Even in 1651-1700, when the percentage of degree-holders in the Ping 6 fang fell to 26 percent, this was still twice the figure attained by any other fang. If we look closely at the figures, however, we find that the degrees held by members of the Ping 6 fang during this 50-year span are quite unevenly distributed, with the Lun 21/2 fang accounting for a disproportionate number. In the eighteenth century, we find another pattern similar to the one we encountered in our analysis of population growth: the Lun 21/3 fang, taken as an aggregate, did not have a particularly high percentage of degree-holders, but one of its component fang, Yü 64, managed to gain degrees for over half of all its members born during this century. And the K'un 12 fang, significant for its population growth from 1700 to 1850, also had a quite high rate of degree-holding during at least the middle 50 years of that period.

TABLE 4.10

*Spearman Rank-Order Correlations Between Percentage of
Degree-Holders in a Given Fang Born During a Particular Fifty-Year Period
and Various Demographic Factors*

Factor correlated with percentage of degree-holders	Ho	Lin	Wu
MPI growth in that fang in the *following* 50 years	.48	.67	.79
Age at birth of first son	.66	.43	.39
Age of wife or concubine at birth of her first son	no data	.07	.38
Number of wives and concubines per man	.51	.52	.63
Number of surviving sons born per wife or concubine	.12	.49	.56

What these data seem to indicate is that fang with higher percentages of degree-holders also had higher rates of population growth. There are good reasons for supposing that men with degrees have more sons; if this is true, degree-holding in one 50-year interval should correlate with growth in the male population index in the next 50-year interval, when those men and their sons are producing children. And when we calculate a measure of association between the two variables, using the Spearman rank-order correlation coefficient (rho) and taking each fang in each 50-year period as a single case, we find exactly that. As indicated in Table 4.10, the Spearman's rho for those two variables in the Ho lineage is .48, a strong positive association.

It is not just in the Ho lineage, however, that this association holds. Table 4.11 shows degree-holding by fang in each 50-year period for the Lin lineage, and Table 4.12 presents similar figures for the Wus. In each case, we again notice that the pattern of degree-holding roughly conforms to the pattern of population growth in the next interval. In the Lin lineage, the big fang, which grew, stagnated, then grew again, showed a similar pattern of examination success: rather high at the beginning, low in the eighteenth century, and higher again in the nineteenth. The second fang, which lost population in the 150 years before 1850, had no degree-holders during two of the three 50-year periods within this time span. And the third fang, though its high percentage of degree-holders in the early years is not matched by population growth, did show a remarkable spurt of degree-holding after 1750, corresponding with its dramatic population growth after 1800.

There is a similar congruence between degree-holding and population dynamics in the Wu lineage. Recall that the lineage, growing rapidly in its

TABLE 4.11

Lin Lineage: Percentage of Degree- and Office-Holders by Fang and Age Cohort,
1601-1850

	Men born:				
Fang	1601-1650	1651-1700	1701-1750	1751-1800	1801-1850
Big fang	13%	3.2%	9.4%	15%	27%
Second fang	11	2	0	13	0
Third fang	50	22	0	36	58
TOTAL	15%	10%	4.8%	21%	42%

TABLE 4.12

Wu Lineage: Percentage of Degree- and Office-Holders by Fang and Age Cohort,
1601-1850

	Men born:				
Fang	1601-1650	1651-1700	1701-1750	1751-1800	1801-1850
Big Chih	0%	67%	0%	0%	extinct
Second Chih					
3	100	42	7	17	12
4	100	33	13	7	10
7	100	78	37	7	6
9	75	45	18	0	0
13	100	73	32	19	13
Third Chih					
1	67	0	0	0	0
2	50	100	0	0	extinct
8	50	40	87	43	53
Fourth Chih					
6	100	39	17	7	6
14	100	27	4	9	50
Fifth Chih					
12	50	0	0	extinct	
TOTAL	77%	41%	20%	13%	18%

first century, showed declining rates of population growth thereafter until
1850. The pattern of degree-holding for the lineage as a whole is just what
we would expect: the percentage of degree-holders declines steadily from
the 1601-50 interval to the 1751-1800 interval. And at the same time, the
only fang that continued to grow during the first half of the nineteenth
century was the eighth fang, whose rate of degree-holding, 43 percent, was
over twice that of its nearest competitor, the thirteenth fang, and more
than three times the rate for the lineage as a whole. As in the case of the
Ho lineage, the general impressions of fit between degree-holding and popu-

lation growth in the Lin and Wu lineages are supported by statistical calculations: the Spearman's rho for these two variables is a very strong .67 for the Lins and an overwhelming .79 for the Wus.

We have established, then, that there is a definite association between degree-holding and the propensity of males to reproduce; and we can surmise that it is degree-holding that facilitates fertility, rather than the other way around, since degree-holding in a certain time interval is correlated with fertility in the next interval. Our next task is to explain this association: what is enabling wealthy, high-status men to have more sons than their poor agnates? We can think of several possibilities, not all independent of one another. For example, wealthy men might be marrying at a younger age, thus lengthening their potential reproductive span (not a negligible factor in a population where many men die in middle age or younger) and increasing the likelihood that members of several generations will be alive at once, thus increasing the population at any one time. Or they may be marrying younger women, thus increasing the reproductive span of the women, an important consideration in any population. Both these variables seem reasonable from what we know about traditional Chinese society: we know that poverty did postpone marriage for both men and women. And furthermore we would expect the two variables to go together: in our own sample, the average age differential between husband and wife was only 4.24 years in the Wu lineage and 2.16 years in the Lin lineage, indicating that men who married young married young women and older men married women close to their own age.

A third possibility is that wealthier men brought in more women to reproduce. Since it was easier for a wealthy man to get a wife, and since concubinage was practically confined to the wealthier classes, this also seems a reasonable hypothesis. Finally, it is possible that the women brought in by men of wealthier fang gave birth to more children per woman. Any or all of these factors might reasonably operate to raise the reproduction rate of wealthier branches of a lineage; let us look at their effects in turn.

First, we can explore the possibility that members of more prosperous fang married younger or, more precisely, that they got sons younger, which ought to be associated (though we have no proof) with younger marriage. The relevant figures for the Ho, Lin, and Wu lineages are set out in Tables 4.13, 4.14, and 4.15. Patterns in this regard are particularly noticeable in the Ho lineage. In Table 4.13, fang with unusually low ages at the birth of the first son are circled. Many of these are the same fang that showed high population growth: Ping 6 in the sixteenth century, Lun 21/3 and especially its component Yü 64 in 1701-50, Yü 64 in 1751-1800, and K'un 12 in 1751-1800. In this lineage we find degree-holding and age at birth of first son negatively correlated (that is, the greater the percentage of de-

TABLE 4.13

Ho Lineage: Age of Father at Birth of First Surviving Son by Fang and Father's
Age Cohort, 1551-1850

Fang	Fathers born:					
	1551-1600	1601-1650	1651-1700	1701-1750	1751-1800	1801-1850
Ping 1	26.3	32.0	33.1	37.1	33.5	29.3
Ping 6	25.1	25.7				
Lun 11			44			
Lun 13			30.0	33.6	29.1	29.8
Lun 14			32.6	36.3	33.5	32.5
Lun 21/2			28.1	28.8	31.6	27.2
Lun 21/3			30.1	25.1	32.6	28.4
Yü 64				22.0	25.4	28.6
Ping 7	32.0	36.4	29.8	33.0	28.5	35.8
Chen 8	32.3	27.1	27.4	29.8	32.3	30.0
Chen 20	32.0	30.8	34.9	31.4	27.9	31.6
K'un 12	35.0	38.3	30.0	28.4	26.6	31.5

TABLE 4.14

Lin Lineage: Age of Father at Birth of First Surviving Son by Fang and Father's
Age Cohort, 1601-1850

Fang	Fathers born:				
	1601-1650	1651-1700	1701-1750	1751-1800	1801-1850
Big fang	18.2	32.1	33.6	31.6	25.4
Second fang	28.2	31.5	30.1	24.8	22.5
Third fang	16	30.5	31.4	27.5	25.5

grees, the lower the age at birth of first son); the rho value is .66, indicating a strong association.

In the other two lineages, patterns are more difficult to find and the measures of correlation are somewhat weaker. Nevertheless, the two variables are negatively correlated in the Lin lineage with a rho of .43 and in the Wu lineage with a rho of .39. And indeed in Table 4.15 we can see that as population index growth rates and rates of degree-holding decline for the Wu lineage as a whole from the seventeenth century to the nineteenth, the average age of fathers at the birth of their first sons rises steadily.

Since it is the woman's reproductive span that ought to be crucial for population growth, we might expect to find an even higher degree of association between degree-holding and the age of the *mother* at the birth of

TABLE 4.15

Wu Lineage: Age of Father at Birth of First Surviving Son by Fang and Father's Age Cohort, 1601-1850

	Fathers born:				
Fang	1601- 1650	1651- 1700	1701- 1750	1751- 1800	1801- 1850
Big Chih	Insufficient	Data			
Second Chih					
3	21	28.5	32.6	27.3	26.3
4	22	27.4	37.3	28.2	35.8
7	40.7	23.7	26.5	33.2	34.5
9	27	24.2	26.4	36	46
13	22	24.2	29.2	32.7	31.8
Third Chih					
1	55	31.6	33.3	27.3	35
2	39	37	32	39	extinct
8	21	34.5	25.3	29.3	33.7
Fourth Chih					
6	33	25.1	27.9	30.7	31.7
14	25	26.3	30.9	39	38.5
Fifth Chih					
12	24	31.7	32	extinct	
TOTAL	27.5	26.8	28.9	31.3	33.1

the first son, especially since wives are usually only a few years younger than their husbands. As a matter of fact, the evidence for the hypothesis that wealthier men are marrying younger women, or more precisely, that the wives of wealthier men are producing children younger, is somewhat equivocal. We have no data for the Ho lineage, since its genealogy does not list birth and death dates of wives, but the relevant figures for the Lin and Wu lineages are given in Tables 4.16 and 4.17. There is no apparent pattern in the Lin table; indeed, the Spearman's rho of negative association between degree-holding and age of mother at birth of first son is only .07, indicating essentially no association. For the Wu lineage there does appear to be an association, though not a particularly strong one: the Spearman's rho is .38. And the table indicates that the age of mothers of first surviving sons did rise slightly, though not dramatically, up to 1800, though there was again a decline in the average age for wives of men born 1800 to 1850. This decline may have led to a population increase in the latter half of the nineteenth century; we cannot tell because of the different data base for calculating the Male Population Index.

Another possibility is that men with more wealth and high status have an easier time acquiring brides and concubines, and thus are likely to have more wives and concubines per man than do their poorer relatives. Tables 4.18, 4.19, and 4.20 show the number of wives per man born in each 50-

TABLE 4.16

Lin Lineage: Age of Mother at Birth of First Surviving Son by Fang and Father's Age Cohort, 1601-1850

Fang	Fathers born:				
	1601-1650	1651-1700	1701-1750	1751-1800	1801-1850
Big fang	19.7	26.9	27.1	26.5	24.8
Second fang	26	26	23.1	21.2	22.5
Third fang	24.5	27	29.3	28.3	25.8

TABLE 4.17

Wu Lineage: Age of Mother at Birth of First Surviving Son by Fang and Men's Age Cohort, 1601-1850

Fang	Men born:				
	1601-1650	1651-1700	1701-1750	1751-1800	1801-1850
Big Chih	Insufficient		Data		
Second Chih					
3	19.2	24.5	27.3	23.8	23.2
4	21.5	26	21	26.5	25.8
7	27	21.7	24.7	25.8	20.3
9	23.5	22.5	24	26.4	29
13	24	23.1	24.7	26.9	27.6
Third Chih					
1	43	29.2	28.5	27.7	33
2		37	21		extinct
8	23.5	26.2	26.6	27.1	n.a.
Fourth Chih					
6	29.2	23.0	25.4	24.5	24.7
14	25.5	24.6	29.2	30.5	26
Fifth Chih					
12	Insufficient		Data		
TOTAL	24.6	23.8	25.3	26.1	24.6

year interval in each fang of the Ho, Lin, and Wu lineages respectively. In all three cases there is a moderately strong to strong positive association. In the Ho lineage, for example, we find the familiar pattern of high rates in Ping 6 at the time of its inception and rapid growth in the sixteenth century, in Yü 64 in the late eighteenth century, and in K'un 12 throughout the eighteenth century. The fact that some rapidly growing fang did not show high average numbers of women brought in, and that some slower-growing fang did, simply points out that more than one factor can produce growth. The Spearman rank-order correlation for these two variables has the moderately high value of .51 for the Ho lineage.

TABLE 4.18

Ho Lineage: Number of Women per Man Brought In to Reproduce,
by Fang and Men's Age Cohort, 1501-1850

	Men born:						
Fang	1501-1550	1551-1600	1601-1650	1651-1700	1701-1750	1751-1800	1801-1850
Ping 1	1.28	1.25	1.44	1.22	0.79	0.89	0.36
Ping 6	1.40	1.61	1.21	1.25			
Lun 11				0.80	0.83	0.14	
Lun 13				1.15	0.89	0.87	0.60
Lun 14				0.96	0.80	0.81	0.63
Lun 21/2				1.61	0.96	0.89	0.83
Lun 21/3				1.11	0.87	1.06	0.65
Yü 64				2.33	1.29	1.37	0.88
Ping 7	1.50	1.12	1.33	0.73	0.36	1.25	0.50
Chen 8	1.25	1.09	1.16	1.09	0.83	0.90	0.72
Chen 20	0.75	1.28	0.88	1.06	0.64	1.22	0.74
K'un 12		0.67	1.33	1.00	1.40	1.36	0.94
Others	1.14	0.91	0.67	0.83	0.86	0.44	

NOTE: The figures represent wives plus concubines who bore children. As in earlier tables, the figures for Lun 11-21/3 are components of the Ping 6 figure for 1651-1700, and the figures for Yü 64 are components of the Lun 21/3 figures.

TABLE 4.19

Lin Lineage: Number of Women per Man Brought In to Reproduce,
by Fang and Men's Age Cohort, 1601-1850

	Men born:				
Fang	1601-1650	1651-1700	1701-1750	1751-1800	1801-1850
Big fang	0.93	0.87	0.97	1.0	0.77
Second fang	1	0.90	0.85	0.73	0.62
Third fang	2	1.4	1.2	1.2	1.0

NOTE: The figures represent wives plus concubines who bore children.

Much the same pattern holds for the Lin lineage. The big fang shows a notable dip in marriage success during the same middle years in which its examination success also declined. The second fang, whose examination success and population both declined steadily, with one exception, shows a steady decline in marriage success. And the third fang, although its early rates of marriage success, before it began to be wealthy and growth, are higher than its later rates, still shows rates during its later, expanding years that are higher than those for either of the other two fang in any of their

TABLE 4.20

Wu Lineage: Number of Women per Man Brought In to Reproduce,
by Fang and Men's Age Cohort, 1601-1850

| Fang | Men born: | | | | |
	1601-1650	1651-1700	1701-1750	1751-1800	1801-1850
Big Chih	2	1.7	0.33	1	extinct
Second Chih					
3	1.7	1.2	0.98	0.81	0.76
4	3	1	0.93	0.83	0.65
7	2	2	1.3	0.77	0.53
9	1.7	1.4	0.76	0.73	0.5
13	1	1.7	1.4	0.90	0.69
Third Chih					
1	2.3	0.9	0.6	2	1
2	1.5	1	0.8	0.25	extinct
8	1.2	1.6	1.4	1.5	1.1
Fourth Chih					
6	2	1.3	0.95	0.72	0.5
14	2	1.6	0.92	0.27	3
Fifth Chih					
12	1.5	1.6	0.8	extinct	
TOTAL	1.83	1.36	1.02	0.84	0.74

NOTE: The figures represent wives plus concubines who bore children.

50-year intervals. The impression of a moderately strong relationship between these two variables is confirmed by a Spearman's rho of .52.

The Wu lineage shows a similar pattern. The one fang that shows examination success and population growth in the nineteenth century, the eighth fang, is also the only fang in which the ratio of wives and concubines to men is greater than unity for either 1751-1800 or 1800-1851. Similarly, the seventh and thirteenth fang, which showed high rates of examination success in 1701-50, also had very high rates of marriage success. Once again the Spearman's rho shows a positive association between examination success and marriage success, with a figure of .63.

Finally, as we have seen, it is possible that men of the wealthier fang not only brought in more wives and brought them in at a younger age, but brought in wives who produced more sons per man (again, the number of daughters is irrelevant because they marry out and their offspring are lost to the lineage). We can test this hypothesis in a familiar way—the relevant figures for the Ho, Lin, and Wu lineages are set out in Tables 4.21, 4.22, and 4.23. We find positive associations in two of the three lineages. There is not much association in the Ho lineage—no pattern is readily discernible in the tables, and the rank-order correlation coefficient is only .12, in-

TABLE 4.21

Ho Lineage: Number of Sons per Woman by Fang and Men's Age Cohort,
1501-1850

Fang	Men born:						
	1501-1550	1551-1600	1601-1650	1651-1700	1701-1750	1751-1800	1801-1850
Ping 1	0.78	1.00	1.38	1.09	1.55	1.06	0.50
Ping 6	1.71	1.38	1.63	1.31			
Lun 11				1.00	1.40	1.00	
Lun 13				1.30	1.08	1.40	1.15
Lun 14				1.35	1.38	1.33	0.80
Lun 21/2				1.28	1.18	1.08	0.86
Lun 21/3				1.37	1.48	1.30	1.04
Yü 64				1.43	1.27	1.32	0.91
Ping 7	1.16	1.16	0.60	2.18	1.40	1.10	1.50
Chen 8	1.80	1.17	1.45	1.19	1.62	1.30	1.17
Chen 20	2.33	1.33	1.37	1.12	1.05	1.22	1.00
K'un 12		1.50	1.25	0.75	1.57	1.20	1.06
Others	0.96	1.23	1.38	1.58	1.21	0.25	

NOTE: The figures represent total number of sons divided by total number of wives plus concubines with offspring. The figures for Lun 11-21/3 are components of the Ping 6 figure for 1651-1700; the figures for Yü 64 are components of the Lun 21/3 figures.

TABLE 4.22

Lin Lineage: Number of Sons per Woman by Fang and Men's Age Cohort,
1601-1850

Fang	Men born:				
	1601-1650	1651-1700	1701-1750	1751-1800	1801-1850
Big fang	2.3	1.3	0.83	0.86	1.4
Second fang	1.3	1.9	0.88	0.91	1.4
Third fang	1.7	0.87	0.81	1.6	1.1
TOTAL	1.8	1.3	0.88	1.1	1.2

NOTE: The figures represent total number of sons divided by total number of wives plus concubines with offspring.

dicating no association. In the Lin and Wu lineages, however, the association is somewhat stronger. In the Lin case, we see no particular pattern in the big fang, but we do see the familiar decline in the second fang and the dip and subsequent rise in the third. And in 1751-1800, when the third fang had its greatest examination success, its wives were far more successful reproductively than the wives of either of the other segments. The Spearman's rho for the Lins is a moderately strong .49. In the Wu case, we see the general decline here as elsewhere, and the eighth fang does have a higher rate in the late eighteenth century. The relationship, however, is

108 STEVAN HARRELL

TABLE 4.23

Wu Lineage: Number of Sons per Woman by Fang and Men's Age Cohort,
1601–1850

| | Men born: | | | | |
Fang	1601-1650	1651-1700	1701-1750	1751-1800	1801-1850
Big Chih	0.5	0.6	2	0	extinct
Second Chih					
3	2.2	1.2	0.86	0.96	1
4	1.2	1.7	1.1	1.2	0.61
7	1.3	1.1	1.2	0.93	1
9	2	1.4	1.1	0.62	0.5
13	2	1.8	0.95	1.2	0.89
Third Chih					
1	1.1	1.4	0.5	0.5	0.5
2	1	1.5	1	2	extinct
8	1.2	0.87	1.1	1.2	1.2
Fourth Chih					
6	1.3	2.1	1.0	0.68	1.4
14	1.7	1	0.86	0.67	0.67
Fifth Chih					
12	1.3	0.67	0.25	extinct	
TOTAL	1.47	1.39	1.00	0.99	0.99

NOTE: The figures represent total number of sons divided by total number of wives plus concubines with offspring.

quite strong: when tested statistically the two variables have a Spearman's rho of .56.

Conclusions

In all three lineages studied, we can demonstrate not only that high social status—as indicated by degree-holding, and probably by wealth as well—contributed to population growth, and that such high status, unevenly distributed among the genealogical branches of the lineage, promoted the growth and dominance of some fang at the expense of others. Furthermore, we know how this differential growth was achieved: in the majority of cases, members of wealthier branches of lineages married earlier, married younger women, married or brought in as concubines more women, and married or brought in more fertile women.

These findings have implications both for the study of the Chinese lineage and for the study of population. The process of growth, segmentation, and stratification in Chinese lineages, previously known primarily by reconstructions from synchronic sources, has now been shown to be traceable over the centuries by the use of genealogies. What this means is that Freedman's original characterization of segmentation in the Chinese lineage as asymmetrical and based on wealth[15] is validated by the study of three lineages over time.

In terms of the study of population, our findings have rather broader and rather less demonstrable implications. We have talked in this paper simply about three lineages, chosen not by any random process but simply by examining the genealogies that appear to contain the best data. Within these three lineages, the rich, as they get richer, get children, and by doing so some of them become poorer. It would be rash to state that this is the model for late Ming and Ch'ing society as a whole—there are a lot more lineages to be studied, and a lot of people who are not members of any lineage.

Yet are these not interesting implications for the population of China as a whole? The lineages, after all, start out as but a minuscule proportion of the population of even a local marketing area in the Sung, Yüan, or early Ming. That they became as large as they did shows they were growing faster than the population as a whole. But by studying large, fast-growing lineages, am I introducing an inherent bias into the study of China's population? My answer is Yes and no. Yes because, as wholes, despite any internal differentiation, these lineages represent the demographically more successful segments of the local population. No because there is differentiation between the more successful and the less successful segments within the lineages, and these differences can be accounted for not by characteristics of the *lineage*, but by characteristics of the *family*. It is the family's wealth that makes it possible to spend a large amount of money on the wedding of a son not yet twenty, that induces a widow to remarry into the family, or that persuades a poor girl's parents to sell their daughter to the family as a concubine.

The resources available in the corporate holdings of the lineage (schooling, examination expenses, sometimes income from the distribution of the proceeds of collectively owned land) may help individual families prosper, and in that sense the sample is biased in favor of wealthy families. But the sample contains members of poor families as well. And insofar as the poor families are also gaining certain benefits from lineage membership, the differences between rich and poor found in this paper are probably understated: we would expect rich families who are members of no lineage to still have the advantages of rich families who do belong to lineages, whereas poor families who are members of no lineage will have none of those benefits. If anything, then, outside of lineage organization the gap between rich and poor would be even wider. For this reason, I think it justifiable to assert, at least as a working hypothesis, that population growth in late imperial China is best explained by the assertion that the rich get children.

FIVE

Rural Migration and Fertility in Tokugawa Japan: The Village of Nishijo, 1773-1868

Akira Hayami

Most demographic studies of Tokugawa Japan that are based on the *shūmon-aratame-chō* (household registers)[1] focus on questions and types of analysis comparable to those found in studies based on European parish registers. However, a good time series of shūmon-aratame-chō may provide data that permit analyses beyond what is possible from the European registers.

The most important aspect of demographic behavior that specialists in European historical demography cannot examine is migration. Migration is, however, within the sphere of the shūmon-aratame-chō, which at least in theory record every demographic event taking place in a given village in a single year. This means we can observe the entire migration process, from entry to exit of every villager registered, as well as his demographic experience and the family context. We can trace individual villagers from birth to death or to permanent departure from the village. We may also carry this process further, and trace the lives of everyone in the village during the period for which records exist. Thus, the shūmon-aratame-chō provide the basis for demographic classification and statistical analysis of entire villages.

In this paper, we will discuss migration in rural Japan as it affected the rural population, with particular focus on fertility. Our case study will be of a village in central Japan for which we have complete registers for the 97 years from 1773 to 1869. This is the farming village of Nishijo, located in northwest of Nagoya, in the midst of a delta fed by three rivers, the Kiso, Nagara, and Ibi. The area is called Wajū (literally, "in the ring") because of its unique topography of hamlets and fields encircled by high embankments. The soil is fertile, and rice, the chief local crop, and also cotton, rapeseed, and other cash crops were cultivated during the period under study, although we have no data on production.

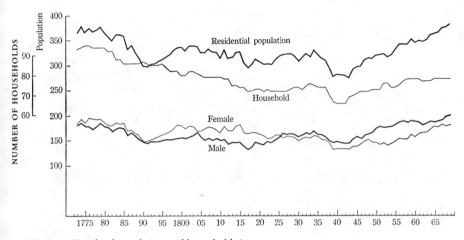

Fig. 5.1. Trends of population and household size

The village was located only four miles from the castle town of Ōgaki, and, during the second half of the Tokugawa period, it was under the control of the Tokugawa government but administered by the domain of Ōgaki. Nishijo was not completely independent, being administered as part of neighboring Niremata village, but it can be considered independent for the purposes of our study. As we shall see, there was considerable migration both in and out of Nishijo during the century for which we have records, and there were very close ties between Nishijo and Niremata in terms of both marriage and employment, with movement between the villages in both directions.

Fortunately, the shūmon-aratame-chō for this village represent a complete, unbroken series from 1773 to 1869.[2] Furthermore, the entries in these registers provide minute details—thus giving as much information as one can expect from such materials. Any change in residence, the reason for the change, the destinations of migrants, and even postmigration movements are all recorded. An analysis of the population of Nishijo derived from the shūmon-aratame-chō provides the following basic demographic information: The total residential population was 366 (181 men and 185 women) in 1772, and 381 (200 men and 181 women) in 1869. The number of households decreased during this time from 93 to 78. Although there was little change in population at either end of the series (as shown in Figure 5.1), a large drop occurred at the end of the 1780's and again in the late 1830's. These two drops in population correspond to the second and third of the three great natural disasters of Tokugawa Japan. The population decrease of the 1780's was caused by the Temmei famine, which fol-

TABLE 5.1

Birth and Death Rates for Nishijo by Decade, 1773-1868

Period	Number of births	Number of deaths	Crude birth rate per M	Crude death rate per M	Rate of natural increase per M
1773-1780	72	61	24.5	20.8	+3.7
1781-1790	87	101	26.1	30.3	−4.2
1791-1800	122	73	38.4	23.0	+15.4
1801-1810	106	76	32.6	23.4	+9.2
1811-1820	92	70	29.6	22.5	+7.1
1821-1830	107	63	34.7	20.5	+14.2
1831-1840	102	110	34.5	37.2	−2.7
1841-1850	102	59	33.8	19.6	+14.2
1851-1860	108	59	32.4	17.7	+15.7
1861-1868	95	50	32.7	17.2	+15.5
TOTAL	993	722	31.9	23.2	+8.6

lowed several years of poor harvests. In the years 1785 to 1789, 51 persons died in Nishijo; the village population dropped from 361 to 299, a decrease of about 17 percent. The second decrease, in the 1830's, caused by the Tempō famine, was due to a poor harvest and an epidemic in the years 1837-38. It is recorded that 28 persons died in the village in 1837, with the crude death rate rising as high as 90 per thousand. As Table 5.1 shows, this is the highest rate for a single year in the period covered.

Except for these two big drops, population movement was rather slow. However, after the drop in the late 1830's, the population recovered quickly, with the annual increase averaging 1.2 percent. Although the total population figures for the village show few discernible trends, the birth rate, at 31.9 per thousand, was much higher than the death rate, which averaged 23.2.[3] Births during the entire period totaled 993 and deaths only 722. Thus there should have been a natural increase of 271 persons during the 97 years. Despite this large natural increase, however, the total population of the village changed little, owing to the high incidence of emigration.

Migration in the Tokugawa Period

Many histories of the Tokugawa period report that peasants were tied to their land and legally barred from migrating. There were, in fact, some institutional restrictions on peasants' movements, and the geographical range of their lives must have been much narrower than at present. This does not mean, however, that peasants spent their entire lives in their native village, or even in its immediate vicinity. On the contrary, analysis of the shūmon-aratame-chō shows that far more migration took place than one might suppose. Though some institutional limitations existed, their practical effect is questionable. Moreover, peasants sometimes ignored the required procedures in leaving the village and once they had entered a big city, they seem never to have been caught.

One might suppose that the undeveloped system of transportation imposed another limitation on migration. There was no public transport on land, and thus ordinary people had to walk. Consequently, long-distance migration took many days and a good deal of money, and the journey was always exhausting. Nonetheless, migration within a ten days' walk was not infrequent, and for migration to a big city the range was even greater.

What concerns us here is the migration of labor, not migration for marriage or adoption. The term *dekasegi* (literally, "leaving home to work") covers both permanent and temporary migration. In part because of the institutional restrictions on permanent changes of abode, all peasants were in principle expected to return home sometime in the future, so the term, which means temporary migration, was applied to everyone. And in fact Japanese laborers tended to relocate for work for a time and then return home, a practice that continued until very recently. Thus, although all migration of labor was recorded as dekasegi (e.g., working temporarily at so and so's house as a servant), in truth both permanent and temporary migrants were classified under this one term, and without following up individual cases, we cannot distinguish permanent from temporary migration.

The causes of labor migration were largely economic. The Tokugawa shogunate and the daimyo spent most of their revenues in the cities and towns, and a large number of merchants and manual laborers gathered there. Given the generally poor living conditions in cities and towns, and particularly their susceptibility to epidemics and famine, urban populations could not be maintained without a constant influx from the countryside. Though the historical demography of Japanese cities is almost completely undeveloped, from surveys conducted by the Tokugawa shogunate between 1843 and 1867 we know that 25-33 percent of the common people of Edo (now Tokyo) were born outside the city.[4] Cities by their very existence fostered migration, and when economic activities increased and the urban population grew, the increase was drawn from rural areas.[5]

Two phases of intervillage mobility can be discerned. The first is the type widely seen up to the eighteenth century, that of the *genin* or servant who migrated to take up long-term employment—in some cases lifelong service. This type of labor, which has been traced to ancient times, began to disappear early in the Tokugawa period. This was due to a nationwide shift to small-scale farm management,[6] which depended chiefly on the labor of family members in the direct line. This was an important change that took hold gradually throughout the seventeenth century.

With the conversion to small-scale management complete, the second phase of migration began. The development of rural handicraft industries requiring a large labor force and the cultivation of cash crops as a sideline also induced migration. Labor was supplied by contract, usually for a year but subject to extension. The Japanese term for persons who worked under yearly (or term) contracts is *nenki-hōkōnin*. Labor migration of this type continued hand in hand with industrial development, creating both areas of labor supply and areas of labor demand. In a well-to-do farmer's household, there were always men and women who were employed as domestic servants on long-term contracts, but there were no more than two or three such households in any one village, so their number was not significant. Emigration for noneconomic reasons also included service, sometimes involuntary, in samurai families.

Migration in Nishijo

On balance Nishijo served as a labor supply area, but there was some demand within the village for outside labor. However, there was a sharp drop in the 1790's from nine or ten households employing servants or workers to only one or two households thereafter, with a corresponding drop in the number of people so employed—from 20 in 1780 to a maximum of four from 1810 on. So few outsiders were employed in Nishijo that in this paper we shall ignore them, and concentrate on the migration of Nishijo residents to other places to work and the effects of this employment.

Good as the Nishijo records are, it is still difficult to determine whether any given individual had, or—even more difficult—did *not* have, the experience of working away from home sometime during his or her lifetime. To be certain a villager died without ever leaving the village to work, we must be able to trace his activities from birth to death. Since our documents cover only 97 years, only a few cohorts can be thus traced. Because very few people left home to work in old age, however—and it is doubtful whether those who are listed as doing so were in fact working—the cohorts born between 1773 and 1825 can be used for our analysis, since the villagers born in 1825 would have been 45 years old in the last record.[7]

The population included in these cohorts comprises 244 males and 250 females, of whom 62 boys and 60 girls died before reaching age 10. If these deaths are subtracted, 182 men and 190 women remain. Of these, 87 men, or 48 percent of the 182 men, and 117 women, or 62 percent of the 190 women, went out to work at some time in their lives. Though there is some difference between men and women, in general the percentage who left the village to work is far higher than we would have expected, and we are not counting people who left their household to work within the village.

TABLE 5.2

Dekasegi Rates by Sex and Landholding Status
of Household, 1773-1869

(percent)

Status	Male	Female
Landlord	39.4%	32.5%
Owner-cultivator	29.6	59.1
Owner-tenant cultivator	27.8	64.7
Tenant	63.1	74.0

NOTE: The percentages represent all those in the category who went out to work at some time during their lifetimes.

Why did so many people leave Nishijo to work? For several reasons. There were many cities in the surrounding area, the rural handicraft industry was well developed, and the village's location on a plain made travel comparatively easy. Also, the village had a high birth rate, which would explain the incentive or need to seek employment away from home.

When we compare the experience of dekasegi by landholding class, how do the percentages vary? Fortunately, the land held within Nishijo by each household is recorded in the shūmon-aratame-chō in terms of the assessed rice output, but because we do not know how much land households held outside the village, landholding by household cannot be accurately assessed. However, if we use the information we have, households can be classified as: (a) landlords, (b) owner-cultivators, (c) owner-tenant cultivators, and (d) tenants.[8] Using this classification for each villager at birth, the proportion of each class that went out to work at some time during their lifetimes is shown in Table 5.2. For the men, the proportion of labor emigrants is far higher among the tenant group than in any other class, but the other three classes show no significant differences. For women too, the proportion of labor emigrants is highest for the tenant group, but the rate gradually decreases as we climb the social scale, with the lowest proportion in the landlord class. Among the tenants, 63 percent of the men and 74 percent of the women left the village to work, and thus we know that the principal source of dekasegi labor was this class. Table 5.3 shows the proportion of households in each class that had at least one member who emigrated to work at three points in time: 1780, 1820, and 1860. This table also shows that the highest proportions of labor emigrants are found in the tenant households.

At what age did the villagers start working outside the village? To observe the conditions on both the labor supply and labor demand sides, we shall classify all the households as either tenants or nontenants. Then, we shall classify the initial destinations as urban or rural. The ages at first de-

TABLE 5.3

Percentage of Households Whose Members Went Out on Dekasegi,
1780, 1820, and 1860

Status	1780	1820	1860	Total
Landlord	33%	33%	60%	39%
Owner-cultivator	30	29	40	32
Owner-tenant cultivator	50	50	45	48
Tenant	46	63	56	54

kasegi are shown in accordance with this classification in Table 5.4. Generally speaking, the mean age in tenant households was rather low; some boys and girls left home to work as young as age six. Slightly fewer went to rural areas than to cities. The lowest age at first dekasegi is found among tenants who went to rural areas, the highest among nontenants who went to cities. Table 5.4 shows that about equal numbers of men went to urban and to rural areas, but a larger number of women went to rural areas. The villagers from the nontenant classes went primarily to big cities.

To ensure accurate figures on dekasegi destinations, in Table 5.5 we analyze participation in terms of man-years. We divided the years between 1773 and 1868 into four periods and dekasegi destinations into three classifications: cities, towns, and rural areas.[9] The total dekasegi reached 6,647 man-years, with an annual average of 68. Dekasegi destinations, however, changed a good deal over time, with increasing numbers seeking work in cities and towns (Figure 5.2). It is significant that women going to work in towns had the highest rate toward the end of the period. From their destinations we know that they were employed by the developing textile industry, which spread over a five- to seven-mile area to the east of the village.[10]

The amount of dekasegi for each year is shown in Figure 5.3. The swing for women is much larger than that for men. For women, the ratio of peak to lowest exodus was 58 : 19, i.e., over 3 : 1. This ratio was 47 : 18, or 2.6 : 1 in the case of men. There were two clear peaks of dekasegi for women, in 1781-95 and 1815-26, whereas for men there was no clear peak, only a gradual leveling-off. The second peak for women reflects the increase of dekasegi to cities and towns, a phenomenon that cannot be explained by population changes within the village. The total population, as seen in Figure 5.1, was low and stagnating. If we look at the sex ratio and age composition, we find no conspicuous change, and after 1840, when dekasegi was at a minimum, we see an increase in the population aged 16-50. Thus, the rise in dekasegi for women may have resulted from better conditions of employment or higher pay available outside the village.

TABLE 5.4

Age at First Dekasegi by Sex, Landholding Status, and Destination

	Tenant		Non-tenant	
Measure	Urban destination	Rural destination	Urban destination	Rural destination
Males				
Range (age)	8-47	6-29	8-33	13-18
Mean	15.9	13.6	16.4	15.8
Mode	11	11	–	–
Sample size	48	46	20	4
Females				
Range (age)	6-24	7-25	9-21	10-18
Mean	14.7	13.4	14.7	14.8
Mode	14	13	–	–
Sample size	42	73	36	5

TABLE 5.5

Distribution of Dekasegi by Sex, Time Period, and Destination

	Destination (*man-years*)				Distribution (*percent*)		
Time period	Rural	Town	City	Total	Rural	Town	City
Males							
1773-1800	309	25	540	874	35.4%	2.9%	61.8%
1801-1825	325	87	501	913	35.6	9.5	54.9
1826-1850	170	115	496	781	21.8	14.7	63.5
1851-1868	138	112	354	604	22.9	18.5	58.6
TOTAL	942	339	1,891	3,172	29.7%	10.7%	59.6%
Females							
1773-1800	405	69	427	901	45.0%	7.7%	47.4%
1801-1825	382	86	577	1,045	36.6	8.2	55.2
1826-1850	377	125	445	947	39.8	13.2	47.0
1851-1868	151	228	203	582	26.0	39.2	34.9
TOTAL	1,315	508	1,652	3,475	37.8%	14.6%	47.5%

Dekasegi to rural areas was declining, but if we combine dekasegi to this village with dekasegi from it, we see that labor migration between villages was characteristic of this period. On the whole, the number of people coming to work in this village was far smaller than those leaving, with a ratio in man-years of 447:2,030. If we examine migration in terms of destination, we observe the interesting characteristics seen in Figure 5.3. As previously mentioned, a larger number of women than men went out on dekasegi. Men mostly went south for dekasegi and then, in terms of frequency, to the north, east, and west, while dekasegi to Nishijo was from

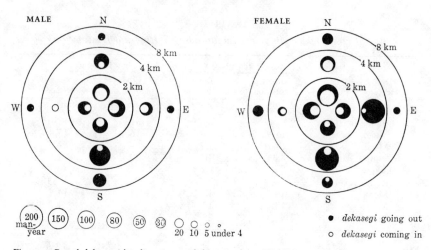

Fig. 5.2. Rural dekasegi by direction and distance from Nishijo

the north, east, south, and west. For women, dekasegi from the village was to the south, east, north, and west, in that order, while dekasegi to Nishijo was from the north, west, south, and east. Women most frequently migrated in from the north, but migrated out to the south and east. Thus there seems to have been a directional trend in labor migration involving Nishijo.

The city of Nagoya is 15 miles southeast of Nishijo, and in the intervening area the textile industry was well developed. As is characteristic of labor migration in a premodern society, labor migration here did not consist of a single journey to a distant place, but involved a series of short moves, first to places nearby. Here it is clear that 80 percent of the migration between villages took place within a 2.5-mile radius and flowed in a definite direction.

The statistics on dekasegi destinations by city calculated in man-years for each period are shown in Table 5.6. Except for the very few who went to Edo, people mostly went to Nagoya, to Ōsaka, 75 miles to the southwest, or to the area between these two major cities, which includes Kyōto. Before 1800, Kyōto was the most popular destination for migrants of both sexes. In the following quarter-century, men continued to go mainly to Kyōto, but women went mostly to Nagoya. After 1826, men too went mostly to Nagoya. In addition to these three cities, other important dekasegi destinations were Ōgaki (men and women), Sakai (men), and Tsu (women).

For dekasegi to towns, the destinations are listed in Table 5.6 in descending order of importance: for men, Yokkaichi and Hamada in Ise province

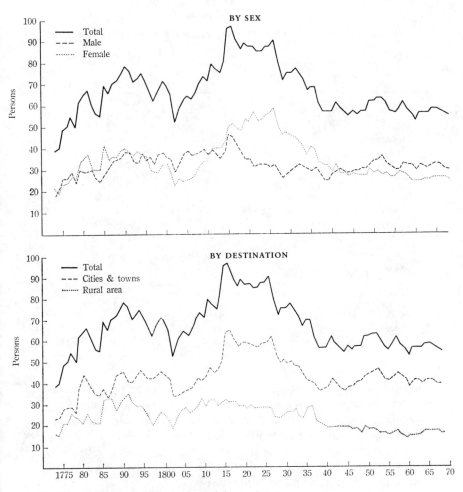

Fig. 5.3. Dekasegi from Nishijo by sex and destination

(100 man-years); Kasamatsu (81), Takehana (65), and Imao (30), all in Mino province; and for women, Takehana (173); Noma in Owari province (108); Kurigasa in Mino province (43); Hamada (42); Hagiwara in Owari province (37); and Kasamatsu (31). These small cities or towns of the Nōbi Plain and the surrounding area formed the administrative, transportation, and industrial centers of the area.

For only a few persons can we accurately measure the length of time worked outside the village. In the 1773-1825 cohorts, 43 men and 92 women terminated work for reasons other than death. The average dura-

TABLE 5.6

Distribution of Urban Dekasegi by Sex, Time Period, and Urban Area

(man-years)

Urban area	1773-1800	1801-1825	1826-1850	1851-1868	Total	Percent
Males						
Edo	45	19			64	3.4%
Nagoya	134	75	199	182	590	31.1
Kuwana				18	18	1.0
Tsu		9	17	2	28	1.5
Ōgaki	13	33	48	19	113	6.0
Hikone		10		17	27	1.4
Kyōto	340	230	34	27	631	33.4
Ōsaka	8	87	148	71	314	16.6
Sakai		38	50	18	106	5.6
TOTAL	540	501	496	354	1,891	100.0%
Females						
Nagoya	117	229	290	91	727	44.2%
Kuwana	12				12	0.7
Tsu	16	39	5		60	3.6
Ōgaki	22	95	17	43	177	10.8
Hikone	9	1	1		11	0.7
Kyōto	223	170	44	18	455	27.7
Ōsaka	27	38	87	51	203	12.3
TOTAL	426	572	444	203	1,645	100.0%

tion of dekasegi for these men and women, by class and destination, is as
follows: for men, 13.3 years for tenants and 8.6 years for nontenants; 8.7
years for those who went to cities and towns, 12.3 years for those who
went to rural areas; and for women, 14.0 years for tenants and 15.2 years
for nontenants; 13.7 years for those who went to cities and towns, 12.5
years for those who went to rural areas. These figures suggest a sharp contrast in the distribution patterns for the two sexes.

For people who went on dekasegi to cities and towns, the records contain only the names of their destination. We have no way of knowing how
long these people continued to work for the same employers. But the names
of employers of people who went to rural areas are recorded, and for them
we can ascertain the length of dekasegi contracts. The largest number were
one-year contracts. In a sample of 261 men, 115 or 45 percent had one-
year contracts, as did 70 women from a sample of 219, or 32 percent. The
longer the contracts, the smaller the percentage of people holding them.
Ninety percent of the men and 68 percent of the women had contracts of
less than five years' duration. The total average employment period was
2.9 years for men and 5.2 years for women, many of whom worked as domestic servants. The contracts tended to increase in duration as time went

TABLE 5.7

Reasons for Terminating Dekasegi

(number of persons)

Reason	Male	Female
Death	62	64
Returned home	48	18
Marriage	5	103
Adoption	8	
Miscellaneous	16	2
Unknown	3	
TOTAL	142	187

NOTE: Another 34 men and 31 women terminated dekasegi after the final year for which we have records.

on. Employment for a year or two as a farmhand decreased, while employment in domestic service increased.

Table 5.7 shows how many people discontinued dekasegi for various reasons. "Continued" means that in the last year of our records, work outside the village had not been terminated. The average age for the termination of dekasegi was 30.3 years for men, 27.8 for women. Among the 329 men and women who stopped work, 126 (38 percent) died while employed, 116 left their positions to marry or for other reasons, leaving only 87 (27 percent) who ever returned to their native village. Fewer women returned home than men—15 percent compared to 34 percent, although the number of women who married and went to other villages was balanced by brides coming into Nishijo. In short, then, it is not really appropriate to think of dekasegi as a temporary interruption in residence in one's native village.

The Relationship of Migration Data to Other Demographic Indices

The practice of dekasegi had a significant impact on the demography of Nishijo, in addition to bringing in income from outside the village and employing people who otherwise might have been unemployed and underemployed. First, it was labor migration that prevented a large increase in the village's population over the century covered by our records. With the average age at which residents first left the village to work 14 or 15, about 30 percent of the labor supply of this age left the village. Nearly one-half the men in this village left at some time in their lives to work elsewhere, and 32 percent of those who survived to 11 years of age eventually became part of the labor force of another area. Twenty-five percent of the women permanently left the village.

Dekasegi also affected the death rate in the village. According to the data for Nishijo, persons who worked away from home had a higher death

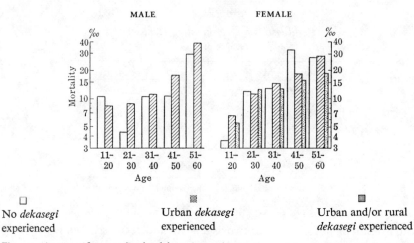

No *dekasegi*
experienced

Urban *dekasegi*
experienced

Urban and/or rural
dekasegi experienced

Fig. 5.4. Age-specific mortality by dekasegi experience

rate than those who remained in the village all their lives. Figure 5.4 shows
the differences in death rates by age group for those who had ever worked
in a city and those who had not. We must take into consideration that
those who had no dekasegi experience included men and women who were
physically handicapped or too weak to work or travel to work elsewhere,
but at least as far as men are concerned, in almost all age groups those who
had ever worked away from home had a higher death rate. For women,
there is evidence of a reverse relationship, which may have occurred because women who remained in the village married at an earlier age and
were more likely to die from pregnancy and childbirth. But what might be
considered the greatest impact of dekasegi was on fertility, which we deal
with below.

The Impact of Dekasegi on Fertility

Dekasegi among women had a negative impact on fertility within Nishijo and, we hypothesize, on most areas of Japan where it was widely
practiced. First, women who worked away from home on average married
later than women who never left their native village. For the cohorts born
between 1773 and 1825, the average age at marriage for women who
never left home was 20.7, whereas women who had worked away from
home married at 26.3. (The difference for men was not significant: for the
same cohorts, men married at 28.2 if they had not worked away from
home and 29.9 if they had.) Age-specific fertility rates obtained through
family reconstitution techniques suggest that women who worked away
from home bore two fewer children than women who did not, with the

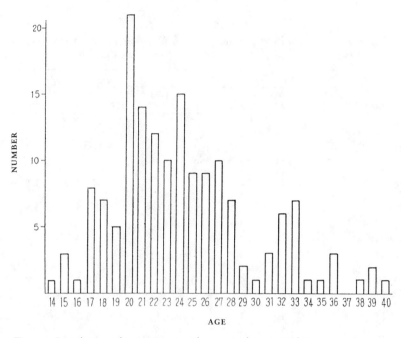

Fig. 5.5. Distribution of age at marriage for women born in Nishijo, 1773-1840

difference attributable to the delay in age at first marriage (see Figure 5.5 and Tables 5.8, 5.9, and 5.10). Since fertility was highest for women in their early twenties, each year marriage was delayed past 20 meant a loss of .3 -.4 children, or a total of about two for the six-year delay among women who left Nishijo to work.

But just as the proportion of the population who worked away from home differed by landholding class, so did the effect of dekasegi on the demographic indices. The number of children in completed families, analyzed by the woman's age at marriage, shown in Table 5.10 did not differ significantly by landholding class. However, if all women who ever went out to work married at 26.3, while those who never did so married at age 20.7, we would see a difference in fertility by class since the proportion of women who worked away from home varied by class. If we apply the differential dekasegi rates found in Table 5.1 to determine the average age at marriage and then average the number of births in completed families for women in each class,[11] the results are as follows: the average number of births would be 5.4 among landlords, 4.9 among owner-cultivators, 4.8 among owner-tenant cultivators, and 4.7 among tenants. These are all figures for completed families, but married life ended for many women before the childbearing years ended (see Tables 5.11 and 5.12).

TABLE 5.8

Age at Marriage of Men and Women According to Whether Subject Ever Worked
Away from Nishijo, 1773-1800 and 1801-1825 Cohorts

	Never left village				Worked away from village			
Age at marriage	1773-1800	1801-1825	Total	Percent	1773-1800	1801-1825	Total	Percent
Males								
16-20	3	1	4	6.3%	1		1	3.6%
21-25	7	5	12	18.8	6	4	10	35.7
26-30	15	15	30	46.9	4	2	6	21.4
31-35	3	9	12	18.8	3	3	6	21.4
36-40	3	1	4	6.3	3		3	10.7
41-45	2		2	3.1				
TOTAL	33	31	64	100%	18	10	28	100%
Average age at marriage	27.8	28.6	28.2		29.8	30.1	29.9	
Females								
-15	4		4	8.3%				
16-20	18	6	24	50.0	10	2	12	14.6%
21-25	10	5	15	31.3	20	14	34	41.5
26-30		2	2	4.2	8	11	19	23.2
31-35	2	1	3	6.3	3	6	9	11.0
36-40						3	3	3.7
41-45					2	3	5	6.1
TOTAL	34	14	48	100%	43	39	82	100%
Average age at marriage	20.1	22.1	20.7		24.5	28.3	26.3	

TABLE 5.9

Age-Specific Marital Fertility Rates

Age group	Number of births	Fertility
16-20	56	0.257
21-25	201	0.319
26-30	225	0.285
31-35	203	0.252
36-40	147	0.201
41-45	65	0.097
46-50	15	0.026

TABLE 5.10
Average Number of Births in Completed Familes by Woman's Age at Marriage

Age at marriage	Number of births	Age at marriage	Number of births
16	7.19	24	4.94
17	6.93	25	4.62
18	6.67	26	4.31
19	6.41	27	4.02
20	6.16	28	3.74
21	5.90	29	3.45
22	5.58	30	3.17
23	5.26		

NOTE: Calculated from Table 5.9.

TABLE 5.11
Average Age at Marriage by Landholding Status, 1773-1835 Cohort

Status	Went out to work	Never left to work	Total
Males (N = 107)			
Landlord	25.5	27.7	27.4
Owner-cultivator,			
Owner-tenant cultivator	26.3	29.2	28.8
Tenant	27.9	28.0	27.9
TOTAL	27.5	28.3	28.1
Females (N = 158)			
Landlord	24.3	21.2	21.6
Owner-cultivator,			
Owner-tenant cultivator	27.2	21.0	24.3
Tenant	25.6	22.3	24.7
TOTAL	25.9	21.5	24.0

TABLE 5.12
Age-Specific Marital Fertility by Landholding Status

Age group	Tenant	Owner-cultivators, Owner-tenant	Landlord	Total	Number of births
16-20	0.182	0.284	0.247	0.257	56
21-25	0.376	0.300	0.313	0.319	201
26-30	0.251	0.292	0.299	0.285	225
31-35	0.231	0.252	0.285	0.252	203
36-40	0.196	0.193	0.232	0.201	147
41-45	0.103	0.082	0.133	0.097	65
46-50	0.034	0.020	0.030	0.026	15

TABLE 5.13

Presence of Heirs by Landholding Status

Status	Inherited	No heirs
Landlord	34	0
Owner-cultivator,		
Owner-tenant cultivator	61	6
Tenant	183	60
TOTAL	278	66

TABLE 5.14

Distribution of Households by Landholding Status, Selected Years, 1780-1869

Status	1780		1810		1840		1869	
	Number	Percent	Number	Percent	Number	Percent	Number	Percent
Landless	68	73.9%	48	62.3%	19	29.7%	31	41.9%
Less than								
2 *koku*			1	1.3	21	32.8	24	32.4
2-5	2	2.2	4	5.2	12	18.8	11	14.9
5-10	10	10.9	16	20.8	7	10.9	3	4.1
10-20	8	8.7	6	7.8	4	6.3	2	2.7
20-50	4	4.3	1	1.3			2	2.7
Over 50			1	1.3	1	1.6	1	1.4
Temples	2		2		2		2	
Guard (?)							1	
Unknown							1	
TOTAL	94	100.0%	79	100.0%	66	100.0%	78	100.0%

NOTE: A *koku* equals approximately 5 U.S. bushels.

A gross reproduction rate of 2.2 was the minimum level for maintaining population in Tokugawa rural society.[12] The reproduction rate in Nishijō, except for landlords, was very close to this rate, and it must have been below it for families in the tenant class. Thus, tenants would have been unable to maintain their numbers and the tenant population would have decreased without interclass mobility. In fact, there were many tenant households that ceased to exist for lack of heirs, and others that had to adopt sons from other households to maintain the family line. As seen in Table 5.13, during the period studied 66 households, 60 of them in the tenant class, became extinct. This represents 32 percent of all changes in household head in the tenant class, and is very high compared to 6 percent in the nontenant classes.

In a balance sheet comparing the number of newly established branch households with the number of lines that became extinct, the landlords and owner-cultivators would receive a plus count, the tenants a minus.

However, the proportion of households in each class in the village changed scarcely at all during the century examined (see Table 5.14), thus providing evidence of a downward mobility of households during the Tokugawa period. When a branch household was established, it was usually of a lower class than the main household. That mobility between classes had a downward trend in this labor-supplying village is a phenomenon worthy of further study.

The Neighboring Villages

To what extent is the village of Nishijo representative of all Japan, or, more modestly, of the Nōbi Plain? Analysis of dekasegi is possible because Nishijo's registers extend in an unbroken series for 97 years, and because they include the particulars of migration. Thomas C. Smith used the shūmon-aratame-chō from Nakahara, a village only two miles from Nishijo, to conduct a superb demographic analysis, which revealed evidence of sex-selective infanticide.[13] But because there is not a single entry pertaining to migration in the Nakahara registers, he could not include it in his study. The omission of dekasegi from the Nakahara registers does not mean there was none. The shūmon-aratame-chō I have collected from villages controlled, like Nakahara, by Ōgaki, all use the same system, based on "permanent residence" rather than continuous registration, in the compilation of the shūmon-aratame-chō.

To determine whether the conditions in Nishijo were characteristic of the Nōbi Plain or not, one must locate villages that entered information on the shūmon-aratame-chō in the same way as Nishijo. These were villages that had adequate records and were, like Nishijo, either shogunate land administered by Ōgaki or areas administered by the shogunate itself. I have records for two villages near Nishijo that fulfill these requirements, Niremata and Ario-shinden. However, the number of years represented in the registers is small, and there are many missing years, so the scope of our investigation is restricted.

The earliest registers for Ario-shinden, which is about three miles west of Nishijo, date from 1685, and the records are highly reliable from 1736 on. Consequently, we can investigate the prevalence of dekasegi in a period earlier than we could for Nishijo. In 1736 eight men and four women are listed as being on dekasegi, a small proportion of the total population of 140 males and 129 females in the village. Since the number of those who entered the village from other villages on labor contracts (*irikasegi*) was 11 men and 23 women, the village was absorbing labor from other areas. Ario-shinden sits on land reclaimed from the river, so a large number of laborers was probably required. If one examines the relationship between the inflow and outflow of labor, the balance tips toward a net outflow for

males from 1742 on, and for females from 1753. After 1753, though the
trend for women frequently reverses direction, the village as a whole becomes a net exporter of labor. In the same year as the first for which we
have records for Nishijo, 1773, dekasegi is greater than irikasegi, for men,
in a ratio of 16 : 11. In the period from 1790 through 1794, when dekasegi
is at its peak, as many as 27 men and 20 women are involved. Conversely,
irikasegi declines in this period, and, at its highest point, embraces five men
and ten women. In 1794 the population of Ario-shinden is 95 males and
104 females. Of the 44 residents aged 16 to 50, 18, or 41 percent, are on
dekasegi. From these figures it is clear that Ario-shinden was a net exporter
of labor at the end of the eighteenth century. Since the village's registers end
in 1800, we cannot investigate later transitions. Even though it was a newly
reclaimed village, during the latter half of the eighteenth century, irikasegi
declined and dekasegi increased. This result suggests that the reciprocal exchange of contract laborers between villages declined, and, in its stead,
dekasegi from villages to cities and towns increased.

The earliest registers from the village of Niremata cover 11 different

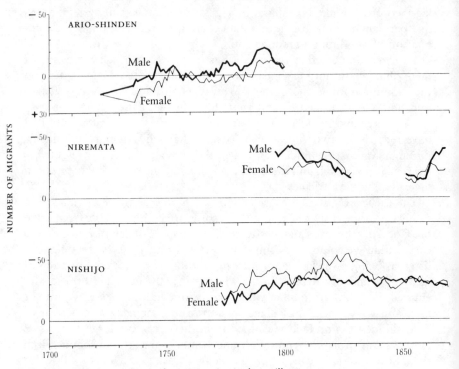

Fig. 5.6. The balance of in- and out-migration in three villages

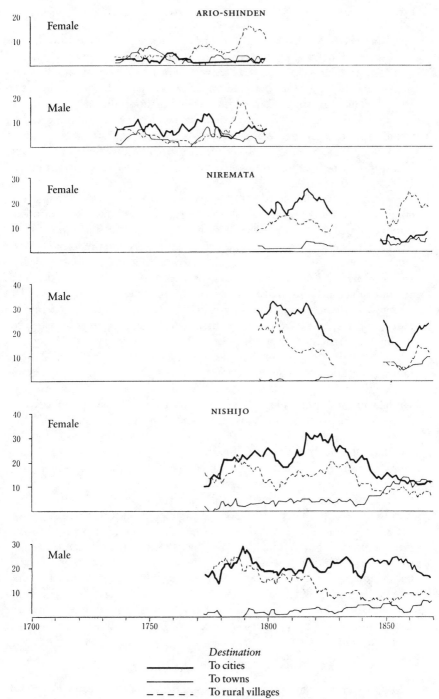

NUMBER OF MIGRANTS

ARIO-SHINDEN

Female

Male

NIREMATA

Female

Male

NISHIJO

Female

Male

1700   1750   1800   1850

Destination
————— To cities
————— To towns
– – – – To rural villages

Fig. 5.7. Dekasegi destinations for migrants from three villages

years between 1638 and 1684, but the entries are incomplete and there is no listing of dekasegi. However, for the two periods 1796-1828 and 1848-68 there are, respectively, 30 and 15 years of shūmon-aratame-chō in existence. The balance between import and export of labor in these two periods tends toward export, as it does in Nishijo in the same periods. In 1803, when dekasegi peaked for men, 60 men left. Of the 69 male and 64 female residents in the 16-50 age group, 49 men and 39 women, or 71 percent and 61 percent of the respective populations, left on dekasegi. Thus, with a population almost the same size as Nishijo's, the amount of dekasegi was equivalent.

From the evidence for Ario-shinden and Niremata, we conclude that conditions in Nishijo were by no means exceptional. The destinations of Niremata men on dekasegi were also nearly the same as Nishijo men's. In both periods under consideration, urban areas were the predominant destinations, with other villages and local towns following in that order. In the later period, dekasegi to local towns increased and to villages declined, so that in some years the former was more prevalent than the latter. Dekasegi by women in the period 1796-1828 was directed, as in Nishijo, to cities, villages, and local towns, in that order. However, in contrast to the Nishijo pattern, in the period 1848-68 labor migration to villages increased, to a level equal to that to cities and towns. Since even in Nishijo labor emigration by women to urban areas declined in the 1850's, some years falling below dekasegi to local towns, the patterns of dekasegi by women in these two villages are not really contradictory. The records of Ario-shinden overlap with those of Nishijo for very few years, and they run out during the period when labor emigration by women was primarily to other villages. In the records' final year, men's destinations are primarily cities, but since, during the preceding ten years the destinations have been primarily villages, the situation was not stable.

Ario-shinden was on newly reclaimed land, so its conditions were not representative. In the latter half of the eighteenth century, there was more dekasegi than irikasegi in Ario-shinden, and the trend was toward the export of excess labor. While there may have been a great demand for labor within Ario-shinden, in Nishijo and Niremata the export of labor to cities had begun earlier, and, by the time of the first surviving records, they had already become villages with a continually high rate of dekasegi. The relationship between dekasegi and irikasegi in these three villages and the transitions in numbers of persons on dekasegi, by destination and sex, are graphed in Figures 5.6 and 5.7.

Labor Migration Elsewhere in Japan

If we extend our field of inquiry beyond the Nōbi Plain, can we conclude that conditions in Nishijo were representative of the country as a whole?

Research using registers where the particulars of labor migration are adequately reported is limited, and it concentrates on the central part of the island of Honshū. Consequently, to obtain a bird's-eye view of the entire country, we are forced to ignore areas where village and regional studies are undeveloped. However, information on dekasegi, particularly from the eighteenth century on, and from villages to cities and towns, is comparatively abundant. Susan Hanley's research on the Okayama area shows that, while there were many changes in the balance of migration in her three villages and the pattern in any one village varied from year to year, there was always labor migration to the city of Ōsaka as well as to the castle town of Okayama.[14] Mark Fruin's study of two villages in Echizen from 1810 to 1865 shows that, although the destination of migrants is unknown, in one, out-migration was greater than in-migration during the entire period, and, in the other, from about 1840 onward.[15] My own study of the Suwa area of Shinano province shows that, particularly among the many villages on the eastern shore of Lake Suwa, especially in the last quarter of the seventeenth century, 20 percent of the adult male working population (aged 16-60) left on dekasegi.[16] Migration to Edo constituted about a third of the total. While labor migration to villages and on samurai labor contracts (as servants in samurai households) decreased with the passage of time, migration to Edo increased. At its peak in the first quarter of the nineteenth century, migration to Edo included 12 percent of the adult male labor force. As in Okayama, dekasegi to cities declined sharply from the middle of the nineteenth century on. In the village of Yokouchi, also in the Suwa area, in the periods 1676-85, 1751-60, and 1826-35, at least one person in each five-year age group left on dekasegi.[17] In the latter part of this period, about a third of the men from 16 to 60 went on dekasegi, almost all of them to Edo.[18]

The phenomena common to all these areas are: that we have records of dekasegi to cities (Edo, Ōsaka, Kyōto, and the principal castle towns); that the proportion of the population involved is fairly substantial; and that it declines toward the end of the Tokugawa period. This last point accords well with Thomas Smith's observation that, in comparison with Europe, Japan's preindustrial period was marked by a decline in the population of cities (his 35 castle towns), and an increase in the population of rural areas and local towns.[19]

Conclusion

During the period 1721-1846, the population of Japan showed decreases in the northeastern area, stayed level in the central area, and increased in the southwestern area.[20] The decrease in the northern area is thought to be attributable primarily to deteriorating natural conditions (i.e., to a harshening climate). In the eastern and central part of Japan, where economic development was greatest and the proportion of urban population highest, no one has explained the stagnation of local populations. What we have observed in this study is that when economic development stimulates urbanization within a region, labor migrates from the rural area to cities and towns. Generally, the higher death rate in the city and the outflow of labor from the labor-supplying areas results in a lowered rural population. According to E. A. Wrigley, this accounts for the "negative feedback" observed between population and economic development in preindustrial societies.[21] That is, the cities drain the surrounding countryside of population, thus creating negative growth rates in their hinterlands despite a positive balance of births over deaths in these same rural areas.

In Nishijo, the death rate was higher for males in the village who went out to work, while the fertility rate for females with work experience elsewhere was lower by an average of two children per woman. These effects were in addition to the impact on the village of the loss to the population of persons who went out to work "temporarily" but who in fact never returned. Thus, for this part of Japan, it was economic development, subsequent urbanization, and the flow of labor to the cities that kept the rural population from growing, and not crop failures or economic distress. While this study has focused on only one village, subsequent studies show that Nishijo was not an isolated case, but that developments in this village were part of a general trend in central Japan during the last century of the Tokugawa period.

SIX

Urban Migration and Fertility in Tokugawa Japan: The City of Takayama, 1773-1871

Yōichirō Sasaki

Until recently, analyses of fertility and reproduction rates for any pre-industrial city in Japan, or for that matter for any preindustrial city anywhere, have rarely been even attempted. The reasons for this clearly lie in the difficulty of obtaining usable records. Fortunately, however, in the case of Japan, we have the *shūmon-ninbetsu-chō* (census registers by religious sect), an excellent source for historical demography; and in recent years, we have found that these records exist for quite a few cities.[1]

In this chapter, we will analyze fertility for the city of Takayama, in Hida province, for the period 1773-1871. The shūmon-ninbetsu-chō for Takayama, one of the best sets of records available, enable us both to estimate fertility in Takayama and to compare its fertility level with those of the rural villages studied to date. On the basis of these records, we will conclude that Takayama could not sustain its population without immigration from rural areas.

A Description of Takayama

For Takayama, we have shūmon-ninbetsu-chō for all the years from 1773 to 1871 for the Ni-no-machi section of the city, and from 1819 to 1871 for the Ichi-no-machi section. There are no gaps in either sequence, and all the records are fully usable. Records for the third section of the city, San-no-machi, are fragmentary, and therefore I have left this section out of my analysis. Any biases that may result from this exclusion are, I believe, negligible.[2]

The total number of people listed in the shūmon-ninbetsu-chō for the first two sections is 40,289. As Table 6.1 shows, the natural increase was negative, though just barely, and the increase in population resulted principally from positive net migration. We should note, however, that the in- and out-migration figures shown in Table 6.1 include intracity migra-

TABLE 6.1

Birth, Death, Immigration, and Emigration Data for Takayama, 1773-1871

Measure	Number of persons
Form of first appearance in the records	
Already in records at first date	
for which there are records	6,415
Born	13,936
Immigrated to the city	19,938
Form of last appearance in the records	
On last set of records as	
living in the city	8,652
Died	14,430
Emigrated from the city	17,207
Net increase in population	2,237

tion. For the period before 1818, migration between Ichi-no-machi and San-no-machi, on the one hand, and Ni-no-machi, on the other, is included, and after 1819, between Ichi-no-machi and Ni-no-machi, taken together, and San-no-machi.

Immigrants from outside the city numbered 11,282, and 8,469 people left the city, for a net in-migration of 2,813, which exceeds the net increase of 2,237 in the city's total population. In the analysis below, migration refers only to movement into and out of the city; unless otherwise indicated, migration within the city is left out of consideration.

During the period covered by our data, Takayama was one of the few cities in Tokugawa Japan to show an increase in population. The primary cause of this increase was immigration, and the majority of immigrants were from farm villages.[3] Also, as we will discuss shortly, a large proportion of the children born were to immigrants from outside the city. Both facts demonstrate the important role villages play in the changes in urban population during the Tokugawa period.

Now let us examine the population trends in the two sections of Takayama we have studied, Ichi-no-machi and Ni-no-machi. In examining the trend line for Ni-no-machi in Figure 6.1, which extends for nearly a century, we note three periods each of increase and decrease and one period of stability. The periods of decline were those of the Temmei famine in the late eighteenth century; the 1830's, during which the Tempō famine occurred; and the last years for which there are data in the nineteenth century, years of unseasonable weather and social tumult, especially around the Meiji Restoration. The period of stability was also a period of unseasonable weather, with frequent poor harvests. That is, unseasonable weather,

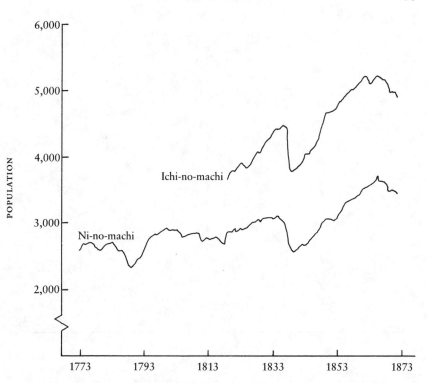

Fig. 6.1. The population of Ichi-no-machi and Ni-no-machi, 1773-1871

poor harvests, and famine caused the death rate to increase, immigration to decline (immigrants were usually young adults), and a decline in the birth rate, all of which contributed to a declining or stable population.

In normal years, by contrast, the opposite factors were at work. The birth rate rose, the death rate declined, and net immigration increased, thus turning the population trend for Takayama to a steady gain. In short, the population of Takayama reacted quite sensitively to agricultural conditions in the surrounding villages. Under normal agricultural conditions, the population of the city tended to increase.

Several characteristics of immigration to Takayama should be noted. First, immigrants came as single persons, rather than in family groups. Second, most immigration involved entry into a family by marriage or adoption; immigration in fulfillment of an employment contract, e.g., as a servant, was rare (2.1 percent of the total). As explained below, Takayama required immigrant labor from rural villages to increase or even maintain its population. It was considered more beneficial and effective to import

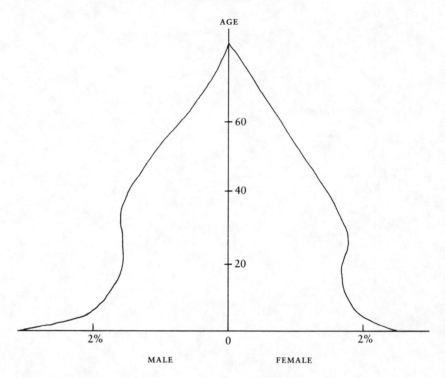

Fig. 6.2. Age composition of Ichi-no-machi and Ni-no-machi, 1773-1871

labor through permanent family ties than to sign contracts good only for a limited period. From this point of view, population movement from the rural areas to the city resulted primarily from "pull" on the part of the city rather than "push" on the part of the countryside. In times of famine, when the economic capacity of Takayama to support its population, let alone newcomers, diminished, there was a decrease in in-migration and an increase in out-migration. Some migrants from Takayama even moved out of Hida province, which in bad years was not self-sufficient with respect to food. In 1870, for example, the largest purchase Hida made from other provinces was 15,000 *koku* of rice, valued at 88,236 *ryō*. Hence emigrants from Takayama in times of famine should not be assumed to be all returning to their native villages in Hida.[4]

We can make similar observations for the population of Ichi-no-machi, except that the rate of increase in this section tended to be higher than in Ni-no-machi. In general, the population trends for about two-thirds of Takayama—Ichi-no-machi and Ni-no-machi—were similar, and thus one

TABLE 6.2

Major Population Indices for Takayama

Measure	Rate per thousand	Rate calculated with death at age 0 included
Crude birth rate	26.32	30.79
Crude death rate	27.26	31.68
Rate of natural increase	−0.94	−0.89
Immigration (including from other sections)	36.49	
Emigration (including to other sections)	29.22	
Net immigration	7.27	
Immigration from outside Takayama	20.15	
Emigration from Takayama	16.35	
Net immigration from outside Takayama	7.44	
Average household size	3.9	

can reasonably assume that the total population of the city also displayed the same trends. During the 98 years for which we have data, the population of Ni-no-machi rose by 708 persons (an annual average increase of 0.25 percent); the population of Ichi-no-machi rose during our 52-year period by 1,550 persons (or .60 percent per annum).

When we turn our attention to Figure 6.2, which presents population by age groups, we note that the graph widens at the middle age ranges and thus resembles the typical urban population pyramid. The difference in the profiles for males and females reflects sex differences in age at immigration. The modal age of male immigrants was 24-28 years, that of female immigrants 20-23. Other factors apart, such an age structure is conducive to high fertility.

Table 6.2 summarizes the major population indexes for Takayama. Here we should remind the reader that the ages referred to in the shūmon-ninbetsu-chō are *kazoe-doshi*, i.e., children were labeled one year old at birth. Since there is no reasonable way to adjust these ages accurately, we simply subtracted one year from the age recorded, a procedure followed throughout this chapter.

Fertility

A prerequisite for reliable estimates of fertility is the ability to determine the number of births, but the shūmon-ninbetsu-chō usually omitted children who died before age 1. If a birth occurred after one year's shūmon-ninbetsu-chō was prepared and the infant subsequently died before the

Fig. 6.3. Infant (age o) death rate in Takayama, 1773-1870

next year's was drawn up, in principle this birth was not recorded. In short, the existence of a birth was recognized only when a baby survived to the next registration.

Crude birth and death rates require the inclusion of the number of deaths below age 1 (age 0). Information from other sources gives us a reference point for inferring the death rate at age 0. Figure 6.3 shows the infant (age 0) death rate for the period 1773-1870, based on Suda Keizō's estimates.[5] The rate exhibits a long-term upward trend, but this can be ascribed to increased accuracy in the basic data rather than to a real increase. Of course, rises in the infant death rate in times of famine are to be expected. Based on these data, the number of deaths at age 0 is derived as follows: (1) the number of deaths at age 0 = the number of estimated births minus the number of children at age 1; (2) the number of births = the number of children at age 1 plus those who died between age 0 and age 1.

By this method, the figure for all births in Takayama from 1773 to 1870 is 16,816, exceeding that for children of age 1 registered in the shūmon-ninbetsu-chō by 2,880, or 20.7 percent. Crude birth and death rates (shown in the second row of Table 6.2) are calculated by adding the infant death figures to those given in the shūmon-ninbetsu-chō. The average infant death rate for the 98-year period in question is 171.0 per thousand. However, given the difficulty of including deaths at age 0 in calculations of age-specific birth rates and the desirability of making the Takayama data comparable to the village data, we calculated fertility on the basis of births that could be verified, that is, babies who survived long enough to be listed in the shūmon-ninbetsu-chō.

Presented in Table 6.3 and Figure 6.4 are the general fertility and marital fertility rates and the proportions married for Takayama. Also included in Table 6.3 and Figure 6.5 for the sake of comparison are the same calculations for the villages of Kando-shinden and Nishijo-mura during the same period.[6] The total number of births to Takayama mothers aged 15-49 was

TABLE 6.3

General and Marital Fertility and Proportions Married in Takayama
and Two Villages, 1773-1871

Age of mother	Number of births (1)	Female population (2)	General fertility (1) ÷ (2)	Married females (3)	Proportions married (3) ÷ (2)	Marital fertility (1) ÷ (3)
Takayama						
15-19	884	22,560	.039	4,872	.216	.182
20-24	2,718	23,234	.117	12,929	.556	.210
25-29	3,453	23,905	.144	17,853	.747	.193
30-34	2,870	22,600	.127	18,042	.798	.159
35-39	1,930	20,736	.093	16,471	.794	.117
40-44	833	18,368	.045	13,768	.750	.061
45-49	251	15,986	.016	10,847	.679	.023
TOTAL	12,939	147,389	.088	94,782	.643	.137
Kando-shinden						
15-19			.025		.066	.377
20-24			.176		.413	.425
25-29			.215		.752	.281
30-34			.174		.811	.215
35-39			.135		.750	.180
40-44			.077		.703	.110
45-49			n.a.		n.a.	.013
TOTAL			n.a.		n.a.	.241
Nishijo-mura						
15-19			.041		.160	.257
20-24			.200		.627	.319
25-29			.217		.762	.285
30-34			.201		.798	.252
35-39			.155		.773	.201
40-44			.074		.776	.097
45-49			.017		.689	.026
TOTAL			.133		.641	.207

12,939, which accounts for 98.4 percent of the 13,148 legitimate births. Table 6.4 shows the distribution of births to mothers in this age group according to the mothers' place of birth. We note the relative importance of immigrant mothers. Nearly 40 percent of all mothers came from rural villages. Furthermore, had we been able to identify the origins of all the mothers, the proportion of mothers who had immigrated to Takayama would doubtless be even higher. We note in passing that immigrants to the city, being mostly young adults, also contributed to reducing the crude death rate in Takayama.

What becomes evident in comparing Table 6.3 and Figure 6.4 is that marital fertility, proportions married, and general fertility are all rather

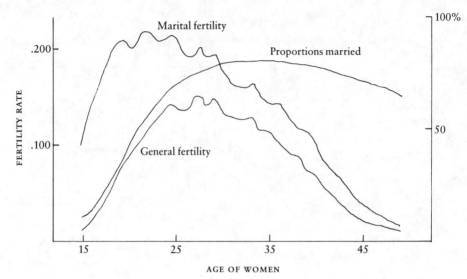

Fig. 6.4. Age-specific general fertility, marital fertility, and proportions married for Taka-yama, 1773-1871

low. It is also clear that the curve for marital fertility and the curve for proportions married have a 14-year difference in their peaks; that is, the peak for marital fertility is at age 22, whereas the peak for proportion married is at age 36. This suggests that if we ignore the level of marital fertility, the pattern of marital fertility is normal. However, among the youngest adults, i.e., those whose marital fertility would have been highest, the proportion married was low, reaching 50 percent only at age 22.6. Even at peak, that is at age 36, the proportion was only 80.9 percent.[7] All this means that for women in the first half of the childbearing years we observe high marital fertility but a low proportion married, whereas for women in the second half of the childbearing years we see low marital fertility but a relatively high proportion married. These phenomena cancel each other out, with the net result being a low general fertility with a relatively flat distribution.

These facts reflect the specific characteristics of the composition of the Takayama population. That is, a relatively high proportion of young adults in the total population canceled out a latent high fertility. Cities are the places to which immigrants from rural villages move, and these immigrants are mostly young adults. This causes the city population to have a higher proportion of young adults than villages have. But even so, urban birth rates are generally lower than village birth rates. This is so both because

TABLE 6.4

*Number of Births to Takayama Mothers Aged 15-49
by Mother's Place of Birth*

Mother's place of birth	Number of births	Percent of all births
Takayama	2,105	16.3%
Outside Takayama	4,747	36.7
Unknown	6,080	47.0
TOTAL	12,932	100.0

there was a larger gap in the cities between the marital fertility rate and the proportion married, and because, as we shall see, the levels of both were lower in cities than in villages.

Table 6.3 reveals no appreciable differences in terms of the proportions married between Takayama and the farming villages. In Kando-shinden, the proportions married in the 15-24 and the 35-44 age groups are lower than in Takayama, and that for the 25-34 age group is only slightly above that for Takayama. In Nishijo-mura, the 15-19 and 35-39 age groups have lower proportions married than in Takayama, but the other age groups have higher proportions married than in Takayama. Under age 24 Kando-shinden has a lower proportion married than Takayama, Nishijo-mura a higher proportion, and the absolute values involved are large. However, for the ages over 25, there is little difference between Takayama and these farming villages. Also the low proportions married under age 24 in Kando-shinden are offset by the high marital fertility in these age groups; thus the general fertility is higher than in Takayama for the age group 20-24, which has the highest fertility.

Consequently, marital fertility is what determines general fertility and the birth rate in both city and village. If we exclude the 45-49 age group in Kando-shinden, the farm villages show higher values than does Takayama. Moreover, in the 20-24 age group, which has the highest fertility, the difference in marital fertility between the villages and Takayama is the greatest (Kando-shinden, .215, Nishijo-mura, .109).

The proportion married observed for Takayama resulted from a relatively late age at marriage and a relatively high rate of divorce and remarriage. For females born in Takayama, the average age at first marriage was 20.6, the same as in Kando-shinden and younger than Nishijo-mura's, which was 23.2.[8] However, the population pool born in Takayama that remains traceable over the years declines as the ages rise (see Table 6.8 below). This introduces a bias in our observations because we cannot observe all the first marriages that might have taken place at relatively late ages. Thus it is likely that average age at first marriage of people born in Takayama was in fact higher than the figure we have.

That is, age at first marriage of women in Takayama differed little from that observed for village women, but women whose marriages are actually recorded in the Takayama records constitute a very limited proportion of the total population. The origins of women whose marriages are recorded were as follows: women born in Takayama, 1,510 (24.2 percent); women who migrated between sections of the city, 891 (14.3 percent); women who migrated in from outside the city, 3,842 (61.5 percent).

Sixty-two percent of the married women of Takayama were immigrants from outside the city, with more than half the women coming from neighboring villages. The average age at marriage of the immigrants—who were a large proportion of the total population—was high, 25.3. This age at marriage was calculated by using the age at immigration if the reason given for immigration was marriage, and, when marriage occurred after immigration, the actual age at marriage. The fact that a high proportion of the married women consisted of immigrants whose marriages occurred at relatively higher ages contributed to the higher age at marriage for Takayama as a whole, in comparison to that of the villages.

The relatively high frequency of divorce also contributed to the high average age at marriage. Of all the couples found in Takayama (15,630), 4,800 of the marriages ended in divorce, 4,433 of the women were widowed, and the remainder, 6,397 couples, remained married until they moved out of the city or the records end. Of course, not all divorced women left the city after their divorce; some remained in the city, and some of these remarried. One out of four women in the shūmon-ninbetsu-chō whose initial marriage could be confirmed is observed marrying again. (Women who were already married at their first appearance in the records were not included in this calculation.)

These divorces and the high frequency of remarriage tend to increase the average age at marriage, as well as to shorten the average duration of marriage. For all married women, the average duration of marriage was only 10.8 years, considerably shorter, for example, than the 17.3 years for Yokouchi-mura in Shinshū in the same period.[9]

To summarize. (1) Married women born in Takayama were almost the same age at first marriage as women in the farming villages, but they are a small proportion of all married women in Takayama. (2) The remaining, larger proportion of married women—that is, women who immigrated into the city—had a higher average age at marriage than their village counterparts. (3) The divorce rate in the city was high. (4) Even for immi-

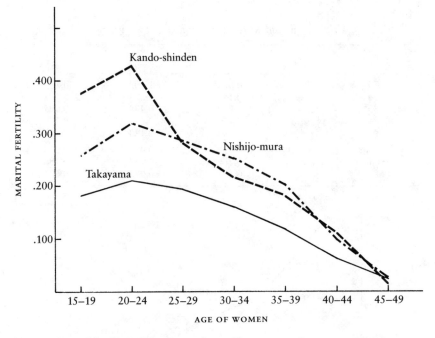

Fig. 6.5. Marital fertility in Takayama and two villages, 1773-1871

grants, divorce per se did not lead to emigration; most divorced persons continued to live in the city, with many of them remarrying, which raised the average age at marriage in Takayama as a whole and shortened the duration of marriage.

The differences in marital fertility between Takayama and the two neighboring villages are statistically significant, as shown in Figure 6.5. What caused the lower marital fertility in Takayama is unclear. One possibility is that infant deaths, unrecorded in the shūmon-ninbetsu-chō, were more frequent in cities such as Takayama than in the villages. Reasonable as this hypothesis seems, we have no way of testing it, since deaths at age 0 were not recorded in the villages either. Another possibility is fertility control in Takayama.

To examine this second possibility, we applied the "Model Fertility Schedule" method developed by A. J. Coale and T. J. Trussell.[10] As is well known, this method uses the m-value, derived from the equation $r(a) = Mn(a)e^{v(a)m}$, to evaluate the extent of fertility control, where $r(a)$ is the observed value of marital fertility for each age group, $n(a)$ expresses Louis Henry's concept of natural fertility, M equals $r(20\text{-}24)/n(20\text{-}24)$,

TABLE 6.5
Values of m *and* M *for Takayama and Two Villages*

Age of mother	Takayama m	Kandō-shinden m	Nishijō-mura m
25-29	0.064	1.102	0.152
30-34	0.153	0.654	0.108
35-39	0.218	0.478	0.095
40-44	0.154	0.237	-0.260
45-49	-0.442	-0.123	-0.211
Mean	0.029	0.470	-0.023
Standard deviation	0.269	0.458	0.196
M	0.457	0.924	0.693

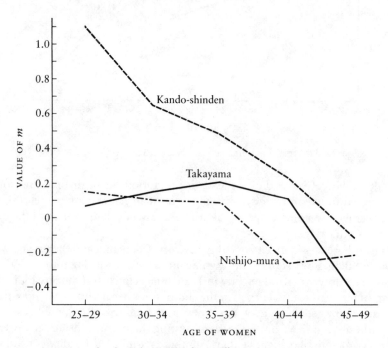

Fig. 6.6. Values of *m* for Takayama and two villages, 1773-1871

and $v(a)$ is the Coale-Trussell constant. The results obtained for Taka-yama, Kando-shinden, and Nishijo-mura are shown in Table 6.5 and Fig-ure 6.6. High standard deviations for the first two may indicate the absence of a uniform sequence of *m*-values over the age groups and a poor fit with the expected pattern of controlled fertility. In every district the value of m between ages 45 and 49 is responsible for raising the standard deviation. In fact, for these ages, m is negative in Takayama and Kando-shinden, and in Nishijo-mura it shows an increase. When this age group is excluded, the standard deviation for Takayama is 0.063, for Kando-shinden 0.365, and for Nishijo-mura 0.191, with corresponding m-values of 0.147, 0.618, and 0.024. It seems clear that birth control was not being carried out in Takayama or Nishijo-mura. There may have been considerable birth control in Kando-shinden; but since the marital fertility of the 20-24 age group, which determines M, has an abnormally high value, we cannot say for sure. Further investigation should tell us more.

One could also hypothesize that the environment of city life somehow affected the frequency of pregnancies and births, but thus far we do not have the historical evidence to support such speculation.

Differences in Marital Fertility by Origin of the Population

We now turn to examining fertility in Takayama by place of origin for those persons who can be clearly established as either natives or immigrants. There was a distinct difference in the marital fertility of the two groups. In Table 6.6 we present general fertility, proportions married, and marital fertility by mother's origin. The same data are presented in Figure 6.7, which also shows differences in the observed value of marital fertility.

Marital fertility, but not general fertility, was higher for those born in the city. Immigrants had a much higher general fertility rate; indeed, the average general fertility rate of the immigrants aged 15-49 is nearly twice that of the native population.

What caused this difference, of course, was clearly the difference in the proportion married. For the age group 15-49, the immigrants' proportion married was 2.2 times that of the indigenous population. Furthermore, as is evident in Figure 6.7, the proportion married among immigrants exceeded 50 percent before their marital fertility rate declined—to be precise, before they reached age 20. For those born in the city, by contrast, the proportion married reached 50 percent only at age 27, by which time their marital fertility rate had already shown a tendency to decline. Similarly, the peak of 91.1 percent married for immigrants was reached at age 30-34, whereas the native-born population reached this peak at age 40-44—and even then the proportion married was only 68.7 percent. The large difference in proportions married was more than enough to swamp the small difference in marital fertility, and the distribution of proportions married by age group contributed to the difference in general fertility.

What differences do we find if we compare the city immigrant population to the village population of the same period? In comparing the data

TABLE 6.6

*General and Marital Fertility and Proportions Married in Takayama
by Mother's Place of Origin*

Age of mother	Number of births (1)	Female population (2)	General fertility (1) ÷ (2)	Married females (3)	Proportions married (3) ÷ (2)	Marital fertility (1) ÷ (3)
Natives of Takayama						
15-19	259	11,331	.023	1,333	.118	.194
20-24	613	7,860	.078	2,685	.342	.228
25-29	546	5,153	.106	2,737	.531	.199
30-34	366	3,404	.108	2,200	.646	.166
35-39	234	2,398	.098	1,646	.686	.142
40-44	75	1,635	.046	1,123	.687	.067
45-49	9	928	.001	575	.620	.014
TOTAL	2,101	32,709	.064	12,299	.376	.171
Immigrants						
15-19	303	4,077	.074	1,851	.454	.164
20-24	1,186	7,276	.163	5,827	.801	.204
25-29	1,652	9,405	.176	8,518	.906	.194
30-34	1,329	9,133	.146	8,322	.911	.160
35-39	847	8,055	.093	7,119	.884	.119
40-44	348	6,602	.053	5,464	.828	.064
45-49	87	5,251	.017	4,025	.767	.022
TOTAL	5,752	49,799	.116	41,126	.826	.140

for Kando-shinden and Nishijo-mura presented in Table 6.3 with the data for Takayama presented in Table 6.6 (general and marital fertility), we find several interesting contrasts. Marital fertility was significantly lower among immigrants. Since the majority of Takayama immigrants were of village origin, why did their marital fertility decline so when they migrated to the city? The answer to this question is important to our understanding of urban populations, but to date we have been unable to find one.

One possible factor is economic status. Most immigrants to the city became part of the lower class; that is, they took up residence not in the old section of Takayama, in which the proportion of homeowners was high, but in the newer section, in which renters constituted a vast majority (see Table 6.7). If we consider the ratio of owners to renters as an index of economic status, it is clear that many people living in the new section (thus many immigrants) must have been poor. We can hypothesize that the poor, living in an inferior environment, may have had higher infant mortality rates, which are not recorded in the shūmon-ninbetsu-chō. But though this hypothesis might explain the low marital fertility among immigrants, it should apply to natives as well.

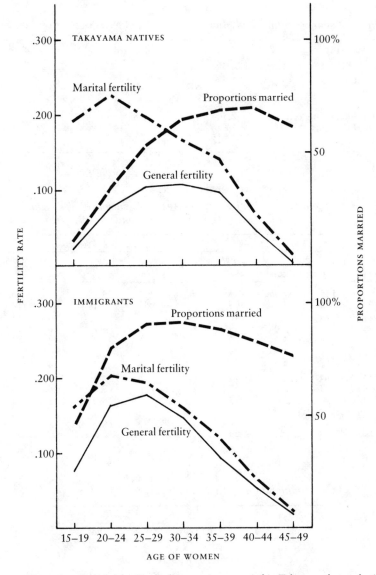

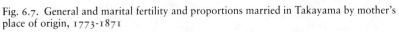

Fig. 6.7. General and marital fertility and proportions married in Takayama by mother's place of origin, 1773-1871

TABLE 6.7

Data on Owning, Renting, and Migration in Old and New Sections of Takayama

Measure	Old section (1)	New section (2)	(2) ÷ (1)
(a) Owners	1,984	2,542	
(b) Renters	4,639	21,581	
(b) ÷ (a)	2.34	8.49	
(c) Immigrants	2,364	8,733	3.7
(d) Emigrants	1,646	5,714	3.5
(c) − (d)	718	3,019	4.2

TABLE 6.8

Death and Emigration by Sex and Age for Residents of Takayama Born in the City Between 1773 and 1796

	Males				Females			
	Died		Migrated		Died		Migrated	
Age	No.	Pct.	No.	Pct.	No.	Pct.	No.	Pct.
0-4	143	39.3%	133	29.5%	116	44.3%	117	26.1%
5-9	32	8.8	103	22.8	37	14.1	65	14.5
10-14	15	4.1	46	10.2	13	5.0	60	13.4
15-19	11	3.0	39	8.7	15	5.7	76	17.0
20-24	19	5.2	49	10.9	15	5.7	52	11.6
25-29	13	3.6	24	5.3	6	2.3	30	6.7
30-34	11	3.0	23	5.1	6	2.3	24	5.4
35-39	13	3.6	14	3.1	8	3.1	7	1.6
40-44	18	5.0	7	1.6	6	2.3	4	0.9
45-49	14	3.9	5	1.1	13	5.0	5	1.1
50-54	8	3.0	2	0.4	5	1.9	3	0.7
55-	67	18.4	6	1.3	22	8.4	5	1.1

TABLE 6.9

Immigration to Takayama by Age and Purpose

	Purpose	
Age	Marriage	Other
0-14	55	871
15-29	2,497	886
30-	704	614
Unknown	17	21
TOTAL	3,273	2,392

Now let us examine the marriage patterns of native-born residents and immigrants. First, it is difficult to trace native-born residents because the longer the period over which one tries to trace them, the larger the number who disappear from the record. For example, if we trace the 815 males and 710 females born in Takayama between 1773 and 1796 who potentially could be traced until age 76, the result is as seen in Table 6.8.

Both the death rate for females under age 20 and the out-migration rate for females under 35 were higher than the corresponding rates for males, which reduced the number of mothers born in the city. The high incidence of out-migration reduced the number of years recorded in the shūmon-ninbetsu-chō for people who lived in the city and are known to have been born there. In contrast, although a briefer average period is recorded for women who migrated to the city,[11] the immigrants were mostly young adults, many of whom came in permanently to marry, as can be seen from Table 6.9. Of those who migrated into the city, 57.8 percent came to marry, a figure that reached 73.8 percent for immigrants aged 15 to 29. Both these percentages would, of course, be higher if all marriages occurring after immigration were included.

These differences in marriage patterns between women native to the city and immigrant women led to the differences observed in the number of births to the two groups. Also, as shown in Table 6.6, the difference in the proportion married between these two populations suggests that men pre-

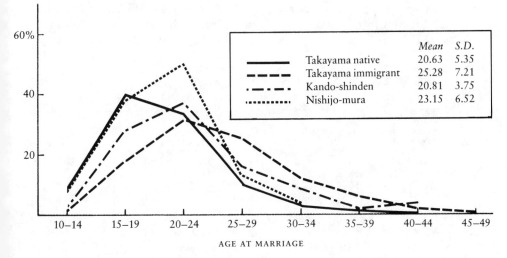

Fig. 6.8. Age at marriage for females in Takayama and two villages, 1773-1871

ferred a wife from outside the city, especially one from a farm village. Perhaps women from the country were healthier than those from the city. Women from the villages had a longer life expectancy at age 1 than those born in Takayama (40.9 vs. 35.5).[12] Why, then, was marital fertility, as shown in Table 6.6, lower among the immigrants?

One possible reason is that some of the female immigrants were migrating for the purpose of remarriage. Figure 6.8 depicts the age at marriage in Takayama for native and immigrant women; for the sake of comparison, the figures for Kando-shinden and Nishijo-mura have been added. The average age at marriage is similar for Takayama-native and Kando-shinden women but is substantially higher for Takayama immigrants and Nishijo-mura women. Furthermore, women from the countryside had the highest average age. Clearly many of them had been married at least once before moving to Takayama, a fact naturally consistent with low marital fertility. The relatively low average age at marriage for women born in Takayama is distorted by the disappearance from our records of women who married after leaving the city. For this reason the true average age at marriage for women born in Takayama is slightly higher than the age shown in Figure 6.8.

The Reproduction Rate

The purpose of this section is to analyze the reproduction rate by introducing survival rates and reexamining fertility, which we touched upon earlier. For the female population, life expectancy at age 0 was 30.9; the highest life expectancy was at age 6, when it reached 47.3. The survival rate reached 50 percent at age 27.3. The gross and net reproduction rates and the intrinsic rate of natural increase shown in Table 6.10 were calculated using the annual number of births per female ($5F_x$) (which was in

TABLE 6.10

Reproduction Rates for Takayama by Mother's Age

Age of mother (x to x + 4)	(1) $5F_x$	(2) Midpoint (x + 2.5)	(3) $5L_x \div l_0$	(4) R_0 (1) × (3)	(5) R_1 (2) × (4)	(6) R_2 (2) × (5)
15-19	0.01905	17.5	2.84662	0.05423	0.94903	16.60803
20-24	0.05716	22.5	2.64810	0.15137	3.40583	76.63118
25-29	0.07064	27.5	2.42919	0.17160	4.71900	129.77250
30-34	0.06193	32.5	2.21323	0.13707	4.45478	144.78035
35-39	0.04546	37.5	2.01323	0.09152	3.43200	128.70000
40-44	0.02218	42.5	1.82249	0.04042	1.71785	73.00863
45-49	0.00768	47.5	1.62550	0.01248	0.59280	28.15800
TOTAL	0.28410			0.65869	19.27129	597.65869

NOTATION: x = age; F_x = daughters ÷ females; L_x = stable population from life table; l_0 = stable population at age zero.

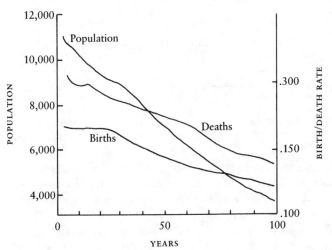

Fig. 6.9. Simulated population trends for Takayama under closed conditions, 1773-1871

turn calculated from the general fertility and the ratio of females born to total births) and the survival rate of females ($5 L_x/l_o$). The gross reproduction rate of 1.4205 is the product of low marital fertility. Similarly, the net reproduction rate of 0.65869 reflects women's low survival rate as well as the low marital fertility rate. Despite the influx of large numbers of young men and women from the farming villages, the low survival rates and low marital fertility made it impossible for the city to maintain its population. Even the preference for brides of village origin, though it helped, did not enable Takayama to maintain its population. In short, Takayama raised its potential for maintaining its population through female immigrants, but even so its net reproduction rate remained below unity. For the population to increase or even remain stable, an even larger number of immigrants from villages would have been necessary.

To trace what would have happened to the population of Takayama in one century under closed conditions, with no in- or out-migration, we have performed a simple simulation[13] whose results are presented in Figure 6.9. The data used in this simulation are observed values for the population born in Takayama, but the survival rates are calculated from age 1. The initial population of 11,040—calculated from the number of births estimated for 1860 and Takayama survival rates—declines after a century to 3,653. The number of deaths is 20,088, compared to only 13,774 births.

To further analyze the reproductive capacity of Takayama, the intrinsic rate of natural increase and the intrinsic birth and death rates were calculated using the values shown in Table 6.10.[14] Table 6.11 shows the results

TABLE 6.11

Birth and Death Rates for Takayama

Measure	Intrinsic rate per M	Crude rate per M
Birth rate	22.43	30.79
Death rate	36.53	31.68
Rate of natural increase	−14.10	−0.89

of these calculations, together with the crude rates obtained from the observed data for Takayama. Since the intrinsic rates are calculated assuming a stable population, the assumed age distribution does not bulge at the middle age groups as was in fact the case in Takayama. Thus there is a big difference between the crude rates calculated from observed data and the estimated rates obtained assuming a stable population, and the difference is greatest between the two sets of birth rates. This large difference of course results from there being a larger number of women of childbearing age in Takayama than would be found in a stable population. In any event, the difference between the crude and intrinsic birth rates is an eloquent indicator of Takayama's reliance on immigrants to maintain its population.

Conclusion

In this chapter we have presented and analyzed data pertaining to the fertility and reproductive capacity of Takayama during the second half of the Tokugawa period. In doing so, we provided evidence demonstrating the inability of an urban population to maintain itself through natural increase because of its low fertility, a phenomenon that to date has been discussed without quantitative evidence. On the basis of his examination of village data, Akira Hayami has hypothesized that in premodern Japan, cities served to suppress the rate of population growth in the countryside.[15] That is, the urban birth rate was lower than the birth rate in the villages; more important, it was lower than the death rate in the cities. Thus, for an urban population to increase or even maintain itself, a city had to have sufficient immigration from rural villages to offset the difference between the city's birth and death rates. Hayami has suggested that more than 50 percent of the villagers who emigrated to the city failed to return, which both lowered the adult population of the village and lowered its birth rate by reducing the number of inhabitants of childbearing age. Further, those persons who did return to the village had a higher age at marriage than those who had never left, another factor contributing to a reduction in the rural birth rate.

As a result, the existence of a city tended to prevent increases in population in the surrounding region, and, of course, the more urbanized a region, the more pronounced this tendency. Using the 1875 data from the *Kyōbu Seihyō* military survey of the population, Hayami demonstrated there was a negative correlation between the proportion of urban population in a region and that region's rate of population growth. In this chapter we have tested Hayami's hypothesis with a simulation and other analyses. The results show that Takayama could not maintain its population without immigration from the countryside. In addition, we learned that the city's low birth rate was the compound result of low fertility and a low female survival rate, and not merely the result of a high death rate, as has often been maintained. Undoubtedly the low survival rate in the city was the product of an urban environment that was not conducive to good health, and the death rate could not be reduced significantly even with a constant inflow of rural immigrants who can be assumed to have been healthy. There were no doubt other factors contributing to low urban marital fertility, factors that remain to be uncovered by further research.

Finally, the proportion married in Takayama was the product of a high average age at marriage, a high rate of divorce, and frequent remarriage, and this leaves us with the question of why the divorce rate was so high in the city. Analyses from sociological and anthropological perspectives might allow us to ascertain the attitudes toward marriage among the urban population and pinpoint the reasons for the high divorce rate. From the economic perspective, we surmise that although rural women constituted a source of labor, unmarried women could not easily support themselves in a village. In the cities, by contrast, wives may not have been an essential part of the labor force but single women could find employment and support themselves.

In conclusion, it must be reiterated that the data presented in this paper are limited to one city, Takayama, during the second half of the Tokugawa period, and we must remain extremely cautious in viewing the results as representative of all Tokugawa cities. Takayama is the first Tokugawa city to be analyzed demographically, and to date we lack the comparable data for other cities that would enable us to understand how representative Takayama was.

SEVEN

Fertility in Prerevolutionary Rural China

Arthur P. Wolf

After noting that Sir George Staunton "startled the faith of many readers" by reporting the population of China to be 333,000,000, Malthus continued: "To account for this population, it will not be necessary to recur to the supposition of Montesquieu, that the climate of China is in any peculiar manner favorable to the production of children, and that the women are more prolific than in any other part of the world."[1] But despite Malthus, such a view of Chinese women was widely accepted and became part of Europe's understanding of what China is like. In part, this was because the notion offered an easy explanation of how China maintained such a large population in the face of frequent epidemics, recurrent famines, and incessant internecine strife, and in part it was because competent scholarly observers like Walter H. Mallory and H. D. Tawney confirmed Montesquieu's supposition. Mallory claimed that "the fecundity of the Chinese is without parallel,"[2] and he and Tawney saw that fecundity as an integral part of "Chinese habit and doctrine." Tawney's version of the argument is worth quoting because he takes an intriguing hypothesis and turns it into an image that sums up the orthodox view of fertility in late traditional China:

Sentiment, hallowed by immemorial tradition, makes it a duty to have sons, and the communism of the patriarchal family dissociates the production of children from the responsibility for their maintenance. Hence prudential restraints act with less force than elsewhere; and population, instead of being checked by the gradual tightening of economic pressure on individuals, plunges blindly forward, till whole communities go over the precipice.[3]

In 1934 E. F. Penrose, reacting to Mallory's claim that "in China the birth rate is abnormally high,"[4] asked, "Is Oriental fertility abnormal?"[5] The answer, he insisted, was to be found in John Lossing Buck's 1921-23 survey of 2,640 farm families in seven provinces of China. Though Buck did not report a fertility rate, he did show that the average size of the farm family was 5.65, which led Penrose to conclude that "certain quantitative investigations based on samples do not indicate that there is anything exceptional in Chinese fertility."[6] Penrose appears not to have known that by the time he published, Buck and his Chinese colleagues had already completed a second survey, which provided all the data needed to calculate a birth rate for rural China. This second survey, commonly referred to as the Chinese Farm Survey, was begun in 1929 and completed in 1931. The portion of the survey relevant to fertility covered more than 40,000 farm families in 119 widely dispersed localities.[7]

What then of Montesquieu's supposition? Was the Chinese birth rate "abnormally high," as Mallory claimed, or are such reports to be passed over as "personal impressions," as Penrose argued?[8] Curiously, the data collected by Buck's team had to wait nearly fifty years for anyone to seriously ask what they had to say about Chinese fertility. Frank Notestein and Chiao Chi-ming reported the survey results in summary form,[9] but the significance of the data was not drawn out until 1976, when George W. Barclay, Ansley J. Coale, Michael A. Stoto, and T. James Trussell completed an analysis initiated by Irene B. Taeuber.[10] Their conclusions regarding Chinese fertility are almost as startling to the faith of contemporary scholars as Staunton's report of the size of the Chinese population was to his readers. After examining the data for internal consistency and finding them free of damning contradictions, the Princeton group (as I will call them for brevity's sake) concludes that "the births reported by the Chinese Farmers . . . provide no support, even after adjustment, for the very large historical family size that has been imputed to the Chinese."[11] It is not just that Chinese fertility is found to fall far short of the level expected by Montesquieu and Mallory; on these new estimates, it is discovered to be moderate compared to the fertility of other agrarian societies. Indeed, Chinese marital fertility, far from being certified as "abnormally high," is now pronounced "very low."[12] Even after adjustments that raise the rate well above the level reported by Buck, it is "only 51 percent of the highest recorded schedule," a situation that is to be expected "only in populations in which some combination of contraception and abortion is practiced."[13]

Though their language is somewhat misleading, the Princeton group does not claim that Chinese peasants controlled their fertility. Nor do they claim that the Buck data are entirely accurate as reported. Rather, their position is that the Buck data provide a basis for estimating Chinese fertility and that the rate so estimated is as low as that found in some contracepting populations. But if the Chinese farmers surveyed by Buck did not practice birth control, why was their fertility as low as in populations that do practice birth control? The Princeton group suggests as possibilities "prolonged breast-feeding among inadequately nourished women" and "reduced coital frequency among couples suffering from chronic fever and other debilities,"[14] but their emphasis is clearly on what Malthus termed preventive rather than positive checks. After noting that "it now appears to be fairly common, perhaps even typical, for marital fertility to be low in . . . populations with nearly universal marriage," they write: "There is reason to expect long established traditions of early and universal marriage to exert a moderating influence on marital fertility. The alternative would be a growth of population so rapid that it could not be indefinitely sustained."[15]

Granting at the outset that Chinese fertility was not so high as to be "without parallel," this paper asks if it was as low as the Princeton group suggests. The question is important because even a small difference may alter our interpretation of Chinese population dynamics. The essence of the Princeton group's argument is that where marriage is late and a large proportion of all women never marry, as in much of Western Europe until very recently, marital fertility can approach the biological limit; but where marriage is early and nearly universal, necessity selects for customs that hold fertility well below its potential. Though it is unclear how and why customs favoring high fertility give rise to customs that check fertility, we must accept the argument if we agree that Chinese fertility was only 60 to 70 percent of that of premodern Europe. But what if it could be shown that the Princeton figures underestimate Chinese fertility by 10 to 20 percent? Not only would this narrow the gap between the Chinese and the Europeans, it would also suggest that the remaining difference is due to positive rather than preventive checks. Since it is clear that the population of China was not growing explosively during the first half of this century, evidence that the Princeton group underestimates fertility would strongly suggest that they also underestimate mortality. This in turn would argue that economic conditions in rural China were even more appalling than the Buck figures indicate, and thus make credible the view that Chinese fertility was constrained more by sickness and poverty than by prophylactic customs.

The Chinese Farm Survey provides two sets of data that can be used to estimate a fertility rate. All the adult women in the surveyed families were asked, first, whether or not they had borne a child during the preceding year, and, second, how many children they had borne in their lifetime. Given the ages of the women and their marital status, the answers to the first question yield both age-specific fertility and age-specific marital fertility for a twelve-month period during the years 1929-31. The advantage of these estimates is that they are not likely to be biased by faulty memory; the disadvantage is that they refer to a brief period of time, the length of which respondents have difficulty in judging correctly and during which fertility behavior may reflect such short-term events as floods and droughts.

TABLE 7.1

Chinese Farm Survey, 1929-1931:
Number of Women by Age and Age-Specific Fertility Rates
Based on Reported Number of Children Born in Year Preceding Survey

Region	Age						Total fertility rate
	15-19	20-24	25-29	30-34	35-39	40-44	
	Number of women						
Southeast Coast	515	406	477	328	374	267	
Southeast Hills	301	291	361	259	297	196	
Southwest Plateau	431	451	384	317	322	252	
Szechwan Basin	625	595	599	455	504	316	
Lower Yangtze	2,254	2,384	2,282	2,013	1,835	1,490	
Northern Plain	3,530	3,320	3,363	2,344	2,722	2,228	
Northern Highlands	499	427	427	342	332	276	
Tibetan Hills	242	214	219	135	162	108	
TOTAL	8,397	8,088	8,112	6,193	6,548	5,133	
	Births per 1,000 women						
Southeast Coast	138	283	214	198	107	41	4.91
Southeast Hills	60	254	233	201	135	61	4.72
Southwest Plateau	91	279	323	281	217	111	6.51
Szechwan Basin	117	308	242	204	157	60	5.44
Lower Yangtze	55	223	248	218	140	75	4.80
Northern Plain	65	246	244	201	166	80	5.01
Northern Highlands	104	220	192	146	111	40	4.07
Tibetan Hills	58	201	247	222	130	83	4.71
TOTAL	74	245	244	208	152	74	4.99

SOURCE: Unpublished tables compiled by Frank W. Notestein on the basis of data collected by J. Lossing Buck.

TABLE 7.2

Chinese Farm Survey, 1929-1931:
Number of Married Women by Age and Age-Specific Marital Fertility
Rates Based on Reported Number of Children Born in Year Preceding Survey

Region	15-19	20-24	25-29	30-34	35-39	40-44	Total marital fertility rate
			Age				
	Number of married women						
Southeast Coast	340	387	457	316	348	225	
Southeast Hills	151	268	339	245	261	168	
Southwest Plateau	237	424	372	304	304	218	
Szechwan Basin	378	560	581	434	463	274	
Lower Yangtze	929	2,144	2,200	1,914	1,674	1,274	
Northern Plain	1,836	3,129	3,236	2,218	2,467	1,913	
Northern Highlands	396	419	417	335	319	249	
Tibetan Hills	105	192	209	129	151	88	
TOTAL	4,372	7,523	7,811	5,895	5,987	4,409	
	Births per 1,000 married women						
Southeast Coast	209	297	223	206	115	49	5.50
Southeast Hills	119	276	248	212	153	71	5.40
Southwest Plateau	165	297	333	293	230	128	7.23
Szechwan Basin	193	327	250	214	171	69	6.12
Lower Yangtze	132	248	257	229	153	87	5.53
Northern Plain	125	261	254	212	184	93	5.65
Northern Highlands	131	224	197	149	116	44	4.31
Tibetan Hills	133	224	258	233	139	102	5.45
TOTAL	142	264	253	219	166	86	5.65

SOURCE: Unpublished tables compiled by Frank W. Notestein on the basis of data collected by J. Lossing Buck.

TABLE 7.3

Chinese Farm Survey, 1929-1931:
Average Number of Children Ever Born by Age of Mother

Region	Age						45 or over
	15-19	20-24	25-29	30-34	35-39	40-44	
	Number of mothers						
Southeast Coast	338	385	453	312	347	224	546
Southeast Hills	147	267	335	242	260	167	385
Southwest Plateau	237	423	372	304	304	218	523
Szechwan Basin	373	560	579	434	462	274	754
Lower Yangtze	923	2,135	2,185	1,907	1,662	1,270	2,761
Northern Plain	1,826	3,103	3,216	2,211	2,452	1,908	4,872
Northern Highlands	389	415	414	334	317	247	584
Tibetan Hills	105	192	209	129	151	88	274
TOTAL	4,338	7,480	7,763	5,873	5,955	4,416	10,699
	Average number of children ever born						
Southeast Coast	.41	1.34	2.57	3.77	4.49	5.00	5.54
Southeast Hills	.28	1.18	2.27	2.54	4.66	4.79	5.81
Southwest Plateau	.32	1.44	2.75	3.90	4.87	5.27	6.30
Szechwan Basin	.45	1.43	2.45	3.31	4.10	4.34	4.88
Lower Yangtze	.27	1.21	2.56	3.70	4.56	5.33	5.50
Northern Plain	.24	1.11	2.24	3.35	4.04	4.72	4.99
Northern Highlands	.38	1.53	2.86	3.92	4.55	5.39	5.71
Tibetan Hills	.30	1.05	2.34	3.57	4.15	5.05	4.99
TOTAL	.30	1.22	2.43	3.56	4.32	4.96	5.36

SOURCE: Unpublished tables compiled by Frank W. Notestein on the basis of data collected by J. Lossing Buck.

Estimates based on the number of children ever borne avoid these problems, but are often biased by faulty memory and deliberate falsification. I know from experience that elderly Chinese women often have great difficulty recalling children who died as infants, and I have found that women married a second time are very reluctant to report the children of their first marriage. To remarry is a disgrace, and thus the children of an earlier marriage become an acute source of embarrassment.

The fertility rates produced by the Farm Survey are shown in their raw form in Tables 7.1-7.3.[16] The only essential difference between these figures and the unadjusted figures published by the Princeton group is that the six regions with the smallest numbers of respondents are not aggregated.[17] My reason for this is to make it clear that the Farm Survey data do not represent China. Of the 10,699 women aged 45 or older who were interviewed, 25.8 percent came from the Lower Yangtze region (see Map 7.1) and 45.5 percent from the Northern Plain region. This leaves only 28.7 percent of the sample to represent all of Fukien, Kiangsi, Kwangtung, Hunan, Kweichow, Szechwan, and Yunnan, and most of Chekiang, Hupeh, Shansi, Shensi, and Kansu. And the peripheral provinces of Liaoning, Jehol, Chahar, Suiyuan, Ningsia, Tsinghai, and Sikang are not represented at all.

The reader should also note that the disaggregated figures in Tables 7.1 and 7.2 show an exceptionally high fertility rate on the Southwest Plateau and an exceptionally low rate in the Northern Highlands. The high rate in the southwest probably reflects the presence there of partly sinicized Chuang, Yi, and Miao, ethnic groups known for their high fertility, while the low rate in the Northern Highlands testifies to the extreme poverty of the area and the debilitating effects of periodic droughts. I mention this because the Princeton group tells us "the very low marital fertility of the Chinese Farmers (half that of the Hutterites) shows only moderate variation between North and South, and among the survey regions."[18] This, I suggest, is only because the data have been aggregated in a gross and arbitrary fashion. How much variation can one expect to find when ethnic boundaries are ignored and such rich areas as the Lower Yangtze are lumped together with such perennially poor areas as Su-pei? I will demonstrate elsewhere that Chinese fertility varied not only between regions but between villages of the same standard marketing community.

I also object when the Princeton group tells us that the Farm Survey data present "a picture of Chinese traditions persisting from the Imperial dynasty of the last century."[19] Though this may be largely true of the data collected in the interior of the country, it is definitely not true of the data from communities along the coast. By 1929, when Buck launched his second survey, family life along the China coast was already subject to the

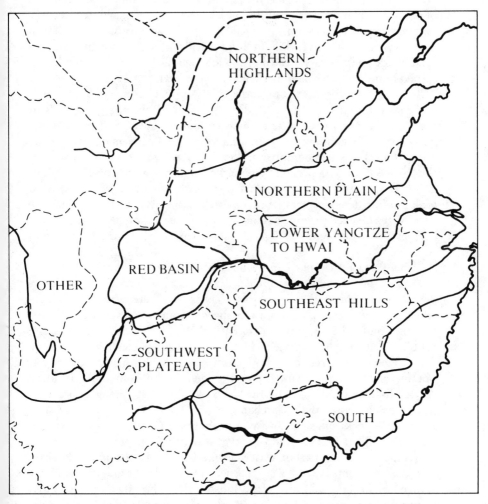

Map. 7.1. Eight regions of China covered by Buck's surveys. Adapted from Irene B. Taeuber, "The Families of Chinese Farmers," in Maurice Freedman, ed., *Family and Kinship in Chinese Society* (Stanford, Calif., 1970), p. 65.

vicissitudes of the world market. The factories and homes of Shanghai drew labor from as far away as the plains of northern Anhwei and the hills of central Chekiang. The result in one of the villages I visited in 1981 was that marriage was commonly delayed because the wife-to-be was employed as a servant in the city, while in another village marital fertility was adversely affected because a third of the married men were barbers who returned home only to celebrate the lunar New Year.

But these objections are tangential to my primary concern. Simply put, it is that I do not trust the Buck data. When the Princeton group tells us that "the data on the Chinese Farmers should no longer be dismissed as a basis for understanding the demography of the China mainland," I demur.[20] I am not a demographer and can only accept their contention that the Farm Survey data present "a remarkably consistent picture,"[21] but this is not enough to convince me that these data provide a clear backward look into the demography of late Imperial China. The means by which the data were collected prompt doubts about their accuracy, and these doubts deepen when one compares Buck's results with those reported from other sources.

In his Preface to *Land Utilization in China*, Buck notes that "the personal approach for investigational work in China is very important in order to ensure information as accurate as possible. There were some villages where surveys were actually started out where the suspicion was so great that they had to be discontinued and other villages chosen."[22] About other problems encountered in the field and the means of dealing with them, Buck is silent. The rest of what I know about Buck's field methods was obtained from Chang Hsin-yi, now President of the Chinese Agricultural Association and once one of Buck's field assistants. Chang either conducted or supervised the research in six localities, four in Kansu and Tsinghai and two in Kwangsi. Chang told me that the first place he surveyed was his native village in Yung-teng county, near Lanchow. He had not visited the village in 18 years, but was welcome because his brother and sister were still residents. Chang's second field site was his grandfather's native village, where he could also claim kinship ties. The other four localities were all the homes of Chang's students, who accompanied him and did most of the interviewing. "I just sat next to them and tried to advise."

Chang was well aware that if the villagers did not have some reason to trust the interviewer, they would not tell the truth. "People wouldn't tell you if there were young men in the family for fear that they would be drafted, and they didn't like to mention young, unmarried women. And when asked about how many children they had, they usually counted only the boys. Asked if they had any daughters, they replied, 'Oh, you want to know about them too?'" But even when the interviewer came recommended by kinship, there were problems, particularly with the fertility schedule. The interviewers were all men, the interviewees were women, and in rural China the subject was a delicate one. Chang found that for the most part he could not even interview women, let alone question them about their fertility. The information he reported was largely obtained from relatives and neighbors. He assumes that his informants did not tell him about children who were killed or died young because they did not know about them.

The extent of the problems encountered in the field was fully appreciated by Frank Notestein, whose skepticism is partly responsible for the caution with which sinologists treat the Farm Survey data. He wrote:

In spite of the care taken to obtain reliable data, examination of the crude birth and death rates for individual localities showed that a number of them had been inaccurately enumerated. Some of the rates were impossibly low, indicating a failure on the part of certain field workers to record all of the births and deaths, and suggesting the possibility of other inaccuracies less easily detected. Such a finding is not surprising when one considers the obstacles facing the investigation of an illiterate peasant population by enumerators with little experience in making field studies and only a hazy idea of the use to which their reports would be put.[23]

Notestein dealt with this problem by discarding the data for those localities "in which it was most obvious that a substantial proportion of the births and deaths had been omitted."[24] After allowing for the possibility that "low rates might be due to specific local conditions or to chance errors arising from small numbers," he ranked the areas enumerated in order of their crude birth and death rates and set aside those that fell beyond the first quartile limits.[25] Altogether, 18 of 119 areas were rejected. The one set of surviving tabulations for these areas shows (see Table 7.4) that the effect was to lower slightly the fertility of the Southeast Hills (obviously, because the rejected areas showed unacceptably low death rates) and to raise substantially the fertility of the Southeast Coast, the Lower Yangtze, the Northern Plain, and the Northern Highlands. The effect for China as a whole was to raise general fertility from 159 to 171 per thousand and general marital fertility from 189 to 201.

Thus what we see in Tables 7.1-7.3 are not in fact the raw data. They are the data from those surveys yielding fertility rates that Frank Notestein found believable. But why should a skeptic accept Notestein's criterion? Why not choose a criterion that raises fertility to a level he finds believable? Though Buck and his colleagues appear to have been generally sensitive to the problems of field research in rural China, they were clearly not sensitive to the particular problems presented by demographic research. They sent young men to interview women, and, when that proved impossible, they settled for information from relatives and neighbors. Not sur-

TABLE 7.4

Chinese Farm Survey, 1929-1931: General and Marital Fertility Rates of Areas Selected for Analysis by Notestein Compared with Rates of All Areas Surveyed

Region	Total number of areas surveyed	Number of areas discarded	Births per thousand women		Births per thousand married women	
			Selected areas	All areas	Selected areas	All areas
Southeast Coast	8	2	171	147	195	167[a]
Southeast Hills	5	1	164	167	196	199
Southwest Plateau	3	0	221	221	256	256
Szechwan Basin	15	0	191	191	220	220
Lower Yangtze	35	8	165	148	200	180
Northern Plain	41	4	170	165	201	196
Northern Highlands	10	3	142	119	153	132
Tibetan Hills	2	0	158	158	196	196
TOTAL	119	18	171	159	201	189

SOURCE: Unpublished tables compiled by Frank W. Notestein on the basis of data collected by J. Lossing Buck.
[a] Area 53 excluded for lack of information.

prisingly, the result was that a number of localities reported impossibly low fertility rates. The Princeton group assumes the problem was solved when Notestein discarded the patently impossible data, but he himself warns of "other inaccuracies less easily detected." My own view is that if 18 of 119 local surveys produced absurd results because the field workers were not prepared for the problems they faced, the likelihood is that the majority of the surveys underestimated fertility by a considerable margin. I can see no reason for assuming that the problems were confined to the 18 worst cases.

The Princeton group is well aware that the Buck data are grossly deficient in several respects. By their own estimate Buck's field workers recorded only 56.0 percent of female deaths and only 52.1 percent of male deaths.[26] The difference between their attitude toward the Farm Survey and mine stems from their conviction that despite these deficiencies, the data can be made to yield reliable estimates of vital rates. How, then, do they estimate fertility? Because "parities reported by women are known to be understated by a widening margin as the age of the women increases,"[27] they suspect that the total number of births reported by the older women

TABLE 7.5
Age-Specific Fertility Rates Estimated by Princeton Group
on the Basis of the Chinese Farm Survey

| | | | Age | | | | Total |
Category	15-19	20-24	25-29	30-34	35-39	40-44	fertility
All women	197	268	262	221	156	74	5.44
Married women	174	287	272	233	171	86	6.12

SOURCE: George W. Barclay et al., "A Reassessment of the Demography of Traditional Rural China," *Population Index*, 42 (1976): Table 5, p. 614.

is too low, and they also suspect that "the low level of fertility reported by the Chinese Farmers during the year before the survey might be due to a contraction of the reference period."[28] But where similar suspicions lead me to dismiss the Buck data as the product of careless field research, the Princeton group argues that reasonably accurate estimates of fertility can be obtained by "combining information from questions about births-last-year and children-ever-born, in order to exploit the advantages of both. In this procedure, the *pattern* of fertility is preserved as indicated by births-last-year, and *level* is determined by average parity reported by women at some fairly early age, say 25-29."[29] In other words, the relative fertility of women of different ages is set by the births reported for the previous year, while the absolute fertility of these women is given by the total number of births reported by women aged 20-29.

The estimates obtained by application of this procedure are shown in Table 7.5, the effect being to raise total fertility from 4.99 to 5.44 and total marital fertility from 5.65 to 6.12. These new estimates are probably closer to the truth than the unadjusted figures reported by Notestein, but I am not willing to accept them as reasonable estimates of fertility in rural China. How can one assume that the information reported for young women is accurate while that reported for old women and for the year prior to the survey is inaccurate? Certainly young women are more likely than old women to remember and report accurately their births, but this does not justify assuming that the parities reported by the Farm Survey are accurate for young women. That would be likely only if the women studied had been interviewed directly, and the evidence says that this was not the case. Though it may be that Chang Hsin-yi was unusual in having to obtain most of his information from his subjects' neighbors, the fact that the interviewers were men makes it all but certain that they did not interview young women. The fertility histories of young women were probably all obtained from other people, and thus there is good reason to think that their parities are the least accurate of those reported.

I have begun with my doubts about the way the Farm Survey was con-

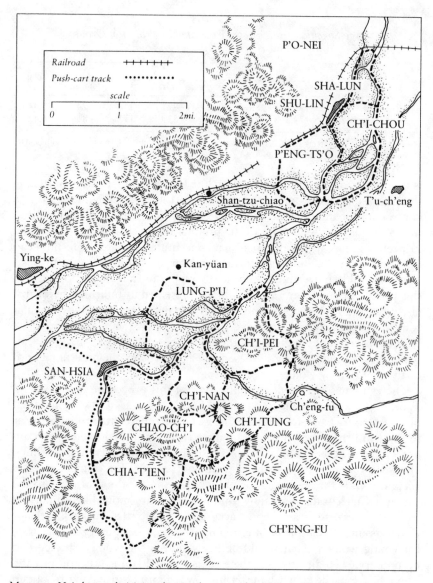

Map. 7.2. Hai-shan and vicinity, showing location of the thirteen districts included in the present study. Adapted from Arthur P. Wolf and Chieh-shan Huang, *Marriage and Adoption in China, 1845-1945* (Stanford, Calif., 1980), p. 50.

ducted and the conclusions were drawn, but these doubts were not the source of my original concern. My suspicion was first aroused when I saw that the Chinese Farm Survey yields fertility estimates well below figures derived from the Japanese household registers for Taiwan. But before we turn to the evidence from the Taiwan registers, I must say a word about what Taiwan was like in 1906 when the registers were initiated. To support their view that the Farm Survey provides "a link with the more remote past," the Princeton group notes that the very early age at marriage found on the mainland in 1929-31 was "rather close" to that of Taiwan in 1906 and "nearly identical" to that of Taiwanese women with bound feet, who "showed a more traditional pattern of early marriage."[30] This implies that by 1905 part of the Taiwanese population had already started down the road to modernization, abandoning the traditions associated with bound feet and early marriage. But in fact all the evidence argues that rural Taiwan did not experience substantial social or economic change until after World War I and did not reach a watershed until the early 1930's. The frequency of foot-binding and its association with early marriage is irrelevant. In 1905 women with large feet were not harbingers of social change; either they were poor or they were Hakka. Women with bound feet married earlier because they were relatively well off or because, being Hokkien, they had been reared by their future husband's family from infancy.

My previous reports of data from the Taiwan registers all refer to nine "villages" (*li*) located in the rich river valley that forms the southwestern corner of the Taipei Basin.[31] I have now added data from two upland villages, Ch'eng-fu and P'o-nei, and two market towns, Shu-lin and San-hsia (see Map 7.2). All are located within a few miles of one another in an area generally known to natives of the region as Hai-shan. Since both the history and the ethnography of the area are easily available to interested readers,[32] here I need only note that until the early 1930's, the residents were mostly farmers and almost universally poor. The fertility rates discussed in the following pages are based on 127,458 years of experience by women aged 15-45. Of this total, 61,143 years (48.0 percent) were passed in landless families, and 35,778 years (28.1 percent) in families paying a land tax of less than five yen. Since families paying less than five yen could not raise enough food to feed themselves on their own land, this means that something more than three-fourths of the population were tenant farmers, farm laborers, coolies, and odd-jobbers of one kind or another. The wealthy formed only a tiny fraction of the total population. The number of years passed in families paying a land tax of 100 or more yen constitute only 1.5 percent of the data.

The Taiwan household registers have also been described elsewhere and need not detain us here.[33] Suffice it to say that although there may be some

TABLE 7.6

Age-Specific Fertility Rates for Hai-shan, Taiwan, 1906-1945

Period	15-19	20-24	25-29	30-34	35-39	40-44	Total fertility rate
			Number of woman-years lived				
1906-1910	2,108	2,449	2,360	1,881	1,600	1,220	
1911-1915	2,463	2,083	2,360	2,203	1,748	1,458	
1916-1920	3,272	2,383	1,989	2,260	2,117	1,608	
1921-1925	3,375	3,138	2,243	1,867	2,175	1,989	
1926-1930	3,754	3,386	3,036	2,138	1,816	2,045	
1931-1935	3,948	3,692	3,263	2,829	2,064	1,724	
1936-1940	4,580	3,770	3,531	3,129	2,683	1,957	
1941-1945	5,597	4,471	3,660	3,412	2,962	2,523	
			Births per 1,000 woman-years				
1906-1910	139	252	231	212	157	86	5.38
1911-1915	123	250	229	206	173	84	5.32
1916-1920	111	252	230	206	159	74	5.16
1921-1925	128	267	251	207	159	76	5.44
1926-1930	139	271	261	222	170	78	5.70
1931-1935	130	255	267	240	175	82	5.74
1936-1940	114	261	270	251	196	93	5.93
1941-1945	88	222	236	208	163	89	5.03

SOURCE: Household registers compiled by the Japanese colonial government.

underregistration of births and infant deaths during the early years, these registers are the most reliable source of data we have for any area of China if not for any area of the premodern world. What do they tell us about fertility in the Chinese countryside? Consider first Table 7.6. We see there that although age at marriage was later in Taiwan than on the mainland, total fertility was 5.38 in 1906-10, 7.8 percent above the level given by the original Farm Survey data. After that the Taiwan rate fell, most precipitously in the aftermath of World War I; recovered in the years 1921-25; and then rose gradually to 5.93 in 1936-40, exceeding the unadjusted mainland rate by 18.8 percent. What we conclude depends on what point of comparison we think appropriate. In 1905 Taiwan was an impoverished, disease-ridden frontier compared with such areas of the mainland as the Lower Yangtze, but by 1940 its standard of living was one of the highest in Asia. And we must allow for the possibility that the rising fertility rate reflects improvement in the household registration system as well as a rising living standard. All we can say with confidence is that the Taiwan registers yield a total fertility rate that is 5-15 percent higher than the rate given by the Chinese Farm Survey.

Turn now to the marital fertility rates shown in Tables 7.7 and 7.8. The aggregate rates shown in Table 7.7 begin in 1906-10 at 6.25, 10.6 percent

TABLE 7.7

Age-Specific Marital Fertility Rates for Hai-shan, Taiwan, 1906-1945

Period	15-19	20-24	25-29	30-34	35-39	40-44	Total marital fertility rate
			Age				
Number of woman-years lived							
1906-1910	954	2,149	2,164	1,662	1,348	924	
1911-1915	962	1,748	2,137	1,988	1,471	1,138	
1916-1920	1,183	1,896	1,793	2,003	1,835	1,280	
1921-1925	1,157	2,341	1,926	1,635	1,844	1,625	
1926-1930	1,291	2,538	2,557	1,836	1,537	1,684	
1931-1935	1,130	2,637	2,698	2,399	1,737	1,401	
1936-1940	1,099	2,534	2,807	2,606	2,257	1,584	
1941-1945	1,232	2,820	2,766	2,691	2,394	2,016	
Births per 1,000 woman-years							
1906-1910	261	263	237	221	171	98	6.25
1911-1915	271	271	243	209	186	95	6.38
1916-1920	245	281	239	212	169	84	6.15
1921-1925	296	306	266	222	160	78	6.69
1926-1930	310	318	282	239	184	84	7.08
1931-1935	336	311	291	259	188	96	7.41
1936-1940	353	337	305	275	213	105	7.94
1941-1945	321	316	283	243	182	100	7.22

SOURCE: Household registers compiled by the Japanese colonial government.

above the mainland rate, and by 1936-40 rise to 7.94, 40.5 percent above the mainland rate. But the real difference between the Taiwan and mainland rates is far greater than these figures reveal. In northern Taiwan marital fertility varied sharply by form of marriage. When the bride was adopted at an early age and reared by her future husband's family for what I call a minor marriage, fertility was far lower than when she was reared by her natal family, regardless of whether she eventually married virilocally in the major fashion or uxorilocally.[34] Since minor marriages were rare in those areas of the mainland covered by the Farm Survey but accounted for approximately 40 percent of all first marriages in northern Taiwan during the Japanese period,[35] comparison of the aggregate figures from the registers with the Farm Survey estimates conceals an important difference. Just how important a difference is shown in Table 7.8. In 1906-10 marital fertility was 6.59 for major marriages and 7.25 for uxorilocal marriages, 14.2 percent and 28.3 percent above the Farm Survey estimates; by 1936-40, the major marriage rate had risen to 8.58 and the uxorilocal rate to 8.40, 51.9 percent and 48.7 percent above the mainland figures. We must conclude that Chinese farmers on Taiwan enjoyed considerably higher fertility than mainlanders or accept the possibility that the Farm Survey data are inaccurate.

TABLE 7.8

Age-Specific Marital Fertility Rates for Hai-shan, Taiwan, by Form of Marriage, 1906-1945

Year	Form of marriage	Number of woman-years lived in married state — Age						Births per 1,000 woman-years in married state — Age						Total marital fertility rate
		15-19	20-24	25-29	30-34	35-39	40-44	15-19	20-24	25-29	30-34	35-39	40-44	
1906-1910	Major	332	903	861	726	640	460	274	287	252	219	189	98	6.59
	Minor	459	990	1,017	730	516	346	244	239	214	211	143	81	5.66
	Uxori.	151	203	183	94	35	18	285	251	263	286	144	221	7.25
1911-1915	Major	374	691	916	801	616	524	238	303	276	205	159	88	6.57
	Minor	428	696	844	855	617	416	227	231	217	199	212	106	5.96
	Uxori.	141	288	222	162	90	34	355	310	207	229	178	147	7.12
1916-1920	Major	430	839	741	881	713	543	261	316	265	229	180	72	6.61
	Minor	604	685	618	716	743	508	232	226	197	184	141	87	5.34
	Uxori.	138	294	297	207	145	69	247	303	263	212	172	144	6.71
1921-1925	Major	422	1,028	870	698	820	628	313	356	277	232	199	76	7.26
	Minor	600	912	618	514	633	641	258	265	236	202	131	78	5.86
	Uxori.	112	304	298	242	172	133	437	270	266	248	174	60	7.27
1926-1930	Major	581	1,243	1,183	822	631	764	348	358	300	251	201	94	7.76
	Minor	605	915	867	549	468	552	273	260	256	222	156	58	6.13
	Uxori.	92	304	342	294	235	140	317	329	304	235	195	136	7.58
1931-1935	Major	515	1,387	1,361	1,116	767	562	371	350	328	271	207	123	8.25
	Minor	502	913	841	759	495	424	281	264	233	235	149	64	6.13
	Uxori.	99	280	348	329	280	218	414	300	281	276	207	110	7.95
1936-1940	Major	552	1,492	1,584	1,366	1,055	702	382	379	325	297	232	101	8.58
	Minor	402	755	803	746	687	465	326	253	269	234	176	97	6.78
	Uxori.	131	228	301	320	325	244	327	359	323	312	231	127	8.40
1941-1945	Major	673	1,839	1,722	1,532	1,244	971	353	344	306	261	195	113	7.87
	Minor	425	636	667	709	687	608	261	242	234	221	160	84	6.01
	Uxori.	109	288	253	292	282	263	340	295	284	216	167	80	6.91

SOURCE: Household registers compiled by the Japanese colonial government.

I fear that some readers will prefer the first option because they regard Taiwan as only marginally Chinese. I admit that Taiwan cannot be regarded as representative of China, not because it is unique among the provinces but because, like all the other provinces, it has its peculiar characteristics. I therefore turn now to evidence I collected in 1980-81 on the China mainland for the explicit purpose of reevaluating the Farm Survey results. My plan was to visit seven of the Farm Survey sites and reconstruct earlier fertility by interviewing women old enough to have married before land reform and collectivization transformed the countryside. I did in fact carry out this plan, to the extent of spending most of a year interviewing old women in seven widely dispersed localities. But because most of the Chinese countryside remains closed to foreigners whatever their purpose, I did not get to any of the communities surveyed by the Buck teams. In each of the seven provinces visited, I had to settle for a model collective in the vicinity of the site I had selected. In Fukien, Kiangsu, and Szechwan, this took me to units that have become models because they are favorably located and richly endowed, while in Chekiang, Shantung, and Shensi I was taken to units that have been set up as models to show what can be done in areas that lack any special advantage. My Peking site is special because it was chosen to pretest my interview schedule rather than as a primary field site.

I will eventually report in detail what I learned of past and present conditions in each of the localities visited. For the present purpose their location and rough characterizations of their pre-1949 economy must suffice. My first field site consisted of two villages in the suburbs of Peking near the Summer Palace; from Peking I traveled to southern Fukien, where I interviewed in a cluster of villages near Chiao-mei in Lung-hai county; from there I moved north to Chekiang, where I worked in several hamlets in the hills south of Shaohsing; after Chekiang I went to Kiangsu, where I was assigned to a commune across the Grand Canal from Yangchou; my next move took me to what is now a model brigade in An-ch'iu county in central Shantung; I then moved inland to another model brigade on the banks of the Ching-ho River in Li-ch'üan county in Shensi; and finally I ended my tour in Ta-yi county, 30 miles southwest of Chengtu in Szechwan.

Prior to 1949 my Peking informants' husbands were wheat and vegetable farmers who added a bit to their incomes by collecting leaves for camel drivers or burying ice to sell in the city in the summer; in Fukien they were rice farmers or were employed in some capacity or other in Southeast Asia; in Chekiang they planted a combination of wheat, rice, and tea if they owned land, and, if they did not, collected firewood in the hills and carried it to market in Shaohsing; in Kiangsu they worked as barbers in Shanghai, as boatmen on the Grand Canal, as cooks in Yangchou, or they farmed; in both Shantung and Shensi they were poor farmers who planted wheat to feed their families and vegetables to sell in the local markets; and in Szechwan they were tenants of the notorious landlord Liu Wen-tsai, whose cruelty is cast in clay in the Rent Collection Courtyard.

In each of the sites visited I asked to interview *all* the women aged 55 and over living in one or more adjacent villages (which in most cases meant that I asked to see all the women living in one brigade).[36] After Peking, my goal was 90 informants per site, this being as many as I could manage in the month allowed for each locality, but in four of the six sites I fell short because I was not allowed to interview women living outside the unit "open" to foreigners. Though I had to use an interpreter in two sites and often needed help in the others, I conducted all the interviews myself and insisted on meeting in the informant's home where family members could be consulted if necessary. On most days my interviews were attended by a member of the Chinese Institute of Sociology in Peking, a member of the provincial social science academy, a foreign affairs officer from either the county or the prefecture, a representative of either the commune or the brigade in which I was working, and a woman assigned to arrange my interviews and interpret when necessary. Though I began by fearing that this formidable entourage would make it impossible to elicit information on emotionally difficult subjects, my final judgment is that it worked in my favor. The presence of representatives from all levels of government created an atmosphere that combined public pressure with some assurance of privacy. On the one hand, my informants saw that my questions were supposed to be answered; on the other, they could see that the information requested was not for local consumption.

I interviewed 580 women born in the years 1896-1927—seven before 1900, 97 in 1900-1909, 201 in 1910-19, and 275 in 1920-27. The women in the first two cohorts were married and bore most of their children under conditions similar to those experienced by the younger Farm Survey women, but the women in the two later cohorts passed these critical years under the worst conditions China had seen since the Taiping Rebellion. Their childbearing years were cross-cut by the horrors of the Sino-Japanese War, the Civil War, land reform and collectivization, and the disastrous Great Leap Forward. Noting the sharp impact of World War II on Taiwanese fertility (see Tables 7.9 and 7.10), one would expect the fertility of my mainland sample to fall well below that of the Farm Survey women. But in fact we find just the opposite. In all seven localities the fertility of my interviewees exceeds that of the Farm Survey women by a substantial margin. Tables 7.9 and 7.10 show that total fertility for the 580 women was 5.78, and total marital fertility 7.03. These figures exceed the Farm Survey figures by 15.0 percent and 20.9 percent.

TABLE 7.9

*Age-Specific Fertility Rates Based on Retrospective Reports by Women Born
Between 1896 and 1927 and Interviewed in China in 1980-1981*

Locality	Age						Total fertility rate
	15-19	20-24	25-29	30-34	35-39	40-44	
	Number of woman-years lived						
Peking	260	260	260	260	260	260	
Fukien	400	400	400	400	400	400	
Chekiang	405	405	405	405	405	405	
Kiangsu	505	505	505	505	505	505	
Shantung	450	450	450	450	450	450	
Shensi	430	430	430	430	430	430	
Szechwan	450	450	450	450	450	450	
TOTAL	2,900	2,900	2,900	2,900	2,900	2,900	
	Births per 1,000 woman-years						
Peking	142	312	312	254	165	27	6.07
Fukien	128	238	293	253	158	55	5.63
Chekiang	119	294	326	205	173	49	5.83
Kiangsu	77	313	283	265	160	54	5.76
Shantung	67	264	269	240	196	80	5.59
Shensi	163	261	268	226	161	54	5.66
Szechwan	69	251	302	273	167	118	5.98
TOTAL	106	275	298	246	169	65	5.78

SOURCE: Interviews conducted by the author in seven mainland localities in 1980-81.

My mainland interviews followed a more or less standard procedure.
After I had been introduced and the purpose of the interview explained, a
local cadre emphasized how important it was for us to know about *all* the
informant's children. "It doesn't matter if they lived or died in a few hours,
if they were boys or girls, if you raised them or gave them away, we want
you to count them all." I then asked the informant to tell me how many
children she had borne, how many had died, and how many had been sold
or given out in adoption. When I had obtained what appeared to be a complete count, I asked the informant to take the births in order and tell me
how old she was when each child was born and how long it had lived. With
this history before me I then inquired about every birth interval of three or
more years. "Why didn't you bear any children during these three years?
Were you ill? Was your husband ill? Were you and your husband living
together?" In sum, I did everything I could to ensure a complete count, but
I did not succeed. The sex ratio for the 3,170 births counted was 114.
Since there is no good reason to assume that all the children missed were
female, the actual fertility of my informants must be considerably higher
than my figures indicate. I estimate a total fertility of at least 6 and total
marital fertility of something over 7.

TABLE 7.10

Age-Specific Marital Fertility Rates Based on Retrospective Reports by Women
Born Between 1896 and 1927 and Interviewed in China in 1980-1981

Locality	15-19	20-24	25-29	30-34	35-39	40-44	Total marital fertility rate
			Age				
Number of woman-years lived							
Peking	142	233	242	237	235	237	
Fukien	147	340	340	341	308	283	
Chekiang	192	357	370	361	358	349	
Kiangsu	137	455	487	481	463	447	
Shantung	120	356	425	419	403	395	
Shensi	290	423	428	421	411	395	
Szechwan	169	409	431	420	396	358	
TOTAL	1,197	2,574	2,728	2,684	2,578	2,468	
Births per 1,000 woman-years							
Peking	261	348	335	279	183	30	7.12
Fukien	346	279	344	294	205	78	7.73
Chekiang	244	331	349	224	190	55	6.97
Kiangsu	285	347	294	277	175	60	7.19
Shantung	249	334	282	255	216	91	7.15
Shensi	241	265	269	230	168	58	6.17
Szechwan	185	274	313	293	190	148	7.13
TOTAL	255	309	308	264	189	76	7.03

SOURCE: Interviews conducted by the author in seven mainland localities in 1980-81.

The primary objection to this conclusion will be that the old women I interviewed were not representative of their cohorts. They were survivors who were probably healthier and heartier as young women than their deceased peers. Assuming then that good health promotes high fertility, it could be that I interviewed only the most fertile representatives of these cohorts. Moreover, it could be that in China women who bear a lot of children live longer because they have several sons to nurture them in their old age. The argument is plausible, but not necessarily correct. Until the early 1960's there were no maternal care facilities of any kind in the Chinese countryside. Women bore their children at home with the assistance of a relative or neighbor who cut the umbilical cord with whatever knife was handy and treated all postpartum problems with traditional concoctions. Under these conditions it could well be that the most fertile women were the least likely to survive the childbearing years. The criticism and the response must stand as alternative hypotheses until further work with the Taiwan household registers allows us to settle the issue.

The data from the Taiwan household registers are of questionable relevance because they come from the edge of the Chinese empire. The data from my mainland interviews are questionable because they were collected so long after the fact. But there is another set of data against which neither of these objections can be raised. In 1931 one of the most experienced of Buck's collaborators, Chiao Chi-ming, joined with one of the leading demographers of the time, Warren S. Thompson, to conduct a four-year study of vital events in Chiang-yin county in central Kiangsu.[37] Older scholars like Tai Shih-kuang and Li Ching-han recommend this study as the best work of the time. Instead of sending untrained students to collect information on their holidays, Chiao and Thompson set up a registration system under the supervision of D. T. Chen. Chen solicited the cooperation of community leaders and eventually enlisted the aid of 180 reporters, each of whom he visited once a month to collect data and personally check on the accuracy of the information reported:

Very often he checked the information given by the people of one village by questioning the people who lived in the neighboring village; thus he often secured additional reporters. He made friends with all sorts of people—midwives, church members, Taoists, quack doctors, sorceresses and others. They all helped in the work of vital registration to some extent. By paying attention not only to the attitudes of the people and their casual talk but also to the number of pregnant women in each village, and the number of married women between ages 15 and 49 the supervisor got an additional check on births. For registration of death he paid attention to the notes written "nothing untouchable" pasted on every door in the village, the spirit tablet sitting against the wall in the house, the remnant of the mat and the bed straw from the deceased's bed burnt outside the village, the half-mourning worn by the people, the new tombs, and the small coffins or straw packets with corpses hanging in the trees.[38]

One might expect somewhat higher fertility in Chiang-yin than in China as a whole because it was located in one of the richest areas of the country, but the years 1931-35 were not good years. In 1931 the county was hit by a flood, followed by violent outbreaks of dysentery and cholera; in 1932 drought succeeded flood and brought another outbreak of cholera; and in 1933 the area was ravaged by one of the worst malaria epidemics in years. And this was on top of severe economic dislocations caused by the Great Depression. But despite the troubled times the fertility recorded by Chiao, Thompson, and Chen (see Table 7.11) exceeds by a wide margin the rates given by the Farm Survey, matching the highest figures from Taiwan. Average total fertility for 1931-34 was 6.38 (27.9 percent above the Farm Survey rate and 7.6 above the highest Taiwan rate), while total marital fertility was 7.41 (31.2 percent above the Farm Survey figure and only 7.1 percent below the highest Taiwan figure).

The reader should note that in comparing the results of the Farm Survey with those of other studies, I use only the unadjusted figures reported by the authors. The reason for this is that I am not attempting to provide a

TABLE 7.11

Age-Specific General and Marital Fertility Rates for Chiang-yin County, Kiangsu,
1931-1935

Year	15-19	20-24	25-29	30-34	35-39	40-44	Total fertility
				Age			
			Number of women				
1931-1932	864	876	782	765	682	535	
1932-1933	842	859	779	737	667	534	
1933-1934	852	814	791	700	688	535	
1934-1935	861	791	802	652	712	535	
TOTAL	3,419	3,340	3,154	2,854	2,749	2,139	
			Number of married women				
1931-1932	334	818	758	734	625	466	
1932-1933	315	796	734	693	601	458	
1933-1934	326	756	764	670	633	469	
1934-1935	331	737	771	628	658	469	
TOTAL	1,306	3,107	3,027	2,725	2,517	1,862	
			Births per 1,000 women				
1931-1932	95	337	330	259	251	95	6.84
1932-1933	67	318	338	242	202	73	6.20
1933-1934	80	273	277	253	179	69	5.66
1934-1935	70	372	343	288	198	95	6.83
TOTAL	78	325	322	260	207	83	6.38
			Births per 1,000 married women				
1931-1932	246	361	340	270	274	109	8.00
1932-1933	178	343	358	257	225	85	7.23
1933-1934	209	294	287	264	194	79	6.64
1934-1935	181	399	357	299	214	109	7.80
TOTAL	203	349	335	272	227	96	7.41

SOURCE: C. M. Chiao, Warren S. Thompson, and D. T. Chen, *An Experiment in the Registration of Vital Statistics in China* (Oxford, Ohio, 1938), Table 32, p. 45.

new estimate of fertility in rural China. That is a task better left to the demographers. My only goal is to show that even after Frank Notestein discarded some of the data as patently deficient, the figures reported by Buck fall well below those reported by others. Whatever the true level of fertility in rural China in the late 1920's and early 1930's, it was considerably higher than any of the figures recorded or derived from the Farm Survey. The sex ratio of the births reported by the old women I interviewed was 114, which indicates that they failed to report a substantial number of female births and suggests a number of male births also went unreported. The Chiao, Thompson, and Chen study is probably closer to the truth because births were recorded as they occurred, but a sex ratio at birth of 112 says that even this very careful study fell short of perfection.[39] This is important because if one were to accept my results and those of Chiao, Thompson, and Chen as essentially accurate, their close agreement with the Princeton estimates would appear to validate those estimates and their source, while in fact the convergence only shows that even when the Buck data are adjusted to the highest plausible level, they only reach the benchmark set by unadjusted data from other sources.

The essence of my criticism of the Princeton group's use of the Buck data can be summed up by noting a certain irony in their argument. Convinced that societies with early and nearly universal marriage cannot tolerate high marital fertility, they nonetheless always choose the line of argument that leads to a high rather than a low estimate of fertility. Not only do they accept Notestein's decision to throw out the data from 18 communities as "impossibly low," they adjust the remaining data upward to match the relatively high level of fertility reported by women aged 20-29. Their justification for this is the belief that reports of young women are more accurate than those of old women, but they might just as well have argued that because the years immediately preceding the Survey were relatively prosperous, the fertility of young women should be adjusted downward to match the more representative experience of the older women. Thus someone sympathetic to the Princeton group's point of view could easily argue that they have not made their best case. My unsympathetic thought is that if the Princeton group had arrived at a lower estimate, their results would have differed so strikingly from the data available from other sources as to discredit the Farm Surveys.

I emphasize these points because the bulk of the Farm Survey data poses a threat. If these data and the estimates derived from them are accepted as reasonably accurate, the evidence from Taiwan and particular mainland communities like Chiang-yin will be set aside as products of local circumstances, and this would be tragic because it is these studies, not the Chinese Farm Survey, that offer us our best chance for a backward look into the demography of late Imperial China. But while I favor dismissing the Farm Survey data as unreliable and beyond salvaging, I do not dispute the general point made by the Princeton group. Montesquieu's supposition was wrong. Though Chinese fertility was considerably higher than the Farm Survey indicates, it was not "without parallel." To the contrary, marital fertility appears to have been only about 75 percent of that of premodern Europe. This difference is not startling (the Princeton estimate is about 50 percent), but it is interesting. Why was the fertility of Chinese women lower than that of European women?

The first point to be made is that whatever the reason for moderate fertility in China, it was not deliberate fertility control. Where Japanese peasants made the family fit the farm, the Chinese assumed they would some-

TABLE 7.12

Age-Specific Marital Fertility Rates for Hai-shan, Taiwan, by Form of Marriage and Number of Surviving Sons, 1906-1945

Form of marriage	Number of surviving sons	Age					
		15-19	20-24	25-29	30-34	35-39	40-44
		Number of woman-years lived					
Major	None	3,027	4,838	2,862	1,632	1,111	867
	One	791	3,365	3,259	2,389	1,663	1,295
	Two	57	1,028	2,076	1,968	1,552	1,111
	Three	4	178	807	1,208	1,086	829
	Four	0	12	203	567	684	572
	Five	0	1	32	176	389	481
Minor	None	3,171	3,432	2,049	1,164	816	643
	One	803	2,292	2,302	1,882	1,382	1,048
	Two	50	713	1,402	1,330	1,248	958
	Three	0	64	437	837	798	716
	Four	0	0	80	269	378	330
	Five	0	0	8	96	225	266
		Births per 1,000 woman-years lived					
Major	None	378	404	273	157	95	31
	One	166	298	314	244	139	62
	Two	–	233	320	295	227	107
	Three	–	–	278	308	274	139
	Four	–	–	–	289	281	149
	Five	–	–	–	–	267	154
Minor	None	294	273	211	146	67	26
	One	149	238	245	203	135	35
	Two	–	185	250	259	186	101
	Three	–	–	222	234	197	115
	Four	–	–	–	279	230	142
	Five	–	–	–	–	240	154

SOURCE: Household registers compiled by the Japanese colonial government.

how make the farm fit the family. Though there is ample evidence of female infanticide in some areas, there is no evidence of controlling family size by limiting the number of sons. Thinking that if a family had four or five sons they would be satisfied and limit their fertility, I used the Taiwan registers to calculate age-specific marital fertility by number of surviving sons. The results show (see Table 7.12) that even with five surviving sons, Chinese farmers did not attempt to control fertility. Women with the maximum number of sons possible at a given age experience relatively low fertility during that age interval because they are still nursing their last-born, but for other women in the age interval, fertility rises steadily with the number of surviving sons. Note in particular the behavior of women aged 40-45. If there was some limit on the number of sons desired, one would expect that

TABLE 7.13

Various Chinese Age-Specific Marital Fertility Rates Compared with Louis Henry's Natural Fertility Rate

Provenance	Age					
	15-19	20-24	25-29	30-34	35-39	40-44
Age-specific marital fertility rates						
Natural fertility	–	435	407	371	298	152
Taiwan, major marriage	331	343	298	252	198	97
Taiwan, minor marriage	261	249	232	214	159	81
Taiwan, uxorilocal marriage	335	302	277	253	193	109
Mainland (Buck)	142	264	253	219	166	86
Mainland (Wolf)	195	301	306	272	197	94
Chiang-yin county	203	349	335	272	227	96
Indexed rates (20-24 equals 100)						
Natural fertility	–	100	94	85	69	34
Taiwan, major marriage	97	100	87	73	58	28
Taiwan, minor marriage	105	100	93	86	64	33
Taiwan, uxorilocal marriage	111	100	92	84	64	36
Mainland (Buck)	54	100	96	83	63	33
Mainland (Wolf)	65	100	102	90	65	31
Chiang-yin county	58	100	96	78	65	28

SOURCE (of natural fertility rate): Louis Henry, "Some Data on Natural Fertility," *Eugenics Quarterly*, 8 (1961): 81-91.

at this age, the fertility of women with four or five sons would be lower than that of women with two or three sons. But regardless of whether they married in the major or the minor fashion, women with four or five sons produced a third more children than women with two or three sons.

That the Taiwanese were not unusual among Chinese in making the most of their fecundity is clearly shown in Table 7.13. While the level of fertility among the populations discussed in this paper falls well below natural fertility, the age pattern displayed by all but one is very similar to the natural fertility pattern.[40] This strongly suggests that whatever the reason for the relatively low marital fertility of the Chinese, it was not contraception, infanticide, or abortion. If families were deliberately limiting the number of children, the age-specific marital fertility rate would fall after the desired number of children had been achieved, producing a concave rather than a convex trajectory (see Figure 7.1). Only Taiwanese major marriages depart from the natural fertility curve by more than a few percentage points, and this is clearly an artifact of age at marriage rather

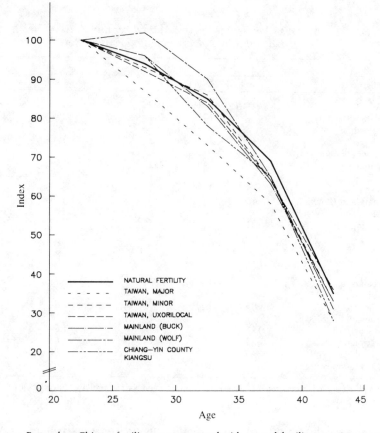

Fig. 7.1. Premodern Chinese fertility rates compared with natural fertility rates (age-specific marital fertility indexed at 20-24)

than evidence of birth control. Where most mainland Chinese women married at 16 or 17 and bore their first child before age 20, Taiwanese women who married in the major fashion commonly married at 18 or 19 and bore their first child early in the 20-24 interval. Consequently, the fertility of the 20-24 interval, which anchors the index figures, is high relative to that of succeeding intervals, producing a curve that mimics the curve found in contracepting populations.

Thus we have a dilemma: Why was marital fertility relatively low in a strongly pronatalist culture? Part of the answer is that despite the heavy-handed emphasis on fertility in traditional Chinese marriage rites, marriage customs sometimes discouraged high fertility by ignoring the natural inclinations of the bride and groom. The most striking case in point is minor marriage in Taiwan, but this is only one of a number of customs that acted as inadvertent checks on fertility. Another example that is important to the demography of North China is the custom of marrying preadolescent boys to 19- and 20-year-old girls. Asked why she had not borne any children during the first five years of her marriage, one of my Shantung informants replied, "How could I have children? My husband was just a child. He didn't sleep with me; he slept with his mother." This woman was more outspoken than my other informants, but her experience was not unusual in rural communities north of the Yangtze River.

Natural disasters also took a high toll on fertility in rural China, particularly in the north, where flood and drought created a recurring cycle of misery. The reader probably has noted that the marital fertility of my Shensi informants falls far short of that of the women interviewed in the other six localities. Although it has been suggested that the low fertility of this area is due to a natural contraceptive in the cottonseed oil used for cooking,[41] my guess is that closer analysis of the data will reveal that the real causes were drought and famine. Many of my older informants told vivid tales of the terrible drought of 1928-31, when rich and poor alike abandoned their homes and fled south in search of something to eat. The strategy in such desperate times was for husband and wife to divide up the children and flee in separate directions. It was understood that what little food they might find would not suffice for the entire family.

The puzzle we face in trying to explain why Chinese fertility was moderate rather than high is accentuated by the fact that in the West, poverty, illiteracy, and low rank have long been associated with a high rather than a low birth rate. In China, however, there is some evidence that this relationship was reversed. Though the Farm Survey data show no differences in the fertility of landlords and tenants, the fertility of families with large farms was somewhat higher than that of families with small farms, particularly in South China.[42] Moreover, a series of urban studies by J. B. Griffing and Herbert D. Lamson shows that literate women with literate husbands bore more children than illiterate women with illiterate husbands.[43] I have therefore been at some pains to discover what the situation was in Taiwan, where the combination of household registers and land records provides accurate measures of both fertility and wealth. My measure of wealth is the amount of the annual land tax paid by each woman's family. To take account of changes in the family's economic fortunes, I have calculated the amount of tax paid every fifth year from 1906 to 1941 and used this figure to assign the women present to one of four tax classes. When changes in the size or quality of the family's estate caused it to move up or down the tax scale, the women were reassigned on the basis of the new assessment. Thus my assignments always reflect a woman's current situation.

Though the calculation of these measures was extremely tedious because of land fragmentation, the results appear to be worth the effort. The data reveal a clear and consistent positive relationship between fertility and wealth. Table 7.14 shows that throughout the period of the Japanese occupation, landless families who paid no tax produced fewer children

TABLE 7.14

Age-Specific Marital Fertility Rates for Hai-shan, Taiwan, by Amount of Land Tax, 1906-1945

Period	Amount of land tax (yen)	15-19	20-24	25-29	30-34	35-39	40-44	Total marital fertility rate
		Number of woman-years lived by married women						
1906-1910	No land	468	1,033	1,190	912	720	500	
	Less than 5	278	632	566	441	362	243	
	5 to 10	71	148	111	85	60	81	
	10 or more	137	336	297	225	206	101	
1911-1915	No land	408	751	949	965	723	543	
	Less than 5	298	554	685	623	496	369	
	5 to 10	91	151	185	115	79	64	
	10 or more	165	292	319	284	173	162	
1916-1920	No land	517	806	739	930	912	645	
	Less than 5	343	495	546	536	487	378	
	5 to 10	95	183	155	186	133	63	
	10 or more	229	413	354	352	302	194	
1921-1925	No land	562	1,013	848	710	911	825	
	Less than 5	277	645	515	464	453	401	
	5 to 10	112	180	152	150	163	142	
	10 or more	207	503	411	310	317	257	
1926-1930	No land	569	1,169	1,182	817	701	837	
	Less than 5	369	703	707	514	477	452	
	5 to 10	117	227	198	161	136	132	
	10 or more	235	440	470	344	223	263	
1931-1935	No land	507	1,175	1,221	1,146	811	673	
	Less than 5	333	722	765	613	459	432	
	5 to 10	103	258	270	208	175	109	
	10 or more	187	482	442	431	291	187	
1936-1940	No land	506	1,161	1,262	1,228	1,079	765	
	Less than 5	353	716	812	757	617	432	
	5 to 10	73	249	381	252	183	186	
	10 or more	166	408	452	368	378	202	
1941-1945	No land	643	1,407	1,351	1,264	1,113	981	
	Less than 5	298	709	676	699	622	508	
	5 to 10	125	239	244	258	270	184	
	10 or more	166	465	496	470	390	343	

TABLE 7.14 *(cont.)*

Period	Amount of land tax (yen)	Age						Total marital fertility rate
		15-19	20-24	25-29	30-34	35-39	40-44	
	Births per 1,000 woman-years in married state							
1906-1910	No land	226	260	221	222	167	114	6.05
	Less than 5	270	260	228	195	171	66	5.95
	5 to 10	352	298	234	154	117	123	6.39
	10 or more	313	262	319	293	199	79	7.33
1911-1915	No land	258	261	234	212	183	87	6.17
	Less than 5	289	258	247	204	180	95	6.36
	5 to 10	296	330	206	217	253	47	6.75
	10 or more	260	291	282	208	191	142	6.87
1916-1920	No land	222	267	222	212	169	96	5.94
	Less than 5	269	259	234	194	152	71	5.89
	5 to 10	211	285	206	194	173	32	5.50
	10 or more	275	332	297	247	195	82	7.15
1921-1925	No land	290	316	256	206	168	84	6.59
	Less than 5	318	290	274	215	165	70	6.66
	5 to 10	277	283	283	233	172	99	6.73
	10 or more	295	316	272	265	177	62	6.94
1926-1930	No land	290	310	272	237	177	79	6.82
	Less than 5	311	336	280	236	178	86	7.14
	5 to 10	332	304	293	267	185	121	7.51
	10 or more	345	318	307	233	215	80	7.49
1931-1935	No land	327	293	294	244	170	86	7.07
	Less than 5	321	292	269	267	216	97	7.32
	5 to 10	310	334	297	270	200	111	7.60
	10 or more	402	374	314	280	189	118	8.38
1936-1940	No land	334	332	287	266	228	119	7.83
	Less than 5	365	336	293	287	190	95	7.83
	5 to 10	396	322	357	261	153	92	7.90
	10 or more	368	363	345	291	238	84	8.44
1941-1945	No land	307	304	262	231	181	102	6.93
	Less than 5	325	316	297	256	174	96	7.32
	5 to 10	311	322	271	252	200	103	7.30
	10 or more	373	348	329	251	184	99	7.92

SOURCE: Household registers compiled by the Japanese colonial government.

than their neighbors who paid a tax. On the average the wives of land-holders paying a tax of ten yen or more bore 13.3 percent more children than the wives of landless laborers and tenant farmers. This is important because it suggests that in China, even small differences in wealth affected marital fertility. The families living in the communities covered by this study included only a few petty landlords. The great landlords who con-trolled nearly half the area's productive land were not local people. Thus

TABLE 7.15

Age-Specific Marital Fertility Rates for Hai-shan, Taiwan,
by Form of Marriage and Amount of Land Tax, 1906-1945

Form of marriage	Amount of land tax (yen)	Age						Total marital fertility
		15-19	20-24	25-29	30-34	35-39	40-44	
		Number of woman-years lived in married state						
Major	No land	1,804	4,215	4,091	3,543	2,921	2,298	
	Less than 5	1,048	2,437	2,551	2,159	1,775	1,480	
	5 to 10	310	830	764	676	564	464	
	10 or more	718	1,940	1,833	1,563	1,226	912	
Minor	No land	1,829	2,952	3,008	2,761	2,413	2,047	
	Less than 5	1,168	1,907	1,722	1,534	1,325	1,029	
	5 to 10	405	622	601	471	399	343	
	10 or more	622	1,019	947	813	708	542	
Uxori.	No land	490	1,091	1,095	1,021	851	652	
	Less than 5	295	683	692	555	422	301	
	5 to 10	62	141	170	169	142	72	
	10 or more	125	274	287	195	148	92	
		Births per 1,000 woman-years lived						
Major	No land	320	328	278	239	187	97	7.25
	Less than 5	343	342	296	249	192	87	7.54
	5 to 10	322	351	297	247	207	108	7.66
	10 or more	343	371	343	286	228	107	8.39
Minor	No land	241	253	228	214	166	81	5.91
	Less than 5	268	238	231	225	160	87	6.04
	5 to 10	286	259	238	198	148	73	6.01
	10 or more	294	253	247	202	141	74	6.06
Uxori.	No land	304	291	271	248	207	124	7.22
	Less than 5	363	310	267	234	156	73	7.02
	5 to 10	354	306	311	307	197	125	8.00
	10 or more	385	328	303	288	216	104	8.12

SOURCE: Household registers compiled by the Japanese colonial government.

the difference we find between the landless and the landed is the difference
between tenant farmers and small holders whose property just managed to
support a family.

Table 7.15 takes the analysis of the relationship between fertility and
wealth a step further by controlling for form of marriage. The comparisons displayed there show that where wealth enhanced the fertility of major and uxorilocal marriages, it had no effect whatever on the fertility of
minor marriages. When husband and wife are reared together from an
early age, their fertility is immune to the stimulus provided by wealth. This
is important not only because it gives us stronger evidence of the influence
of wealth on fertility in the other two forms of marriage, but also because

it suggests why it is that wealth usually stimulates higher fertility. The generally lower fertility of minor marriages is best interpreted as expressing a sexual aversion aroused by early and intimate childhood association.[44] Thus the difference in the way the three forms of marriage respond to wealth is probably related to coital frequency. Major and uxorilocal marriages respond with higher fertility because coital frequency rises with a little more leisure and a little better diet; minor marriages remain at the same level of fertility because coital frequency is regulated by negative emotions rather than by the time and energy available for sex.

I will conclude by summing up what I call the neo-orthodox position on fertility in premodern rural China. Chinese fertility was not as high as the vivid language of Mallory and Tawney suggested, but not as low as the Princeton group proposes. Though it is too early in the development of Chinese historical demography to settle on figures for any period, my estimate is that in the first half of this century, total fertility in China averaged six births and total marital fertility seven and a half births. But I hasten to add that there is more at stake than numbers. I take my position on the orthodox side of the debate because I feel that however much they exaggerated the birth rate, Mallory and Tawney were closer to understanding the role of fertility in Chinese society than the Princeton group. The suggestion that in China low marital fertility was a consequence of early and universal marriage misses entirely the motive for these customs. Marriage was early and universal because the Chinese wanted as many children as possible. The problem for the future is not to explain how the Chinese compensated for their marriage customs; it is to discover how the desires expressed in those customs were frustrated.

EIGHT

Fertility in Rural China: A Reconfirmation of the Barclay Reassessment

Ansley J. Coale

Arthur Wolf's essay on "Fertility in Prerevolutionary Rural China" is based, I believe, on a misunderstanding of two major points in the article by Barclay et al., which undertook a reassessment of the Lossing Buck survey of some 200,000 Chinese agriculturalists in 1929-31. One misunderstanding concerns the position taken in the reassessment about the accuracy of the data in the survey; the other misunderstanding involves the significance assigned to the moderate level of fertility that was finally estimated.

First, the reassessment did not assert that the survey data were accurate; nor were the figures on fertility and mortality as given in the survey accepted. Rather, the reassessment subjected the survey data to a battery of analytic techniques developed in the last thirty years for extracting valid demographic information from incomplete and inaccurate data.[1]

Second, the misunderstanding with respect to the interpretation of the moderate fertility level that was estimated arose in part because in the reassessment, it was stated that the level of marital fertility was only 51 percent of the highest recorded schedule, a low level that "would be expected by demographers only in populations in which some combination of contraception and abortion is practised." This sentence could mislead the unwary. It was preceded by an extended discussion of the age structure of fertility in China showing that fertility was "natural," meaning that Chinese couples did *not* take deliberate steps such as contraception and abortion to stop having children when the desired family size had been attained. This point was a principal one. The moderate level of fertility in the absence of contraception constitutes a demographic puzzle. It was noted that somewhat similar characteristics (high proportions married and low marital fertility) have been found in other populations, especially in the Central Asian Republics of the Soviet Union, which in 1897 and 1926 had high proportions married, low age at marriage, and low marital fertility, very similar to our estimates for the Chinese farmers.

I turn now to more extended comments on these two points.

Forms of Analysis Used in Estimating Demographic Characteristics of the Chinese Farm Population

It is unfortunate that Frank Notestein discarded some of the data from the Buck survey and that these data cannot now be recovered. It was understandable that Notestein, writing before techniques for correction had been worked out, felt that data from the areas in which the birth and death rates were several standard deviations lower than in the other districts Buck surveyed should not be taken seriously. It is especially ironic that these data are lost, because the very methods of analysis that were applied in the reassessment would have made evident the deficiencies in these data, and quite probably would have produced estimates of the degree of understatement, and by correction, produced usable estimates. In other words, our checks would likely have revealed the need for major corrections to both the fertility and the mortality schedules in the areas in which the birth and death rates were so conspicuously low.

To repeat, the reassessment did not assert that the survey was accurate, and did not accept the figures on fertility or mortality as given. Rather, the reassessment subjected the survey data to corrections that emerge from the data themselves. Two sets of fertility estimates were made. First, age-specific fertility schedules were constructed from the number of births reported as occurring the previous year, adjusted for understatement. This calculation accepts as correct the *proportionate distribution* by age of mother of the rate of childbearing, recorded in the form of the number of births occurring in the year before the survey to women of each age. However, the *completeness* of these reported numbers of births is not accepted. Rather, the degree of understatement is calculated by cumulating the recorded rates of births for younger women to determine how many children on average they would have borne by ages 20-24 and 25-29. This calculated cumulative fertility is compared with the average number of children ever born as reported by women in these age intervals. The entire schedule of fertility rates is then inflated by the multiplier needed to bring cumulated fertility in line with the number of children ever born reported by the younger women. The rationale is that the omission of children ever born to date in each woman's life ordinarily does not become consequential until women are older, when often they misunderstand the need to report as children persons who are now adult and no longer at home. Older women may also omit children who died long ago. Worldwide experience with reports on children ever born shows that in most contexts the numbers reported by women under 30 are reliable. In such reports an accurate perception of whether or not births occurred in the last year is not required, and the numbers of children ever born that are reported are relatively small. It is highly unlikely that women under 30 have forgotten births, all relatively recent, that have occurred to them. This standard procedure, when applied to other bodies of faulty data, leads to upward adjustments in the rates of childbearing by as much as 30-40 percent. In the application of this procedure to the data from the Buck survey, the overall upward adjustment was only 9 percent, but it was 12 in the south and 24 percent in one region (which after this large adjustment still had a total fertility rate below 6).

The second method of estimating the overall rate of childbearing involved an application of stable age distributions. In a population (like the Chinese) with an age distribution little affected by time trends in birth and death rates, the birth rate can be reliably estimated by employing a model stable population that incorporates the appropriate level of infant and child mortality and that has the same proportion under ages 5, 10, 15, 20, . . . , 35, as the given population. Combining the child mortality level with the cumulative proportion under successive ages leads to a succession of estimated birth rates, which are uniform if ages are not severely misreported and if the age distribution is genuinely stable. When this technique was applied to the age distribution from the Chinese farm population and the estimates (very high) of infant and child mortality (derived by a method to be described in a moment), the succession of estimated birth rates was uniform. The seven estimates derived from the proportions under 5, 10, 15, 20, 25, 30, and 35 years of age were 41.0, 41.2, 40.9, 40.2, 40.1, 40.8, and 40.4 per thousand, an unusually consistent sequence. The average estimate of the birth rate agreed very closely with that derived from the corrected age-specific fertility schedules (the birth rate derived from the age distribution was 40.5 per thousand, compared to 41.2 from the adjusted age-specific fertility schedule). The agreement in the estimates was good not only for the area covered by the survey as a whole, but also for the separate regions for which estimates could be constructed.

If the survey had not included data on births in the preceding year, we might have estimated the age-specific fertility schedule by assuming that the married women were subject to a typical "natural" fertility schedule (with rates for five-year age intervals from 15-19 to 45-49 of 0.411, 0.460, 0.431, 0.395, 0.322, 0.167, and 0.024), then calculating the resultant number of births, and finally reducing the fertility schedule by a multiplier that would bring the total number of births into line with the stable population estimate of the birth rate. The result is shown in Table 8.1.

In short, our fertility estimates are very close to those that would be estimated from infant and child mortality and the age distribution, combined with the age structure of natural fertility—a strong confirmation of the validity of the estimates.

Analysis showed that the data on mortality were much less complete than those on births the previous year. Infant and child mortality was esti-

TABLE 8.1

Fertility Rates from Farm Survey Data as Calculated by Barclay et al. and from "Natural" Fertility and Proportion Married

Age interval	Fertility rates as calculated by Barclay et al.	Fertility rate from "natural" fertility and proportion married
15-19	.107	.123
20-24	.268	.245
25-29	.262	.238
30-34	.221	.216
35-39	.156	.169
40-44	.074	.082
45-49	.011	.011
TOTAL FERTILITY RATE	5.50	5.42

mated by a procedure that has proved very robust when applied to data from many parts of the world. This procedure accepts as accurate the reported number of children ever born and the reported number still surviving, at least for younger women. The responses in the survey to these questions indicated a very high infant mortality rate (with 30 percent of the children dying in the first year)—just about twice the infant mortality that was reported in response to direct questions about births and deaths under age one in the year preceding the survey.

Reported mortality above age 5 was corrected through a technique that combines the age distribution of reported deaths with the age distribution of the population. This procedure also indicated severe underreporting of deaths in response to a question about deaths within each household in the preceding year. Only about 54 percent of the deaths above age 5 were reported.

Comparison of Fertility Data from the Reassessment with Data Provided by Wolf

Wolf compares the fertility rates derived from the Buck study with data taken from registers that he reassembled from the Hai-shan region in Taiwan. He has calculated age-specific fertility rates and age-specific marital fertility rates from the registers in this area from 1906 to 1945, arguing, I think convincingly, that these registers were essentially complete.

If we compare the fertility data for Hai-shan with adjusted age-specific fertility rates that Barclay et al. give as their best estimate, they are astonishingly close. In the upper panel of Figure 8.1, the age-specific fertility rates (as corrected in the reassessment) of the Chinese farmers are com-

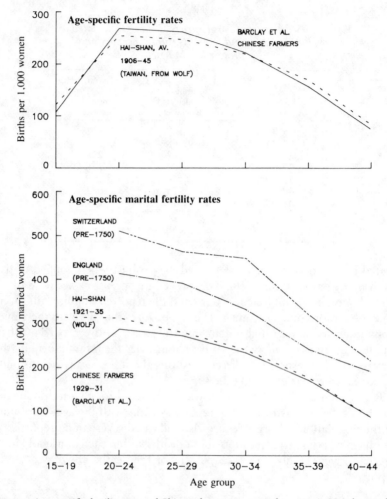

Fig. 8.1. Age-specific fertility rates of Chinese farmers compared to rates in Hai-shan and in preindustrial Europe

pared with the average age-specific fertility rates for 1906-45 Hai-shan. In the lower panel, the age-specific marital fertility rates for the Chinese farmers and for Hai-shan in the period 1921 to 1935 are compared. Also shown are the highest and lowest age-specific marital fertility schedules from a set of pre-1750 European data. The underlying similarity of the Chinese farmers to the Taiwanese data is evident; the divergence at ages 15-19 in marital fertility rates is an exception that could be the result either of a somewhat higher incidence of adolescent subfecundity in the Chinese farmers, or of some form of minor bias in the Taiwan data (the re-

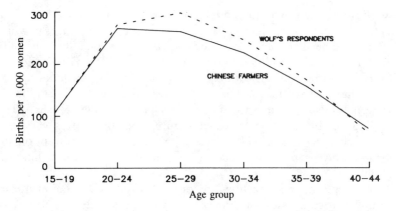

Fig. 8.2. Age-specific fertility of Chinese farmers compared to retrospective fertility of Wolf's older respondents

ported high fertility at 15-19 is not ordinarily found in early-marrying populations). I find it genuinely astonishing that there should be such close conformity between the accurately recorded data from Taiwan and the adjusted data for the Chinese farmers. The contrast between the moderate marital fertility rates in these two Chinese populations and the much higher marital fertility in preindustrial Europe is very conspicuous. At the same time, note that the age structure of the different marital fertility schedules is comparable from age 20 to age 44, a consistency which implies that all these populations were subject to "natural" fertility and were not characterized by a high degree of voluntary control through the practice of contraception and abortion.

In Figure 8.2 the age-specific fertility rates of the Chinese farmers are compared with the rates Wolf derived from the histories of the older women he interviewed in seven villages of rural China. The women were over 55 in 1981, and most of their childbearing at ages above 30 or 35 occurred after World War II. Note that the agreement between the corrected Buck survey and his retrospective data is very good at the first two age groups and only slightly divergent thereafter. This slight divergence may indicate slightly higher marital fertility experienced in the later years, say in the 1940's and 1950's, as compared with the 1930's.

The average total fertility rate for the period 1906 to 1945 for Hai-shan is 5.46, for the Chinese farmers 5.50, and for Wolf's respondents 5.76. The Taiwanese population therefore had a total fertility that was 99.2 percent that of the Chinese farmers, and Wolf's respondents a total fertility rate just over 4 percent greater than the Chinese farmers. Again, this seems to me surprisingly strong confirmation of the probable validity of the adjusted data for Chinese farmers.

Wolf notes that the fertility in the northern Taiwan area from which he took the registers was reduced by the high incidence of marriages in which the wife had been adopted in infancy and raised in the family of her ultimate husband. The fertility of these "minor" marriages was some 20 percent lower than the fertility of major marriages, and he concludes that on the mainland, where this form of marriage was much less prevalent than in northern Taiwan, fertility should have been higher than in Hai-shan. This is a plausible but not conclusive conjecture, since there are a variety of ways in which fertility is held in check in the absence of contraception and abortion, only one of which is lack of sexual attraction between husband and wife.

Contraception and abortion are ordinarily parity-related measures, meaning that couples use such measures with special intensity to restrict childbearing after the desired number of children have already been born. As noted above, the age pattern of childbearing among the Chinese farm population conforms to the typical age structure of fertility among couples that are *not* employing parity-related restriction of fertility. However, "fertility not affected by parity-related limitation varies a great deal in level because of such health-related factors as reduced sexual activity in populations subject to chronic fevers, high rates of miscarriage for anemic women, and sterility caused by venereal disease or tuberculosis. It is also reduced by periodic separation of spouses associated with seasonal migration, or by periods spent away from home by fishermen, herdsmen, or hunters." [2]

Another important factor is breastfeeding. Nursing delays the resumption of ovulation and hence the next conception. The duration of amenorrhea varies from three or four months when the baby is not breastfed to 18 months in Bangladesh and Indonesia, where breastfeeding is prolonged. The most extended interbirth intervals (almost four years on the average) reliably recorded in the absence of contraception occur among the !Kung tribesmen in Southwest Africa. Intensive observation of a number of !Kung mothers shows that nursing not only continues until the child is more than three years old, but also is very frequent (on average every 15 minutes). [3] Taboos on sexual intercourse may also intervene. Many societies forbid sexual relations for a nursing mother. The period of prescribed postpartum abstinence sometimes extends beyond the period of nursing, particularly in West Africa.

There is a theme running through much of Wolf's paper to the effect that fertility is associated negatively with poverty and positively with level of living. For example, he argues that one might expect somewhat higher fertility in Kiang-yiu than in China as a whole because it was located in one of the richest areas of the country. As a general proposition, I think the assumption of a close association between level of living and fertility is erroneous. At one time Rose Frisch made a persuasive case that undernourishment leads to amenorrhea and prolonged interbirth intervals. Subsequent investigations of the period of amenorrhea in Bangladesh and Guatemala bring this contention into serious doubt. The difference in the period of postpartum amenorrhea between well-nourished and poorly nourished women in Guatemala is slight, and the relation in Bangladesh between various indices of malnourishment and the duration of postpartum amenorrhea is also a very weak one. Clearly, if there is actual starvation, menstruation ceases and fertility is greatly reduced, but long-lasting malnutrition above the level of starvation seems to have very little effect.

Interpretation of the Moderate Fertility Found in the Reassessment

The assertion that early and universal marriage led to or was associated with lower marital fertility is based on a rather complicated argument. The statement does *not* mean that in traditional societies in which marriage was early some form of contraception or abortion was followed, or that couples in these societies wanted to have fewer children. Rather, the argument is that if early marriage were combined with very high fertility, the resultant very high overall fertility would lead to very rapid population growth, were it not for the fact that rapid growth is not possible in a traditional society over a long period and that high fertility must therefore be associated with high mortality.

In an essay composed for inclusion in the Proceedings of a conference on the European Fertility Project that was held in Princeton in 1979,[4] I proposed a general explanation of why fertility is only moderately high in preindustrial populations. The argument is as follows:

The high birth rates that according to Notestein were an inevitable feature of preindustrial societies were not nearly as high as can be imagined by picturing a situation in which separate high fertility characteristics reliably recorded in different populations are combined in one population. The highest reliably recorded rates of childbearing by married women are found among twentieth-century Hutterites (an Anabaptist sect settled in the north central part of the United States, adhering to a religious prohibition of contraception or abortion), and the French Canadian population of the seventeenth century. Age of marriage was not very early in these two populations. Early marriage and high proportions currently married at potentially fertile ages *are* found, on the other hand, in many Asian and African populations. If the high marital fertility of the Hutterites were combined with the high proportions married of rural China, the total fertility rate would be over 10. No population has ever been observed to have a total fertility rate close to 10. The level of fertility actually achieved by . . . preindustrial populations . . . is only 40 to 60 percent of what might be possible.

Although very high fertility can be imagined and could in principle be achieved, it would not be advantageous to the welfare or even to the survival of preindustrial populations. Facing the constraints of limited technology and territory, a population with a total fertility rate of 8 to 10 would increase at annual rates of more than 1 percent, if its expectation of life at birth were over 20 years; in no more than a few centuries, overcrowding would drive its growth rate back to zero as expectation of life at birth fell to 13 to 17 years, at which point only 20 to 25 percent of women would survive to the mean age of childbearing. The long-run combination of very high fertility and very high mortality is not a combination that best fits a society to cope with adversity or rival groups. A population would have more resilience and vitality if its fertility and mortality were only moderately high. Optimal fertility in preindustrial populations, it may be suggested, would be no higher than is consistent with zero growth at the greatest average duration of life that can be achieved in the given culture and environment. Maintenance of the lowest achievable mortality is easier if fertility responds in a homeostatic fashion to increases or decreases in the population; i.e., if fertility falls when the population overfills its habitat, and rises when the population is decimated, but maintains a modest average level.

The statement that traditional societies developed customs that promoted high fertility or faced extinction should therefore be amended to say that traditional societies developed customs that kept fertility at *moderate* levels, avoiding both fertility so low that negative growth would make the population shrink to zero, or so high that positive growth would lead to an overcrowded habitat, and hence to higher mortality and greater vulnerability to catastrophe or rival groups.[5]

The advantages of moderate fertility in a different context with some analogous features are known to biologists. The reproductive strategy that confers genetic advantages on animal species sometimes requires moderate rather than very high fertility. Evolutionary theorists postulate two polar strategies that are optimal for contrasting categories of animal life. Species of small body size, short life span, and short intergenerational intervals, with a limited area of foraging and a highly variable habitat, survive successfully through a capacity for very rapid multiplication when their habitat is sparsely populated; species of large body size, long life span, and long intergenerational intervals, with an extensive area of foraging and a stable habitat, persist successfully with limited reproduction that maintains a population of stable size, permits adequate care for a modest number of young during their long period of maturation, and avoids surpassing the capacity of the niche.[6] . . . The genetically governed reproductive strategy that is advantageous for large, slowly maturing organisms in a stable habitat has as its analog nongenetically governed reproductive strategies of human societies. In both instances, it is a moderate rate of reproduction rather than a very rapid rate that is advantageous. Moderate reproduction is attained among larger mammals and birds by various genetically programmed restrictions on fertility, and in human populations by various social customs or practices.[7]

Conclusion

In sum, the estimates of the level and age pattern of fertility for the Chinese farm population are virtually identical with the fertility data recorded in the registers for Hai-shan, and little different from the retrospective fertility based on the recollections of older women interviewed by Wolf. Fertility estimates independently derived from the age distribution and the mortality estimated for young children are also very nearly the same as the estimates based on corrected numbers of births for the year before the survey.

How anomalous are these low rates? They are perfectly consistent with the long-run slow increase that one necessarily associates with the population of traditional China, given the quite high estimated mortality rates (an average duration of life of only 24 years, and an infant mortality rate of 300 deaths under one year per 1,000 live births).

If estimates of fertility were higher, still higher mortality would be implied. The only possibility of higher fertility (given the consistency of the estimates derived from corrected births for the previous year and from the age distribution) is that dead children might have been underreported, and also omitted from the reports of children ever born as well. Had there been such omissions, the estimates of child mortality would be too low, as would the correction to the reported number of births the previous year. An infant death rate of 0.300 and an expectation of life at birth of only 24.2 years stipulate a very stiff regime of mortality. If we imagine 35 percent instead of 30 percent of babies dying before their first birthday, and imagine that the underreported 5 percent of dead children are also omitted from the reported number of children ever born, the estimated total fertility would be increased from 5.50 to 5.78. It may be that such a slightly higher figure is correct, but I see no compelling reasons for assuming that mortality was even higher than the very high levels already estimated.

NINE

Family and Fertility in Four Tokugawa Villages

Susan B. Hanley

The Japanese today are often perceived as a people who act within a very narrow set of norms, who weigh public consensus very heavily in making decisions, and who fit, perhaps better than most groups, the economist's ideal of the rational actor. If one considers the behavior of the Japanese in the eighteenth and nineteenth centuries as reflected in demography, one also finds the Japanese family constrained within narrow limits by powerful social and economic forces. It is the purpose of this paper to analyze what these norms and patterns were during the second half of the Tokugawa period and to suggest what forces may have led the Japanese to act as they did.

As in early modern Europe,[1] the family in premodern Japan was more than a social and kinship unit; it formed the basic legal and economic unit in society as well. This unit, called the *ie* in Japanese, has no direct equivalent in English, although it is most often translated as household; depending on the context, however, it may also be translated as family or even, as used by the aristocracy, house. R. J. Smith defines the Japanese ie as follows: "The household was conceived to be a corporate body, and its members were expected to sacrifice personal desires and accept all major decisions of the household head. The headship passed to one child, in principle the eldest son of the incumbent, to whom both authority and property were transferred."[2]

The household in Tokugawa Japan, not the individual, was the basic legal unit in society, in most cases the basic economic unit, and for all practical purposes, the basic social unit. The head had not only legal authority over all the members, but legal responsibility for them as well. Should a member of the family defy the head's wishes, he could be expelled from the family and disinherited, and, if living in a village, forced to leave the community, thus losing the only form of social security that existed in Tokugawa Japan.

From the late sixteenth century on, the basic economic unit in rural Japan was the family farm. To maximize taxes, the government fostered the growth of independent farmers who held sufficient land to form an economically viable unit. Official policies toward this end included prohibiting the formation of branch families—i.e., division of the family's landholdings—unless there was sufficient capital or land to meet government regulations.[3] But farmers were themselves reluctant to divide up their land. Three to five *tan* (.75 to 1.25 acres) seems to have been the amount of land a nuclear family could work without using hired labor, thus making this size of landholding optimum, that is, providing the highest return for a family's labor. According to a model of farm economics for a village in the domain of Okayama, the area that is the focus of this chapter, a family of five with two adult males, or a family of three comprising a man, his wife, and child, would fare at least as well as a leading family with large landholdings farmed by hired labor.[4]

Furthermore, it can be argued that the household's status (*kakaku*) provided an important incentive for limiting dependents. Each family wanted to maximize per capita income in order to maintain its standard of living and its social rank. Although status was not solely a reflection of economic position, it was almost always tied to power, which was at least partly economic. Not only did status determine who held village offices, it even determined who sat where at the village's annual meetings. On the negative side, a poor family that had to presume on others because it could not meet its share of the tax burden or could not feed itself before harvest could not live comfortably in a small, closed society in which charity or welfare came only from relatives, neighbors, or village leaders.[5]

Thus, on the one hand, people had to have children to provide labor for their farm, to care for them in their old age, and to carry on their line of descent. On the other hand, they had to make the family fit its resources. A large number of children on a small farm was almost as disastrous as no children at all. And even for well-to-do farmers with sufficient land to establish a branch headed by a younger son, to divide the family resources was to weaken the ie as an economic and social unit and to divest it of at least some of its economic and political clout, particularly vis-à-vis up-and-coming neighbors. In sum, the Japanese family was extraordinarily "conservative": it wanted to perpetuate itself and preserve its relation to its own resources.

In this paper I will examine data from four farming villages dealing with population changes, with family size and composition, and with demographic behavior that affected the ie: fertility and attempts to control it, marriage, adoption, and other means of regulating family membership. My purpose is to determine what the priorities of Japanese families were, how they acted to realize them, and what effect outside stimuli, such as changes in the economy or natural disasters, had upon them. From a broader perspective, we would like to find out how the Japanese resembled or differed from their Chinese neighbors, with whom they had much in common culturally, and from their Western European counterparts, with whom they later shared industrialization.

The Four Sample Villages

The data for this analysis come from the *shūmon-aratame-chō*, household registers, used in the other studies on Japan in this volume, from four villages in west central Japan. The most detailed analysis will be of Fujito in Okayama, the village for which we have the best records and the most information on social and economic conditions. Wherever possible comparable data will be provided for two other villages in the same domain of Okayama and for a village in the Mikawa region.

While the registers for these villages were devised and used for the same purposes as those studied by Hayami, Sasaki, T. C. Smith, and R. J. Smith, they appear to contain more information than those extant for other areas and may be more reliable. A major difference between the registers for Okayama and many of those extant for other domains is that births were included in Okayama, certainly for those children who survived to their first New Year. Thus it is possible to obtain birth dates with considerable accuracy, and fertility estimates can be considered at least as reliable as those obtained for any other area in premodern Japan.

Although the methods of registration were nearly the same for all three Okayama villages, their population growth rates and patterns varied tremendously (see Figure 9.1). The four villages studied are as follows:

1. *Fujito*, a farming village that seemingly had economic problems in the late eighteenth century but a growing economy in the nineteenth. It was located in the southernmost district of Okayama on a major route from the castle town (the domain's administrative center), to Shimotsui, a major port on the Inland Sea. The village became involved in the cotton industry, and in the nineteenth century the weaving of cotton cloth formed an important secondary source of employment in the village. Also, the arable land in the village was increased by about 20 percent in the early nineteenth century through reclamation. Data are available for this village for 42 of the years between 1775 and 1863. In this period the population of the village grew, though not steadily, from just under 600 persons to slightly over 700.

2. *Fukiage*, a fishing village on the Inland Sea that grew rapidly in the eighteenth century as its neighbor, Shimotsui, became a port on the shipping circuit from western Japan to Ōsaka. Thirty-one registers, scattered

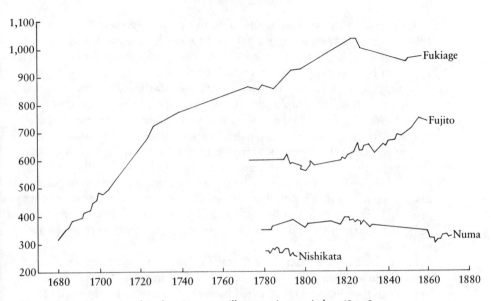

Fig. 9.1. Population growth in four Japanese villages, various periods, 1680-1870

throughout the two centuries from 1683 to 1869, still exist for this village. During this period the population of Fukiage tripled, increasing from 308 in 1685 to 932 in 1860.

3. *Numa*, a landlocked farming village that showed a nearly stable total population of slightly over 300 from 1780 to 1871, a century during which data exist for 33 years. Although it was located in the plains area on the road to the castle town, Numa did not have the opportunities for economic expansion of either Fujito or Fukiage.

4. *Nishikata*, a farming village adjacent to Mikawa Bay off the Pacific coast and next to a post station on the Tokaido, the most traveled road in Japan. Records exist for this village for the crucial famine years of the 1780's, and although they cover only 15 years, they are continuous from 1782 to 1796. Nishikata's population dropped during this period from 271 to 248, around 9 percent.

Since our focus is on the village of Fujito, let us first examine in more detail the changes that occurred in this village during the 90-some years for which there are data. The year 1775, the first for which we have records, had not only the largest amount of both in- and out-migration of any year, but also the largest amount of hired labor used within the village; 43 people came into the village to work, who, combined with people who worked in households other than their own, produced a total of 50 hired laborers within the village; at the same time, 27 people went outside the village to work. Then there is a gap in the records of several decades, but an analysis of the 1794 records indicates that the Temmei famine of the 1780's did not negatively affect Fujito's birth rate.

During the first period for which there are nearly continuous records, 1794-1810, the demographic data evoke a village in which economic conditions were harsh: the villagers were clearly trying to minimize population growth by postponing marriage for many young people and sending out more brides than were brought in. Emigration was high, particularly among men in the peak working ages. Most who left did so illegally. The cause of the economic stress such behavior indicates was not famine or disease; indeed, the death rate was lower in these years than in many other periods. The population of the village fell by some 10 percent during these years, although this was due to out-migration rather than a negative natural increase.

In contrast, by the 1820's, the next period for which we have population records, the economy was on the upswing. The amount of arable land belonging to the village was increased by perhaps 20 percent, through reclamation, and commerce and home industry developed at an accelerated rate. This was the only period in which younger brothers were allowed to marry, and the increased number of marriages resulted in a higher birth rate, which would have created an even greater increase in population than occurred had an epidemic not struck village children in 1832. By the late 1830's the Tempō famine was taking a visible toll on the population, although the population lost in this health crisis was less than that lost in the economic crisis at the turn of the century.

Despite the crop failures and epidemics of the 1830's and 1840's, the village economy experienced substantial development, bringing with it a new prosperity. Along with increases in the arable land in the village came an increase in the average size of landholdings, and these developments were paralleled by an increase in commercial activities. The leading family in the village, the Hikasa, was instrumental in developing shipping, fertilizer production, and cotton dyeing, and most villagers became involved in the cotton industry. By 1837, 20 percent of the cultivated land in Fujito was planted in cotton, and by 1842 the village had an average of one loom per household, with some households working as many as three. In the 1840's, weaving became the primary income source for many families; largely untaxed, it could be more profitable than farming.

With heightened prosperity came a sharp drop in emigration and a jump in the standard of living. Not surprisingly, net migration for employment stood at zero just after the Tempō famine, but both in- and out-migration remained low in the 1840's, with a net immigration of only four or five persons per year. This increased only slightly in the 1850's, with net immigration for employment usually between five and eight persons per year through 1863. The demand for labor within Fujito made it unnecessary for villagers to leave their homes, much less the village, to find employment, and the similar situation in neighboring villages made attracting labor from other villages difficult.

As early as 1823, village headmen in the district were complaining that the prevalence of secondary employment made it difficult for them to obtain hired farm labor, but the government of Okayama refused to ban such activities because of the increased income they brought to farm households. Only in the Tempō period did it try to limit the number of looms to one per household, and this was because officials feared the weaving industry might draw too many workers from farming, upon which the tax system rested.

Prosperity was reflected in the kind and number of consumer goods offered for sale in the village. In the seventeenth century, the major market in each domain was the castle town, and villagers relied on peddlers for their necessities. By the mid-eighteenth century, not only had towns developed in the countryside, but the peddlers carried an increasing variety of goods, and village shops gradually opened on a part- or full-time basis, depending on demand. In the early nineteenth century, an Okayama villager could purchase from a village shop a wide variety of daily necessities, including both farm tools and food staples, and also luxury goods such as funeral requisites: cakes, tea, tobacco, etc. After the mid-nineteenth century, villagers could buy perfume, cosmetics, and incense, and the richer among them were importing linen from Echigo, medicine from Etchū and Toyama, expensive furniture from Nōtō, and sugar from southern Japan.[6]

Although the specific economic conditions differed in the other three villages examined in this study, they reflected the same general economic and social trends. Fukiage, located just to the Inland Sea side of Fujito, grew rapidly in the eighteenth century as part of a booming port economy. Numa, while in the southern half of Okayama, and thus in the half enjoying accelerated economic growth, had fewer opportunities for growth within the village, a fact reflected in a stagnant population during the nineteenth century and negative migration rates from 1800 on. We have less information about Nishikata than the other villages, but the fifteen years for which there are data are significant; beginning just before the Temmei famine and continuing for half a decade after its end, they provide a good sample of population changes during a major mortality crisis. But despite the differences in geographic situation, in period covered by the extant data, and in economic trends, the major demographic indices for all four of these villages present startling similarities, as we will see in the next section.

An Analysis of the Quantitative Records

In this section we will first examine the demographic data as they pertain to changes in family size and composition over time. We will look at household size over time, family type, and the composition of families in terms of the members' relation to the head. Next, we will investigate possible reasons for the types and sizes of households in these villages, including both those factors over which the villagers had little control, primarily death rates, and those over which they exercised considerable control: age at marriage, number of married women of childbearing age per household, adoption, and limitations on the number of children born or raised.

The data from all four villages show a remarkably consistent trend in the number of households in each village over time. Given the difficulties and expense involved in erecting dwellings, one would not expect to find sharp fluctuations from year to year, but the consistency in the number of households transcends periods of economic difficulties, famine, and even growth and prosperity. Tables 9.1 and 9.2 present data on total population, number of households, and average household size for the four villages.[7]

Just as the number of households in each village tended to remain constant over time, so did the average number of people in each household, falling in most villages very slightly over the course of the eighteenth century and the first half of the nineteenth. Average household size varied by village, but the averages for each period are all within the same narrow range, undoubtedly a result of the small sample sizes. By the mid-nineteenth century, the averages ranged from a low of 3.7 for Fukiage to 5.5 for Fujito.

In Fujito, despite the growth of the population and economic changes in the village, the average household size was remarkably stable from the 1770's through the 1860's, with an average of just over five persons for the entire period. In Fukiage, the average household size rose from 5 in the 1680's to 7 by 1712, and then showed a steady decline for the remainder of the Tokugawa period, falling from just over 5 in the 1730's to just over 4 from the 1770's through the 1820's, and to 3.6 from 1854 to 1869. Average household size in Numa fell gradually but steadily from 5.8 in 1780 to just over 5 in the early 1830's. From 1860 to 1871 it dropped from 4.8 to 4.3. Nishikata's stood at just over 4 through the 1780's and then dropped to 3.7 by 1796.

The standard deviation was large for all the villages, so to show the range of family size, I have drawn up a frequency table of households by family size for Fujito (Table 9.3). The mean and mode of family size were close in value throughout most of the period. In 1775, 43 percent of the

TABLE 9.1
Population and Average Household Size in Fujito, 1775-1863

Year	Population	Number of households	Average household size	Standard deviation
1775	596	110	5.418	5.545
1794	600	111	5.405	5.708
1797	605	111	5.450	5.801
1798	585	110	5.318	5.628
1799	585	110	5.318	5.632
1800	580	110	5.273	5.608
1801	576	109	5.284	5.574
1802	570	109	5.229	5.558
1803	560	109	5.138	5.539
1804	560	109	5.138	5.487
1805	559	111	5.036	5.375
1806	555	111	5.000	5.370
1808	567	111	5.108	5.444
1809	577	112	5.152	5.476
1810	566	111	5.099	5.439
1825	586	112	5.232	5.703
1826	591	112	5.277	5.784
1827	590	113	5.221	5.755
1828	600	113	5.310	5.843
1829	608	114	5.333	5.722
1830	619	115	5.383	5.757
1831	637	118	5.398	5.741
1832	650	118	5.508	5.876
1833	619	118	5.246	5.642
1834	622	118	5.271	5.661
1835	636	118	5.390	5.818
1837	640	119	5.378	5.838
1841	614	119	5.160	5.580
1844	637	118	5.398	5.741
1845	628	118	5.322	5.581
1846	642	120	5.350	5.567
1847	645	120	5.375	5.584
1848	649	122	5.320	5.470
1850	669	123	5.439	5.580
1852	664	125	5.312	5.349
1856	679	126	5.389	5.541
1857	685	126	5.437	5.593
1859	716	128	5.594	5.756
1861	714	130	5.492	5.657
1863	706	132	5.348	5.551

TABLE 9.2

Population and Average Household Size in Nishikata, Numa, and Fukiage for Selected Years, 1683-1871

Year	Population	Number of households	Average household size	Standard deviation
Nishikata				
1782	295	70	4.214	4.597
1787	310	72	4.306	4.684
1792	295	73	4.041	4.475
1796	268	72	3.722	4.108
Numa				
1780	337	58	5.810	6.300
1803	350	61	5.738	6.356
1814	376	66	5.697	6.172
1825	381	68	5.603	6.069
1832	356	68	5.235	5.588
1860	330	69	4.783	5.247
1871	315	73	4.315	4.491
Fukiage				
1683	308	65	4.738	4.707
1694	421	73	5.767	6.044
1706	494	81	6.099	6.567
1712	547	77	7.104	7.642
1727	678	129	5.256	5.225
1741	763	140	5.450	5.498
1773	827	190	4.353	4.353
1791	724	171	4.234	4.268
1801	896	210	4.267	4.270
1821	1,011	240	4.212	4.301
1860	932	255	3.655	3.705

families in Fujito had either five or six members (exclusive of servants), and while there was a greater spread in family size in later years, the mode was either 5 or 6 for most years until 1856, when it changed to 4—the figure at which it remained through 1863. In all years there were more families with four persons or fewer than with seven or more.

Large families were not common. In most years there were no more than 15 families in Fujito with more than eight members, though the inclusion of servants would make a few additional households exceed this size. On the other hand, there was a surprising number of one- and two-person households. The peak in the number of one-person households came during 1800-1810, when there was an average of 12 such households per year. From 1845 on, the number of very small households declined, so that by the late 1850's there were only two one-person households. Thus, in the late Tokugawa years when the average number of persons per household was falling, there was also a decrease in very small households, which created a more leptokurtic distribution.

TABLE 9.3

Frequency Table of Households Headed by Males (Females) by Size of Family in Fujito for Selected Years, 1775-1847

Number in family	1775	1794	1808	1825	1833	1841	1847
1	5 (1)	4 (2)	10 (1)	4	4 (4)	5 (5)	1 (3)
2	3 (1)	8	5	12 (1)	8 (1)	9 (2)	4 (3)
3	9	12	10 (1)	14	13	15	14 (1)
4	9 (1)	11	16	14	17	10 (1)	14 (1)
5	23	18	14	20	15	23	23
6	22	13	18	11	21	17	19 (1)
7	10	15	13	10	7	9	11
8	7	8	6	9	5	6	5
9	5	3	4	4	9	4	5
10	3	6	4	6	6	3	3
11	5	1	3	1	1	1	5
12	2	4	2	2	2	3	4
13	1	1	0	0	0	2 (1)	1
14	0	1	0	0	1	0	1
15	0	0	1	0	0	0	0
16	2	1	0	1	0	1	0
17	0	0	0	1	1	1	0
18	0	0	1	0	1	0	0
19	0	1	0	1	0	0	0

Although the number of one- and two-person households in the early nineteenth century is larger than expected, it is not hard to explain. First, averages cloak individual differences. Second, houses and house lots were hard to obtain, and most villages show an almost constant number of houses over time, even when there were extreme fluctuations in population. Given that the stem family was the most prevalent type, it was likely that many families would be reduced to just one or two members at some point in the life cycle. During periods of economic stress, most people were in no position to increase family size through marriage or adoption, as is evidenced in the large number of one- and two-member families in both 1808 and 1841. But the relative prosperity and population growth of the late Tokugawa period led to more households that could support at least three members.

In Fujito, the size of each household tended to remain constant over time. The relatively constant mean in household size over the nine decades for which there are data was due in large part to the small fluctuation around the mean in the number of family members per household. In short, a family in which the modal or mean number was 4 tended to return to this number whenever membership either exceeded or fell below 4. The same constancy was true for families of every size.

TABLE 9.4
Coefficient of Variation for Changes in Family Size over Time by Household in Fujito, 1775 - 1863

Household	Mean	S.D.	Coef. of variation	Household	Mean	S.D.	Coef. of variation	Household	Mean	S.D.	Coef. of variation
1	5.36	0.99	.185	30	5.00	1.29	.258	59	6.09	2.35	.386
2	9.19	2.96	.322	31	7.20	2.05	.285	60	12.50	0.88	.070
3	4.58	1.07	.234	32	5.48	2.00	.365	61	5.53	2.69	.487
4	5.30	1.40	.264	33	4.69	1.17	.249	62	7.66	2.49	.325
5	5.58	1.77	.317	34	4.29	1.45	.338	63	6.72	2.97	.442
6	4.46	1.51	.337	35	3.57	1.75	.490	64	3.86	2.44	.633
7	5.67	1.12	.198	36	2.86	2.47	.864	65	3.15	0.76	.241
8	9.05	1.84	.203	37	6.36	1.72	.271	66	5.73	1.55	.271
9	4.83	2.06	.427	38	4.79	2.05	.428	67	4.05	1.36	.336
10	6.73	1.30	.193	39	5.91	2.03	.344	68	5.70	0.95	.167
11	5.86	1.02	.174	40	6.57	1.64	.249	69	5.23	1.17	.224
12	4.39	0.62	.141	41	1.07	3.91	.366	70	5.73	1.88	.328
13	5.56	1.47	.264	42	8.26	4.03	.488	71	2.93	1.19	.407
14	5.07	0.94	.185	43	7.81	1.79	.229	72	7.38	2.78	.377
15	7.22	3.09	.428	44	5.36	1.62	.302	73	4.18	1.14	.273
16	3.63	1.83	.504	45	4.27	1.59	.373	74	4.97	0.31	.062
17	7.65	2.34	.306	46	8.69	2.54	.292	75	4.03	1.27	.316
18	6.67	2.57	.385	47	4.56	1.36	.298	76	6.03	1.59	.264
19	7.12	0.87	.122	48	7.00	1.65	.236	77	5.27	2.03	.385
20	5.62	1.23	.219	49	7.84	2.44	.311	78	7.05	1.97	.279
21	7.12	3.30	.464	50	5.46	1.66	.304	79	4.13	1.42	.344
22	5.26	2.20	.418	51	16.76	2.49	.149	80	1.92	1.30	.677
23	7.62	3.31	.434	52	6.10	1.84	.302	81	7.08	2.79	.394
24	4.81	1.16	.241	53	6.01	1.91	.318	82	5.53	1.67	.302
25	7.73	2.29	.296	54	3.43	0.31	.090	83	2.37	1.20	.418
26	3.59	1.85	.515	55	3.61	1.21	.335	84	2.69	1.54	.572
27	3.93	2.88	.733	56	6.83	1.85	.271	85	3.56	1.71	.480
28	4.53	1.51	.333	57	11.67	1.57	.135	86	4.50	1.27	.282
29	7.55	2.91	.385	58	5.66	1.35	.239	87	4.51	1.41	.312

This tendency has been statistically tested by calculating the coefficient of variation for each household over time (see Table 9.4). Only those households that could be identified over several decades were used in the sample, which comprised 87 families identified from at least as early as 1825 and found in registers until the end of the period under observation. Of these families, 24 had a coefficient of variation of less than .25; 50 had a coefficient of variation of less than .33; and 80 had a coefficient less than .50. Thus, the annual variation in each family's size was small. I believe the reason for this constancy was that the fixed economic base of each household tended to change relatively little over time. Moreover, any changes were usually shared by other households, thus necessitating that each household maintain the same number of members—the optimum economically—in order to maintain its position within the village. That the fixed capital base in terms of land tended to remain constant is evident in Figure 9.2; of the 142 women in Cohort Groups G and H, only eight, from seven households, came from families that changed landholding class between 1851 and 1863.

The average-size household was small and grew even smaller over time because it comprised primarily members of an elementary or stem family. Table 9.5 shows that in Fujito nearly three-quarters of all households were limited to elementary or stem families. Calculations for the other three villages show the same results. Remarkably, in no village in any year for which records are extant do we find a single frereches or joint family (with household headship shared by two or more married brothers), and contrary to what one would expect in a premodern farming village, there were substantial numbers of solitary households. Only a small fraction of the families could be classified as grand in any of the villages except for Fukiage in the late seventeenth and early eighteenth centuries, its period of rapid growth. After the mid-eighteenth century, this type of family was unusual in all the villages and particularly rare in Nishikata.

The "unknown" category in Table 9.5 contains both households that could not be categorized and households that fell outside the categories used for the conference for which these papers were prepared. The major type of family omitted was composed of related persons who did not form an elementary family, primarily siblings living together. Also excluded are unrelated persons living together, which in these villages usually meant members of religious orders. As Table 9.5 shows, only a very small percentage of all households belonged in this category.

Clearly the vast majority of rural Japanese in central and western Japan lived in elementary or stem families for most of their lives (Table 9.6). The prevalence of the elementary family is particularly striking for Nishikata, where at least 49 percent of all families can be so classified in each of the

Description	Sample size
Cohort group:	
(A) Those married women who had reached age 39 (or 39 by 1778) but were no more than 55 by 1775.	34
(B) Women of childbearing age but less than 39 who appeared in the records only in 1775-78.	20
(C) Childbearing women aged 18-38 in 1775 (or 18 by 1778) who could be identified in the 1794 records.	34
(D) Married women aged 23-44 in 1794 and who were married prior to 1794 (but who did not appear in the 1775-78 records).	56
(E) Women whose marriages were contracted between 1794 and 1810. This group includes six women whose marriages were terminated prior to 1810.	51
(F) Married women aged 31-45 in 1825 who did not appear in records prior to that year.	42
(G) Women who were married between 1825 and 1841. Below, this cohort group has been further divided into five classes by the kokudaka size of the household in which each woman lived.	80
(H) Women who were married (or who bore children without recorded husbands) after 1841 but who reached age 44 or whose marriage had terminated by 1863. This cohort group, too, has been further subdivided into classes by the kokudaka size of her household.	62
(I) Women who were married or who bore children without recorded husbands after 1844 but who were still of childbearing age and married in 1863.	44

Kokudaka class:
- (I) Households with no recorded landholdings
- (II) Households holding land assessed at one koku or less
- (III) Households holding land assessed at 1-3 koku
- (IV) Households holding land assessed at 3-6 koku
- (V) The remaining households, consisting of the following groups:
  - (1) Households containing ten or more members for the entire period under observation
  - (2) Households holding land assessed at 6-10 koku
  - (3) Households holding land assessed at more than 10 koku (only the Hikasa and Hoshijima lines were in this category from 1825-1863, the period for which the classifications were made)
  - (4) Households that changed kokudaka classes from 1851 to 1863, most often switching between the 1-3 and 3-6 kokudaka classes.

Fig. 9.2. Cohort groups and kokudaka classes for Fujito, 1775-1863

years for which there are data, and where at least 48 percent of all persons lived in elementary families. And in this village, in every sample year, at least 10 percent of the families were classified as solitary. Despite the fact that this was a late-eighteenth-century farming village, in distribution of family type, it looks like a modern urban population.

Since most people lived in elementary or stem families, it follows that most were classified as members of the head's nuclear family, that is, as

TABLE 9.5

Relative Frequency of Households by Family Type in Fujito for Selected Years,
1775-1863

Year	Number of families	Family type				
		Solitary	Elementary	Stem	Grand	Unknown
1775	110	.05	.46	.31	.13	.05
1778	95	.05	.43	.32	.14	.06
1794	111	.05	.46	.32	.13	.05
1799	110	.10	.49	.25	.14	.02
1800	110	.11	.49	.25	.14	.01
1804	109	.12	.50	.21	.16	.02
1805	111	.12	.48	.21	.14	.05
1810	111	.08	.41	.31	.14	.06
1825	112	.04	.57	.21	.13	.05
1829	114	.04	.53	.25	.16	.04
1830	115	.03	.49	.26	.17	.05
1834	118	.06	.47	.27	.14	.05
1835	118	.06	.43	.28	.17	.06
1841	119	.08	.44	.26	.16	.06
1844	118	.08	.39	.30	.18	.06
1848	122	.02	.44	.28	.17	.08
1850	123	.02	.47	.29	.16	.06
1857	126	.02	.52	.27	.16	.03
1859	128	.02	.50	.26	.19	.04
1863	132	.02	.45	.27	.18	.08

TABLE 9.6

Relative Frequency of Persons by Family Type in Fujito for Selected Years,
1775-1863

Year	Number of persons	Family type				
		Solitary	Elementary	Stem	Grand	Unknown
1775	604	.01	.42	.33	.22	.02
1778	540	.01	.37	.36	.25	.02
1794	619	.01	.38	.36	.24	.01
1799	592	.02	.45	.28	.24	.01
1800	600	.02	.45	.28	.25	.00
1804	572	.02	.43	.26	.28	.01
1805	568	.02	.42	.27	.26	.03
1810	590	.02	.33	.38	.25	.03
1825	609	.01	.47	.25	.25	.02
1829	621	.01	.41	.28	.30	.01
1830	650	.00	.38	.30	.30	.02
1834	647	.01	.38	.33	.27	.02
1835	664	.01	.35	.30	.31	.02
1841	631	.02	.36	.30	.29	.02
1844	648	.01	.32	.32	.31	.03
1848	682	.00	.35	.30	.29	.05
1850	694	.00	.38	.31	.28	.03
1857	720	.00	.42	.32	.24	.02
1859	734	.00	.39	.31	.28	.02
1863	707	.00	.35	.33	.27	.04

TABLE 9.7
Percentage of Persons Classified as Elementary and Stem Family Members in Fujito for Selected Years, 1775-1863

Year	Percentage elementary	Percentage stem and elementary	Year	Percentage elementary	Percentage stem and elementary
1775	63.4%	77.1%	1837	58.6%	71.9%
1794	64.4	75.8	1841	61.5	76.9
1802	67.9	77.1	1844	60.5	75.0
1810	65.0	77.2	1848	63.9	75.6
1825	63.8	73.4	1856	65.4	78.8
1833	64.9	74.5	1863	63.0	77.6

NOTE: Elementary family members are here defined as household head (male or female), wife, son, and daughter. Stem family members include the preceding plus parents (of head), grandparents, grandchildren, son-in-law, daughter-in-law, and great-grandchildren.

head, wife, son, or daughter (see Tables 9.7 and 9.8). The percentage is even higher if persons in the nuclear families of the present, former, and future heads, that is, in the direct line of succession, are included. The percentage is highest for Nishikata, where nearly everyone lived in elementary families.[8]

Although I have calculated age distribution by family type and family transitions, creating pages of computer output, I have not included the results, primarily because they are very unenlightening. Since the predominant family types were the elementary and the stem, the transitions tend to be back and forth between these two types. The other types of transitions occurred only in very low frequencies in any period and are therefore not significant.

Such regularity in household size and composition for the four scattered villages in this sample over the span of several hundred years—not to mention other samples gathered for the same period—would lead us to believe that the Japanese were deliberately controlling family size and composition. What strategies could they adopt and within what parameters were they working?

First, the Japanese from these samples faced relatively low crude birth and death rates (Table 9.9). The mean death rate varied little by village. There was a larger range for birth rates, which reflected the economic conditions in each village in the periods for which data were calculated. Even if one argues that these rates are lower than they would be if infants who died before they were registered were included, the addition of these infants would not alter the natural increase rate for each village. Both Fujito and Fukiage had small net natural increases in population over time, and

TABLE 9.8

Categories of Kinsmen in Fujito for Selected Years, 1775-1863, in Declining Order of Frequency Seen in 1775
(Percent of total population)

Relationship	1775	1794	1810	1825	1835	1845	1863
Son	19.0%	19.5%	22.5%	16.8%	16.3%	16.6%	18.5%
Head	17.8	18.0	18.8	18.7	17.8	17.2	17.2
Daughter	14.6	14.7	12.9	14.8	14.8	14.2	14.4
Wife	11.4	11.8	10.9	13.1	12.8	12.1	11.5
Mother	6.4	6.2	5.8	5.3	4.3	4.8	2.6
Younger brother	4.7	4.7	5.3	5.3	3.9	4.5	3.0
Younger sister	2.9	2.2	2.1	2.0	2.5	2.2	1.9
Nephew (son of younger brother)	2.0	1.3	1.2	1.9	2.5	2.6	1.9
Grandson	1.9	1.2	1.6	1.2	1.7	2.4	4.2
Niece (daughter of younger brother)	1.7	1.5	1.6	1.0	1.3	1.3	1.6
Granddaughter	1.5	1.0	1.4	1.0	1.3	2.6	3.0
Son's wife	1.5	1.0	1.6	0.7	1.1	1.4	2.6
Younger brother's wife	1.5	1.3	0.9	1.5	1.3	1.4	0.9
Father	1.3	1.7	0.7	0.7	1.7	1.6	0.4
Cousin (son of uncle)	1.2	0.8	1.4	1.0	0.8	0.8	0.4
Older brother	0.8	1.7	0.4	1.2	1.0	0.6	0.6
Nephew (son of older brother)	0.7	1.7	0.7	1.7	2.1	1.4	0.1
Second cousin (male)	0.7	1.3	0.4	1.0	1.7	0.6	0.9
Older brother's wife	0.5	0.5	0.5	1.0	1.1	0.0	0.1
Older sister	0.3	0.8	1.2	0.3	0.3	0.5	0.7
Adopted son	0.2	0.8	0.4	2.2	0.8	0.8	0.3

NOTE: This list includes only those relationships held by at least 1 percent of the population for more than one year. The only major omission is that in 1863, 1.4 percent were female heads, 1.3 percent adopted brothers, and 1.0 percent yoshimuko (daughters' husbands who were adopted into the family).

TABLE 9.9

Crude Birth and Death Rate Averages for Four Japanese Villages
in Selected Periods, 1693-1871

Village and period[a]	No. of yrs. with available data	Crude birth rate average per thousand	Crude death rate average per thousand
Fujito			
1794-1799	4	20.2	20.5
1800-1804	5	15.4	16.8
1805-1810	5	22.3	17.0
1825-1829	5	25.2	20.5
1830-1834	5	33.1	29.0
1835-1841	3	23.3	25.8
1844-1848	5	28.5	21.6
1850-1857	4	28.6	26.4
1859-1863	3	18.3	19.2
1794-1863	39	24.2	21.8
Nishikata			
1782-1786	5	19.9	14.5
1787-1791	5	18.6	29.2
1792-1795	4	16.7	26.9
1782-1795	14	18.5	23.3
Fukiage			
1693-1700	5	31.0	15.9
1702-1712	5	26.3	21.1
1727-1741	3	31.9	30.8
1773-1781	3	25.4	24.6
1791-1801	3	26.0	20.3
1821-1826	3	18.4	19.4
1854-1860	3	19.4	22.2
1693-1860	25	26.0	21.5
Numa			
1785-1803	7	24.9	–
1814	1	23.9	–
1819-1832	13	19.3	22.8
1860-1871	10	15.7	16.6
1785-1871	31	19.6	20.1

SOURCE: S. B. Hanley, "Fertility, Mortality, and Life Expectancy in Pre-modern Japan," *Population Studies,* 28, 1 (1974), 131.
[a]The period average is the mean of the means.

Numa and Nishikata small net decreases, during the years for which there are data.

All evidence suggests that the Japanese achieved their relatively low birth rates through conscious population control, using methods that not only limited the number of children born, but limited the composition of

TABLE 9.10

Percentage of Population Composed of Wives of Persons Not in Main Line of
Descent for Four Japanese Villages in Selected Years, 1683-1871

Fujito		Fukiage		Numa		Nishikata	
Year	Percentage	Year	Percentage	Year	Percentage	Year	Percentage
1775	2.85%	1683	0.00%	1780	4.15%	1782	0.36%
1794	2.83	1702	3.77	1801	3.72	1789	0.00
1810	2.47	1730	1.82	1831	3.66	1796	0.00
1825	4.08	1773	0.96	1861	2.22		
1837	4.07	1801	0.88	1871	1.27		
1844	3.28	1821	1.19				
1863	2.28	1860	0.87				

NOTE: Percentages were obtained by dividing the number of wives other than those of the head or his father, son, or grandson by the total population of the village.

families to the stem type. First the Japanese controlled who could marry. Table 9.10 indicates that very few men were allowed to marry except those in the main line of descent. In Nishikata, it was virtually unheard of in the late eighteenth century for a man other than the head or his successor to marry and stay in the family. Many of the married persons in a household who were not in the stem family were relatives who joined the household long after they had married, such as a widowed sister-in-law with her children who had nowhere else to go. In a very few cases, a brother of the head was allowed to marry, but in these cases the head remained single, as witnessed by the fact that there was not a single frereches family in any of these samples.

Even more revealing of the control the Japanese exerted over their households is the percentage with women of childbearing age (Table 9.11). Whereas on the average each household had one woman of childbearing age, with the exception of Nishikata, the percentage of these who were wives and therefore subject to having children varied considerably by village and period. Only 52 percent of the households in Nishikata had married women of childbearing age just prior to the Temmei famine, and this percentage dropped by ten points during the famine years. The percentages in Numa dropped steadily over the course of the 90 years for which there are data. Both Fukiage and Fujito have percentages over 70, but only in two sample years, and these were both during periods of economic expansion—during Fukiage's development as a port and Fujito's period of land reclamation.

Table 9.12 reveals more clearly how the people in these four villages used marriage to regulate growth in the family, either by increasing adult

TABLE 9.11

Average Number of Households Containing Married Women of Childbearing Age in Four Japanese Villages in Selected Years, 1683-1871

Year	Number of households	Percentage of households with wives 15-44	Avg. no. of married women 15-44 per household
Fujito			
1775	110	56.4%	0.99
1794	111	66.7	1.12
1810	111	49.5	1.01
1825	112	71.4	1.13
1837	119	67.2	1.17
1844	118	63.6	1.14
1863	132	61.4	1.17
Fukiage			
1683	65	64.6	1.12
1702	78	76.9	1.36
1730	134	68.7	1.10
1773	190	54.2	0.96
1801	210	50.0	0.90
1821	240	51.7	0.94
1860	255	32.5	0.69
Numa			
1780	58	77.6	1.07
1801	63	71.4	1.16
1831	70	58.6	1.04
1861	69	44.9	0.87
1871	73	33.7	0.90
Nishikata			
1782	67	52.2	0.88
1796	68	42.6	0.71

membership or by incurring the risk of children. There were large fluctuations in the percentage of women in the most fertile age group who were married. In 13 of 21 years sampled from the four villages, the percentage of women aged 20-24 who were married was under 40. In fact, the fluctuations in the percentage of 20-24-year-old women married are more revealing of the actions affecting fertility in response to economic conditions than any other statistics compiled. While the total percentage of women aged 15-44 who were married hovered around 60 for the 21 sample years, the percentage in the 20-24 age group ranged from 14.3 to 81.8. And while the total percentage married was affected by the unintentional disruption of marriage through death, nearly all the unmarried women aged 20-24 had never been married.

TABLE 9.12

Percentage of Women Married by Age Group for Four Japanese Villages in Selected Years, 1683-1871

Age group	Fujito						
	1775	1794	1810	1825	1837	1844	1863
15-19	7.7	4.5	0.0	0.0	6.1	13.0	2.6
20-24	38.5	20.0	32.0	44.4	53.6	38.2	47.6
25-29	81.3	84.2	66.7	70.6	75.0	70.8	62.1
30-34	92.9	82.6	84.6	96.1	91.7	78.9	64.0
35-39	93.3	100.0	72.7	77.8	94.1	84.2	88.2
40-44	83.3	90.0	73.6	93.3	72.4	73.3	87.5
TOTAL	56.9	59.7	49.1	63.0	57.6	56.0	52.6
TOTAL NO. OF WOMEN	109	124	112	127	139	134	154

Age group	Fukiage						
	1683	1702	1730	1773	1801	1821	1860
15-19	26.3	0.0	7.1	3.2	6.3	9.8	5.9
20-24	37.5	21.0	50.0	38.9	21.9	34.1	45.5
25-29	100.0	92.3	72.0	71.4	57.1	70.3	43.8
30-34	71.4	81.8	83.3	75.6	75.6	76.3	53.8
35-39	60.0	76.0	88.5	74.1	86.1	75.0	75.0
40-44	90.0	70.0	84.2	84.6	85.7	79.3	61.5
TOTAL	57.5	56.6	62.2	56.6	55.3	55.0	47.2
TOTAL NO. OF WOMEN	73	106	148	182	190	225	176

Age group	Numa					Nishikata	
	1780	1801	1831	1861	1871	1782	1796
15-19	9.1	0.0	5.0	7.1	0.0	27.3	0.0
20-24	81.8	29.4	55.6	40.0	14.3	50.0	25.0
25-29	66.7	84.6	66.7	37.5	50.0	60.0	55.6
30-34	100.0	90.0	80.0	80.0	77.8	69.2	90.9
35-39	100.0	90.9	90.0	83.3	50.0	85.7	80.0
40-44	88.3	100.0	85.7	83.3	90.0	66.7	62.5
TOTAL	72.6	61.6	56.2	51.7	43.9	57.6	60.4
TOTAL NO. OF WOMEN	62	73	73	60	66	59	48

The two extremes of this range come from Numa, where nearly 82 percent of the 20-24 group and 73 percent of all women aged 15-44 were married in 1780. The total percentage married dropped through the following century, reaching 44 in 1871, when only 14.3 percent of the 20-24 year olds were married. Less than 30 percent of the 20-24 year olds were married in 1801, but nearly 56 percent were in 1831. Two factors can be seen at work here. First, the village seems to have been at its maximum population in the late eighteenth century and thereafter the total population in the village ceased to grow. To achieve this "zero population growth," the number of marriages permitted within the village had to be gradually reduced on a long-term basis, and hence the steady but gradual decline in the percentage of women married. But short-run economic conditions also affected marriages. There seems to have been a recession in the villages of Okayama around the turn of the nineteenth century, and persons who would otherwise have married either postponed marriage or remained single. In Fujito and Fukiage the percentage married of women aged 20-24 was also at a low at that time; the villages were in the 20-30 percent range around 1800. However, from the 1820's on, conditions improved, and more marriages were contracted. In the 1830's the percentage of 20-24-year-old women married rose to over 50 in Numa and Fujito, probably partly in response to the increase in secondary industries, which began to boom at this time.

Although the percentage of women who never married was higher than it is today, large numbers of Tokugawa women were not forced to remain single for life. The percentage of women aged 30-39 who were currently married was usually over 80. But having the highest proportions of women married in their thirties, when fewer children were born—witness the early age of last childbirth—and comparatively few in their early and mid-twenties obviously had the effect of reducing births considerably. The high average age at first marriage in Europe is well known as one of the most effective means of reducing fertility; it seems to have been equally effective in Japan. Again, this was not a custom introduced in the late Tokugawa period as a short-term measure for reducing births; in Fukiage in 1683 only 37.5 percent of the women aged 20-24 were married, but 100 percent of the women aged 25-29 were living with husbands.

Fluctuations in the age at marriage should reveal the same patterns as Tables 9.11 and 9.12. However, the average age at first marriage is not especially illuminating for two reasons. First, because of gaps in the data, it is difficult to filter out second and even third marriages. Second, it was customary to formally register a marriage only after it was clear that a bride could get along with her new family (i.e., with her mother-in-law) or she was pregnant and an heir assured. Thus the women's average age at marriage as seen in the registers nearly coincides with average age at first birth. The average age at first marriage as far as could be determined (with women over 30 excluded) was 23.3 in Fujito, 23.4 in Fukiage, 23.4 in Nishikata, 23.5 in Numa. Thus, average age at marriage was not only consistent, it was also high compared to standards prevailing in much of the world, though not in Europe. Even if one subtracts a year or more to account for the period between the religious ceremony, after which the bride and groom began living together, and the legal registration of the marriage, it is clear that there were very few teenage brides and that women did not begin bearing children until well past 20.

Tokugawa villagers not only regulated fertility by controlling who could marry when, but all evidence points to their controlling fertility within marriage as well. It was within the context of the broader social controls over population growth that individuals controlled their own fertility. To maintain their standard of living and status within the village, families had every reason to keep nonworking members to a minimum, in other words, to have as few children as possible. This was strongly reinforced by pressure to conform to the village's social norms. In some communities a family was mocked if it had more than three children, and it was considered inappropriate for a woman to bear and raise a child if she had been divorced, if she had a daughter or daughter-in-law living with her who was also bearing children, or if the family could not provide a suitable banquet to celebrate the birth of the child.[9] Thus, even if a woman wanted to have a large number of children, she was likely to be subject to pressure not to both from her own family and from the village at large. And if the pressure to conform was anything like what it is in modern Japan, it was very strong.[10]

The net result of these pressures was a very small number of children in the completed family, as can be seen in Tables 9.13 and 9.14. These averages, of course, are lowered by the exclusion of infants who died soon after birth, but nevertheless one does not expect to find the average number of children born to be three or less. Clearly these people were practicing some kind of birth control.

The practice of abortion and infanticide in Tokugawa Japan is now fairly well documented,[11] so I will only summarize the findings. First, the sex ratios of last-born children indicate that in Fujito parents preferred sons, and when their desired family size had been attained or nearly so, they "returned" unwanted girls when they were born. The data suggest that people in Fukiage and Nishikata were doing the same, but for these villages the samples are too small to assert this with confidence. Numa showed an excess of female births over male, but the number of children born was small, as in the other villages, and the best hypothesis is that people in Numa were practicing abortion (see Table 9.15).

The mothers' average ages at first and last birth (Table 9.16) reveal that women had a short span of childbearing. Even women who bore five or more children in Fujito on average bore their last child before they were 40. The mean length of childbearing for most cohorts in this village was only a decade. Given the large amount of quantitative evidence on abor-

TABLE 9.13

Distribution of Completed Family Size in Fujito
for Selected Cohort Groups of Families with Children

Cohort group and no. of children	No. of families by no. of children ever born	No. of families by no. of children who survived
Women aged 23-44 in 1794 (Cohort Group D)[a]		
0	–	1
1	5	9
2	8	10
3	16	10
4	15	17
5	5	4
6	3	4
7	2	0
8	1	0
Average	3.53	3.11
Women married 1825-1841 (Cohort Group G)		
0	–	3
1	11	15
2	4	13
3	17	21
4	19	16
5	15	6
6	8	2
7	2	0
8	0	
Average	3.72	2.76
Women married after 1841 (Cohort Group H)		
0	–	0
1	10	13
2	16	18
3	8	10
4	9	11
5	8	6
6	8	1
Average	3.22	2.69

[a]See Figure 9.2 for explanation of Cohort Groups.

tion and infanticide practices, measures to prevent these practices, reasons for them, and their extent, the best hypothesis to explain the mothers' low age at last birth and the small completed family size is that the Japanese were widely using such methods.

If families were limiting marriage within the household to the direct

TABLE 9.14

Distribution of Family Size in Fukiage and Numa
at Various Dates, 1773-1871

Village and no. of children	No. of families by no. of children ever born	No. of families by total no. of children at any one time
Fukiage, 1773-1801		
0	24	15
1	25	27
2	51	50
3	42	51
4	38	38
5	15	13
6	10	12
7	2	3
8	2	0
Average	2.73	2.82
Numa, 1814-1832		
0	7	4
1	7	9
2	15	18
3	14	15
4	16	14
5	4	5
6	2	0
Average	2.69	2.63
Numa, 1860-1871		
0	3	2
1	3	4
2	5	3
3	13	13
4	3	6
5	0	0
6	0	0
7	1	0
Average	2.89	2.61

heir, and if the heir and his wife were limiting the number of children they raised to an average of two or three, then many families must have found themselves without an heir. The Japanese solved this problem through adoption. Although there were a number of couples in Fukiage and Numa who bore no children, there were no families in either of these villages or in Fujito who raised no children. More common than the adoption of children was the adoption of young adults, either a husband for a daughter in a family with no sons, or a young man who would himself become the heir.

TABLE 9.15

Sex Ratios of Last-Born Children for Four Japanese Villages in Various Periods,
1693-1871

Village and cohort group	Sample size	Sex ratio (M/F)	Village and cohort group	Sample size	Sex ratio (M/F)
Fukiage, 1683-1730			Fujito		
I[a]	82	1.41	A	33	1.20
II[b]	104	1.36	B	18	2.60
Numa, 1814-1832			C	33	1.75
I	22	.83	D	54	1.45
II	40	.90	E	43	1.15
Numa, 1860-1871			F	38	1.00
I	10	.67	G	76	1.30
II	24	.85	H	60	1.70[c]
Nishikata, 1782-1796			Total for Fujito	355	1.40[c]
I	17	1.83			
II	30	1.50			

[a]Mothers who lived with their husbands to age 44.
[b]Mothers married to age 39 or whose marriages were ended prior to that age by the death of either spouse.
[c]Sex ratio is outside the 95 percent confidence interval.

That the household and continuation of the family as a social and economic unit were more important than the continuation of the blood line is evidenced by the statistics on adoption in premodern Japan. Adoption was common among samurai, but it was even more frequent among commoners. Of 105 families in Fujito for whom records exist for at least two generations, 56 families, or 53 percent, adopted sons or other relatives—e.g., brothers—for the purpose of continuing the family line. This is easily twice the rate of adoption found for the *hatamoto* class of samurai.[12] And this percentage is undoubtedly an underestimate because there was a tendency for the term "adopted" to be dropped from the records within a few years of the event, particularly when referring to a household head who had been an adopted son.

Adoption was so common that in Numa in the period 1860-71 there were more adoptions recorded than marriages. The incidence of adoption varied by village and period, but it was never rare. In many years the number of adoptions exceeded 50 percent of the number of marriages. Because most of those adopted were adult males and because of the practice of dropping the designation "adopted" after a few years, I did not attempt to compile rates of adoption or age at adoption and instead compiled figures on the incidence of adoption compared to marriage (Table 9.17).

In addition to assuring the continuation of family lines, adoption created an outlet for excess sons in a family already assured of an heir. The

TABLE 9.16

Average Ages at First and Last Births in Fujito by Cohort Group and
Kokudaka Class

	Average age at first and last birth by cohort group			
Cohort group	First birth	S.D.	Last birth	S.D.
A	–	–	36.0	4.9
B	21.5	2.8		
C	23.0	4.4	35.9	5.1
D	24.6	4.1	34.3	4.5
E	24.4	4.6		
F	26.5	4.2	36.6	4.4
G	22.8	3.0	33.1	6.0
H	23.1	4.8	31.8	6.5
I	22.3	3.6		
All	23.6	4.3	34.1	5.7

	Average age at first birth for women by kokudaka class for cohort groups G and H			
Kokudaka class	Group G	S.D.	Group H	S.D.
I	25.3	3.3	25.3	2.9
II	22.4	2.6	25.9	6.5
III	22.0	2.7	24.3	6.0
IV	22.4	2.9	21.2	2.9
V	23.2	2.8	21.5	4.0
All[a]	22.8	3.0	23.0	4.8

	Average age at last birth of women who bore five or more children		
Cohort group	Age	S.D.	Sample size
A	39.5	3.6	8
C	39.4	2.5	13
D	38.8	2.1	12
E	37.1	3.3	8
F	38.8	3.5	11
G	38.3	3.1	24
H	35.8	3.0	17
All[a]	38.1	3.3	93

[a]The total averages are weighted averages.

custom of adoption was so widely accepted that at least two families in
Fujito permitted their younger sons to leave home or be adopted, and,
when their own heirs subsequently died, took in adopted sons to succeed
the head rather than have their own children return. The importance of the
family name and the continuation of the line in Japan has long been stressed
by anthropologists, but a crucial difference between Japan and, for ex-

TABLE 9.17

Incidence of Adoption Compared to Marriage in Four Japanese Villages in Selected Periods, 1693-1871

Period	Number of adoptions			Number of marriages			Adoptions as percentage of marriages
	In	Out	Total	In	Out	Total	
			FUJITO				
1775-1810 (15)[a]	12	8	20	54	58	112	17.9%
1825-1841 (13)	24	23	47	54	44	98	48.0
1844-1863 (12)	31	24	55	51	41	92	59.8
			FUKIAGE				
1693-1741 (13)	11	7	18	56	40	96	18.8
1773-1860 (12)	71	45	116	65	54	119	97.5
			NUMA				
1780-1832 (22)	14	14	28	67	57	124	22.6
1860-1871 (10)	29	25	54	23	24	47	114.9
			NISHIKATA				
1782-1796 (15)	13	10	23	20	16	36	63.9

[a]Number of years during the period for which there are data.

ample, India, is that in Japan any male in the family, whether adopted or not, is eligible to become head, to carry on the family name and business, and to say prayers and care for the tablets of deceased family members.[13]

The practice of adoption ensured families of continuity and thereby gave a certain stability to the village, but it was not itself rigid. Adoption was no more irrevocable than marriage. An adopted son was theoretically to leave his own family behind and become part of the new family just as a bride did, but in reality people returned home when the arrangement proved unsatisfactory. Thus in Nishikata in the 15 years under survey, there were 13 adoptions into Nishikata families and 10 out, for a total of 23 (compared to 36 marriages), but during the same period 16 persons who had been adopted out returned home. Adoption seems to have been somewhat more successful in Fujito, where it increased over time. In the 15 years for which there are records before 1810, 12 persons were adopted out and 8 in. In contrast, from 1825 to 1863, in the 25 years for which there are records, 57 people were adopted in and 47 out, with the average number of adoptions per year double that of the earlier period. Only one person came back from an unsuccessful adoption in the first period, six in the second. The largest number of adoptions took place in the 1840's and 1850's, just after the Tempō famine and ensuing epidemics.

Fertility in Relation to Landholding Class in Fujito

If land was the primary fixed asset in Fujito, we should expect to find differences in the number of children born and raised according to the size of the family's landholding. For Fujito it is possible to examine fertility among women grouped according to the size of their household's landholding. *Nengumai toritate sanyō-chō*, or Records for the Collection of the Rice Tax, are available for six scattered years during the nineteenth century.[14] These records provide a breakdown in *koku* produced of the landholdings of individual families within the village (one koku equals approximately five bushels). Because the population records exist for every year from 1825 to 1835 and nearly every other year after that until 1863, women from these registers were divided into two cohort groups and then further subdivided into five *kokudaka* classes. (See Figure 9.2 for a complete description of these.) Cohort Group G consists of women who were married between 1825 and 1841, while Group H comprises women who were married or who bore children without recorded husbands after 1841 but who reached age 44, or whose marriages had terminated, prior to 1863. The kokudaka classes range from no landholdings (Class I) to three to six koku (Class IV) and a miscellaneous category for large landholders, those who switched classes, etc. (Class V).

In Table 9.18, we find for Cohort Group G that the average number of children in the completed family for each kokudaka class is within .2 percent of the mean for the entire Cohort Group, which was 3.5. In Cohort Group H, however, Class III, comprising women from households holding land assessed from one to three koku, had an average of only 2.6 children; Class V, including women from the largest landholding household and households containing ten or more members, had an average of 4.2 children, though the mean for the entire Cohort Group was still 3.4. Looking at Table 9.19, we see that the average age at first birth was just over 22 for Cohort Group G as a whole and close to it for most of the classes within it, with the exception of women who came from families holding no land at all, who on the average married at 25. For Cohort Group H, the average age at marriage tended to fall as the amount of land held by the bride's family rose. Thus women from families with larger fixed assets married at just over 21, whereas those from families with very little or no land married at over 25.

If we turn to sex ratios of children born to these two Cohort Groups (Table 9.19), we find that only for women married between 1825 and 1841

TABLE 9.18

Average Number of Children in the Completed Family in Fujito by Cohort Group and Kokudaka Class

Cohort group	Number of children	Kokudaka class	Number of children	
			Cohort group G	Cohort group H
A	3.5	I	3.6	3.3
C	4.0	II	3.5	2.9
D	3.6	III	3.5	2.6
E	2.9	IV	3.7	3.5
F	3.5	V	3.4	4.2
G	3.5	TOTAL[a]	3.5	3.4
H	3.4			

[a]The total averages are weighted averages.

TABLE 9.19

Sex Ratios of Children Born in Fujito by Cohort Group and Kokudaka Class of Mother

Cohort group		Sample size	Sex ratio (M/F)
A		139	1.28
B		45	.96
C		137	1.36
D		203	1.26
E		132	1.23
F		132	1.00
G	I	25	.56
	II	39	.77
	III	52	1.00
	IV	100	2.23[a]
	V	57	1.04
Total for G		273	1.21
H	I	23	.92
	II	23	.92
	III	29	1.07
	IV	73	1.35
	V	46	1.42
Total for H		194	1.20
I		81	1.38
Total for all groups		1,336	1.24[a]

[a]Sex ratio is outside the 95 percent confidence interval.

into families with one to three koku of land (G, IV) is the sex ratio of all children so distorted, at 2.23 (sample of 100), as to point conclusively to sex-selective infanticide. But if we look at the sex ratios of last-born children (Table 9.15), we can say with 95 percent confidence that the sex ratio of 1.7 for Cohort Group H does not come from the natural universe, in

TABLE 9.20
Incidence of Infant and Child Mortality in Fujito by Kokudaka Class

Kokudaka class	Number of children	Number who died at age 10 or less	Percentage who died at age 10 or less
For children born to women married 1825-1841 (Cohort Group G):			
I	25	10	40%
II	39	7	18
III	52	18	35
IV	8	3	38
V 1)	110	23	23
2)	26	5	19
3)	10	1	10
4)	13	3	23
TOTAL	283	70	25%
For children born to women married after 1841 (Cohort Group H):			
I	23	2	9%
II	23	2	9
III	29	4	14
IV	17	3	18
V	101	21	21
TOTAL	193	32	17%

which the sex ratio is near unity. The sex ratio of last-born for Group G is 1.3, a figure which we cannot statistically reject as abnormal but which is suspiciously high. Thus it seems highly likely that these two Cohort Groups and no doubt others were practicing "postpartum birth control" to some extent.

Families may have used a third method for reducing family size in addition to abortion and infanticide—intentional or inadvertent neglect of undesired children, which might show up in differential infant and child mortality figures (see Table 9.20). For Cohort Group G, 25 percent of the children registered died before the age of 10, in part because of the epidemic of 1832. The percentages of children dying before 10 vary by kokudaka class, reaching 40 percent among landless families, but even this figure can be assumed to be within the same universe as the total, using a 95 percent confidence interval. The percentages are lower for Cohort Group H (a total of 17 percent), but if anything the death rates rose with size of landholding. We cannot conclude from these percentages, however, that any one group faced statistically higher infant and child mortality rates than the others.

Two conclusions can be drawn from the foregoing comparison of fertility by landholding class: First, despite slight variations, such as the age at marriage of women married after 1841, it is difficult to discern major class differences in fertility in Fujito. This lends credence to the idea that Japa-

226 SUSAN B. HANLEY

nese across the board limited their families, and that they raised only wanted families. Making the decision whether to raise a child before or immediately following birth is less economically and socially wasteful than limiting families through neglect of children already being raised.

Second, the actions of families to maintain optimum family size over time no matter whether the family was large or small, combined with the fact that fertility control did not vary significantly by landholding class, suggest that in many cases the fixed capital base of land may not have been the determining economic factor in optimum family size. One would expect to find this situation only in a society in which land was not the only or most important asset. Thus families with no land but thriving businesses would find it profitable to maintain large families to assure themselves of a ready supply of labor in a labor-short economy, whereas a family with modal holdings and few possibilities of secondary employment might find it necessary to limit children to two in order to maintain or improve their standard of living.

Demographic behavior witnessed in the shūmon-aratame-chō indicates that the small fluctuation in family size over time was not coincidental. Families were almost certainly limiting the number of children they raised, but they also tried not to fall below a certain optimum size, a size determined by the conditions within each household. For example, in the same year that a family lost an adult member, it would replace this member with another adult of the same sex. This was frequently accomplished by taking in a bride for a son in the same year that an adult daughter married out of the family. Adoption was a common means of reducing the size of some families and increasing the size of others. Adoption also served as a welfare measure, which is most apparent in the years following the Tempō famine, when adoptions of people of all ages, even elderly women, were common.

Given the low death rates of Fujito, most families had to limit the number of members in order to maintain a stable size. Not only poorer families dependent on limited amounts of land had incentives to limit family size; so did the rich. Large landowners had sufficient land to permit the establishment of branch families by younger sons, but to do so would dissipate their wealth. Thus we find that although the large landowners in Fujito tended to marry younger than did the average villager, they had on the average no more children. The number of these families is too small to make any statistics compiled on them significant, but still it is striking that there was not a single large family among them.

Conclusion

Based on the demographic data from four villages, all evidence points to the conclusion that the Japanese were attempting, successfully, to control the size of their communities and their families. In most cases they were trying to limit growth, but at times they acted to increase the size of their families or villages. In either case they were striving for the optimum number of members for the financial resources and economic opportunities available. The methods used included adoption; limitations on who could marry; regulating the age at first marriage, especially for women; and almost certainly abortion and infanticide. Through a relatively late age at marriage and short span of childbearing for women, marital fertility was reduced to about three children who lived long enough to be registered.

I believe that much of this low growth rate should be attributed to the multi-faceted role of the family in the society and economy of the later Tokugawa period. The family in question should not be defined as a group of persons closely related by blood who shared a dwelling, but rather as a corporate body whose status and perpetuation as a body was more important than any one of its members, including the head. Although ideally the ie comprised the blood descendants of the founder, the ability of each successor to maintain the corporate body and if possible increase its wealth and status was of such overriding importance that, whenever necessary, a successor was selected on the basis of ability rather than birth order. Just as the absence of a suitable successor was a threat to the future of the line, so were too many potential successors, who during the years they were growing up would be a drain on the family's resources while eventually contributing little to the family's success since they would somehow have to be provided for, in most cases in another business or location.

In terms of their demographic behavior, the Tokugawa villagers were not concerned with perpetuating the blood line as much as with perpetuating the household or ie, and it is this focus that I believe made the crucial difference between the growth rate of Japan's population in the eighteenth and nineteenth centuries and that of other nations in a comparable stage of economic growth. Families not only responded to their own economic situation and goals, they were extremely responsive to economic conditions in the community and region. Thus we see the tendency for each household to remain constant in size over time, owing to the difficulties of substantially changing a family's economic base within a short period. On the other hand, while women were made to postpone marriage in times of economic difficulty, they were not forced to remain single throughout life. For men marriage was limited to the heir except when there was economic development that seemed likely to be long-term or permanent, such as the addition of substantial amounts of reclaimed land to the village arable, the large-scale demand for port facilities, or secondary employment.

Whereas the Chinese perceived a large number of children as potentially contributing to a family's wealth, the behavior of the Japanese reflected

not their ideals, but their assessment of economic realities. They were constrained from behaving as if their own family was all that mattered by
strong, concerted pressure from their fellow villagers and by the domain
government. Like the Japanese today, those of Tokugawa times seem to
have been constrained to follow widely shared norms and to act within
very narrow limits. All this had the result of controlling population in an
already very populous nation and of fostering economic growth and maxi-
mizing per capita income in a country of limited natural resources and in a
period of insignificant foreign trade.

TEN

Fertility and Mortality in an Outcaste Village in Japan, 1750-1869

Dana Morris and Thomas C. Smith

About ten kilometers from the medieval city of Sakai and just east of the port of Kishiwada on Ōsaka Bay lies Minami Ōji.[1] Today it is part of the city of Izumi. In the Tokugawa period it was a village in its own right, all of whose inhabitants belonged to the *eta* class, the outcastes of Tokugawa society. Minami Ōji nonetheless kept an annual population register like other Japanese villages after 1721, and a sufficiently long series of these registers survives to make possible estimates of vital rates for the community. This is a possibility of some general interest. We know of no other outcaste village for which population data of comparable length and breadth survive; and of the many social distinctions in Tokugawa Japan, those between outcastes and the rest of the population were among the most severe. One therefore might expect to find behavior in Minami Ōji rather different from that in the handful of Tokugawa communities so far studied.[2]

All communities so far studied fall roughly in the region between Lake Suwa on the north and Okayama on the south, on the Pacific coast side of Honshū. On the whole, by comparison with Western European parishes in preindustrial times, these communities show moderate fertility, moderate mortality, and a mean age at first marriage roughly midway between the late marriage characteristic of Western Europe and the early marriage found in much of the rest of the world. On general grounds one may doubt that this pattern approached universality. Diversity rather than uniformity marks the population patterns of preindustrial England and France, and ecological conditions in Japan were strikingly different from one region to another. Population in fact declined in the northeast, increased in the southwest, and changed remarkably little in the central region, where local studies have so far been concentrated. The most direct and obvious way to test the variety of demographic behavior in Tokugawa Japan is to push investigation into unknown regions, but an equally effective way may be to

study communities socially and economically as different as possible from
those so far investigated.

Minami Ōji meets the difference test on two grounds. As an outcaste
village it was socially as deviant a community as we are likely to find; and
unlike the populations previously studied, its people earned their living
mainly by wage labor rather than agricultural employments. It turns out—
to anticipate our major findings—that the inhabitants of Minami Ōji also
married earlier, divorced more often, had more children at the same ages,
and died earlier than the people of the villages with which comparison is
possible. Before considering these findings and what they may mean, however, we must say something about the economy and overall population
movements of Minami Ōji, and comment on the reliability of its population registers.

The Village

The population of Minami Ōji approximately tripled between 1750 and
1869, a startling increase if our belief is well-founded that an outcaste village would have been among the poorest anywhere in the country. Nor
does anything we know about the economy of the village counter the impression of poverty. Between half and three-quarters of all households at
different dates were landless (mudaka), and those with land (hyakushō)
often held no more than a house site. In most years the largest holding in
the village was less than fifteen koku, the median under one koku (representing on average about 0.145 hectares in this village), and not all of this
land could be used for farming. One-quarter of the total was taken up with
house sites in 1753, when village population was still relatively small
(Okuda-ke monjo, 1 : 17). Scarcity of land led families to rent fields in non-
outcaste villages nearby. The neighboring village of Ōji, for example, with
nearly ten koku of land per household (7: 872-73), rented half its land to
residents of Minami Ōji. Altogether, Minami Ōji families tenanted in seven
neighboring villages about three times as much land as they held collectively at home (1: 44-45; 8: 483).

We do not know what crops were grown outside, but in the village the
main crop was rice in the summer and wheat in the winter until the early
eighteenth century, when cotton began to encroach on these crops. Cotton
was probably grown as a commercial crop, with raw cotton, yarn, and
cloth being sold in the local markets for which Izumi was famous. Thus
cottage industry may have provided some off-season employment for village families. If so, this work would have reached a peak in 1837, when 39
percent of paddy in Minami Ōji was planted to cotton; after that date, a
depression settled over the Kinai cotton industry and land planted to cotton in Minami Ōji declined by 1860 to a mere 5 percent of the total.

But neither farming nor handicrafts were the major source of income for the village. A document that appears to come from the 1830's attributes no more than 16 percent of income in Minami Ōji to farming, including tenant farming in other villages. Nearly all of the remainder was said to come from work by the day at wages (4: 601).[3] This included farm work, transport, work at local shrine festivals, and the cutting of bamboo on Mount Shinoda in the winter.

But at least in the eyes of other villages the chief nonagricultural occupation of Minami Ōji was the disposal of dead animals (chiefly horses and oxen) from nearly all of Izumi province (4: 479, 530, 588-90; 12: 399 ff). As outcastes, the villagers were legally charged with this duty by the Bakufu government. The village's response to challenges to this monopoly by other outcaste villages demonstrates how jealously it guarded the right, which therefore must have been profitable (4: 591-93). The documents do not disclose the sources of this profit, but villagers may have been paid a fee for each carcass they removed. In any case, we know that the hides were used to produce leather goods; and there is some evidence that at least on occasion villagers consumed the meat (4: 593).[4]

There are, then, reasons aside from the status of the inhabitants to believe that Minami Ōji was an extremely poor village, and it is not surprising to discover that the villagers were frequently in need of famine relief. During the third month of the terrible famine year of 1837, for example, 888 persons of a total population of 1,794 were listed as "destitute" and receiving relief (6: 602-6). By the fifth month the figure had reached 1,336 and included 66 percent of landholding and 78 percent of landless families (6: 653-55). There was another major famine in the winter of 1850-51, when the number of persons on relief reached 875 (6: 691-758). The 1860's saw a series of famines, with something of a record being reached in 1866 when the number of persons on relief rose to 1,585, representing 62 percent of all landholding and 87 percent of all landless families (7: 74-135).

Two other, rather ambiguous indications of poverty in Minami Ōji may be mentioned. There were frequent arrests of villagers, mostly for theft, but occasionally for acts of violence and general rowdiness. In 1832, for example, a total of 15 persons from the village were arrested for theft in eight separate incidents (5: 335-55). This was perhaps an unusually high number, but not unprecedented; indeed, it fell well below the level of the previous year, when 41 villagers, including all four village officials, were temporarily held in connection with a single incident.

The marked instability of the family is another possible indication of poverty. A glance at the register shows that many households contained unmarried members with children, mainly as a result of divorced daughters and sisters returning home with children. Indeed, 34 percent of 552 first marriages between 1830 and 1863 are known to have ended in divorce, and others whose outcomes are hidden from observation by the end of the record may have done so as well. During the years of record from 1830 to 1869 there were 410 divorces against 1,022 marriages. Three or four marriages was not a rare total for either sex, and a few people married as many as seven or eight times.

The Record

Population registers (*shūmon-aratame-chō*) survive for Minami Ōji for fifty-seven of the years from 1750 to 1870 (1: 47-925; 2: 1-1180; 3: 1-1107). They are typical of documents of this type, listing in the same month each year the inhabitants by household, age, sex, and relationship to the household head. Aside from certain awkward gaps in the series, the Minami Ōji registers have but one notable defect: only after 1829 are entries and exits between annual registrations listed by cause. Our calculations of mortality therefore are necessarily based on the period 1830-69 only.[5] Births, though not explicitly recorded before 1830, cause no problems, since children born to residents can be distinguished from other entries by age. Hence estimates of fertility cover the entire period of record.

Thirty-eight registers survive for the period 1750-1829, 18 from the period 1830-69.[6] With some important exceptions registers survive from alternate years only, an odd pattern with a simple explanation. There were two headmen in the village who made up the annual register in alternate years, and the surviving registers come overwhelmingly from one of the two series. The resulting alternate-year pattern is not invariable, however; there are a few multiple-year gaps and also, fortunately, several clusters of consecutive years of record as well.[7] The consecutive years permit us to test the reliability with which exits and entries are recorded in the period from 1830 on, when entries and exits are recorded by cause. Comparing one year to the next and identifying every person who appears in both records, we can determine how many people appear or disappear without explanation. As Table 10.1 shows, unexplained entries and exits in the years of comparison varied from a high of 1.7 percent of the registered population to a low of 0.4 percent.

Another test of the reliability of registration is the consistency of ages, which we have checked in two ways. Table 10.2 compares the ages of all persons in the record in 1869 either with their birthdates or (in the case of mudaka born before 1830) with their ages in 1830. Table 10.3 compares the ages of all hyakushō in 1830 with their birthdates. Both tables show that recorded ages were consistent to the year in over 60 percent of all cases, and consistent to within three years in 95 percent. Inconsistencies of more than three years were about equally distributed between too old and

TABLE 10.1
Unexplained Exits and Entries Between Years of Consecutive Registers in Minami Ōji, 1830-1837

Years compared	Popu-lation	Number of exits			Number of entries		
		Explained	Unex-plained	Pct. un-explained	Explained	Unex-plained	Pct. un-explained
1830/31	1,753	118	7	5.6%	87	0	0%
1831/32	1,722	195	18	8.5	161	5	3.0
1836/37	1,791	226	26	11.5	161	4	2.4
Average				8.7%			2.2%

TABLE 10.2
Discrepancies in Recorded Ages of Villagers Between 1830 and 1869

Discrepancy in 1869 register	Correct age in 1869 (standard age)						Total (≥20 only)
	7-19	20-29	30-39	40-49	50-59	≥60	
≥4 years too young	5	4	4	12	5	5	30
3 years too young	6	10	1	4	4	3	22
2 years too young	10	16	5	12	8	8	49
1 year too young	65	63	17	25	22	4	131
Correct age	492	301	146	139	89	50	725
1 year too old	34	32	24	27	16	14	113
2 years too old	8	10	5	9	6	3	33
3 years too old	4	5	2	2	6	4	19
≥4 years too old	2	7	3	5	4	5	24

TABLE 10.3
Discrepancies in Recorded Ages of Landholding Family Members in 1830

Discrepancy in 1830 register	Correct age in 1830 (standard age)						Total (≥20 only)
	7-19	20-29	30-39	40-49	50-59	≥60	
≥4 years too young	0	0	3	1	3	3	10
3 years too young	0	1	3	2	0	0	6
2 years too young	0	3	3	2	1	2	11
1 year too young	12	10	8	2	8	6	34
Correct age	227	83	61	41	15	21	221
1 year too old	17	6	13	7	2	6	34
2 years too old	4	0	3	0	1	0	4
3 years too old	1	3	3	1	2	0	9
≥4 years too old	1	0	0	1	1	3	5

too young. None of the recording errors revealed in this way affects our calculations since all have been corrected, but the exercise confirms our general impression of the record's reliability.

The Population of Minami Ōji

As Figure 10.1 shows, the population of Minami Ōji grew from just under 700 in 1750 to nearly 2,000 in 1869, and growth was remarkably steady. There was a faltering only in the last decade of record together with two earlier setbacks, the first from an epidemic in the early 1770's and the second from a food shortage in 1837-39. We can say very little about the demographic causes of the loss of population during the two declines. The first occurred before deaths were being recorded; the second centered on the year 1838, when deaths from the famine year of 1837 would have been recorded, and the annual register for that year is missing. How much of the decline during 1838 was attributable to mortality is uncertain; clearly not all, since the age pattern of disappearances strongly suggests some emigration.

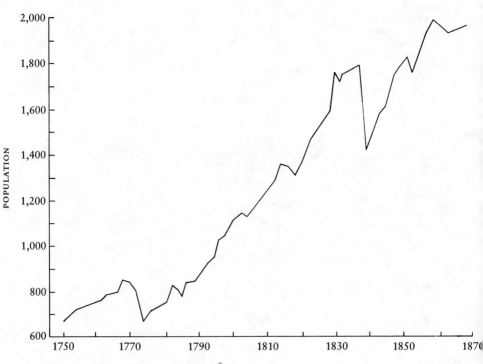

Fig. 10.1. The population of Minami Ōji, 1750-1870

With the exception of the gap between 1837 and 1839, the larger movements of population after 1830 seem to reflect clearly the movement of birth and death rates, as shown in Table 10.4 and Figure 10.2. The figure shows moving averages for five record years; and both rates are adjusted to take account of infants who died before registration, a problem of all registers of the type used here.

It is clear that much or all of the increase in population after 1830 was the result of the excess of births over deaths. Comparing Figures 10.1 and 10.2 for the period after 1830, we see that population growth ceased in the mid-1850's only when death and birth rates—the former falling, the latter rising—converged. In Table 10.5 we check the impression this gives that population growth was thus attributable overwhelmingly to natural increase. In each of four subperiods we subtract the rate of natural increase (b) from the rate of actual increase (a), and attribute the difference, plus or minus, to migration.

Over the whole period there was a slight net loss of population through emigration. Only in the final period, when birth and death rates were nearly in balance, did emigration have any sizable effect on overall population. In the three periods of rising population the rise came almost wholly from natural increase. This is not to say that there was little or no emigration in these periods, only that its net effect was negligible.

A possible error of estimation must be mentioned. Both birth and death rates were necessarily based on years of record, whereas the actual rate of population increase reflects the experience of all years. Hence the contribution of natural increase may be overestimated or underestimated, depending on birth and death rates during gap years. But we know of no reason to think these years were significantly different from years of record, with the exception of the gap year 1838, when most of the deaths resulting from the 1837 famine would have been recorded; for this reason the year 1838 has not been included in the calculations for Table 10.4. We can say with some confidence, therefore, that population between 1830 and 1837, and between 1839 and 1869, grew almost entirely through the excess of births over deaths. For the period before 1830, when deaths cannot be recovered, we can make no estimate of natural increase.

The explosive growth of the population of Minami Ōji is the more striking when we compare it with the movement of population in Izumi province, where Minami Ōji was located; in the Kinki region, of which Izumi was a part; and in the nation as a whole. The population of Izumi and of the Kinki region—both of which had a highly commercial, technically advanced, and remarkably productive agriculture—fluctuated gently but changed remarkably little between the first Tokugawa administrative census in 1721 and the last one in 1846; indeed, both the province and the

TABLE 10.4
Crude Birth-Rates, 1750-1869; and Crude Death Rates, 1830-1869,
for Minami Ōji

Year	Population	Crude birth rate	Year	Population	Crude birth rate	Crude death rate
1750	668	51.6	1812	1,289	42.5	
1752	683	28.4	1814	1,363	35.4	
1754	704	37.6	1816	1,355	24.6	
1762	761	43.9	1818	1,311	28.6	
1764	777	51.8	1820	1,378	52.1	
1766	795	43.8	1821	1,421	26.8	
1768	841	37.3	1822	1,466	33.0	
1770	835	47.1	1826	1,534	54.6	
1772	801	32.8	1828	1,585	45.2	
1774	672	11.1	1829	1,610	23.5	
1776	708	35.8	1830	1,753	81.5	24.4
1780	763	38.0	1831	1,722	39.1	40.9
1782	816	57.8	1832	1,757	48.7	38.5
1784	800	37.4	1836	1,791	30.6	15.2
1785	795	39.2	1837	1,794	40.5	33.2
1786	834	45.8	1839	1,424	21.6	27.2
1788	844	32.7	1841	1,495	55.3	32.8
1790	864	47.3	1843	1,578	59.4	23.2
1792	910	35.8	1845	1,629	50.7	43.1
1794	957	73.2	1847	1,736	71.4	37.0
1796	1,026	62.6	1849	1,792	54.0	33.8
1798	1,058	63.0	1851	1,813	42.6	33.6
1800	1,112	51.2	1853	1,755	40.7	37.4
1802	1,142	30.3	1857	1,930	49.1	24.9
1804	1,127	35.5	1859	1,990	40.8	34.6
1806	1,175	49.9	1863	1,931	35.8	46.4
1808	1,207	32.3	1865	1,940	48.5	26.8
1810	1,242	32.3	1869	1,961	31.7	35.3

TABLE 10.5

Rates of Natural and Actual Increase in the Population of Minami Ōji,
1829-1869

Period	(a) Rate of actual population increase	(b) Rate of natural population increase	Net migration effect (a) − (b)
1829-1837	+13.6	+15.4	−1.8
1839-1849	+23.3	+21.7	+1.6
1849-1859	+10.5	+9.4	+1.1
1859-1869	−1.4	+1.6	−3.0
1839-1869	+11.8	+12.0	−0.2

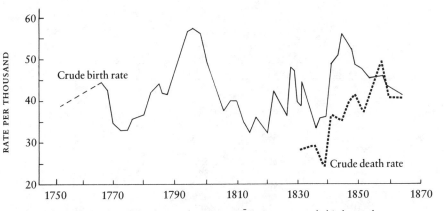

Fig. 10.2. Crude birth and death rates for Minami Ōji. Average crude birth rate from 1750 to 1754; then five-(record-)year moving averages from 1762 to 1869 for crude birth rates and from 1830 to 1869 for crude death rates; expressed in rates per 1,000.

region recorded a slight loss of population during the intervening century and a quarter.[8] Other provinces and regions were demographically more changeable, though most only moderately so, and increases and decreases tended to cancel out. Over the entire period the national population increased a bare 3 percent; at the corresponding annual rate of 0.03 percent it would require over two thousand years for the population to double.

Mortality

The heavy excess of births over deaths in Minami Ōji after 1830 was not because the death rate was particularly low. Indeed, the death rate was on the high side for Tokugawa Japan, running at over 35 per thousand in most years and often over 40. But the birth rate was considerably higher: over 45 in most years and around 50 in the decade after 1840. This is very high compared to other Tokugawa communities for which we have estimates, where rates below 35 and even 30 are usual. It is also rather surprising in view of Minami Ōji's famine relief record. Before attempting to comment further on fertility and mortality, however, let us essay age-specific estimates of both.

Table 10.6 reflects the mortality experience of the Minami Ōji population during the 18 years of record from 1830 to 1869. This life table exhibits the same pattern seen in the village of Nakahara: a high level of mortality in the middle years of life, which if graphed would give a curve with a flat or shallow appearance as compared to the Coale-Demeny Model West population at the same level of mortality.[9] This suggests that infectious and parasitic diseases were a more frequent cause of death in Minami Ōji than

TABLE 10.6

Minami Ōji Life Table, 1830-1869

	Survivors per thousand births		Life expectancy (in years)	
Standard age	Male	Female	Male	Female
1	1,000	1,000	37.1	38.4
5	836	811	40.1	42.9
10	758	731	38.9	42.4
15	738	709	34.9	38.6
20	699	680	31.7	35.2
25	661	642	28.5	32.1
30	606	592	25.8	29.6
35	536	543	23.8	27.0
40	489	492	20.9	24.6
45	439	439	18.0	22.2
50	373	408	15.8	18.8
55	319	364	13.0	15.7
60	264	325	10.2	12.3
65	201	276	7.6	9.1
70	113	189	6.6	7.1
75	60	107	5.3	5.6
80	30	41	3.1	5.8
85	3	27	3.0	2.5

NOTE: Tokugawa population registers did not enter births until average age 1; hence both the birth and death of infants dying before age 1 are lost. For a detailed discussion of Tokugawa registration and an effort to estimate mortality below age 1 for the village of Nakahara, see Thomas C. Smith, *Nakahara: Family Farms and Population in a Japanese Village, 1717-1830* (Stanford, Calif., 1977), pp. 15-31, 45-58.

in modern populations, and that the outcastes of Minami Ōji probably died from the same kind of diseases as the people of Nakahara. Also, as in Nakahara, women of all ages enjoyed an advantage in life expectancy over men, though the advantage was less marked, especially below age 5.

Readers familiar with Tokugawa population registers will recall that births were usually not recorded as they occurred, but at the first annual registration following the first New Year's after birth. On average nearly a year passed between birth and registration, and infants who died in the meantime went unregistered. This is why our life table begins at age 1 rather than 0. We can, however, complete the life table by estimating mortality between 0 and 1 as was done for Nakahara.[10] Since the level of mortality in Minami Ōji, though higher at the older ages, does not depart markedly from that of Nakahara until the middle years of life, we have used the rate of infant mortality estimated for Nakahara as a reasonable approximation for Minami Ōji as well. This estimate was that 20 percent of all children born died before age 1. On this basis we estimate life expectancy at birth in Minami Ōji at 30.6 years for males, 31.6 for females.

TABLE 10.7

Life Expectancy at Age 0 and Age 10 in Minami Ōji
and Selected European Parishes

Village	Life expectancy in years	
	At age 0	At age 10
Crulai, France, 1675-1775	30.3	37.6
Brittany and Anjou, France		
1740-1749	28.2	41.5
1750-1759	31.3	43.9
1760-1769	30.6	43.0
Tourouvre-au-Perche, France		
1670-1719	25.0	36.9
1720-1769	33.1	43.0
Colyton, England		
1538-1624	43.2	n.a.
1625-1699	36.9	n.a.
1700-1774	41.8	n.a.
Minami Ōji, 1830-1869	31.1	40.7

SOURCES: Étienne Gautier and Louis Henry, La Population de Crulai, paroisse normande: Étude historique (Paris, 1958), pp. 162, 190-91; Y. Blayo and Louis Henry, "Données démographiques sur la Bretagne et l'Anjou de 1740 à 1829," Annales de démographie historique (1967), p. 264; Hubert Charbonneau, Tourouvre-au-Perche au XVIIIᵉ siècle (Paris, 1956), p. 194; E. A. Wrigley, "Mortality in Preindustrial England: The Example of Colyton, Devon, over Three Centuries," Daedalus, 97 (1968): 558, 574. Figures are medians where high and low estimates are available.

TABLE 10.8

Life Expectancy at Age 1 in Selected Japanese Villages, 1711-1869

Village	Life expectancy in years	
	Male	Female
Minami Ōji, 1830-1869	37.1	38.4
Fujito, 1800-1810, 1825-1835	48.8	51.5
Iinuma, 1711-1781	41.8	39.7
Nakahara, 1717-1830	46.1	50.8
Nishijō, 1773-1800	34.6	34.4
Nishikata, 1782-1796	44.0	59.2
Yokouchi, 1726-1775	42.7	44.0

SOURCES: Susan B. Hanley, "Fertility, Mortality, and Life Expectancy in Premodern Japan," Population Studies 38:1 (1974), 139; Smith, Nakahara, p. 51; Akira Hayami, "Nōshu Nishijō mura no jinkō shiryo," in Kenkyū kiyō (Tokyo, 1972), p. 181; "Tōnō ichi sanson no jinkō tōkei," in Kenkyū kiyō (Tokyo, 1973), p. 204.
NOTE: Dates for all villages except Minami Ōji and Nakahara refer to birth cohorts. Figures for Fujito and Iinuma are unweighted averages of estimates by Hanley for five-year periods.

When we attempt to characterize the level of mortality shown in the life table, much depends on what is used for comparison. In Table 10.7 we compare life expectancy at ages 0 and 10 in Minami Ōji with a few seventeenth- and eighteenth-century French and English parishes for which we have estimates. Mortality in Minami Ōji appears to be at about the same level as in these communities, though it is notably higher (and life expectancy lower) than in Colyton, England, where mortality was exceptionally low. But in saying this we should keep in mind the possibility that we may have somewhat underestimated mortality in Minami Ōji in consequence of the gap year 1838, and possibly other gap years as well.

Table 10.8 compares Minami Ōji with other Japanese villages for which estimates of life expectancy at standard age 1 are available. In this context, mortality in Minami Ōji appears rather high. Only two villages, Nishijō and Iinuma, have as high or higher mortality. All others show a distinct advantage over Minami Ōji, ranging from 5.6 years for both sexes in Yokouchi to nine years for men and twelve years for women in Nakahara.

Fertility

The most important measure of fertility is marital fertility. There are few societies in which single women contribute significantly to overall fertility, and Minami Ōji does not seem to be one of these.[11] But several factors that affect the proportion of women married need also to be considered if we are to get a reasonably balanced picture of fertility. Before turning to marital fertility, we consider three of these factors briefly: age at marriage, divorce, and widowhood.

Marriage took place early for men and women of both classes in Minami Ōji. For the whole population over the period 1830-69, mean age at first marriage was 17.9 for women and 21.1 for men.[12] This is 1.7 years younger for women and 6.0 years younger for men than in Nakahara, which is about average in this respect for all Tokugawa villages known to us. Hyakushō tended to marry earlier than mudaka: 17.0 as against 18.3 for women, 20.4 as against 21.4 for men. The only significant change over time occurred after 1850 among mudaka, whose mean age at first marriage rose from 17.5 in 1830-49 to 19.3 in 1850-69 for women and from 20.7 to 22.0 for men. This rise, which may have been a response to the increasing pressure of numbers on resources, probably contributed significantly to the fall in the crude birth rate after 1849 (see Figure 10.2).

The effect of early marriage on fertility was offset to some extent by divorce and widowhood. Roughly 40 percent of all marriages ended in divorce in the period 1830-69, and death also took its toll. Women in the period were often widowed early and spent some years in this condition before remarrying or growing too old for childbearing. We have been un-

TABLE 10.9
Percentage of Women in Minami Ōji Currently Married at Selected Ages,
1830-1869

Period and	Age (standard age)						
class	20	25	30	35	40	45	50
1830-1849							
Hyakushō	52%	68%	76%	72%	75%	70%	62%
Mudaka	54	71	75	78	79	64	61
1850-1869							
Hyakushō	44	69	81	74	71	49	55
Mudaka	41	62	70	66	63	59	53
1830-1869							
Both	48	67	74	72	71	61	57

TABLE 10.10

Age-Specific Marital Fertility in Minami Ōji, *1746-1868*

Period and class	Age group (standard age)							Total fertility[a]
	15-19	20-24	25-29	30-34	35-39	40-44	45-49	
1746-1768								
Hyakushō	.573	.406	.358	.373	.296	.194	.052	8.4
Mudaka	.445	.502	.408	.343	.235	.159	.031	8.4
1769-1788								
Hyakushō	.484	.498	.299	.299	.316	.222	.000	8.2
Mudaka	.404	.444	.296	.273	.260	.074	.056	7.0
1789-1808								
Hyakushō	.371	.391	.394	.340	.340	.206	.019	8.5
Mudaka	.755	.545	.374	.364	.325	.228	.081	9.6
1809-1828								
Hyakushō	.320	.427	.380	.324	.212	.139	.063	7.7
Mudaka	.782	.440	.372	.309	.265	.104	.043	7.7
1829-1848								
Hyakushō	.453	.418	.386	.317	.262	.130	.055	7.8
Mudaka	.615	.513	.388	.348	.338	.177	.059	9.1
1849-1868								
Hyakushō	.436	.419	.374	.280	.261	.126	.024	7.4
Mudaka	.645	.403	.366	.312	.240	.187	.048	7.8
1746-1808								
Hyakushō	.451	.437	.354	.330	.320	.206	.023	8.4
Mudaka	.523	.499	.358	.332	.274	.164	.057	8.4
1809-1868								
Hyakushō	.407	.421	.380	.308	.248	.133	.048	7.7
Mudaka	.667	.456	.375	.324	.279	.160	.050	8.2
1746-1868								
Hyakushō	.420	.427	.367	.317	.274	.159	.037	7.9
Mudaka	.619	.471	.367	.327	.277	.161	.052	8.3
Both	.518	.459	.367	.323	.276	.160	.045	8.15

[a]Age 20-49 only. Derived from the age-specific marital fertility figures at left, this figure represents the average number of live children that would hypothetically be born to a woman married continuously from age 20 through age 49.

able to study these interruptions of marriage in the detail they deserve. But given the early age and near universality of marriage, the combined effects of divorce and widowhood may perhaps be seen in the declining proportion of women over 30 who were currently married. The proportion for hyakushō and mudaka together falls from 74 percent at age 30 to 57 percent at age 50 (see Table 10.9). The factors working to this end clearly constituted some restraint on fertility

Marriages in Minami Ōji were not only early but remarkably fertile Age-specific marital fertility by period and landholding is shown in Table 10.10. The estimates have been adjusted to take account of children who may be presumed to have died without registration between ages 0 and 1; this required inflating births at a rate of 20 percent. The most striking feature of the age-specific rates is, of course, that they were high, and we will return to this in a moment. But first it will be useful to note changes in fertility over time and differential fertility between the two classes.

Hyakushō fertility was relatively stable, though slowly declining, and the decline was largely responsible for the slight overall fall in fertility for the entire period. Mudaka fertility, if its movements here are not exaggerated by random fluctuations, was more volatile but showed no overall decline. Overall mudaka fertility exceeded hyakushō by some 5 percent, and during its peak periods the difference rose as high as 15 percent. One would not have predicted this. In other Tokugawa villages fertility appears

TABLE IO.II

Age-Specific Marital Fertility in Selected Japanese Communities During the Tokugawa Period

Place and period	Age group (standard age)							Total fertility, age 20-49
	15-19	20-24	25-29	30-34	35-39	40-44	45-49	
Yokouchi								
Before 1700	.204	.382	.358	.266	.264	.164	.028	7.3
1701-1750	.168	.275	.240	.232	.146	.071	.026	5.0
1751-1800	.188	.205	.226	.161	.116	.078	.101	4.0
After 1800	.306	.264	.231	.202	.092	.042	.011	4.2
Kandō-shinden								
After 1800	.471	.531	.351	.269	.225	.138	.016	7.7
Nishijo								
1773-1835	.321	.399	.356	.315	.251	.121	.032	7.4
Nakahara								
1717-1830	.214	.326	.304	.300	.221	.122	.034	6.5
Minami Ōji								
1829-1868	.542	.449	.377	.318	.276	.160	.048	8.1

SOURCES: Hayami, *Kinsei nōson*, p. 218; Akira Hayami, "Demographic Analysis of a Village in Tokugawa Japan," *Keiō Economic Studies* 5 (1968): 78; Hayami, "Jinkōgakuteki shihyō ni okeru kaisōkan no kakusa," in *Kenkyū kiyō* (Tokyo, 1973), p. 182; Smith, *Nakahara*, p. 60.

NOTE: Dates for places other than Nakahara and Minami Ōji refer to birth cohorts of mothers.

TABLE 10.12

Age-Specific Marital Fertility in Minami Ōji and Selected European Parishes

Place and period	Age group (standard age)							Total fertility, age 20-49
	15-19	20-24	25-29	30-34	35-39	40-44	45-49	
Colyton, England								
1647-1719	.500	.346	.395	.272	.182	.104	.020	6.6
1770-1837	.500	.441	.361	.347	.270	.152	.022	8.0
Crulai, France								
1674-1742	.320	.419	.429	.355	.292	.142	.010	8.2
Le Mesnil-Beau-mont, France								
1740-1799	.452	.524	.487	.422	.329	.135	.017	9.6
Thezels-St. Sernin, France								
1700-1792	.208	.393	.326	.297	.242	.067	.000	6.6
Meulan, France								
1660-1739	.585	.519	.507	.503	.379	.157	.014	10.4
1740-1789	.492	.493	.477	.403	.294	.111	.015	9.0
Anheusen, Germany								
1692-1799	n.a.	.472	.496	.450	.355	.173	.037	9.9
Minami Ōji								
1829-1868	.542	.449	.377	.318	.276	.160	.048	8.1

SOURCES: E. A. Wrigley, "Family Limitation in Preindustrial England," *Economic History Review* 19 (1966): 89; Gautier and Henry, *La population de Crulai*, p. 105; Ganiage, *Trois villages d'Ile-de-France au XVIIIe siècle* (Paris, 1963), p. 82; Valmary, *Familles paysannes au XVIIIe siècle en Bas-Quercy* (Paris, 1965), p. 120; Lachiver, *La population de Meulan* (Paris, 1969), p. 218; Knodel, "Two and a Half Centuries of Demographic History in a Bavarian Village," *Population Studies* 24:3 (1970).

to have been positively correlated with economic well-being; here the relationship is negative. Nevertheless, this pattern should occasion no great surprise, since we frequently see higher fertility among the poorer strata of the population in contemporary societies.

The same pattern appears when we compare Minami Ōji with other Tokugawa villages that were presumably better off (Table 10.11). Fertility was higher in Minami Ōji than in any of these communities, including Kandō-shinden, a village with expanding arable land and the highest marital fertility previously reported. This is not, incidentally, a reason in and of itself for questioning the reliability of the Minami Ōji data. Fertility was not dramatically higher than in Kandō-shinden; moreover, as Table 10.12 shows, it was not particularly high compared to the fertility of preindustrial European communities.

Conclusions

Do the estimates of birth and death rates from Minami Ōji throw light on the larger movements of Tokugawa population? Fortunately these

movements are not themselves in doubt. National population grew vig-
orously in the seventeenth century, changed scarcely at all between 1700
and 1850, and grew powerfully again thereafter; but how and why are
most uncertain.

Until recently it was the common view that these movements reflected
secular changes in the economy. In this view fertility remained consistently
high until well into the twentieth century, presumably at or near the physi-
ological maximum, while mortality fluctuated with variations in food supply and other necessities. Thus, it was held, mortality was unusually low
during the economic expansion of the seventeenth century following the
establishment of the Tokugawa regime, rose again when the economy
ceased to grow about 1700, and then declined in the mid-nineteenth century when the economy began to grow under the influence of international
trade and technological borrowing.

Two scholarly developments of the past fifteen years make this Malthu-
sian view seem less plausible. One is the emergence of a conviction among
many younger historians that during the eighteenth and nineteenth centuries the Japanese economy in fact expanded substantially. The other is
that scattered demographic soundings have consistently shown low to
moderate fertility and mortality during the eighteenth century. As a result,
population is now believed by some to have been held in check in the last
half of the Tokugawa period by a combination of unconscious and conscious controls over fertility. These, it has been argued, permitted a slow
growth in per capita income, which was useful and possibly crucial to later
industrialization.

Although evidence for this belief is somewhat stronger than for the earlier view, which was totally unsupported by age-specific rates, it is nevertheless remarkably fragile. As noted earlier, the handful of demographic
soundings so far taken leave the greater part of the country unrepresented;
and though no one doubts that some regional economies grew strikingly in
the latter half of the Tokugawa period, the significant overall growth of the
economy is a matter of considerable doubt.

The Minami Ōji estimates seem on the whole to strengthen the low fertility explanation of population stagnation, however the economy may
have been moving. Given the extreme poverty of Minami Ōji, the un-
healthy occupation of its inhabitants, and the location of the village in an
area of dense settlement on a major road south from Ōsaka, mortality is
not likely to have been much higher anywhere in the country—at least not
for any very large population over a period as long as two or three decades.
Yet mortality in Minami Ōji was far below the level of fertility. In the years
1829-69, when exits can be identified by cause, the crude death rate ran
24 percent less than the crude birth rate. Over the whole period 1758-

1869 the population of Minami Ōji approximately tripled, apparently with little or no aid from immigration. The failure of population to grow over the country as a whole, therefore, would seem to have been because fertility was considerably lower elsewhere, not because mortality was higher. Or to express the matter somewhat differently: if fertility had been as high elsewhere, an unlikely crude death rate of over 50 would have been required to offset it. And if fertility was indeed lower elsewhere, as we believe, the low rate is less likely to have been the result of lower fecundity than of tighter controls over reproduction.

On the other hand, in taking Minami Ōji to represent a kind of national maximum for mortality (and minimum for fecundity), we may exaggerate its poverty. We may have been mistaken in regarding the frequency and scope of famine relief as signs of chronic malnutrition. Instead they may signify an unusual degree of protection against food shortages that would have brought greater loss of life in other parts of the country. It is clear from the documents that the inhabitants of Minami Ōji ate meat, as non-outcaste populations presumably did not. We do not know how often or in what quantities meat appeared in their diet; nor do we know that non-outcastes abstained wholly from meat, since food shortages may well have overcome their dietary prejudices. Still, in some measure mortality and fecundity in Minami Ōji may have been favorably affected by peculiarities of diet or famine relief.

If they were not, we must return to the probability of differential controls over reproduction. These may well have stemmed from economic differences. The people of Minami Ōji lived mainly by wage labor, whereas the inhabitants of agricultural villages worked on family farms, and this difference may have affected nuptiality and marital fertility in several ways.

(1) Marriage in Nakahara (to use that village to stand for agricultural villages generally) was delayed by the necessity of waiting for the inheritance of a farm, or for parental consent based on the prospect of such inheritance. In Minami Ōji, judging from the early age of marriage for both sexes, marriage required no more than the ability to do an adult's work at one or more low-skill jobs. (2) In Minami Ōji a greater number of children in a family could earn their keep than in Nakahara, where labor demand was limited by farm size. (3) Additional children in farm families increased the pressure or the temptation to partition property and so carried a threat to the integrity of the production unit in a way not felt in nonfarm families. (4) Male children in Minami Ōji tended to marry and stay in the village, whereas in Nakahara second and third sons, who rarely inherited, tended to emigrate. Thus, parental security in old age varied with family size in Minami Ōji. In Nakahara it depended less on the number of children, or having children at all, than on the soundness of the farm to be

handed down. If only the farm were of sufficient size, the prospect of support in old age was good, whether or not there were children: an heir
could always be adopted and, if carefully selected, might be as reliable a
support as a natural heir. If there was little or no land, on the other hand,
children could not help much and might not even stay in the village.

If the fertility differential between Minami Ōji and Nakahara reflects
not a difference in fecundity but a difference in family strategy between
wage-earning and farming villages generally, it has important implications
for Japanese demographic history. It suggests that fertility in farming villages was held at far below biological potential; this would help account
for the stagnation of population during the later half of the Tokugawa period, when perhaps 75 percent of the population was engaged primarily in
farming and the area under cultivation was nearly static. It also suggests
that these restraints on fertility may have been released to some extent by
the growth of nonagricultural employment during the Meiji period. As industry developed, an increasing proportion of the population may have
moved away from the patterns of nuptiality and marital fertility characteristic of Nakahara and toward those characteristic of Minami Ōji. This
would have brought a sizable overall rise in fertility. Some part of the increase in population between about 1850 and the first census in 1920,
then, may have been generated in this way rather than by a fall in mortality. This has always been a theoretical possibility, of course, but the contrast between the Minami Ōji and Nakahara models lends concreteness to
the possibility.

ELEVEN

Transformations of Commoner Households in Tennōji-mura, 1757-1858

Robert J. Smith

From the mid-seventeenth century until 1868 the central government of Japan required that commoners be registered annually, usually in the third month of the year. Although the great majority of these records have been lost, those that survive contain a wealth of information of interest to the historical demographer. Kept by administrative unit, they are valuable above all for the serial nature of the data, which permits us to follow the transformations of a given household over time. There is no need to reconstitute families, nor is it difficult to trace a household through the years.

This paper represents a small part of the analysis of 36 annual registers for two wards (*machi*) of an administrative unit called Tennōji-mura that are scattered over the 102 years from 1757 through 1858. The registers take the form of books in which the individual members of each household are listed on either one or two pages, depending on the size of the residential unit.

Tennōji-mura

Although its official designation is that of village (*mura*), the place from which the registers come has for centuries been a satellite town of the great city of Ōsaka. There is little historical material on Tennōji in the Tokugawa period (1603-1868), but a great deal on earlier years and for the period after the Meiji Restoration of 1868.

Horikoshi and Kubo, the communities for which some registers survive, were two of the seven hamlets that in pre-Tokugawa times are usually referred to as belonging to Shitennōji, the temple complex established in A.D. 593 by Shōtoku Taishi. Sometime after 1684 the seven were merged into the administrative unit officially designated Tennōji-mura.[1] It is significant, however, that on the covers of the registry books Horikoshi and Kubo are identified as machi (wards or towns) rather than as *buraku* (hamlets), as one might expect if they were rural communities. During the Tokugawa

period, Tennōji-mura was assessed at 7,209 *koku*, of which 1,490 were
allocated to the temple itself and the remainder directly to the Bakufu,
which administered it through an official called *daikan*.[2]

Not until the early Meiji period do we have any information on the occupations of the residents of Tennōji-mura. In 1876, at the time of a revi-
sion of the land registers (*kaisei tambetsu*) and 18 years after the last register in our series, Tennōji-mura is defined as comprising an area 28 *chō* by
50 *chō* (the east-west and north-south dimensions, respectively). In round
numbers, the occupations of its 2,825 households are given as follows: agriculture (*nōgyō*), 800; artisanry (*shokkō*), 600; commerce (*shōgyō*), 900;
fishing (*gyogyō*), 25; miscellaneous (*zatsugyō*), 500.[3] Thus, about one-
third of the households are by this account engaged in agriculture and
fishing. The only clue to occupational differentiation at an earlier period is
the remark that sometime around the 1820's some struggling tenants (*ko-
sakunin*) opened *chaya*, small eating establishments, to serve the pilgrims
to the temple and those attending the periodic cattle market held in the
community.[4]

Tennōji-mura retained its administrative identity until very recently. It
was only in 1897 that about 300 chō of the northern part of the community were merged with Ōsaka's Minami-ku (ward), which is said to have
left only about 385 houses with a population of some 1,347. By 1925,
when the rest of the community was incorporated into Ōsaka, the population of Tennōji-mura, not otherwise defined, is estimated to have been
about 50,000.[5]

There is an earlier analysis of the Tennōji registers by Yōichirō Sasaki,[6]
whose author and I share the conviction that the place described in the
registers is essentially urban for the following reasons. The household heads
are designated as houseowners (*iemochi*) or tenants (*shakuya*), terms not
used in rural areas. Furthermore, whole families move in and out of the
place, and there are a large number of house-names (*yagō*), both indications of its urban character. And, of course, Tennōji lay on the edge of expanding Ōsaka.

Before proceeding to my own treatment of these materials, it will be
worth pausing a moment to summarize Sasaki's article, which will serve as
context for what follows. There are some minor discrepancies between our
sets of figures, but they are unlikely to have any serious effect on the comparability of our findings. For example, I have 5,214 occurrences, Sasaki
5,136. I record 1,730 *genin* (servants), Sasaki 1,752. My aggregate population is 20,377; his is 20,044.

The peak of population of Tennōji-mura's Horikoshi and Kubo wards
occurs in 1806. During the first half of the 102 years we are dealing with,
the population rises 69.3 percent, an annual average increase of 1.06 per-

cent. During the last 52 years, the population falls 40.3 percent, an average annual decrease of 0.87 percent. The change in population of Ōsaka itself is less dramatic; from a peak of about 420,000 in 1765, the number declines gradually to 330,000 in 1856. The population of Tennōji-mura exhibits one very dramatic jump of 14.7 percent between 1837 and 1838. One year earlier, the population of Ōsaka had risen 8.5 percent, its most drastic increase in this period.

Except for 1848, there are more males than females in Tennōji-mura, which Sasaki takes to be yet another indication of its urban character,[7] and sharp increases or decreases in total population are usually attributable to fluctuations in the number of genin. It is worth pointing out that their number is very small after 1844, and Sasaki asks whether this might not actually indicate that the place became more rural in character as the population of Ōsaka declined.

I have said that there is no information about the place of origin of people moving into Tennōji. The exception is the first register for 1757, which reveals the very narrow range of neighboring communities from which Tennōji's brides, grooms, and household servants came:[8]

Place of origin	Grooms	Brides	Male servants	Female servants	Total
Ōsaka	–	3	–	–	3
Tennōji	11	19	11	7	48
Settsu	–	6	5	2	13
Harima	–	1	18	13	32
Kawachi	1	2	1	–	4
Kii	–	–	3	3	6

Sasaki points out that there is no way to determine mortality rates; and that since there is no indication whether any given marriage (defined as the appearance of a wife in the register) is the husband's first, second, or third, it is impossible to determine age at marriage. He tries anyway, but for the five subperiods into which he divides the registers he comes up with the admittedly unlikely ages for males and females, respectively, of 37.3 and 28.5, 33.4 and 28.9, 31.0 and 27.3, 32.8 and 20.4, and 31.9 and 27.0.[9] He also has grave doubts about the fertility rates arrived at for the same periods of 18.5, 28.2, 28.6, 26.0, and 28.2—an average of 25.3. These figures are far too low because children who died between one register and the next are unrecorded, and because there is considerable doubt whether all children under the age of 5 were registered routinely.

We are both struck by the very high rate of residential mobility indicated. His five periods are 1757-67, 1784-98, 1802-17, 1831-50, and 1851-58, for which he finds net changes of individuals of 36.4, 41.3, 32.9,

30.9, and 27.4 percent, respectively. Furthermore, whole-family migration is very common, and it seems to increase as the period advances.

Some comment on the quality and character of the data is in order. These registers are disappointingly barren of background information on the individuals and the households listed. For the most part they give only the name (and occasionally what appears to be the occupation) of the household head, and the personal names and ages of the other residents and their relationships to the head. Date of death is given rarely, date of birth never. Occasionally an adoptive relationship is so identified, but usually only in the year of its establishment. In all other matters the registers are silent.

The examples that follow are representative. The first two appearances of a Horikoshi owner household, with a gap of two years, are as follows:

1757 Jirobei	38		1760 Jirobei	39	
Seibei	22	younger brother	Seibei	25	younger brother
Ichi	53	mother	Ichi	55	mother
Jōmatsu	13	servant (genin)	Sōshichi	21	servant (genin)

From the Kubo owner registers, here is a more complex household with a wider gap:

1806 Tōbei	45		1816 Tōbei	55	
Tōzō	25	son	Tōzō	35	son
Tsune	21	son's wife	Tsune	32	son's wife
Yuki	4	son's daughter	Yuki	14	son's daughter
Tōshichi	21	son	Seibei	22	servant (genin)
Toyokichi	21	servant (genin)	Yoshibei	26	servant (genin)
Tōkichi	19	servant (genin)	Kyūzō	16	servant (genin)
Yasu	16	servant (gejo)	Tōkichi	18	servant (genin)
Fuki	14	servant (gejo)	Genkichi	14	servant (genin)
			Yasu	18	servant (gejo)

These two examples suggest that there is a high degree of internal consistency, although occasionally the ages of the very young and very old go awry. There are a great many young children in these registers, and in this respect the Tennōji data appear to be more complete than those for many other parts of the country.[10]

In addition to an array of kin terms ranging from grandfather to cousin, there are a limited number of other categories of household resident. I cannot offer a satisfactory definition of them all, but the list in its entirety follows:

dōke: "co-resident"
inkyo: retiree (all of the very few cases of the appearance of these persons are in "religious" households—see below)

genin, genan, gejo: servant (in some years, *genin* is used for male servants, in others *genan*; *gejo* is invariably used for female servants)

"Religious terms"

so: priest (Buddhist)   *deshi*: disciple (Buddhist)

ama: nun (Buddhist)   *dōshinsha*: "co-believer"

The category *dōke* is the most complex of the lot. They may be unmarried persons of almost any age living with solitary heads of households or with either elementary or stem families. They never occur in households headed by religious persons. Occasionally there are dōke married couples, and more rarely whole families of dōke. These are found in all categories of family form, again excepting the religious ones. Curiously enough, dōke sometimes—although in only a handful of cases—actually become heads of households, either displacing the (usually married) head entirely or relegating him to another status in the family. In a few instances, persons listed as dōke in one register are listed in others as uncles, nephews, and the like.

The category of servant is less ambiguous. Male servants never change status in the household; female servants may, though the cases are few. Some women who are designated *gejo* throughout a series of registers for a given family (in all cases a conjugal family, form D in Fig. 11.1 below) are clearly the mothers of the small children of the head. Occasionally such a gejo eventually is entered as the wife of the head. In one startling case, a woman listed as the wife of the head for several years becomes a gejo for the remainder of the family's appearances; the children continue to be listed, and no other woman is brought in as wife.

I do not know what the term *dōshinsha* means. All of them are male, and the only clue to their identity may lie in the one case where a priest (*so*) in one year is designated dōshinsha thereafter. My guess is that they—and perhaps many of those called priests and nuns as well—are members of the laity who have adopted Buddhist names, rather like the *o-kyō-yomi* (sutra-readers) of the countryside who have no formal training but who do conduct Buddhist rites for a fee.

In any event, the population of all three categories is very small. Servants account for only 8.5 percent of the aggregate population of 20,377, dōke for 1.4 percent; and there are only 12 dōshinsha.

The registers that survive are from the following 36 years of the 102-year span:

```
1757 . . . .
1760 1761 1762 . . . . 1765 1766 1767 . . . .
1784 1785 . . . . 1788 . . . .
1795 . . . . 1797 1798 . . . .
1802 . . . . 1805 1806 . . . .
```

1816 1817
1831 .... 1834 .... 1837 1838 ....
1840 .... 1843 1844 .... 1847 1848 1849
1850 1851 1852 .... 1854 1855 1856 1858

They come from two wards of Tennōji, Horikoshi and Kubo, for each of which there are two registers: one for house-owners (*iemochi*) and one for tenants (*shakuya*).

I have done two things with these materials, and a word about the definitions used is in order here. First, I have taken every appearance of every household in every year as a unit of analysis and called it an "occurrence." By this reckoning there are 5,214 occurrences. I am aware of the statistical impropriety involved, for the occurrences are not truly independent units. Nevertheless, because so many of them are of such short duration and because there are so many gaps in the series, the procedure seems defensible.

Second, I have sorted the 5,214 occurrences of households into sequences; and where it can be established that a given household appears in more than one register, I have arranged things so that its transformations can be analyzed for all registers and years for which it is listed. Some households are present over the entire 102 years, others appear only once, and most last for only a few years. By this reckoning, there are 1,095 separate households. In these terms the distribution is as follows:[11]

Register	Number of occurrences	Number of households	Number of people
Horikoshi owners	812	98	
Kubo owners	1,747	190	
All owners	2,559	288	11,229
Horikoshi tenants	1,499	431	
Kubo tenants	1,156	376	
All tenants	2,655	807	9,148
TOTAL	5,214	1,095	20,377

I have categorized the households by what I have called *family form*. Figure 11.1 shows the basic version of each form. Since forms J and M, four-generation households with heads in the first and fourth generation, respectively, never occur in the registers, I have omitted them from the figure and all the tables.

One final note has to do with what I have called "transformations." Every time a household of one form assumes a different one, it is counted as a transformation. Thus, if a given household is form A in 1757, form C in 1760, and form C again in 1761, it has marked one transformation in the three occurrences. The analysis necessarily involves the use of the aggregated 5,214 occurrences of the 1,095 households over the span of 102

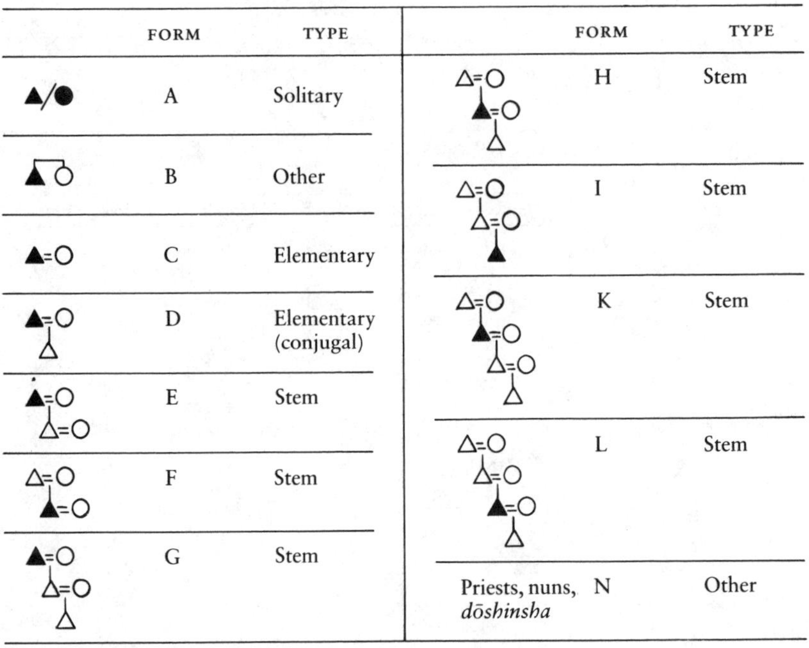

	FORM	TYPE		FORM	TYPE
▲/●	A	Solitary	△=○ ▲=○ △	H	Stem
▲○	B	Other	△=○ △=○ ▲	I	Stem
▲=○	C	Elementary			
▲=○ △	D	Elementary (conjugal)	△=○ ▲=○ △=○ △	K	Stem
▲=○ △=○	E	Stem			
△=○ ▲=○	F	Stem	△=○ △=○ ▲=○ △	L	Stem
▲=○ △=○ △	G	Stem	Priests, nuns, *dōshinsha*	N	Other

Fig. 11.1. Family forms and types. Black figures are household heads. The "Type" column is supplied in the interest of comparability with the Chinese materials in this volume; see also Table 11.2 below.

years. I have ignored the gaps in the series, which do produce a few bizarre leaps in form, but a sampling of only those transformations that occur in contiguous years yields not very different results.

Analysis

Tables 11.1 and 11.2 show the breakdown by ward and household status (owner or tenant) of the 5,214 occurrences of households. Several striking findings are evident. Solitary (A) households account for 17.5 percent of the total, and conjugal families (D) for another 42.1 percent. The elementary (C and D) type accounts for almost half (48.7 percent) of all occurrences. Of all the forms making up the stem type, F and G (two-generation households with junior heads and three-generation households with senior heads) account for about half.

The differences between owners and tenants are particularly apparent with respect to the proportion of three-generation stem families (G, H, and I), which account for 18 percent and 8.6 percent, respectively. Married couples and conjugal families (C and D) are 40 percent of the total for owners, 57 percent for tenants.

An apparent anomaly that I cannot explain is the high rate of solitary

TABLE 11.1

Summary of All Occurrences of Family Form in Tennōji by Ward and Household Status for Various Years, 1757-1858

(N = 5,214)

Family form	Horikoshi				Kubo			
	Owners		Tenants		Owners		Tenants	
	Number	Percent	Number	Percent	Number	Percent	Number	Percent
A	173	21.3%	240	16.0%	294	16.8%	204	17.6%
B	14	1.7	38	2.5	23	1.3	41	3.5
C	35	4.3	141	9.4	84	4.8	83	7.2
D	304	37.4	760	50.7	601	34.5	532	46.0
E	23	2.8	8	0.5	29	1.7	3	0.3
F	62	7.6	177	11.8	224	12.8	150	13.0
G	69	8.5	55	3.7	89	5.1	42	3.6
H	113	13.9	58	3.9	165	9.4	58	5.0
I	7	0.9	4	0.3	16	0.9	8	0.7
K	6	0.7	–	–	7	0.4	–	–
L	6	0.7	8	0.5	10	0.6	–	–
N	–	–	10	0.6	205	11.7	35	3.0
TOTAL	812	99.8%	1,499	99.9%	1,747	100.0%	1,156	99.9%
% of N	15.6%		28.7%		33.5%		22.2%	

Family form	Owners		Tenants		Total		
	Number	Percent	Number	Percent	Number	Percent	
A	467	18.2%	444	16.7%	911	17.5%	
B	37	1.4	79	3.0	116	2.2	
C	119	4.6	224	8.4	343	6.6	
D	905	35.4	1,292	48.6	2,197	42.1	
E	52	2.0	11	0.4	63	1.2	
F	286	11.2	327	12.3	613	11.8	
G	158	6.2	97	3.7	255	4.9	
H	278	10.9	116	4.4	394	7.6	
I	23	0.9	12	0.5	35	0.7	
K	13	0.5	–	–	13	0.2	
L	16	0.6	8	0.3	24	0.5	
N	205	8.0	45	1.7	250	4.8	
TOTAL	2,559	99.9%	2,655	100.0%	5,214	100.1%	
% of N	50.9%		49.1%		100%		

(A) households among the Horikoshi owners. It should also be noted that virtually all the households of form N (priests, nuns, *dōshinsha*) are found among the Kubo owners, whereas there are none at all among the Horikoshi owners.

Tables 11.3, 11.4, and 11.5 deal with the relative importance of family form in 11 selected years. Among the owners (Table 11.3), the percentage of solitary (A) households more than doubles over the 102 years, with a sharp increase after 1784. Elementary (C and D) households decline from

TABLE 11.2

Summary of All Occurrences of Family Types in Tennōji by Ward and Household Status for Various Years, 1757-1858

(N = 5,214)

Family type	Horikoshi				Kubo			
	Owners		Tenants		Owners		Tenants	
	Number	Percent	Number	Percent	Number	Percent	Number	Percent
Solitary	173	21.3%	240	16.0%	294	16.8%	204	17.6%
Elementary	339	41.7	901	60.1	685	39.2	615	53.2
Stem	286	35.2	310	20.7	540	30.9	261	22.6
Other[a]	14	1.7	48	3.2	228	13.1	76	6.6
TOTAL	812	99.9%	1,499	100.0%	1,747	100.0%	1,156	100.0%

Family type	Owners		Tenants		Total	
	Number	Percent	Number	Percent	Number	Percent
Solitary	467	18.2%	444	16.7%	911	17.5%
Elementary	1,024	40.0	1,516	57.1	2,540	48.7
Stem	826	32.3	571	21.5	1,397	26.8
Other[a]	242	9.5	124	4.7	366	7.0
TOTAL	2,559	100.0%	2,655	100.0%	5,214	100.0%

[a]116 siblings (Form B) and 250 priests, nuns, etc. (Form N).

about half to 36.8 percent over the period. There is almost no change in the proportion of households of the stem type (E, F, G, H, I, K, and L). From about one-third (35.3 percent) in 1817 to more than half (57.3 percent) in 1767 of all persons of owner households lived in elementary families.

Among the tenants (Table 11.4) solitary (A) households range from a low of 7.7 percent in 1848 to a high of almost one-third in 1757. The proportion of persons living in elementary (C and D) families among the tenants ranges from a low of 56.6 percent in 1858 to a high of 75.5 percent in 1838, but before 1858 never falls below 60 percent of the population.

Table 11.6 shows the ages of heads of households without regard to sex. The heads of solitary (A) households are in some ways the most interesting, for they are represented in every age group from 0-4 years to 80-84 years, with a median age of 39. This finding raises some questions—which I cannot answer to my satisfaction—about the nature of the headship, for whereas we might expect a certain number of adult males and females to end up living alone, how are we to account for the presence of so many very young unmarried male and female household heads? In this connection, note that households composed of unmarried siblings (B) have heads in only a slightly less broad spectrum of ages, the median age being 28.

Married couples without children (C) clearly fall into two categories:

TABLE 11.3

Relative Importance of Family Form among Owners' Families in Tennōji in Selected Years, 1757-1858
(percent)

Year	Number of households	Family form											
		A	B	C	D	E	F	G	H	I	K	L	N
1757	83	12.0	2.4	7.2	42.2	2.4	8.4	3.6	16.9	—	—	—	4.8
1767	80	7.5	—	8.8	43.8	2.5	16.3	7.5	3.8	—	1.3	1.3	7.5
1784	75	12.0	2.7	8.0	29.3	—	13.3	6.7	13.3	4.0	1.3	—	9.3
1788	78	20.5	3.8	5.1	29.5	1.3	9.0	3.8	14.1	1.3	—	2.6	9.0
1798	72	18.1	—	4.2	31.9	1.4	11.1	4.2	16.7	1.4	—	1.4	9.7
1806	70	15.7	2.9	1.4	32.9	1.4	10.0	11.4	10.0	—	1.4	2.9	10.0
1817	68	17.6	—	4.4	30.9	1.5	8.8	13.2	14.7	—	—	1.5	7.4
1831	68	17.6	2.9	4.4	27.9	5.9	13.2	7.4	10.3	2.9	—	—	7.4
1838	72	22.2	—	2.8	33.3	1.4	12.5	8.3	11.1	—	—	—	6.9
1848	65	24.6	3.1	7.7	30.8	4.6	7.7	1.5	9.2	1.5	—	1.4	7.7
1858	66	25.8	3.0	4.5	31.8	—	9.1	9.1	9.1	—	—	1.5	7.6

Year	Number of persons	Percent of persons living in owners' households of form:											
		A	B	C	D	E	F	G	H	I	K	L	N
1757	335	3.0	1.8	4.8	45.7	3.0	8.4	6.6	25.7	—	—	—	1.2
1767	365	1.6	—	6.8	50.4	2.5	12.9	14.0	3.6	—	2.2	1.9	4.1
1784	367	2.5	1.9	5.7	36.2	—	10.1	9.0	19.1	6.5	2.5	—	6.5
1788	367	4.4	2.7	4.4	36.5	3.0	9.5	6.0	20.7	1.1	—	4.6	7.1
1798	365	6.0	—	2.2	37.8	2.2	10.1	7.9	24.4	0.8	—	1.9	6.6
1806	364	3.8	1.9	3.8	36.0	1.6	9.3	18.1	15.1	—	2.7	3.3	4.4
1817	348	3.4	—	2.6	32.8	2.0	6.9	20.7	23.0	—	—	3.2	5.5
1831	336	3.6	1.2	3.0	35.1	6.8	15.8	12.8	15.2	1.8	—	—	4.8
1838	292	5.5	—	1.4	43.8	3.4	12.0	11.0	16.8	—	—	—	4.8
1848	238	6.7	2.5	5.0	47.5	5.0	7.1	2.9	13.4	1.3	—	1.4	5.5
1858	233	7.7	2.6	3.0	42.5	—	7.7	16.7	14.6	—	—	2.9	5.2

TABLE 11.4

Relative Importance of Family Form among Tenants' Families in Tennōji in Selected Years, 1757-1858

(percent)

Year	Number of households	Family form											
		A	B	C	D	E	F	G	H	I	K	L	N
1757	56	32.1	1.8	21.4	30.4	1.8	3.6	1.8	1.8	—	—	—	5.4
1767	72	18.1	—	8.3	50.0	1.4	9.7	1.4	4.2	—	—	—	6.9
1784	81	16.0	2.5	9.9	48.1	1.2	13.6	1.2	6.2	1.2	—	—	—
1788	72	12.5	2.8	8.3	47.2	—	20.8	2.8	4.2	1.4	—	—	—
1798	88	17.0	2.3	5.7	47.7	1.1	13.6	3.4	8.0	—	—	—	1.1
1806	104	19.2	—	4.8	54.8	—	9.6	3.8	6.7	1.0	—	—	—
1817	73	20.5	1.4	8.2	56.2	—	6.8	2.7	4.1	—	—	—	—
1831	64	23.4	7.8	14.1	40.6	1.6	6.3	4.7	1.6	—	—	—	—
1838	58	19.0	1.7	8.6	56.9	—	8.6	5.2	—	—	—	—	—
1848	65	7.7	4.6	6.2	55.4	—	13.8	6.2	4.6	—	—	1.5	—
1858	65	21.5	3.1	7.7	41.5	—	13.8	3.1	6.2	1.5	—	—	1.5

Year	Number of persons	Percent of persons living in tenants' households of form:											
		A	B	C	D	E	F	G	H	I	K	L	N
1757	122	14.8	1.6	20.5	44.3	3.3	5.7	4.1	3.3	—	—	—	2.5
1767	220	6.8	—	5.5	62.7	2.7	10.9	1.8	6.4	—	—	—	3.2
1784	276	7.2	1.8	6.9	59.4	1.4	12.3	1.8	8.3	0.7	—	—	—
1788	257	7.0	1.9	5.1	55.6	—	18.7	5.1	5.1	1.6	—	—	—
1798	310	6.1	1.3	3.9	56.1	1.0	15.5	4.8	11.0	—	—	—	0.3
1806	393	6.4	—	2.8	67.2	—	8.4	6.4	8.4	0.5	—	—	—
1817	273	7.0	2.2	5.1	68.9	—	9.2	2.6	5.1	—	—	—	—
1831	204	10.8	7.4	12.7	52.0	2.0	7.4	4.9	2.9	—	—	—	—
1838	196	6.6	2.6	5.1	70.4	—	8.7	6.6	—	—	—	—	—
1848	265	3.0	5.3	3.8	58.9	—	10.2	7.9	8.3	—	—	2.6	—
1858	219	8.7	2.3	5.0	51.6	—	13.2	4.6	11.9	1.8	—	—	0.9

TABLE 11.5

Relative Importance of Family Form among All Families in Tennōji in Selected Years, 1757-1858

(percent)

Year	Number of households	Family form											
		A	B	C	D	E	F	G	H	I	K	L	N
1757	139	20.1	2.2	12.9	36.7	2.2	6.5	2.9	10.8	—	—	—	5.8
1767	152	12.5	—	8.6	46.7	2.0	13.2	4.6	3.9	—	0.7	0.7	7.2
1784	156	14.1	2.6	9.0	39.1	0.6	13.5	3.8	9.6	2.6	0.6	—	4.5
1788	150	16.7	3.3	5.7	38.0	0.7	14.7	3.3	9.3	1.3	—	1.3	4.7
1798	160	17.5	1.3	5.0	40.6	1.3	12.5	3.8	11.9	0.6	—	0.6	5.0
1806	174	17.8	1.1	3.4	46.0	0.6	9.8	6.9	8.0	0.6	0.6	1.1	4.0
1817	141	19.1	0.7	6.4	44.0	0.7	7.8	7.8	9.2	—	—	0.7	3.5
1831	132	20.5	5.3	9.1	34.1	3.8	9.8	6.1	6.1	1.5	—	—	3.8
1838	130	20.8	0.8	5.4	43.8	0.8	10.8	6.9	6.2	—	—	0.8	3.8
1848	130	16.2	3.8	6.9	43.1	2.3	10.8	3.8	6.9	0.8	—	1.5	3.8
1858	131	23.7	3.1	6.1	36.6	—	11.5	6.1	7.6	0.8	—	—	4.6

Year	Number of persons	Percent of all persons living in households of form:											
		A	B	C	D	E	F	G	H	I	K	L	N
1757	457	6.1	1.8	9.0	45.3	3.1	7.7	5.9	19.7	—	—	—	1.5
1767	585	3.6	—	6.3	55.0	2.6	12.1	9.4	4.6	—	1.4	1.2	3.8
1784	643	4.5	1.9	6.2	46.2	0.6	11.0	5.9	14.5	4.0	1.4	—	3.7
1788	624	5.4	2.4	4.6	44.4	1.8	13.3	5.6	14.3	1.3	—	2.7	4.2
1798	675	6.1	0.6	3.0	46.2	1.6	12.6	6.5	18.2	0.4	—	1.0	3.7
1806	757	5.2	0.9	1.8	52.2	0.8	8.9	12.0	11.6	0.2	1.3	1.6	3.4
1817	621	5.0	1.0	3.7	48.6	1.1	7.9	12.7	15.1	—	—	1.8	3.1
1831	540	6.3	3.5	6.7	41.5	5.0	12.6	9.8	10.6	1.1	—	—	3.0
1838	488	5.9	1.0	2.9	54.5	2.0	10.7	9.2	10.0	—	—	0.8	2.9
1848	503	4.8	4.0	4.4	53.5	2.4	8.7	5.6	10.7	0.6	—	2.8	2.6
1858	452	8.2	2.4	4.0	46.9	—	10.4	10.8	13.3	0.9	—	—	3.1

TABLE 11.6

Age of Family Head by Family Form in Tennōji

(N = 4,946)

Age	A	B	C	D	E	F	G	H	I	K	L	Total No.	Total Pct.
0-4	3	–	–	–	–	5	–	–	2	–	–	10	0.2%
5-9	13	5	–	–	–	18	–	1	4	–	–	41	0.8
10-14	22	8	–	–	–	25	–	–	3	–	–	58	1.2
15-19	53	13	2	2	–	83	–	10	11*	–	–	164	3.3
20-24	67	17	21	23	–	138	–	10	8	–	4	288	5.8
25-29	105	21*	70	129	–	134*	–	41	4	–	8*	512	10.4
30-34	96	12	45	263	–	93	–	82	2	–	8	601	12.2
35-39	102*	13	53*	307	1	66	–	88*	–	–	3	633	12.8
40-44	88	11	37	404*	3	29	8	82	–	–	1	663*	13.4
45-49	71	7	32	379	4	13	10	59	–	5	–	580	11.7
50-54	61	2	19	298	13	4	29	25	–	4*	–	455	9.2
55-59	68	5	25	213	13*	3	58	5	–	1	–	391	7.9
60-64	62	1	20	101	13	2	60*	1	–	3	–	263	5.3
65-69	52	–	11	44	12	–	46	–	–	–	–	165	3.3
70-74	27	–	4	19	4	–	31	–	–	–	–	85	1.7
75-79	9	–	2	7	–	–	9	–	–	–	–	27	0.5
80-	5	–	–	1	–	–	4	–	–	–	–	10	0.2
TOTAL	904	115	341	2,190	63	613	255	394	34	13	24	4,946	99.9%
% of N	18.3%	2.3%	6.9%	44.3%	1.3%	12.4%	5.2%	8.0%	0.7%	0.3%	0.5%	100.2%	
Median age (starred in table)	39	28	39	44	57	26	61	39	19	52	29	41	

NOTE: Form N (priests, nuns, etc.) has been omitted along with 18 heads whose age is unknown. Median age groups are starred.

TABLE II.7

Ages of Senior and Junior Family Heads of Stem Family Forms in Tennōji

$(N = 1,397)$

Age	Senior heads (E,G)		Junior heads (F,H,I,K,L)		Cumulative percent	
	Number	Percent	Number	Percent	Senior	Junior
0-4	–	–	7	0.6%	–	0.6%
5-9	–	–	23	2.1	–	2.7
10-14	–	–	28	2.6	–	5.3
15-19	–	–	94	8.7	–	14.0
20-24	–	–	160	14.8	–	28.8
25-29	–	–	187	17.3	–	46.1
30-34	–	–	185	17.1	–	63.2
35-39	1	0.3%	157	14.6	0.3%	77.8
40-44	11	3.5	112	10.4	3.8	88.2
45-49	14	4.4	77	7.1	8.2	95.2
50-54	42	13.2	33	3.1	21.4	98.4
55-59	71	22.3	9	0.8	43.7	99.2
60-64	73	23.0	6	0.5	66.7	99.7
65-69	58	18.2	–	–	84.9	–
70-74	35	11.0	–	–	95.9	–
75-79	9	2.8	–	–	98.7	–
80-	4	1.3	–	–	100.0	–
Unknown	–	–	1	0.1	100.0	99.8
TOTAL	318	100.0%	1,079	99.8%		

TABLE II.8

Sex of Family Head by Family Form in Tennōji

$(N = 5,214)$

Family form	Male		Female		Total	
	Number	Row pct.	Number	Row pct.	Number	Column pct.
A	692	76.0%	219	24.0%	911	17.5%
B	104	89.7	12	10.3	116	2.2
C	338	98.8	4	1.2	342	6.6
D	2,115	96.2	83	3.8	2,198	42.1
E	63	100.0	–	–	63	1.2
F	609	99.3	4	0.7	613	11.8
G	243	95.3	12	4.7	255	4.9
H	385	97.7	9	2.3	394	7.6
I	35	100.0	–	–	35	0.7
K	13	100.0	–	–	13	0.2
L	24	100.0	–	–	24	0.5
N	178	71.2	72	28.8	250	4.8
TOTAL	4,799	92.0%	415	8.0%	5,214	100.1%

most are in their twenties and thirties, and the rest are older couples who live alone. Conjugal families (D), whose heads' median age is 44, hold few surprises, but the stem families are a different story. It is in forms E and F (two-generation stem families with senior and junior heads, respectively) that the differences appear most sharply. The median age of the heads of families of form E is 57, of form F only 26. Similarly, in the three subforms G, H, and I (three-generation stem families with senior, middle, and junior heads, respectively) the median ages are 61, 39, and 19. The direction in which a household may shift has everything to do with which of the subforms it represents.

Table 11.7 presents a further refinement of the foregoing analysis. Comparing the stem families with senior heads (E and G) with those with junior heads (F, H, I, K, and L), we can see some striking differences. The columns showing cumulative percentages reveal that 63.2 percent of the latter are 34 years old or younger, whereas 100 percent of the former are 35 or older.

Table 11.8 shows the distribution of family form by sex of head. One-quarter (219) of all solitary households are women, accounting for more than half of all female-headed households. Of the religious households, 72 (28.8 percent) are headed by nuns. The other female household heads (124) are of considerable interest; 83 (66.9 percent) are widowed heads of conjugal families (D), 12 (9.7 percent) are the senior heads of three-generation stem families (G), and a like number are heads of households composed only of siblings. Overall, women account for only 8 percent of all heads, including the nuns.

Marital status and sex of household head are the subjects of Table 11.9, which excludes households of a religious character. Of the total of 4,964 households, 93.1 percent are headed by males of all marital statuses, but only 57.9 percent are headed by married men. Never-married men head 85.2 percent of all two-generation stem families with junior heads (F) and 88.6 percent of the small number of three-generation stem families with junior heads (I). All these appear to represent cases in which the succession has passed to a male child on the death of the household head before the marriage of the successor could be arranged.

Not one of the 4,964 households is headed by a married woman. Never-married women do head 161 households, 90 percent of them solitary (A). Widowed or divorced women head 182 households, 40.7 percent of them solitary (A) and 45.6 percent conjugal (D).

Table 11.10 shows the distribution of the population by family form and the average size of households. For owners the average number of persons per household is 4.39; for tenants the figure is 3.45. The subform differences are more striking. Whereas the range among the owners, exclud-

TABLE 11.9

Family Form by Sex and Marital Status of Family Head in Tennōji

(N = 4,964)

Family form and N	(1) Married male		(2) Widowed or divorced male		(3) Never married male		(2) + (3) Single male		(4) Widowed or divorced female		(5) Never married female		(4) + (5) Single female	
	Number	Row pct.	Number	Row pct.	Number	Row pct.	Number	Row pct.	Number	Row pct.	Number	Row pct.	Number	Row pct.
A (911)	–	–	46	5.0%	646	70.9%	692	76.0%	74	8.1%	145	15.9%	219	24.0%
B (116)	–	–	–	–	104	89.7	104	89.7	–	–	12	10.3	12	10.3
C (342)	335	98.0%	3	0.9	–	–	3	0.9	4	1.2	–	–	4	1.2
D (2,198)	1,888	85.9	199	9.1	28	1.3	227	10.3	83	3.8	–	–	83	3.8
E (63)	44	69.8	19	30.2	–	–	19	30.2	–	–	–	–	–	–
F (613)	79	12.9	8	1.3	522	85.2	530	86.5	–	–	4	0.7	4	0.7
G (255)	143	56.1	100	39.2	–	–	100	39.2	12	4.7	–	–	12	4.7
H (394)	347	88.1	28	7.1	10	2.5	38	9.6	9	2.3	–	–	9	2.3
I (35)	4	11.4	–	–	31	88.6	31	88.6	–	–	–	–	–	–
K (13)	12	92.3	1	7.7	–	–	1	7.7	–	–	–	–	–	–
L (24)	23	95.8	1	4.2	–	–	1	4.2	–	–	–	–	–	–
TOTAL	2,875	57.9%	405	8.2%	1,341	27.0%	1,746	35.2%	182	3.7%	161	3.2%	343	6.9%

NOTE: Form N (priests, nuns, etc.) has been omitted.

TABLE 11.10
Average Size of Household by Family Form in Tennōji
(N = 5,214)

Family form	Owners			Tenants			All			
	Number of households	Number of persons	Average size	Number of households	Number of persons	Average size	Number of households	Number of persons	Average size	Percentage of persons living in household
A	467	508	1.09	444	595	1.34	911	1,103	1.21	5.4%
B	37	123	3.32	79	254	3.22	116	377	3.25	1.9
C	118	352	2.98	226	512	2.27	344	864	2.51	4.2
D	906	4,910	5.42	1,290	5,409	4.19	2,196	10,319	4.70	50.6
E	52	296	5.69	11	47	4.27	63	343	5.44	1.7
F	286	1,165	4.07	327	1,107	3.39	613	2,272	3.71	11.1
G	158	1,151	7.28	97	481	4.96	255	1,632	6.40	8.0
H	278	1,828	6.58	116	613	5.28	394	2,441	6.20	12.0
I	23	111	4.83	12	29	2.42	35	140	4.00	0.7
K	13	107	8.23	–	–	–	13	107	8.23	0.5
L	16	110	6.88	8	48	6.00	24	158	6.58	0.8
N	205	568	2.77	45	53	1.18	250	621	2.48	3.0
TOTAL	2,559	11,229	4.39	2,655	9,148	3.45	5,214	20,377	3.91	100.0%
% of N	49.1%	55.1%		50.9%	44.9%		100%	100%		100.0%

TABLE 11.11

Number of Tennōji Households Having at Least One Kinsman or Other Resident of Various Types, by Family Form

(N = 5,214)

Relationship	Family Form and N												Total (5,214)
	A (911)	B (116)	C (342)	D (2,198)	E (63)	F (613)	G (255)	H (394)	I (35)	K (13)	L (24)	N (250)	
Head (male)	692	104	338	2,115	63	609	243	385	35	13	24	—	4,621
Head (female)	219	12	4	83	—	4	12	9	—	—	—	—	343
Priest	—	—	—	—	—	—	—	—	—	—	—	166	166
Nun	1	—	—	—	—	1	—	—	—	—	—	72	74
Dōshinsha	—	—	—	—	—	—	—	—	—	—	—	12	12
Wife	—	—	335	1,888	44	79	143	347	4	12	23	24	2,899
Son	—	—	—	1,770	11	—	38	299	—	1	19	22	2,160
Daughter	—	—	—	1,485	12	—	77	265	—	5	10	15	1,869
Successor	—	—	—	—	63	—	191	5	—	13	—	—	272
Successor's wife	—	—	—	—	62	—	186	5	—	10	—	—	263
Father	—	—	—	—	—	60	—	76	—	3	3	—	142
Mother	—	—	—	—	—	603	—	353	19	11	8	2	996
Grandfather	—	—	—	—	—	—	—	1	—	—	3	—	4
Grandmother	—	—	—	—	—	—	—	—	35	—	22	—	57
Grandson	—	—	—	1	—	—	162	—	—	8	—	—	171
Granddaughter	—	—	—	—	—	—	172	—	—	7	—	2	181
Elder brother	—	2	—	1	—	4	1	2	—	—	—	—	10
Younger brother	—	47	17	70	—	206	—	47	11	—	1	—	399
Elder sister	—	40	5	16	—	72	2	7	1	—	—	—	143
Younger sister	—	63	22	68	—	203	3	58	6	—	4	—	427
Uncle	3	2	1	5	—	4	—	1	—	—	—	—	16
Aunt	20	12	1	12	—	27	—	1	—	—	—	—	73
Nephew	5	5	5	3	—	15	—	9	—	—	—	—	42
Niece	7	3	1	21	—	16	2	3	—	—	—	—	53
Cousin (m.)	2	—	—	1	—	3	—	—	—	—	—	—	6
Cousin (f.)	1	—	—	—	—	1	—	—	—	—	—	—	2
Wife's sister	—	—	—	6	—	1	—	—	—	—	—	—	7
Inkyo (m.)	—	—	—	—	—	—	—	—	—	—	—	9	9
Inkyo (f.)	—	—	—	—	—	—	—	—	—	—	—	14	14
Unknown (m.)	5	—	1	2	—	1	1	—	—	—	—	—	10
Unknown (f.)	2	—	2	3	—	1	1	—	—	—	—	—	10
Servant (m.)	24	13	56	266	25	70	69	111	8	7	6	61	716
Servant (f.)	19	7	40	237	20	48	58	85	5	7	6	15	547
Co-resident (m.)	30	20	10	48	1	26	6	3	5	—	1	—	151
Co-resident (f.)	20	6	5	18	—	7	11	5	—	—	—	—	73
Disciple (m.)	—	—	—	—	—	—	—	—	—	—	—	68	68
Disciple (f.)	—	—	—	—	—	—	—	—	—	—	—	37	37

TABLE 11.12

Categories of Kinsmen in Tennōji Households in Declining Order of Frequency

(5,214 households)

Term	Number	Rank order	Term	Number	Rank order
Wife	2,899	1	Aunt	73	13
Son	2,160	2	Grandmother	57	14
Daughter	1,869	3	Niece	53	15
Mother	996	4	Nephew	42	16
Younger sister	427	5	Uncle	16	17
Younger brother	399	6	Inkyo (female)	14	18
Successor	272	7	Elder brother	10	19
Successor's wife	263	8	Inkyo (male)	9	20
Granddaughter	180	9	Wife's sister	7	21
Grandson	171	10	Cousin (male)	6	22
Elder sister	143	11	Grandfather	4	23
Father	142	12	Cousin (female)	2	24

ing forms A, B, and N, is from 2.98 (C) to 8.23 (K), among the tenants it is only 2.27 (C) to 6.00 (L). Note that the average size of household is larger among the owners in every category except A.

Table 11.11 lists all the categories of kinsmen and other household residents that appear in these registers. It is somewhat sparse, which is to say that the range of kinsmen looks quite contemporary. The figures in the table are not the number of persons of each category, but the number of households having at least one person of that category. The two are identical only in the cases of the male head, female head, and wife, for there can be only one of each in any household. What stands out clearly is how very few households had any kinsmen beyond sons, daughters, and mothers of the head. Far more households had male or female servants (716 and 547, respectively) than had any secondary category of kinsman.

Table 11.12 lists the categories of kinsmen proper in declining order of frequency of appearance, including *inkyo* (retirees) on the grounds that they probably were kinsmen of some description.

The duration of family forms is shown in Table 11.13. Forms A, B, C, E, I, K, and L overwhelmingly appear in the registers for fewer than ten years; the range in these forms is from 91.3 percent to 100 percent. The conjugal family (D) is far and away of the longest duration, yet 77.6 percent of these households also last fewer than ten years. Observe, however, that this table includes only those cases where there is a transformation from one form to another.

Table 11.14 returns to the 5,214 occurrences, and shows the average duration in years of each form. With the exception of the "religious" households, their terms are very brief. In no case does any form last longer on

TABLE 11.13
Duration of Family Forms in Tennōji
(N = 1,812)

Family form	Number of years											Total	
	1-9		10-19		20-29		30-39		40-49				
	Number	Percent	Number	Percent	Number	Percent	Number	Percent	Number	Percent		Number	Percent
A	345	91.3	27	7.1	5	1.3	1	0.3	—	—		378	20.9%
B	57	96.6	2	3.4	1	—	—	—	—	—		59	3.3
C	203	98.5	2	1.0	1	0.5	—	—	—	—		206	11.4
D	503	77.6	100	15.4	37	5.7	5	0.8	3	0.5		648	35.8
E	39	97.5	1	2.5	—	—	—	—	—	—		40	2.2
F	189	85.9	28	12.7	3	1.4	—	—	—	—		220	12.1
G	71	82.6	12	14.0	3	3.4	—	—	—	—		86	4.7
H	118	86.1	18	13.1	1	0.7	—	—	—	—		137	7.6
I	21	95.5	1	4.5	—	—	—	—	—	—		22	1.2
K	6	100.0	—	—	—	—	—	—	—	—		6	0.3
L	10	100.0	—	—	—	—	—	—	—	—		10	0.6
TOTAL	1,562	86.2	191	10.5	50	2.8	6	0.3	3	0.2		1,812	100.0%

NOTE: If a sequence starts after a break or ends during one, it is given no credit for any years of the break. Therefore, the results are biased in several ways: (1) if a sequence actually continued into a break, its length will be underestimated; (2) if a sequence started and ended during a break, it will not be counted at all; (3) if a sequence started and ended during a break, and by some coincidence the same family form recurred after the break ended, its length will be underestimated. This table includes only those cases where there is a transformation from one form to another.

TABLE 11.14

Number of Independent Occurrences and Duration of Family Forms in Tennōji

(N = 1,841)

Family form and N	Independent occurrences		Family years		Average duration of occurrence in years
	Number	Percent	Number	Percent	
A (911)	378	20.5%	1,322	15.4%	3.50
B (116)	59	3.2	136	1.6	2.31
C (343)	206	11.1	426	5.0	2.07
D (2,197)	648	35.2	3,889	45.3	6.00
E (63)	40	2.2	81	0.9	2.03
F (613)	220	12.0	935	10.9	4.25
G (255)	86	4.7	443	5.2	5.15
H (394)	137	7.4	641	7.5	4.68
I (35)	22	1.2	44	0.5	2.00
K (13)	6	0.3	15	0.2	2.50
L (24)	10	0.5	27	0.3	2.54
N (250)	29	1.6	623	7.3	21.48
TOTAL	1,841	99.9%	8,582	100.1%	

TABLE 11.15

Transformations of Family Forms in Tennōji: Owners

(N = 446)

To From	A	B	C	D	E	F	G	H	I	K	L	N	Number	Percent
A	2	–	12	7	–	4	–	–	–	–	–	–	23	5.2%
B	11	–	3	6	–	3	–	–	–	–	–	–	14	3.1
C	8	6	18	37	20	2	25	7	1	–	1	–	50	11.2
D	–	–	–	–	–	38	16	7	1	–	–	–	124	27.9
E	7	4	10	2	–	5	16	29	2	–	–	–	31	6.9
F	1	1	1	13	4	–	–	15	2	1	–	–	65	14.6
G	1	–	–	17	4	4	6	–	2	4	3	–	46	10.3
H	1	–	1	43	4	6	1	3	2	1	5	–	69	15.5
I	–	–	1	–	–	1	1	3	1	–	–	–	10	2.2
K	–	–	1	2	–	1	1	2	–	1	–	–	5	1.1
L	–	–	–	–	–	–	–	3	–	–	–	–	9	2.0
N	–	–	–	–	–	–	–	–	–	–	–	–	–	–
TOTAL	31	11	46	127	28	64	49	66	9	6	9	–	446	
Percent	7.0	2.5	10.3	28.5	6.3	14.4	11.0	14.7	2.0	1.3	2.0	–		100.0%

the average than six years. By way of explanation, an independent occurrence of a form is defined as beginning with a transformation to that form. Thus the 911 occurrences of form A include 378 independent occurrences of the form; and these 378 independent occurrences cover a total of 1,322 family years, for an average duration of 3.50 years. It is noteworthy that 45.3 percent of the family years are accounted for by the conjugal family (D) and that the next highest percentage is the number of years accounted for by solitary (A) households.

We come at last to the question of transformations. In Tables 11.15, 11.16, and 11.17 the 748 shifts between family forms are given for owners and tenants. The first row of Table 11.15 is read as follows: form A shifted to form C 12 times, to form D 7 times, and to form F 4 times. In all, there were 23 transformations from form A to some other form. The "Total" row indicates that there were 31 transformations from other forms to form A.

The owners (Table 11.15) show 446 transformations. Of these, 124 (27.9 percent) are from the conjugal family (D), primarily to more complex forms (E through L). There tend to be many more transformations to complex forms among owners than among tenants; but once having achieved the stem family type, owners do not sustain it with any regularity. In short, there is no tendency to oscillate among the subforms of the type.

Among the tenants (Table 11.16), who show 302 transformations, again the most common (32.5 percent) is from the conjugal form (D). Like owners, tenants who achieve a stem family are generally unable to sustain it. There is a preponderance of shifts back to elementary families among this group.

The transformations shown in these tables have one curious feature: shifts to a given form are roughly equal in number to shifts from that form. This feature is most noticeable among the owners, but only slightly less so for tenants. It appears that there may be a more or less regular pattern of oscillation between forms of the family, but at the moment I cannot say why this should be so.

Table 11.18 puts the issue of transformations in another context, for it includes information on the form of families at the time of their disappearance from the registers. The first column of its top segment is read as follows: among the owners, no family of form A is transformed into a family of form B, whereas 12 families of form A become form C (slightly more than half of the 23 families of form A that are transformed at all); 105 (82 percent) of form A owner families that do not simply recur in the next register in the same form disappear from the registers. Among the tenant families of form A the proportions of transformations and disappearances are similar. But a glance at form D reveals a striking difference between the

TABLE 11.16
Transformations of Family Forms in Tennōji: Tenants
(N = 302)

From \ To	A	B	C	D	E	F	G	H	I	K	L	N	Number	Percent
A	12	4	8	18	—	4	—	—	—	—	—	—	46	15.2%
B	9	—	—	4	—	1	2	1	—	—	—	—	17	5.6
C	13	2	—	42	—	—	—	—	—	—	—	—	57	18.9
D	2	—	21	29	7	29	2	8	—	—	—	—	98	32.5
E	—	4	1	—	—	—	—	—	—	—	—	—	5	1.7
F	10	—	3	10	—	1	1	15	—	—	—	—	40	13.2
G	1	—	—	7	—	2	—	—	1	—	—	—	11	3.6
H	—	1	—	3	—	3	14	—	1	—	1	—	23	7.6
I	—	—	—	—	—	—	—	—	—	—	—	2	2	0.7
K	—	—	—	—	—	—	—	—	—	—	—	—	—	—
L	—	—	—	1	—	—	—	—	—	—	—	—	1	0.3
N	—	—	—	2	—	—	—	—	—	—	—	—	2	0.7
TOTAL	47	11	33	116	7	40	19	24	2	—	1	2	302	
Percent	15.6	3.6	10.9	38.4	2.3	13.2	6.3	7.9	0.7	—	0.3	0.7		99.9%

TABLE II.17

Transformations of Family Forms in Tennōji: Owners and Tenants

(N = 748)

From \ To	A	B	C	D	E	F	G	H	I	K	L	N	Number	Percent
A	—	4	20	36	—	8	1	—	—	—	—	—	69	9.2%
B	14	—	3	10	—	4	—	—	—	—	—	—	31	4.1
C	20	—	—	79	—	5	2	1	—	—	—	—	107	14.3
D	21	8	39	—	27	67	39	15	2	—	2	2	222	29.7
E	—	—	—	5	—	5	18	7	1	—	—	—	36	4.8
F	17	8	11	23	—	—	—	44	2	—	—	—	105	14.0
G	1	1	4	24	4	8	—	15	—	—	—	—	57	7.6
H	2	1	—	61	4	—	6	—	3	—	3	—	92	12.3
I	3	—	1	—	—	1	1	3	—	1	5	—	12	1.6
K	—	—	1	—	—	—	1	4	1	—	—	—	5	0.7
L	—	—	1	3	—	1	1	3	—	1	—	—	10	1.3
N	—	—	—	2	—	—	—	—	—	—	—	—	2	0.3
TOTAL	78	22	79	243	35	104	68	90	11	6	10	2	748	99.8
Percent	10.4	2.9	10.6	32.5	4.7	13.9	9.1	12.0	1.5	0.8	1.3	0.3		99.9%

TABLE 11.18

From	To	Owners		Tenants		Total	
		Number	Percent	Number	Percent	Number	Percent
A	B	–	–	4	8.7%	4	5.8%
	C	12	52.2%	8	17.4	20	29.0
	D	7	30.4	29	63.0	36	52.2
	F	4	17.4	4	8.7	8	11.6
	G	–	–	1	2.2	1	1.4
	Transformations (Column %)	23 18.0%	100.0%	46 21.1%	100.0%	69 19.9%	100.0%
	Disappearances (Column %)	105 82.0%		172 78.9%		277 80.1%	
B	A	2	14.3%	12	70.6%	14	45.2%
	C	3	21.4	–	–	3	9.7
	D	6	42.9	4	23.5	10	32.3
	F	3	21.4	1	5.9	4	12.9
	Transformations (Column %)	14 82.0%	100.0%	17 44.7%	100.0%	31 56.4%	100.1%
	Disappearances (Column %)	3 18.0%		21 55.3%		24 43.6%	
C	A	11	22.0%	9	15.8%	20	18.7%
	B	–	–	–	–	–	–
	D	37	74.0	42	73.7	79	73.8
	F	2	4.0	3	5.3	5	4.7
	G	–	–	2	3.5	2	1.9
	H	–	–	1	1.8	1	0.9
	Transformations (Column %)	50 81.0%	100.0%	57 43.2%	100.0%	107 55.2%	100.0%
	Disappearances (Column %)	12 19.0%		75 56.8%		87 44.8%	
D	A	8	6.5%	13	13.3%	21	9.5%
	B	6	4.8	2	2.0	8	3.6
	C	18	14.5	21	21.4	39	17.6
	E	20	16.1	7	7.1	27	12.2
	F	38	30.6	29	29.6	67	30.2
	G	25	20.2	14	14.3	39	17.6
	H	7	5.6	8	8.2	15	6.8
	I	1	0.8	1	1.0	2	0.9
	L	1	0.8	1	1.0	2	0.9
	N	–	–	2	2.0	2	0.9
	Transformations (Column %)	124 69.0%	99.9%	98 23.1%	99.9%	222 36.8%	100.2%
	Disappearances (Column %)	56 31.0%		326 76.9%		382 63.2%	
E	D	2	6.5%	3	60.0%	5	13.9%
	F	5	16.1	–	–	5	13.9
	G	16	51.6	2	40.0	18	50.0
	H	7	22.6	–	–	7	19.4
	I	1	3.2	–	–	1	2.8
	Transformations (Column %)	31 100.0%	100.0%	5 50.0%	100.0%	36 87.8%	100.0%
	Disappearances (Column %)	– –		5 50.0%		5 12.2%	
F	A	7	10.8%	10	25.0%	17	16.2%
	B	4	6.2	4	10.0	8	7.6
	C	10	15.4	1	2.5	11	10.5
	D	13	20.0	10	25.0	23	21.9
	H	29	44.6	15	37.5	44	41.9
	I	2	3.1	–	–	2	1.9
	Transformations (Column %)	65 78.0%	100.1%	40 32.5%	100.0%	105 51.0%	100.0%
	Disappearances (Column %)	18 22.0%		83 67.5%		101 49.0%	

Transformations and Disappearances of Family Forms in Tennōji

From	To	Owners Number	Owners Percent	Tenants Number	Tenants Percent	Total Number	Total Percent
G	A	1	2.2%	–	–	1	1.8%
	B	1	2.2	–	–	1	1.8
	C	1	2.2	3	27.3%	4	7.0
	D	17	37.0	7	63.6	24	42.1
	E	4	8.7	–	–	4	7.0
	F	4	8.7	1	9.1	5	8.8
	H	15	32.6	–	–	15	26.3
	I	2	4.3	–	–	2	3.5
	K	1	2.2	–	–	1	1.8
Transformations (Column %)		46 90.2%	100.1%	11 40.7%	100.0%	57 73.1%	100.1%
Disappearances (Column %)		5 9.8%		16 59.3%		21 26.9%	
H	A	1	1.4%	1	4.3%	2	2.2%
	B	–	–	1	4.3	1	1.1
	D	43	62.3	18	78.3	61	66.3
	E	4	5.8	–	–	4	4.3
	F	6	8.7	2	8.7	8	8.7
	G	6	8.7	–	–	6	6.5
	I	2	2.9	1	4.3	3	3.3
	K	4	5.8	–	–	4	4.3
	L	3	4.3	–	–	3	3.3
Transformations (Column %)		69 84.1%	99.9%	23 51.1%	99.9%	92 72.4%	100.0%
Disappearances (Column %)		13 15.9%		22 48.9%		35 27.6%	
I	A	1	10.0%	2	100.0%	3	25.0%
	F	1	10.0	–	–	1	8.3
	H	3	30.0	–	–	3	25.0
	L	5	50.0	–	–	5	41.7
Transformations (Column %)		10 83.3%	100.0%	2 22.2%	100.0%	12 57.1%	100.0%
Disappearances (Column %)		2 16.7%		7 77.8%		9 42.9%	
K	C	1	20.0%	–	–	1	20.0%
	G	1	20.0	–	–	1	20.0
	H	2	40.0	–	–	2	40.0
	I	1	20.0	–	–	1	20.0
Transformations (Column %)		5 83.3%	100.0%	– –		5 83.3%	100.0%
Disappearances (Column %)		1 16.7%		–		1 16.7%	
L	C	1	11.1%	–	–	1	10.0%
	D	2	22.2	1	100.0%	3	30.0
	F	1	11.1	–	–	1	10.0
	G	1	11.1	–	–	1	10.0
	H	3	33.3	–	–	3	30.0
	K	1	11.1	–	–	1	10.0
Transformations (Column %)		9 100.0%	100.0%	1 100.0%	100.0%	10 100.0%	100.0%
Disappearances (Column %)		– –		– –		– –	
N	D	–	–	2	100.0%	2	100.0%
Transformations (Column %)		– –	–	2 12.5%	100.0%	2 8.7%	100.0%
Disappearances (Column %)		7 100.0%		14 87.5%		21 91.3%	

TABLE 11.19

Recurrences of Family Form Without Transformation in Tennōji

(N = 3,364)

Family form	Number of occurrences	Number of recurrences	Percent of recurrences
A	884	538	60.9%
B	112	57	50.9
C	325	131	40.3
D	2,145	1,541	71.8
E	60	19	31.7
F	604	398	65.9
G	251	173	68.9
H	379	252	66.5
I	35	14	40.0
K	13	7	53.8
L	24	14	58.3
N	243	220	90.5
TOTAL	5,075	3,364	66.3%

NOTE: Excludes the 139 families appearing in the first register for 1757.

TABLE 11.20

Family Form at First Appearance of Family in the Tennōji Registers

(N = 956)

Family form	Owners		Tenants		Total	
	No.	Pct.	No.	Pct.	No.	Pct.
A	104	50.7%	167	22.2%	271	28.3%
B	6	3.0	28	3.7	34	3.6
C	13	6.3	92	12.3	105	11.0
D	39	19.0	321	42.7	360	37.7
E	–	–	2	0.3	2	0.2
F	18	8.8	90	12.0	108	11.3
G	5	2.4	9	1.2	14	1.5
H	9	4.4	24	3.2	33	3.5
I	3	1.5	8	1.1	11	1.2
K	–	–	–	–	–	–
L	–	–	–	–	–	–
N	8	3.9	10	1.3	18	1.9
TOTAL	205	100.0%	751	100.0%	956	100.2%
Present in 1757 (excluded)	83		56		139	

two. Among the owners, 69 percent of families of form D are transformed, whereas only 23.1 percent of the tenant families are.

Table 11.19 takes up the question of recurrences. As noted above, one of three things may happen to a family in successive years. It may be transformed or disappear or recur in the same form. The table gives the number of recurrences for each form, excluding the occurrences in the first register for 1757. Thus, of the 884 occurrences of form A, 538 (60.9 percent) are recurrences.

Table 11.20 shows the form of each family entering the registers, excluding those that appear in the first register for 1757. It is hardly surprising that over 80 percent of them are accounted for by the four least complex forms. What is more interesting is that almost exactly half the entering owner families are solitary (A), whereas over half (55 percent) of the entering families among the tenants are either childless married couples (C) or married couples with children (D).

Conclusion

The evidence is unambiguous. Both owner and tenant families and households were small, and neither was on the average likely to remain resident in the wards of Tennōji for very long. Where they came from and where they went cannot be determined from the registers. Only 13 of the 1,095 separate households that resided in these wards between 1757 and 1858 were present for the entire period.

The family transformations of the two populations are somewhat different, but both tend to oscillate between elementary and stem types, the former of much longer duration than the latter. "Whole" three- and four-generation households are rare; that is, intact married couples are seldom found in all generations, and a frequent version of the more complex types is that headed by an unmarried male or a widow.

There is an astonishingly high rate of solitary families in both owner and tenant groups, but there is no evidence to suggest what conditions produced this effect. The number of servants is small, and they are found in households of all categories of both owner and tenant groups.

Two kinds of information would go a long way toward clearing up some of the questions raised by the findings on transformations, but neither can be calculated with any assurance. One is the mortality rate, which simply cannot be determined since we are not told whether disappearances from the register are the result of death or emigration. The other, of course, is the fertility rate. Here the various analytic techniques commonly used in such cases unfortunately produce results that bear no resemblance to rates for other populations in Japan or anywhere else.

We are left, then, with the bare record of the transformations themselves. Surely one of the most arresting discoveries is that none of the forms of the family clearly prefigures a particular other form. Any given form may be succeeded by as few as four or as many as ten others; and even when one transformation is predominant, it almost never accounts for as many as half of all the transformations. Indeed, the most common one very often accounts for something closer to one-third of the total.

There is an entirely unexpected scatter effect that suggests several potentially productive lines of inquiry.

It seems obvious that there is less regularity of transformation than the putative rules of inheritance and descent would seem to ensure. Whereas custom may well have prescribed for any family its next preferred form, the registers afford us a rather close look at how a large number of families, each faced with its own peculiar circumstances, managed (and often did not manage) to continue its existence. The options available to it were many, and it is the result of the exercise of those options that the registers record. Dry as the bare data seem, one can actually get caught up in the drama of the story they reveal. Thus I found myself despairing for one aging couple with two adult sons who did not marry, for as the years passed it became increasingly clear that something had gone wrong. Sometimes a family that seems well on its way is suddenly overwhelmed by the premature death of its head; or an adopted husband vanishes, leaving a woman and her small children for only a year or two before they disappear from the record altogether.

I am indebted to Thomas C. Smith for pointing out to me a consequence of the theoretical ability to change in any one of several directions. However a transformation occurred, whether by choice or by chance, every transformation meant a change in the composition, and perhaps the size, of the family. Each transformation must have brought about more or less fundamental changes in the structure of authority, in the organization of the work force, in the allocation of living space, and in personal relationships between family members. It seems unlikely that all these complicated adjustments could follow a generally prescribed pattern. Here at least a considerable amount of discretion must have been involved, if only to make allowance for individual family circumstances.

It is accordingly important to know how often a family confronted the necessity for making such adjustments. If transformations occurred infrequently—say, once in a generation—we can readily conceive of life proceeding in well-understood customary channels, with each generation repeating essentially the experience of its predecessors. But if they occurred very frequently, we must see this population as less stable and less serene than we have thought.

As we have seen, the transformations occur very frequently indeed. Excluding the religious households, the average duration of any family form runs from two to six years, with an average of 4.3 years for all forms combined. The decisions referred to above were made very frequently—often, it appears, the result of a need or desire to seek a better livelihood. The overwhelming impression is one of flux at both the community level and the family level.

TWELVE

Marriage among the Taiwanese of Pre-1945 Taipei

Sophie Sa

While early Western observers of Chinese society had made known to us a wide range of variation in the behavior of the Chinese with regard to family formation, we have only recently become aware of the extent to which segments of even "traditional" China deviated from the supposed norms. Much of this new knowledge has resulted from research done on Taiwan, thanks to the island's accessibility to fieldwork and to the availability and completeness of economic and demographic data, particularly those gleaned from the household registers. The registers, which were instituted by the Japanese colonial government in 1906 and adopted by the Nationalist government when Taiwan reverted to Chinese rule in 1945, continue to exist today, essentially unchanged in format and content.

One of the recent findings of greatest interest to social demographers is Arthur Wolf's discovery of the extent to which female adoption was practiced in northern Taiwan. Of all the girls born between 1906 and 1915 in the townships he studied, fully 70 percent were given out in adoption as *simpua* (little daughters-in-law or prospective daughters-in-law) to be raised in the home of their future husband by his parents. Although for various reasons not all girls adopted as simpua ultimately married the son of their adoptive parents, "minor marriages" (i.e., those uniting a simpua with her foster brother) nevertheless constituted 45 percent of all marriages occurring in the area between 1916 and 1925.[1]

Wolf's findings not only challenge assumptions about the "preferred" marriage form in China as a whole, they also have significant implications for the study of social demography in Taiwan. A minor marriage unites two people who have been raised as brother and sister and who, in confirmation of Edward Westermarck's theory, in many cases develop a mutual sexual aversion.[2] Where minor marriages constitute a large portion of all marriages, the divorce rate is much higher, and the birth rate lower, than in areas where almost all wives first enter their husband's home as adults on the day of marriage. Obviously, then, for people interested in rates of marriage and divorce, fertility and births, knowledge of the forms of marriage prevailing among particular segments of the population being studied is crucial.

Although household registers are available from 1906 to the present, this analysis is limited to the "dead" registers from the Japanese period. This means that our coverage of a particular household ends with the last change of household head before 1945, or with the last pre-1945 move of the household from the areas sampled. Thus, for example, my record of a household whose last head before 1945 died in 1907 and whose next head did not die until after 1946 extends only through 1907. Similarly, the records of some households begin well after 1906 because they only became households (e.g., through family division) after the registration system had started.

The samples I draw come from the two sections of Taipei City of earliest settlement. The first is today part of Lungshan district and is still referred to by Taiwanese as Bankha, a homophone of the name by which it was known before the 1700's. The second sampled area is part of what is now Yenping district, and is still referred to by Taiwanese by its pre-Japanese name, Toatotia:. The specific core areas within the two districts correspond roughly to what are now Ting-hsin, Lung-shan, Yü-ying, and Liao-kuan wards (*li*) in Lungshan; and Chien-ch'ang, P'ing-le, An-le, and Ch'ang-le wards in Yenping. The wards were selected after consultation with Chinese scholars, local residents, and officials, on the bases of earliness of settlement, representativeness and intrinsic interest of the resident families, and geographic contiguity with other wards. They were also chosen because informants had suggested they contained a relatively high percentage of higher-status families, a criterion to be discussed later.

Situated as they were halfway between the confluence of the Hsintien and Tamsui rivers to the north and the Ta-han River to the south, Bankha and Toatotia: were economically dependent on commerce from early times, and developed into urban centers of northern Taiwan well before the island was ceded to Japan in 1895.[3] Although significant Chinese settlement in Bankha began only after 1709, it was already a place of exchange between Chinese from the mainland and Taiwanese aborigines in the late seventeenth century.[4] Bankha achieved military importance in 1759, when the Ch'ing government moved the military garrison there. It achieved political importance when the government moved the seat of the assistant county magistrate responsible for the Taipei region there in 1809.[5] By the 1810's it had become the undisputed commercial center of northern Taiwan, exporting to China such items as hemp, deerskin, sweet potato, and betel; and importing finished goods such as silver and gold paper used in religious rituals, porcelain and pottery, silk and cotton cloths, bricks, and dry goods.[6] Government establishment of an official public granary followed in 1831, an official academy in 1841, and a *paochia* registration system around the same time.[7] By the mid-nineteenth century, in short, Bankha had become the political, military, and commercial center of northern Taiwan.

Although Bankha continued to be the center of activity in the northern region until the Japanese occupation, it gradually lost its dominant position in commerce to Toatotia:, the second area under analysis. The main reasons for Bankha's decline were civil war in the 1850's between groups originating from different parts of Fukien, which sapped the area's strength and vigor, and forced large numbers of people to flee; xenophobia on the part of local residents, which drove Western traders away; and the silting of the Tamsui River, which made Bankha increasingly inaccessible to large ships.

The site where the defeated Taiwanese and rebuffed Westerners converged was Toatotia:. Downstream from Bankha, Toatotia: was not affected by the Tamsui's silting until the turn of the century. Although much of Toatotia:'s rapid economic development is attributable to the vigorous efforts of local merchants, the most important factor was probably the influx of English, American, German, and Spanish trading firms. The Dodd and Brown companies established offices in Toatotia: in 1869, and by 1872 Jardine Mathieson and Tait had opened branches as well.[8]

Most of the Western merchants who came to Taiwan in the early 1860's were attracted by the island's camphor and sugar. However, with the discovery that northern Taiwan's climate and soil were ideal for growing tea and the introduction of several new tea strains by John Dodd in 1865, the tea trade quickly became the most lucrative. By 1869, some 200,000 catties of tea from northern Taiwan were shipped to New York alone, and Toatotia: was at the center of that trade.[9]

The development of Toatotia: received additional impetus from the investments of Taiwan's progressive first governor, Liu Ming-ch'uan, who made Taipei the focus of a program to modernize the island. He established a military arsenal in Taipei, constructed a railroad extending from Toatotia: north to Keelung, and began another from Taipei southward to Tainan. In addition, he designated Toatotia: as an area for foreign residents, encouraged the formation of a tea guild with headquarters in the area, and established a customs office there to collect taxes on tea. When Liu's term as governor ended in 1891, Toatotia: had become the commercial center of northern Taiwan and possibly of the whole island.[10]

Toatotia:'s heyday, then, came on the eve of the cession of Taiwan to Japan in 1895. Although it continued to be the center of the tea trade and tea-processing in the north, it gradually lost its lead as the most advanced area of northern Taiwan because the Japanese developed their own area of trade and industry in Senglai, a third section of Taipei City.

The decline of both Bankha and Toatotia: was, of course, gradual and relative. Both areas continued to flourish. From about 18,700 in 1895, Bankha's population rose to more than 29,000 by 1904, an increase of almost 56 percent in eight years. Toatotia: grew from an area with 900-plus households in 1889 to one with more than 22,600 persons in 1896, and more than 48,600 in 1904.[11] Few Japanese lived in these two areas, so the population increase was due almost entirely to natural increase and the in-migration of Taiwanese from other parts of the island.[12]

Social Status and Household Composition

Because the population under study here is an urban one, containing a greater diversity of occupations and social strata than the rural populations usually studied in fieldwork on Chinese society, we have an unusual opportunity to compare families of different socioeconomic status living in the same area in terms of their demographic behavior. My focus is on the various forms of marriage practiced by Taiwanese in Taipei before 1945, and relates choice in form of marriage to socioeconomic status. My underlying assumption is that families of different social strata behave differently when confronted with the same question of arranging a marriage for a son or a daughter. This is likely to be so because demographic choices of this sort are not simply biological arrangements made with regard only to members of the affected households, but social choices that both reflect and express social status.

Implicit in this analysis is the idea that the household is a rational actor, making decisions on the basis of available information, in the light of prevailing risks, and with a view toward definable rewards and goals. Since the kinds and amounts of information available to a particular household vary with the status of that household, the decisions it makes should reflect its status. High-status households, for example, have wider information networks and can afford longer search procedures than low-status households when looking for spouses for their children. They also respond to a different, more sophisticated set of criteria. Similarly, households of different socioeconomic status face environments with differing degrees of risk and differing attitudes toward risk. Finally, households of different status differ in the nature and size of the stakes most salient to them. High-status households are interested in maintaining their prestige in the community and can afford to do so. At the other extreme, low-status households, while they want to meet their social demographic obligations honorably, must basically be concerned with physical survival. These cumulative advantages of high-status households, and the corresponding cumulative disadvantages of low-status ones, should lead to significantly different strategies for forming families and continuing family lines.

Households, of course, do not exist in a vacuum. Rather, they exist within specific societies and cultures. As members of a particular social-cultural system, they subscribe to a common set of values and norms and strive toward certain shared goals. But the degree of conformity to those norms and the degree of success households have in achieving those goals depend on the resources available to them, as well as on the position they hold within the larger system. Social-cultural norms and values, in other words, establish the limits of acceptable behavior; household socioeconomic status demarcates, within those limits, what is appropriate and possible.

Marriage among the Taiwanese lends itself particularly well to the present analysis. First, we know that continuation of the male line of descent was the most fundamental goal of the Chinese family, and that marriage, as the only legitimate means to that end, was considered a universal imperative. Second, we also know the alternative ways by which a Chinese living in Taiwan could marry, as well as how these compared in terms of social prestige and economic cost. In addition, the detailed information in the household registers, used in conjunction with historical writings and biographies, makes it possible to classify the sampled households into distinct socioeconomic strata, even though neither income level nor "status" were categories used in household registers.

For inclusion in the high-status category in this study, a household had to satisfy one or more of the following conditions: it included at least one person who is mentioned by name as having been politically, economically, or socially important in writings about the period;[13] it included at least one concubine and one bondservant or two of either (an indication of wealth); it included at least one member who held a *hsiu-ts'ai* or *chü-jen* degree (which conferred status on the household). In addition, a high-status household could not have a head who had a low-status occupation, such as that of clerk or laborer.

Middle-status households were classified mostly on the basis of occupation. They include households of businessmen or shopkeepers, school teachers, physicians, and the like. Only households of such people as coolies and other manual laborers, street vendors, rickshawmen, and, in the case of women, laundresses, gold- and silver-paper pasters, and tea-leaf sorters were included in the low-status category. Since the criteria are admittedly crude, and since this study is an attempt to highlight differences between status groups, I excluded from the sample households that seemed on the borderline between status groups—households with one concubine or one bondservant, which might have had upper-middle status, and those whose heads held lower-middle-status positions, such as office workers and policemen.

My original design was to choose a random stratified sample of 200 high-status, 200 middle-status, and 200 low-status households from the selected wards in Lungshan and Yenping, with half of each status group coming from each district. In assembling these 600 households, however, I found only about thirty that met my criteria for elite status. In order to achieve a more evenly stratified sample, I had to go outside the core areas of the two districts to include all the high-status households that could be found in the dead registers for eastern Lungshan and southern Yenping. Even so, the final sample contains only 97 high-status households all told: 63 from Lungshan, 34 from Yenping. What these figures indicate is that the criteria used for assigning households to the high-status category were sound: certainly they are more consistent with the exclusivity of elite status than was my original expectation of finding 100 such households in each of two relatively small geographical areas. The final sample contains 190 middle-status households—104 from Lungshan, 86 from Yenping— and 196 low-status households—96 from Lungshan, 100 from Yenping.[14]

Single-member households that never acquired additional members were excluded from the start, since the biographical data needed for the analysis depend in large part on information in the registers of others entering the household. Except in cases of uxorilocal marriage, for example, a man's marriage is not recorded on his own register. To know about a man's virilocal marriage, we need his wife's register, which notes when and in what manner she married in. Similarly, to know whether a woman bore children, we need the children's registers, which state their birthdates and their parents' names. If a child died or otherwise left a household before the household entered the sample, we have no record of its birth.

The sample includes some of the most prominent families and households in the history of Taipei. In Bankha, for example, we have the descendents of Wang I-teh (1796-1858), who had come to Taiwan in his late teens or early twenties after his family in Ch'üan-chou had suffered severe reverses. I-teh built up a significant shipping business, which in time became one of the largest such enterprises in Bankha. He amassed an impressive fortune and, through his generosity and public spirit, earned the respect and affection of the people of Bankha as well.[15]

The household whose register I have is that of Wang Shun-ch'ing (1847-1912, no. 3 in Figure 12.1), son of I-teh's eldest son Tse-shu (1820-1849), who had been a scholar before he died at 29 and whose wife is listed in the Tamsui Prefecture Gazetteer (*Tan-shui T'ing Chih*) as a "virtuous woman." It is not clear what Shun-ch'ing's occupation was, but we know that he was

Male
Foster son adopted from unrelated persons
Female
Concubine
Female adopted as prospective daughter-in-law
Female adopted as foster daughter
Female obtained as bondservant
Died before January 1, 1906
Marriage

△×○ Illicit relationship, and resulting child illegitimate
(M) Person married out
(T) Person left the household to become bondservant in another household
(D) Died after January 1, 1906
(A) Was given out in adoption
HHH Head of household

(Number above symbols refers to order of person's appearance in household register.)

Legend to Figs. 12.1, 12.2, and 12.3

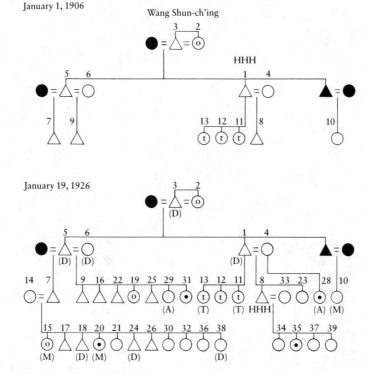

Fig. 12.1. The Wang family of Bankha

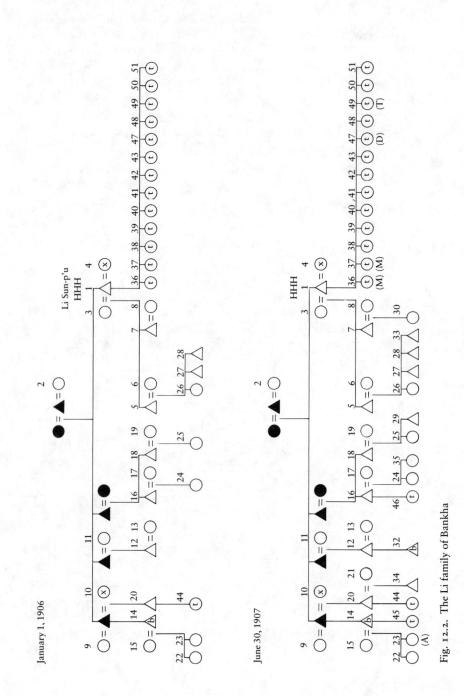

January 1, 1906

Li Sun-p'u
HHH

June 30, 1907

HHH

Fig. 12.2. The Li family of Bankha

January 1, 1906

Ching-sheng

May 31, 1925

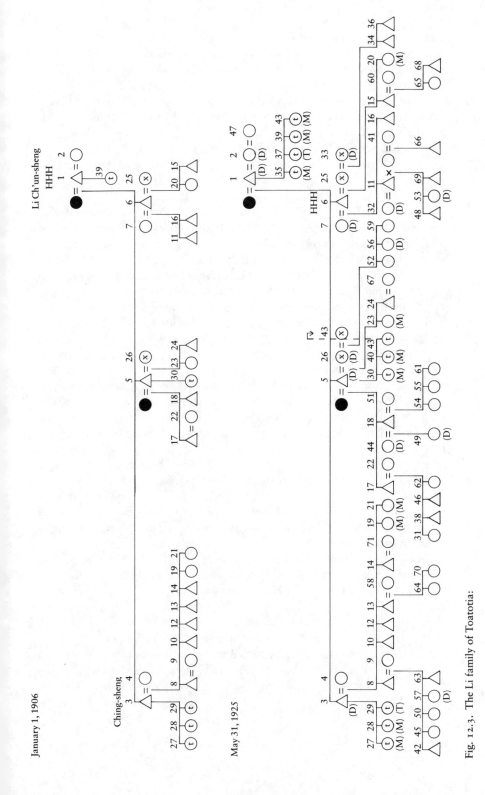

Fig. 12.3. The Li family of Toatotia:

well-known and respected for contributing to local public works and that
he occupied many honorable and honorary positions in the city. The Wang
household was not very large, relative to some other high-status households, but it had all the elements of the Chinese "grand family," with a
man, his wife, their sons, and their sons' wives and children all living
under the same roof. In addition the household included three female
bondservants.

The Bankha sample also includes the descendents of Li Po-ch'ou (1756-
1855), who had been a Confucian scholar in Ch'üan-chou when a geo-
mancer advised him to go as far as possible from his native land. Although
Po-ch'ou started a business in Taiwan, it was his son Chih-ch'ing (1822-
1902) who began the trading company called Li Sheng Fa which eventually
became one of the largest in Bankha. Of Chih-ch'ing's six sons, the first
and last did not survive to adulthood, but the others all distinguished
themselves in scholarship. His fourth son served for a time as assistant
county magistrate. However, only the fifth son, Sun-p'u (1858-1911), out-
lived his father, and it was he who expanded the family business to such an
extent that they were said to be the wealthiest family in the Taipei area,
and their influence is alleged to have surpassed that of the Tamsui Sub-
prefectural Defense.[16]

In 1906, Li Sun-p'u was heading an undivided household, which included his stepmother; the widows, children, and grandchildren of his second, third, and fourth elder brothers; as well as his own wife, concubine,
sons, sons' wives, etc., for a total of 27 family members and 14 bondservants (Figure 12.2). Family division took place just 18 months after the
registers began, and in those 18 months, 15 changes were made in household composition: ten new members entered through birth, marriage,
adoption, or purchase; and five departed through marriage, adoption,
sale, or death. The rate and frequency of these changes gives an idea of the
level of activity in such households. Each individual event would have
thrown an ordinary household into turmoil, not to mention debt, since we
know what elaborate and expensive preparations usually accompanied a
birth, marriage, or death.

Among the elite of Toatotia:, the sample includes the household of Li
Ch'un-sheng (1837-1924), who represented what might be called the
"new breed" of Taiwanese, whose success was due directly to their role as
compradors for Western merchants. Born in Amoy just four years before
the signing of the Treaty of Nanking, which opened that city to Western
commerce and missionaries, Li was converted to Christianity at 15. He became fluent in English through association with missionaries, and came to
know several English merchants with trading companies in Amoy. He began to work for John Dodd, who subsequently brought him to Taiwan,

first to Kao-hsiung in southern Taiwan to open a branch of Dodd's company there, and then to Toatotia: in the mid-1860's to manage the local branches of both Dodd and Boyd companies. Li eventually went into business for himself, amassing a vast fortune through his dealings in tea, petroleum, camphor, and other major exports.[17]

Li Ch'un-sheng was one of three men chosen to head public security in Taipei after Taiwan's cession to Japan, and was subsequently decorated by the Japanese government for his contribution to local affairs, which included acting as informal adviser to the Japanese on matters concerning Taipei's Western community.

Li's eldest son, Ching-sheng, like the sons of many of Taiwan's successful businessmen, excelled in scholarship, but he was active in other fields too, becoming counselor to the Taipei prefectural government under the Japanese and president of the Hsin-kao Bank. His sons distinguished themselves also. One became a provincial assemblyman, another became a banker after returning from studies in the United States.[18] In 1906, Li Ch'un-sheng was still head of his household, which included his three sons, their wives and concubines, their children and children's wives, and five female bondservants (Figure 12.3).

The above typify the elite households in our sample in first establishing themselves through commerce and then becoming prominent in other spheres as well. Most contributed large sums of money to public works. Wu Ch'ang-ts'ai, whose household is in the Bankha sample, initiated the reconstruction of Lungshan Temple in 1920, to which his family firm donated 5,000 gold *yuan*. Ku Hsien-jung of Toatotia: gave 20,000 gold yuan to the same cause; Ch'en T'ien-lai and his father, also of Toatotia:, gave more than 700.[19] Li Ch'un-sheng was a Christian and took no part in temple reconstruction, but he built two churches in the Taipei area.

In addition, all these families sought the prestige traditionally accorded scholars by encouraging sons and nephews to obtain high degrees. Bankha produced four chü-jen degree holders who passed Ch'ing government examinations at the provincial level. Forty-odd others succeeded at the prefectural level and received hsiu-ts'ai degrees.[20] Toatotia: produced even more degree-holders. After the Japanese take-over, many families sent their sons abroad to study. To cite just two examples, one grandson of Li Ch'un-sheng studied in Japan and then in the United States; a son of Wu Ch'ang-ts'ai obtained a degree in economics from the University of Washington.[21]

Few Bankha or Toatotia: residents held high public office, under either the Ch'ing or the Japanese, but both governments sought their support because of their great local influence. Some served in advisory capacities, while others were appointed to regional and local positions. As mentioned

TABLE 12.1

Frequency of Household Sizes by Household Status in Taipei, January 1, 1906

(percent)

Household status	Number of households	Number of members in household			
		1–5	6–10	11–15	16 or more
High	88	21.6%	38.6%	23.9%	15.9%
Middle	150	64.7	34.7	0.7	0
Low	134	83.6	15.1	1.4	0

NOTE: Members include bondservants but exclude others who were unrelated to the head of household by blood, marriage, or adoption, such as servants and employees.

TABLE 12.2

Frequency of Household Types by Household Status in Taipei, January 1, 1906

(percent)

Household status	Number of households	Household type				
		Solitary	Elementary	Stem	Grand	Frereches
High	88	0.0%	38.6%	19.2%	25.0%	17.0%
Middle	150	2.0	49.3	39.3	5.3	4.0
Low	134	0.8	70.1	25.4	2.2	1.5

NOTE: *Solitary*: one person living alone. *Elementary*: married couple, married couple with unmarried children, man or woman with his/her children; includes households with one or more unmarried relatives. *Stem*: married couple and a married child and child's spouse; includes no more than one married pair in any generation, and includes broken families (e.g., widow and married son). *Grand*: two or more married pairs in the second or third generation. *Frereches*: two or more married pairs in the senior generation.

TABLE 12.3

Frequency of Household Depths in Generations by Household Status in Taipei, January 1, 1906

(percent)

Household status	Number of households	Number of generations				
		One	Two	Three	Four	Five
High	88	2.3%	50.0%	35.2%	10.2%	2.3%
Middle	150	4.7	59.3	34.7	1.3	0
Low	134	11.9	66.4	21.6	0	0

earlier, Li Ch'un-sheng was entrusted with Taipei public security and acted as adviser to the Governor-General on relations with Western commercial interests in Taipei. One of his sons was at one time district chief (Japanese *kuchō*, Mandarin *ch'ü-chang*) of Toatotia:. Wu Ch'ang-ts'ai served successively as city assemblyman, adviser to the Governor-General's Office, and Bankha district chief.[22] Ch'en T'ien-lai sat on various Taipei government committees and was appointed Inspector of the Taipei Central Market. His son Ch'en Ch'ing-po became a Taipei city assemblyman in 1934, and later served as chairman for the local administrative reform committee.[23] Besides holding various offices, Ku Hsien-jung attained perhaps the highest honor open to a Taiwanese under the Japanese: in 1934, he was elected to the Japanese House of Peers.[24]

The men described above were some of the most prominent in Taipei. Let us now compare their households with other high-status households in my sample and with households of the other two status groups: Are their households typical of high-status households, and how different are they from middle- and low-status households? Tables 12.1-12.3 classify the households by size, by structural type, and by depth at one point in time: January 1, 1906.

In sheer numbers, the two Li households mentioned above were among the three largest in my sample on that date, containing 41 and 31 members, but they are clearly more similar to other high-status households than to low- or middle-status households. High-status households taken as a group are consistently larger and more complex and have greater depth, and are therefore closer to the stereotypical Chinese ideal regarding family size than are middle-status households, which are, in turn, more "grand" than low-status households. While only 16.5 percent of the low-status households and 35.4 percent of the middle-status households had more than five members, 78.4 percent of the high-status households did. Additionally, no low- or middle-status household had more than 15 members, while 15.9 percent of the high status had 16 or more. The same pattern holds when we look at the number of generations within households, as well as the complexity of the households.

Forms of Marriage on Taiwan

The preceding section established that households of the three status groups differed in appearance, i.e., in size and composition. Did they also behave differently when it came to one of their most important goals: assuring the continuation of their descent line? This section will describe briefly the forms of marriage on Taiwan. The next section will set forth my expectations regarding the relative frequencies of these forms within each group and report what the data indicate.

Depending on the newly wed couple's place of residence, anthropologists distinguish at least three forms of marriage: virilocal, in which the woman enters as a member of her husband's family; uxorilocal, in which the man becomes a resident member of his wife's family; and neolocal, in which the couple establishes an independent household away from both natal families. Neolocal marriage among the Chinese is a recent trend and rare among the sampled households. The three forms of marriage I will examine are uxorilocal marriage and the two principal variants of virilocal marriage found on Taiwan: the "major" and "minor" forms. The basic difference between the last two forms is that, while the bride in a major marriage enters her husband's household for the first time, as an adult, on the day of their marriage, the bride in a minor marriage has already been a member of her husband's household for years, having been adopted and raised by her husband's family from childhood as a simpua. It is clear from writings about marriage among the Chinese and from conversations with Chinese themselves, that major marriage was the culturally preferred form and the way every Chinese would have wished to marry. In fact, however, many marriages among the Chinese of Taipei did not take this form. The ultimate reason for this is uncertain, but there are several related factors that made major marriage difficult for some segments of the population.

There was, first of all, a shortage of women in the Taipei region. The earliest figures I have, dating from 1896, indicate that for Bankha, Taototia:, and Senglai, which together made up urban Taipei, the sex ratio of the total population was 139.10 males per 100 females, while that for Taiwanese only was 129.37 (Table 12.4). Second, the survival rate of females was lower than that of males. As George Barclay observed in his book *Colonial Development and Population in Taiwan*,

the chances of surviving through infancy and childhood had been extremely poor for girls before 1895, and . . . this handicap disappeared only gradually in later years. . . . [By] the time they were nearing age 20—the range when most of them married—there were not enough women to furnish wives for the eligible men. In 1920, for example, there were nearly 20 "surplus" males for every 100 females in the age group 15-19, who could not find wives from the same age group, and would have had difficulty in finding them from any younger groups of girls which had suffered similar high mortality.[25]

Although Barclay was citing census figures for all Taiwan, the differential survival rate no doubt applied to Taipei's population as well. Third, what women there were were unequally allocated because concubinage allowed some men more than one woman. Although only 56 women in my sample entered the 97 high-status households as concubines between 1876 and 1935, other concubines died or were otherwise removed from the sampled households before my record of them began, so that the actual number was undoubtedly higher. In addition, I purposely excluded from the sample households with only one concubine or one female bondservant. Whatever the actual numbers involved, the taking of concubines by some men could only have aggravated the shortage of marriageable women. Whether or not it was competition that pushed up the cost of acquiring an adult bride, a further reason why major marriage was not universally practiced had to do with its cost.

TABLE 12.4

Sex Ratio of the Population of Taipei City, 1896 and 1905-1946

(males per 100 females)

Year	Total population	Taiwanese only	Year	Total population	Taiwanese only
1896[a]	139.10	129.37	1926	108.11	98.63
1905[b]	116.81		1927	108.12	98.57
1906	120.55		1928	107.69	98.06
1907	121.68		1929	107.87	98.03
1908	121.64		1930	108.05	98.36
1909	122.24		1931	106.57	98.01
1910	120.92		1932	105.95	99.24
1911	120.16		1933	105.17	99.20
1912	120.98		1934	105.08	100.23
1913	120.14		1935	104.78	98.84
1914	119.56		1936	105.09	99.44
1915	111.68	100.65	1937	104.01	99.56
1916	110.85	100.39	1938	102.61	98.68
1917	109.48	100.46	1939	103.24	100.39
1918	109.81	100.95	1940	103.65	101.15
1919	109.52	101.37	1941	104.92	102.20
1920	111.95	101.63	1942	103.88	101.70
1921	112.61	101.27	1943	103.68	101.14
1922	111.20	100.18	1944	102.40	101.06
1923	110.65	99.74	1945	101.90	100.89
1924	108.79	98.94	1946	99.48	96.87
1925	109.12	99.55			

[a]Figures are for the urbanized area of Taipei City commonly referred to as the "three towns of Taipei," Bankha, Taototia:, and Senglai. Based on Huang Te-shih, *Tai-pei shih yen-ko chih kao* [Draft records of the development of Taipei City] (1961), p. 86.
[b]My source did not differentiate people by place of origin prior to 1915. Based on *T'ai-pei shih-cheng-fu chu-chi shih*, 1950, 4.

Briefly, the marriage ritual consisted of initial inquiries by the boy's family about the potential bride and her family, exchanges of genealogical and horoscopic charts between the two families, betrothal and exchanges of gifts and money, setting the marriage date, and finally, the transfer of the bride to the groom's home and the marriage ceremony.[26] Although the ceremonies could be more or less elaborate depending on the resources of the two families, major marriage always involved large expenses. In addition to those incurred by both sides for the go-betweens who were essential to every exchange between the families, the banquets punctuating each rite, and the fortunetellers, the groom's family had to provide bridewealth and the bride's family a dowry. According to Suzuki Seiichiro, a Japanese observer writing in the 1930's, the average family paid 600 yuan in bridewealth for an average bride, and 1,000 yuan or more for a pretty girl with the equivalent of a high school education. Given that skilled and semi-skilled laborers at the time earned at most 2.5 yuan a day, or an average of less than 500 yuan a year,[27] it took years for families of laborers to set aside enough money to obtain a bride for one of their members, even if bride-wealth amounted to only one-half or one-third the 600 yuan quoted by Suzuki.

We have no comparable figures for the average bride's dowry. However, Suzuki says that some wealthy households felt it such a point of honor to demonstrate that their daughter would never burden her husband's family that they provided her not only with the usual items of furniture, clothing, and jewelry, but with a lifetime's supply of rice, soy sauce, toiletries, and firewood, as well as money to be set aside for her eventual funeral. In addition, the bride's family might give her some real estate and a sum of "private money" for her personal use: "several thousand yuan was not uncommon and several tens of thousands was not unheard of." [28]

Another Japanese observer, Ikeda Toshio, witnessed the marriage of a daughter of "a certain family" in Bankha in 1922. Apparently he was also privy to the list of articles she took as her dowry. These included 8 pieces of furniture; 16 silk dresses, skirts, and trousers; pillows, blankets, and quilts; bolts of silk and cotton cloth; cups, saucers, bowls, lacquer trays, flower vases, candlesticks, silver wine cups and flasks; drapes, scrolls, screens, and mosquito nets; several dozen silk and cotton handkerchiefs; a dozen pairs of slippers and shoes; purses, handbags, and strongboxes; mirrors, cosmetics, shoe and tooth polish; about 500 yuan; pearl and gold hair ornaments, assorted jade jewelry, and 40 pieces of gold jewelry.[29] It goes without saying that families of middle and low income gave their daughters less lavish dowries. Since providing "appropriate" dowries was a matter of family face, however, even poor people felt compelled to make sacrifices so that they and their daughters would not be looked down on by their friends, neighbors, and in-laws.

In minor marriage, a man marries a woman who was adopted as a child and raised by his family. The sequence of events and rituals leading from the initial inquiries to the marriage itself was essentially the same as that for major marriage, but the transfer of the bride-to-be took place at betrothal rather than just prior to the marriage ceremony, and the interval between betrothal and marriage naturally tended to be much longer—to allow time for the children to grow up. In addition, the rituals were generally less elaborate and thus less costly, even when wealthy families were involved. Again according to Suzuki, the boy's family might send no more than a string of cash amounting to two to four yuan for the simpua and some simple food for her family. It might also give the girl's family money, but this was a very small sum and was sometimes omitted altogether if the girl was very young, say 2 or 3 years old, since the major expense of raising her would have been borne by the adoptive family. It might give the family of a 7- or 8-year-old girl as much as 100 yuan as "reimbursement" for having raised her thus far,[30] but even that is clearly much less than bridewealth for an adult bride. A simpua's dowry was similarly very modest and sometimes consisted of no more than a new suit of clothing for herself.

When the young people were old enough to marry, a propitious date was picked, and a private ceremony called "a marriage within the household" (*ho-lai hun-in*) was held, involving simply the worship by the young couple at the groom's family altar, accompanied by a communal feast that included only the immediate family of the groom.

In addition to its low cost, there were other advantages to minor marriage. Particularly important in a woman-short society was the assurance the adoption gave the groom's family that it would not lose out altogether in the competition for brides. It also meant the family acquired an extra person who would be useful around the house, particularly as she grew older. Further, the family acquiring the simpua acquired a child who would develop strong emotional ties to her foster family and so would not cause divisiveness in her husband's household.

On the other hand, minor marriage also had its disadvantages. One was its lower prestige, although this could be overcome somewhat by an elaborate public wedding feast. A second problem was the simpua's survival to adulthood. Wolf's figures show that the death rate of adopted daughters was much higher than that of either sons or daughters raised by their own families.[31] Even if a simpua survived, she would not necessarily make a good daughter-in-law. More important, although a close relationship might develop between the girl and her foster-mother/mother-in-law, she might not make a good wife for her foster-brother/husband. One reason that people liked to adopt a baby girl before their son was weaned stemmed from the belief that children suckled by the same woman would be especially close emotionally. The saying was *sang-cng leng-thau kha sang-sim*, to suckle at the same breast leads to the same heart.[32] However, while the boy and girl might indeed love each other as brother and sister, Wolf has found strong support for Westermarck's thesis that early and close childhood association produced sexual aversion, a condition that jeopardized the major family goal of marriage, that of producing descendants.[33]

The high rate of premarital pregnancy found for simpua of upper-status households who married in the minor fashion suggests that the Taiwanese were well aware of this danger (Table 12.5). That is, a simpua and her foster brother may have been encouraged to test their sexual compatibility before the marriage ceremony was held. The girl's pregnancy provided unmistakable proof of mutual attraction, or at least, sufficient toleration to produce progeny. The much higher incidence of such pregnancies among the high-status households probably does not reflect a greater awareness

TABLE 12.5

*Frequency of Premarital Pregnancy by Status among Women Born 1886-1925
Marrying in the Minor Fashion in Taipei*

Status and measure	Wife's year of birth				Total
	1886-1895	1896-1905	1906-1915	1916-1925	
High					
No. of marriages	15	7	3	2	27
Wife pregnant at marriage:					
Number	3	3	2	1	9
Percent	20.0%	42.9%	66.7%	50.0%	33.3%
Middle					
No. of marriages	16	11	1	0	28
Wife pregnant at marriage:					
Number	2	2	1	–	5
Percent	12.5%	18.2%	100.0%	–	17.9%
Low					
No. of marriages	9	5	5	1	20
Wife pregnant at marriage:					
Number	1	2	2	–	5
Percent	11.1%	40.0%	40.0%	–	25.0%

of, or concern for, possible aversion between foster siblings. More likely it
indicates that high-status households were better able to pursue alternatives if the couple proved incompatible, so that many couples who failed
the compatibility test were never forced to marry. Middle- and low-status
families, with their more limited resources, might have realized that their
simpua and her future husband would not be happy with each other but
could do little but hope for the best.

The third form of marriage found on Taiwan is uxorilocal marriage,
whereby the "summoned husband" (*chio-fu*) becomes a member of his
wife's family. The rituals involved are again variants of those for major
marriage, except that they were usually simplified and reversed, in that it is
the groom who gets "looked over" by the bride's family and who is
ultimately transferred from his natal home to that of his wife with *his*
"dowry." The terms and conditions imposed on the summoned husband
differed, however, from those for the in-marrying bride in several important ways.

First, not all the children born to the uxorilocally married couple auto-
matically belonged to the wife's family. Depending on agreements made
before marriage, some or all of the children might take the man's surname

TABLE 12.6

Surname Styles of First-Born Sons of Uxorilocal Marriages by Household Status, Taipei Sample, 1906-1945

Household status	Number born	Mother's surname		Father's surname		Double surname	
		Number	Percent	Number	Percent	Number	Percent
High	1	0	–	1	100.0%	0	–
Middle	18	7	38.9%	10	55.6	1	5.6%
Low	21	6	28.6	14	66.7	1	4.8
TOTAL	40	13	32.5%	25	62.5%	2	5.0%

and thus belong to his patriline, although we are uncertain what the usual arrangement was. Suzuki says that in most cases the first son belonged to the man's line and the second to the wife's, while another authority claims the reverse was true.[34] Of the first-born sons of uxorilocal marriages in my sample, more than 60 percent took their father's surname (Table 12.6). Second, while virilocal residence for the in-marrying woman lasted as long as she lived or until she was divorced, the uxorilocal residence of the summoned husband was usually limited by contract, so that after the specified five, ten, or more years had elapsed, he could take his wife and those children assigned to his lineage and set up an independent household with himself as head. Alternatively, he could return to his own father's household. A third difference between the virilocally married woman and the uxorilocally married man was that the former became a member of her husband's line at marriage and thereafter worshiped his ancestors, whereas except in rare instances, the uxorilocally married man did not sacrifice to his wife's family's ancestors or inherit property from that family. By the same token, he did not lose the right to sacrifice to his father's ancestors or the right to his patrimony. The exception was the man who "wrote a contract of severance" (*hsia-tng*), thereby breaking all relations with his patriline and acquiring the right to remove his personal tablet from his paternal altar and place it on the altar of his wife's family.[35]

Although the lot of the summoned husband may seem more tolerable than that of the in-marrying bride, in a patriarchal society like China's uxorilocal marriages were considered not only abnormal by definition, but inferior. The general male attitude toward such marriages is summed up by the saying "So long as I have one bowl of rice to eat, I will not be a summoned husband."

For people without sons, the uxorilocal marriage of daughters or foster daughters gave them a way to extend their descent line without adopting male children. Some people who had sons late in life or whose sons were sickly might arrange uxorilocal marriages for older daughters as insurance against the possibility that their sons would not produce heirs. In either case, the family with the summoned husband also had access to the labor and earnings the man could provide. There was a third reason for bringing in a son-in-law: some parents loved their daughter too much to see her marry out. However, because the marriage was considered so contrary to the natural order of things and because only socially and economically inferior men would even contemplate such a marriage, it was unlikely that anyone would resort to it unless there was no other choice.

Household Status and Marriage Form

The reader will recall that the fundamental premises of this paper are that households are rational actors making decisions about how a son or a daughter should marry on the basis of the costs and benefits involved, and that households of different socioeconomic status will behave differently precisely because of their status differences. I also said, however, that households do not exist in a vacuum but rather as members of a sociocultural system that delimits the range of behaviors considered acceptable and arranges the available options on a scale of cultural preferability. In general, I would expect that the higher the status of a household, the more likely its behavior is to cluster at the top end of the scale, and the lower the status, the more likely its behavior is to cluster at the bottom end. But I would also expect that even the very-low-status households would not go off the scale altogether. Thus, for example, while marriage might have been difficult for some people, few Chinese would never marry and few households would fail to arrange marriages for their offspring because the culture declared it imperative that every man marry and every male line have a successor.

In fact, marriage was almost universal for Taiwanese men and women both, at least during most of the period under study (Table 12.7). That being the case, how did the men of Taipei, and in particular the men from low-status households, marry, given the shortage of women and the costliness of major marriage? Did they marry women who were considered less than ideal in terms of physical appearance, age, or social acceptability— former prostitutes, for example, or the previously married? Did they delay marriage until enough money could be saved to afford an adult bride? Or did they resort to the less prestigious forms of marriage?

The household registers did not rate people on physical appearance. Only scanty information is available for a person entering a particular household for the first time unless his or her previous household happened to be among those already in my sample. In most cases, then, it is impos-

TABLE 12.7

Proportions of Taiwanese Ever Married by Age and Sex, 1905-1935

Age	1905	1915	1920	1925	1930	1935
			MALES			
10-14	0.1	0.0	0.2	0.1	0.1	0.1
15-19	10.2	5.7	6.3	5.3	7.3	5.7
20-24	45.7	40.1	42.8	44.7	51.6	49.8
25-29	77.4	72.9	76.5	78.2	82.9	83.1
30-34	89.4	88.1	88.6	89.7	91.3	91.9
35 and over	95.3	95.4	95.5	95.8	96.2	96.0
			FEMALES			
10-14	2.3	0.7	0.6	0.4	0.5	0.4
15-19	47.3	34.7	32.8	29.4	32.6	28.1
20-24	91.6	87.4	86.6	84.4	86.3	83.0
25-29	98.2	96.6	96.9	96.2	96.1	95.9
30-34	99.2	98.5	98.5	98.3	98.0	97.7
35 and over	99.7	99.5	99.4	99.3	99.3	99.0

SOURCE: George W. Barclay, *Colonial Development and Population in Taiwan* (Princeton, N.J., 1954), p. 211.

sible to determine a person's attractiveness, social background, or previous marital status. One can, however, compare the ages of husbands and wives. Table 12.8 does this for men and women who married in the major fashion between 1896 and 1925. Interestingly, although native informants and foreign observers alike state that the ideal was for the husband to be three or four years older than the wife,[36] my figures show that this was often not the case in practice: 26 percent of the men of high-status households were *younger* than their wives, as opposed to 13 percent for men of middle status, and 7 percent for men of low status. On the other hand, while only 15 percent of the high-status men were more than five years older than their wives, the figure for middle-status men was 33 percent, low-status men 44 percent. Whatever constituted the true ideals of the Chinese of Taipei, if we accept as "ideal behavior" the behavior exhibited by high-status households, men of low-status households were most "deviant."

With respect to age at marriage, our sources tell us that early marriage was an ideal in late traditional and early modern China.[37] This time the data corroborate their claims. For those born between 1876 and 1905 who married in the major fashion, 92 percent of the men of high-status households married before the age of 25, as compared with 71 percent of the men of middle status and 67 percent of the men of low status (Table 12.9). Correspondingly, while more than 5 percent of the low-status men married after age 35, this was true of just slightly more than 2 percent of the middle-

TABLE 12.8

Age Differences Between Husbands and Wives by Household Status in Taipei Sample's Major Marriages, 1896-1925

Direction and degree of difference	High status		Middle status		Low status	
	Number	Percent	Number	Percent	Number	Percent
Wife is older by:						
>1-5 years	19	11.2%	7	7.6%	2	2.8%
>0-1 year	25	14.8	5	5.4	3	4.2
SUBTOTAL	44	26.0%	12	13.0%	5	7.0%
Husband is older by:						
>0-1 year	29	17.2%	9	9.8%	8	11.1%
>1-5 years	71	42.0	41	44.6	27	37.5
>5-10 years	15	8.9	18	19.6	23	31.9
>10-15 years	9	5.3	12	13.0	7	9.7
>15 years	1	0.6	0	0	2	2.8
SUBTOTAL	125	(74.0)%	80	87.0%	67	93.0%
TOTAL	169	100.0%	92	100.0%	72	100.0%

TABLE 12.9

Age at Marriage by Household Status for Men in Taipei Sample Born 1876-1905

Man's age at marriage	High status		Middle status		Low status	
	Number	Percent	Number	Percent	Number	Percent
>15	2	1.2%	2	2.3%	2	3.5%
>15≤20	81	47.9	28	32.2	13	22.8
>20≤25	73	43.2	32	36.8	23	40.4
SUBTOTAL	156	92.3%	62	71.3%	38	66.7%
>25≤30	9	5.3%	18	20.7%	13	22.8%
>30≤35	1	0.6	5	5.7	3	5.3
>35	3	1.8	2	2.3	3	5.3
SUBTOTAL	13	7.7%	25	28.7%	19	33.4%
TOTAL	169	100.0%	87	100.0%	57	100.1%

status men, and less than 2 percent of the high-status men. Thus it does seem that men of low status tended to delay marriage, and it seems likely that they did so because poverty compelled them to.

With regard to form of marriage, I would expect, first, that for all the households studied the frequencies of marriage forms would vary with their prestige value, and that major marriages would therefore account for the largest portion of marriages; that minor marriages would be the next most frequent; and uxorilocal marriages least frequent. Differentiating the households by status, I would expect that members of high-status households would most often marry in the major fashion, because it was the culturally preferred form and because they would both be able to afford such marriages and covet the prestige associated with them. I would expect that low-status households would most need to avoid the expenses of a major marriage and be the most concerned to ensure as early as possible the availability of a bride for their sons and would therefore resort most often to minor marriages. Finally, I would expect that uxorilocal marriages would be rare among every status group, but especially rare among high-status households who could afford to bring in concubines to increase their chances of having sons. In short, my expectations are that the frequency with which households practiced one form of marriage or another would vary directly with the status of the household and the prestige value of the marriage form.

The findings bear out my expectations. Table 12.10 says that, for all men born between 1886 and 1925 who were born or adopted into the sampled households and who were known to be marrying for the first time, 80.8 percent married in the major fashion, 15.7 percent in the minor fashion, and 3.6 percent uxorilocally. Further, except for one age cohort among low-status men, the same relationship of major to minor to uxorilocal marriages held within each status group and for every age cohort. That is, there were more major marriages than minor marriages, which were in turn more numerous than uxorilocal marriages. The one exception was the cohort of low-status men born between 1886 and 1895, among whom there were as many uxorilocal as minor marriages. While one might speculate on the reasons for this, the figures are in any case consistent with what might have been expected, given the particular sex imbalance of Taipei's population between 1896 and 1915 (see Table 12.4), during which period these men would have reached marriageable age.

Finally, the findings substantiate my expectation that the higher the status of a household, the more likely it would be to arrange major marriages for its sons and the less likely it would be to arrange minor or uxorilocal marriages. And conversely, the lower the status of a household, the less likely it would be to arrange major marriages and the more likely it would be to arrange minor and uxorilocal marriages. That the behavior of middle-status households was generally closer to that of low-status households highlights the social distance between the elite and the rest of society.

That there were any uxorilocal marriages among men of high-status households deserves comment and closer examination. Part of the explanation may be that Table 12.10 does not distinguish between men who were recorded simply as having "married out" and men who were specifiedly "summoned out." In fact, of the three high-status men who left their parents' households at marriage (including one who falls outside the birth

TABLE 12.10

Frequency of Marriage Forms by Husband's Household Status and Date of Birth
for Men Born or Adopted into Sample Taipei Households, 1906-1945

Household status and man's date of birth	Number of marriages	Form of marriage					
		Major		Minor		Uxorilocal	
		Number	Percent	Number	Percent	Number	Percent
All statuses							
1886-1895	153	115	75.2%	30	19.6%	8	5.2%
1896-1905	101	80	79.2	17	16.8	4	4.0
1906-1915	65	59	90.8	6	9.2	0	–
1916-1925	19	19	100.0	0	–	0	–
TOTAL	338	273	80.8%	53	15.7%	12	3.6%
High status							
1886-1895	75	61	81.3%	13	17.3%	1	1.3%
1896-1905	56	50	89.3	5	8.9	1	1.8
1906-1915	28	25	89.3	3	10.7	0	–
1916-1925	10	10	100.0	0	–	0	–
TOTAL	169	146	86.4%	21	12.4%	2	1.2%
Middle status							
1886-1895	42	28	66.7%	12	28.6%	2	4.8%
1896-1905	30	21	70.0	8	26.7	1	3.3
1906-1915	23	23	100.0	0	–	0	–
1916-1925	7	7	100.0	0	–	0	–
TOTAL	102	79	77.5%	20	19.6%	3	2.9%
Low status							
1886-1895	36	26	72.2%	5	13.9%	5	13.9%
1896-1905	15	9	60.0	4	26.7	2	13.3
1906-1915	14	11	78.6	3	21.4	0	–
1916-1925	2	2	100.0	0	–	0	–
TOTAL	67	48	71.6%	12	17.9%	7	10.4%

cohorts listed in Table 12.10), only one was specifically said to have been
"summoned." Of the two who simply "married out," one later returned to
his natal household with his wife and two children, and still later split
away from his elder brother. In other words, he had not relinquished his
inheritance rights. The other married a Japanese woman and moved to
Tokyo. Since marrying into one's wife's family was not considered demean-
ing in Japan, and since Taiwan was under Japanese rule at the time, perhaps this was a case where Japanese rather than Chinese cultural ideals
prevailed. The one man from a high-status household who was specifically
listed as having married uxorilocally was 12 years old and living in the
household of his father's elder brother when the household registers began
in 1906. No other member of his immediate family was present, so he
probably was the sole survivor of his father's line. His uxorilocal marriage
at the advanced age of 43, together with his family background, suggests

he was a poor relation who was not considered a true member of the household, and whose marriage was therefore not considered consequential enough to undermine the household's prestige.

The Taipei sample includes the households of 17 men of all statuses whose first marriages were uxorilocal. The exact composition of the households of three of these men at their time of marriage is not known, but of the 14 others, only one, the high-status man who married out to Japan, had both parents living. Five (36 percent) of the 14 did not have fathers; two had no mothers; and six (43 percent) had neither father nor mother. Obviously for a man who lacks the support of parents necessary to make a normal, virilocal marriage, uxorilocal marriage is a rational step. Furthermore, unlike women who were economically dependent on their own husband's family, men had the means to support themselves. Thus they also had the means to extricate themselves from an unsatisfactory marriage. It is this freedom that makes uxorilocal marriages the least stable of the three forms, as Wolf's data and mine indicate.[38] That there were so few of these marriages, despite the advantages they offered and their reversibility, shows how strongly cultural ideas influenced behavior.

Looking at the marriages of women born and adopted into the sampled households who remained in the households until they married, we find that, at least among those women born between 1886 and 1925, major marriages predominated (Table 12.11). We again find a correlation between the status of the household and the frequency of major marriage: the higher the status, the greater the relative frequency of major marriage. We find, however, that while the same relative importance of major, minor, and uxorilocal marriages held for women of high- and middle-status households as obtained for men, it did not hold for low-status women: more women of low-status households married in the uxorilocal fashion than in the minor fashion. In fact 23.6 percent of all women of low status who married did so uxorilocally, and the percentage is even higher if we exclude adopted daughters and look at only the natural daughters of the households.

Significantly, of the 60 uxorilocally married women born or adopted into the sampled households who were born between 1876 and 1925, only two (3.3 percent) had older brothers, while 23 (38.3 percent) had younger but not older brothers, and 35 (58.3 percent) had no male siblings at all (Table 12.12). Of the two who had older brothers, one had been adopted as a simpua by a middle-status household when she was three days old, at which time her foster brother, an only son, was six months old. It seems likely that the two children were originally intended to marry each other. Instead, a husband was summoned in for the girl when she was 14, her foster-brother 15, and her foster-father 44 years old. This seems early for

TABLE 12.11

Forms of First Marriage by Household Status for Women Born 1886-1925
Who Were Born or Adopted into Taipei Sample Households

Household status and category	Form of marriage						Total married[a]
	Major		Minor		Uxorilocal		
	Number	Percent	Number	Percent	Number	Percent	
High status							
Natural daughters	65	100.0%	0	–	0	–	65
Adopted daughters	46	59.7	29	37.7%	2	2.6%	77
TOTAL	111	78.2	29	20.4	2	1.4	142
Middle status							
Natural daughters	39	86.7	0	–	6	13.3	45
Adopted daughters	35	48.6	28	38.9	9	12.5	72
TOTAL	74	63.2	28	23.9	15	12.8	117
Low status							
Natural daughters	27	73.0	0	–	10	27.0	37
Adopted daughters	35	50.7	19	27.5	15	21.7	69
TOTAL	62	58.5	19	17.9	25	23.6	106

[a]Excludes female bondservants.

TABLE 12.12

Sibling Set at Marriage by Household Status for Women Born 1876-1925
in Taipei Sample Who Married Uxorilocally

Measure	Household status			Total
	High	Middle	Low	
No. of women	3	28	29	60
Sibling set				
No siblings	1	9	9	19
Percent	33.3%	32.1%	31.0%	31.7%
Sisters but no brothers	0	9	7	16
Percent	–	32.1%	24.1%	26.7%
Younger but no older brothers	2	9	12	23
Percent	66.7%	32.1%	41.4%	38.3%
At least one older brother	0	1	1	2
Percent	–	3.6%	3.4%	3.3%

NOTE: Includes women born and adopted into sampled households, but not bondservants. Sibling sets include foster siblings.

the foster siblings to have discovered they were sexually incompatible (although my sample does include people who married at age 12), and also too early for their father/foster-father to have been anxious about the birth of a grandson. Since the records show that the son died at age 32 without ever marrying, the likeliest explanation for the early, uxorilocal marriage of the girl is that her foster brother was sickly, and a husband was brought in for her because the family needed the help of a healthy adult male and the assurance of descendants.

The other woman who married uxorilocally even though she had older brothers was a low-status woman whose brothers were 21 and 23 years older than she. When she married at the age of 17, her brothers were 38 and 40 years old, and neither had produced any children. In fact, the elder of the two died a bachelor at 56, the younger was left a childless widower at 43. The parents of these three probably realized they had little chance of obtaining grandchildren through their sons and so finally placed their hopes on their daughter.

What the sibling sets of the uxorilocally marrying women and the details about the two women above indicate are that those households who arranged uxorilocal marriages for their daughters did so because they had little other choice. They needed the labor and income that an able-bodied adult male could provide, and they had to rely on their daughters for the continuation of their descent lines. Far from being useless drains on family resources who grew up only to produce sons for other people's lineages, as Chinese adages would have us believe, *some* daughters at least were very important to their natal families; indeed, they were crucial to their family's survival.

The tables above told us how children of the various households actually married. They indicate that the stereotypes regarding marriage practices as expressed by elite ideology, Western and Chinese scholars, and even local informants do not give a complete account of the range of behavior found among the population of even a small area in Taiwan. Although Taipei's high-status households conformed more closely to Chinese social norms and ideals than did middle- and low-status households, even they sometimes resorted to the less prestigious forms of marriages. On the other hand, it is clear that the same norms that dictated the behavior of the elite group also had relevance for the population at large. Households of middle and low status did not achieve the ideals as frequently as the high-status group, but even among people of low status, the relative frequency of the three forms of marriage was directly related to the prestige value of the forms, as Table 12.13 shows. In addition, major marriages accounted for well over half of all marriages for all status groups, whether one looks at the entire period under discussion as a whole or broken down by decades.

It might be argued that some of the low- and middle-status households backed into conforming to elite ideology. That is, the fact that major marriages occurred so frequently among these two groups arose not from their subscription to elite ideals, but rather from a lack of choice. Some households may have preferred minor marriages but were too destitute even to

TABLE 12.13

Frequency of Marriage Forms by Receiving Household Status for Taipei Sample,
1896-1945

Household status and year of marriage	Number of marriages[a]	Marriage form					
		Major		Minor		Uxorilocal	
		Number	Percent	Number	Percent	Number	Percent
High status							
1896-1905	75	67	89.3%	6	8.0%	2	2.7%
1906-1915	71	55	77.5	16	22.5	0	0.0
1916-1925	56	50	89.3	5	8.9	1	1.8
1926-1935	24	22	91.7	2	8.3	0	0.0
1936-1945	19	17	89.5	1	5.3	1	5.3
TOTAL	245	211	86.6%	30	12.2%	4	1.6%
Middle status							
1896-1905	69	41	59.4%	15	21.7%	13	18.8%
1906-1915	59	41	69.5	11	18.6	7	11.9
1916-1925	32	20	62.5	10	31.2	2	6.2
1926-1935	36	29	80.6	1	2.8	6	16.7
1936-1945	13	12	92.3	0	0.0	1	7.7
TOTAL	209	143	68.4%	37	17.7%	29	13.9%
Low status							
1896-1905	58	34	58.6%	16	27.6%	8	13.8%
1906-1915	42	26	61.9	6	14.3	10	23.8
1916-1925	31	18	58.1	5	16.1	8	25.8
1926-1935	18	11	61.1	4	22.2	3	16.7
1936-1945	4	4	100.0	0	0.0	0	0.0
TOTAL	153	93	60.8%	31	20.3%	29	19.0%

[a]Includes only marriages in which both partners are marrying for the first time. Only marriages occurring within sampled households are included, thus excluding marriages in which a household member marries out.

adopt prospective daughters-in-law; or they may have adopted a simpua with the intention of marrying her to their son but she died in childhood; finally, they may have wanted to adopt simpua but lost out in the keen competition for young girls.

Table 12.14 lists the boys born or adopted into the sampled households by whether they were matched with foster sisters whom they might have married. All boys whose parents/adoptive-parents adopted a girl no more than ten years younger and no more than five years older than the boys were considered "matched," and no distinction is made between girls adopted in as simpua (prospective daughters-in-law) and those adopted as *yong-lu* (foster daughters) because the Taiwanese of Taipei did not themselves seem to make clear distinctions between these two categories, and because, in any case, the status of a yong-lu could have been officially changed to that of simpua, and vice-versa, if the household so desired.

TABLE 12.14
Males in Taipei Sample Born 1896-1925 Who Were Matched with Foster Sisters,
by Household Status

Household status and year of birth	Number of males	Matched males	
		Number	Percent
High status			
1896-1905	173	39	22.5%
1906-1915	262	50	19.1
1916-1925	154	12	7.8
TOTAL	589	101	17.1%
Middle status			
1896-1905	146	50	34.2%
1906-1915	146	33	22.6
1916-1925	90	18	20.0
TOTAL	382	101	26.4%
Low status			
1896-1905	65	16	24.6%
1906-1915	87	18	20.7
1916-1925	87	17	19.5
TOTAL	239	51	21.3%
All statuses			
1896-1905	384	105	27.3%
1906-1915	495	101	20.4
1916-1925	331	47	14.2
TOTAL	1210	253	20.9%

NOTE: Includes males born and adopted into sampled households. "Matched" males include all those who had foster sisters no more than ten years younger and no more than five years older.

Of 1,210 boys born between 1896 and 1925, 253 (20.9 percent) were ever matched with a possible candidate for minor marriage. Overall, high-status households matched their sons somewhat less frequently than low-status households, which in turn matched fewer sons than middle-status households. But except for the cohort of boys born between 1916 and 1925, the differences between groups were not large and do not permit any obvious conclusions.

If we next look at the incidence of death among adopted females, we find that the proportion was higher among matched females of low-status households than of the other two groups: 9.8 percent of the low-status matched females died before their prospective husband reached age 15, as compared with 5.9 percent for middle-status females, and 4.0 percent for the high-status females (Table 12.15). This suggests that, had the survival rate of prospective daughters-in-law been equal for the three status groups, there would have been relatively more minor marriages among the low-

TABLE 12.15

Incidence of Death among Girls in Taipei Sample Matched to Boys Born
1896-1925 by Household Status and Intended Husband's Year of Birth

Household status and year of birth	Number of matched males	Deaths of matched girls	
		Number	Percent
High status			
1896-1905	39	1	2.6%
1906-1915	50	3	6.0
1916-1925	12	0	–
TOTAL	101	4	4.0%
Middle status			
1896-1905	50	1	2.0%
1906-1915	33	1	3.0
1916-1925	18	4	22.2
TOTAL	101	6	5.9%
Low status			
1896-1905	16	1	6.2%
1906-1915	18	2	11.1
1916-1925	17	2	11.8
TOTAL	51	5	9.8%

NOTE: Deaths were counted when the girl died before her intended husband reached age 15.

status households, who in fact more often had recourse to adopted daughters than the other groups. On the other hand, the completion rate of minor marriages (Table 12.16) indicates that, for all status groups, many more such marriages could have taken place than actually did, although the rate was higher for low-status households (21.9 percent) than for the other two status groups (11.8 percent for middle-status households, 11.4 percent for those of high status).

It is still possible that, in Taiwan's female-short population, the competition for adoptable girls was so great that it contributed to the relative infrequency with which people matched their sons and so, indirectly, to the low rate of minor marriage. Although one's own daughters were dispensable, other people's daughters were highly desirable for a number of reasons other than their value as future daughters-in-law: rich people needed bondservants, who were almost always female; childless people, both married and single, adopted foster children for companionship and support in old age, and in fact preferred girls to boys because the former were considered easier to raise and more loyal; couples without sons adopted girls in the widely held belief that the latter had the power to induce male births; some people even adopted girls because they wanted daughters.

Table 12.17, which controls for mortality and loss of households to the sample, shows that for all girls born between 1906 and 1935, the overall

TABLE 12.16

Completion Rate of Minor Marriages by Household Status for Matched Boys in
Taipei Sample Born 1896-1925

Household status and year of birth	Number of matched boys	Completed minor marriages	
		Number	Percent
High status			
1896-1905	31	5	16.1%
1906-1915	31	3	9.6
1916-1925	8	0	–
TOTAL	70	8	11.4%
Middle status			
1896-1905	33	8	24.2%
1906-1915	23	0	–
1916-1925	12	0	–
TOTAL	68	8	11.8%
Low status			
1896-1905	10	4	40.0%
1906-1915	11	3	27.3
1916-1925	11	0	–
TOTAL	32	7	21.9%
All statuses			
1896-1905	74	17	23.0%
1906-1915	65	6	9.2
1916-1925	31	0	–
TOTAL	170	23	13.5%

NOTE: Excludes pairs in which either the girl or boy died or otherwise was lost to the sample before the boy reached age 15.

TABLE 12.17

Probability of Adoption by Age 15 of Girls in Taipei Sample Born 1906-1935 by
Household Status and Composition of Sibling Set at Birth

Household status and category	Sibling set				
	None	One	Two	Three or more	Overall
High status					
No. of girls born	83	64	61	127	335
No. adopted out	12	16	16	44	88
Probability of adoption	0.22	0.29	0.32	0.42	0.36
Middle status					
No. of girls born	87	47	43	53	230
No. adopted out	13	11	15	21	60
Probability of adoption	0.23	0.28	0.51	0.55	0.37
Low status					
No. of girls born	64	48	47	35	194
No. adopted out	8	12	14	17	51
Probability of adoption	0.20	0.40	0.39	0.64	0.38

NOTE: "Sibling set" includes all natural siblings as well as all male foster siblings, but excludes all female foster siblings. The method used to arrive at these probability figures was one developed by Arthur P. Wolf. A detailed explanation of the method can be found in Arthur P. Wolf and Chieh-shan Huang, *Marriage and Adoption in China: 1845-1945*, Stanford, Calif., pp. 205-8.

probability of out-adoption by age 15 ranged from 36 percent to 38 percent. That probability was higher among girls born to low-status households and increased with birth order, but even girls with three or more siblings in the Taipei sample were much less likely to be given out in adoption than girls born in Hai-shan, where Wolf conducted his study and where the probability of adoption for girls born 1906-15 with three or more siblings was about 83 percent.[39] This means that, at least in Taipei, there were a large number of girls who could have been adopted but were not, and therefore that the demand for girls must not have been great enough to squeeze out low-status households.

That low-status households did not resort to minor marriage more often, then, reflects a preference on the part of the household's decision-makers and was not the result of circumstances that left them no choice.

Conclusion

I began this analysis of the household register data by emphasizing how different the three status groups were: in size of household, household structure, and the number of generations within the household. I end with the observation that while the three status groups differed significantly in some respects, they were remarkably similar in several others. Major marriages predominated in every group; households of every group matched their sons with future daughters-in-law to almost the same extent; and, most surprising of all, high-status households were about as likely to give out their daughters in adoption as low-status households. Considering that the high-status households in my sample include the wealthiest, most elite of Taipei and perhaps of Taiwan, while the low-status households include the poorest and lowliest coolie laborers, the narrowness of the range of variation exhibited by the households is perhaps the more interesting finding, as the introduction to this volume points out. What emerges from this study is not only that there is a consistent relationship between socioeconomic standing and choice among demographic alternatives,[40] but also that the use of an approach that treats households as rational actors can provide valuable explanatory insight into the workings of a sociocultural system, and, in some instances, predict how particular members of the system will behave.

THIRTEEN

On the Causes and Demographic Consequences of Uxorilocal Marriage in China

Burton Pasternak

"In Shang-nan county there is a custom by which people who have no sons but who do have a daughter call a son-in-law into the family. He is customarily known as *shang-men-hsu*, 'the son-in-law at the door.' The in-marrying man and his parents-in-law must prepare a written agreement, and he must pay them 20 strings of cash or 24 ounces of silver. Moreover, he must agree to live with his wife's parents, to look out for them during their lifetimes, and to attend to their funerals when they die. When children are born the eldest son is assigned to his maternal grandfather's line, while the second son takes his descent from his father. Each inherits the property of his own line. In the case in which there is only one son, he succeeds to both lines and inherits both estates."[1]

Like most descriptions of uxorilocal marriages, the foregoing says that they were arranged by families who had daughters but no sons. This implies that they were usually motivated by what might be called preservative (as against practical) concerns. It also implies that they were rare since a population could contain a large number of sonless families only if fertility was very low or childhood mortality very high, and under these conditions there wouldn't be many men available to marry into their wife's family. This essay has two purposes. One is to show that uxorilocal marriages actually served many purposes in China, and that as a consequence their frequency differed from one area to another.[2] The second is to suggest that this variation in the nature and frequency of uxorilocal marriages has demographic consequences; it affects such things as fertility, age at marriage, frequencies of divorce and remarriage, rates of daughter adoption, and even mortality.

My interest in these questions was aroused during field research in Chung-she, a small Hokkien-speaking village in central Taiwan. I was struck by the fact that uxorilocal marriages were very common among older inhabitants of the village, but less common among younger people. It came as a surprise to discover a community in which uxorilocal marriages were common because Chinese and foreign observers alike have so often reported that the Chinese look down upon such marriages and that they are uncommon. Uxorilocality is said to be a marital option exercised only by the relatively small number of poor couples who are unable to bear or adopt a son; it is a less than optimal way to ensure familial and patrilineal continuity. The poor are also said to be more inclined to this solution than the well-to-do because calling in a husband is relatively inexpensive for all parties. The groom usually is not required to produce bridewealth, little if any dowry is expected from the bride's family, and the marriage ceremony, if there is one, is simple. Given a pattern of equal inheritance among sons, a poor family may have difficulty providing many sons with a workable inheritance. Arranging a uxorilocal marriage for one or more of their sons would relieve some of the pressure since a called-in husband acquires usu-fruct rights over the family estate of his wife in exchange for agreeing to allow one or more of his children to carry the maternal surname and to continue her patriline.

Economic advantages notwithstanding, uxorilocal marriage is from all accounts contracted at a high cost in individual and familial status. The groom enters his wife's family like a bride, and indeed is commonly said to *ju-chui*, "enter as a parasite." By agreeing to allow one or more of his children to carry on the maternal line, he turns his back on his own ancestors, an unforgiveable act in Chinese terms even when involuntary. Uxorilocal marriage is undesirable from the point of view of the bride's family as well, since called-in husbands often violate initial understandings and agreements, especially once their children are born or their parents-in-law have passed away. It is for such reasons that uxorilocal marriage is believed to be not only rare but also intrinsically unstable.

Because uxorilocal unions have this reputation, I was amazed to discover in conversations with villagers that they were common in Chung-she during the Japanese colonial period, a fact confirmed by the household registers. Although I was not primarily interested in forms of marriage at the time, I subsequently noted Chung-she's peculiarity in a comparative study of Chinese communities and proposed a tentative explanation:

Uxorilocal marriages . . . were once common in Chungshe. Data from the household registers show a decline in the number of such marriages over the years, but during each of the periods covered there were more *ju-chui* (i.e., uxorilocal husbands) than male adoptions. In many cases, especially prior to 1930, *ju-chui* entered families that had already provided an heir. In a number of instances their entry into a family resulted in joint form. In still other cases, they were brought into families by marriage with a widow. Two points are worth making here. First, whereas uxorilocal marriages were always rare in Tatieh, they were common in Chungshe until 1930 and thereafter became more infrequent. Second, whereas such marriages mainly provided an alternative mechanism for family perpetuation in Tatieh, many that took place in Chungshe could not have been so motivated, since they involved girls whose brothers had already fathered sons. These facts taken together suggest that uxorilocal marriages may have served an additional purpose in Chungshe—they may have satisfied a need for adult male labor, a need linked to Chungshe's dependence on rainfall. Indeed, in most cases known to me in Chungshe, *ju-chui* were called into families deficient in male labor.[3]

Chung-she's poor clay soils required unusual amounts of water and labor to plow and prepare for cultivation. In contrast to practices described for other Chinese villages, in Chung-she before 1930, agriculture was almost entirely dependent on rainfall irrigation; water was obtained not from canals or ponds, but directly from the heavens. The weather permitted only one crop of rice a year. As a result, families had larger holdings than cultivators elsewhere who could grow two or more crops a year using canal irrigation (which allowed some control over the timing of water allocation). When it rained in Chung-she, families had to plow and prepare for transplanting at the same time, so labor exchange between families was rarely possible.

Reliance on rainfall intensified labor demand in Chung-she and in most other villages on the Chia-nan Plain (an area of some 5,000 square kilometers). Because everyone was under pressure to plow and harrow when it rained, the period of preparation was relatively short and labor-intensive. And since the number of days between transplanting and harvest was fixed, the harvest was also short and labor-intensive. Everywhere in China field preparation involves tasks performed only by adult males. It was the unusually short period of field preparation in Chung-she that intensified the usual demand for adult male labor.

Between 1925 and 1930, Japanese authorities constructed a highly integrated system of canals on the Chia-nan Plain (see Map 13.1). Thereafter water was collected and stored in a central reservoir and gradually allocated across the plain in accord with a complicated rotation schedule. The consequences were immediate and profound. Apart from the obvious need to articulate the activities of families within and between communities, and the need for some managerial presence to maintain the irrigation system and limit water theft, labor requirements were affected. Because water was now stored and allocated on a rotational basis, the period of field preparation (and therefore of harvest) was longer, labor could be exchanged, and the demand for labor was lower than before. Thus, I believe that the need for adult males during the period of rainfall dependence was responsible for the unusual frequency of uxorilocal marriages, and that these marriages became less common once the irrigation system had been completed.

How variable was the frequency of uxorilocal marriage in Taiwan? Was

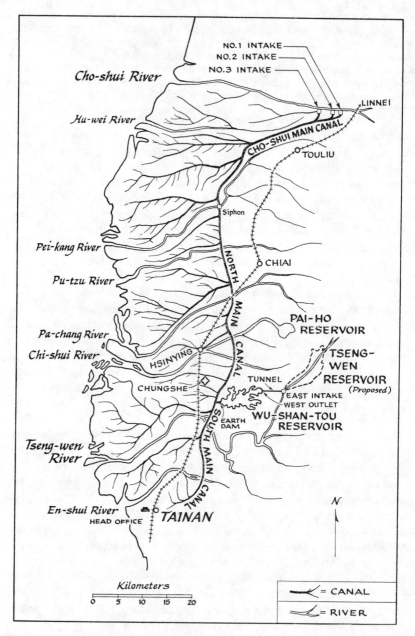

Map. 13.1. The Chia-nan irrigation system. Reproduced from Burton Pasternak, *Kinship and Community in Two Chinese Villages* (Stanford, Calif., 1972), p. 40.

Chung-she typical of the island during the early years of Japanese occupation, or was I right in suspecting that the frequency of such marriages varied with local conditions? Were there any distinctive demographic correlates? For example, these marriages might have been less unstable and perhaps more fertile than uxorilocal marriages elsewhere if they were stimulated primarily by practical rather than preservative concerns. If they were mainly a response to labor needs, we might also anticipate that daughters were less commonly given in adoption than elsewhere. I was in no position to answer such empirical questions on the basis of data available to me at the time I wrote *Kinship and Community in Two Chinese Villages*. What was needed to test these hypotheses was a more systematic analysis of Chung-she's household registry and comparison with records from other localities.

I have now compared Chung-she's registers with those from two other Taiwanese localities—Hai-shan (nine Hokkien-speaking districts in northern Taiwan), and Lung-tu (a Hakka-speaking district in southern Taiwan).[4] In 1935 Chung-she's population was 565. In the same year Lung-tu district had 4,131 people and the six districts of Hai-shan studied by Arthur Wolf had 11,073.[5] Analysis of Lung-tu's household registry is only now fully under way. I draw upon findings from this incomplete analysis because they suffice to show that Lung-tu was different from both Chung-she and Hai-shan, in relative frequency of marriage forms and in the level of fertility. This paper is only a first step toward an explanation of differences between Chinese localities, and a preliminary indication of what the consequences of these differences may have been. The comparative data will at the very least suggest that the sources, extent, and consequences of variation in Chinese marriage customs are more complex than many of us imagined.

The inhabitants of Chung-she, Hai-shan, and Lung-tu have much in common. Their ancestors all came to Taiwan from southeastern China, and they are all poor farmers who make their living from rice and subsidiary crops. But there are differences that, for our purposes, are more important. Ecologically, Hokkien-speaking Hai-shan had more in common with Hakka-speaking Lung-tu than with Chung-she. Farmers in the first two localities could expect two reasonably reliable harvests each year, while rainfall dependence limited those in Chung-she to a single precarious harvest. Irrigation canals were well developed in both Lung-tu and Hai-shan. Ahern described the situation in Hai-shan as follows:

Although it seems certain there was considerable cooperation among surname groups to construct the irrigation network in the beginning, it also seems likely that minimal cooperation was necessary to regulate the system once it began operating, for the area's rainfall is not only plentiful, averaging 83 inches a year, but also fairly evenly distributed throughout the year, with about 60 per cent falling during the five months May through September. In addition, access to water is well distributed.[6]

Rainfall was less plentiful in Chung-she and Lung-tu. It was also available during a more concentrated period. Around Chung-she 87 percent of the annual rainfall fell from May through September; the percentage was 90 around Lung-tu.[7] Chung-she lacked Lung-tu's canals and groundwater resources, however, and was therefore far more at the mercy of nature's whims. At the same time Chung-she shared with Hai-shan a Hokkien cultural restraint on labor from which the Hakka of Lung-tu were free. In Chung-she and Hai-shan women had bound feet and rarely participated in field labor. The people of Lung-tu, like Hakka elsewhere, avoided footbinding; females there participated extensively in the weeding, harvesting, and processing of grain. In short, the limited availability of water intensified periods of labor demand in Chung-she, while, paradoxically, cultural constraints limited the village's ability to respond effectively. Although the peoples of Hai-shan and Lung-tu spoke different languages and had different customs, they were both spared the periodic labor shortages endemic to Chung-she.

Analysis of Chung-she's household registers has confirmed that uxorilocal marriages were more common before canals were introduced than after. Comparison with the registers of Hai-shan and Lung-tu further indicates that the initial frequency of these marriages was higher in Chung-she. Table 13.1 says that while major marriages were most popular in all three localities, uxorilocal unions were unusually common in Chung-she while minor marriages (in which the groom's family adopted his future bride while she was a young child) enjoyed unusual popularity in Hai-shan. The data in Table 13.2 suggest that the relative proportion of the various marital forms did not change very much over time in Lung-tu. In terms of expressed values and actual frequencies, Lung-tu seems to have been the most "traditional" of our three localities. Uxorilocal marriages were uncommon in Lung-tu; people married this way significantly less often than in Hai-shan.[8] Minor marriages were also less common there than in Hai-shan and Chung-she,[9] whereas ideologically more respectable major marriages were more common.[10]

Taken alone, the data in Table 13.1 could mean that Chung-she was unique. Was it the only community in this part of central Taiwan with so many uxorilocal marriages, or did other communities share this characteristic? A partial answer to this question is provided by the Japanese vital statistics. Although the boundaries of the t'ing listed in Table 13.3 have no relation to social custom, the figures show considerable variation in the popularity of this form of marriage in Taiwan. In general, these marriages

TABLE 13.1

Form of First Marriage by Sex and Birth Cohort in Three Taiwan Localities

Year of birth and locality	No. of first marriages	Form of first marriage (percent)		
		Major	Minor	Uxorilocal
MALES				
1886-1905				
Lung-tu	356	91.9%	2.0%	6.2%
Chung-she	75	58.7	8.0	33.3
Hai-shan	1,475	48.5	40.5	10.9
1906-1915				
Lung-tu	294	94.6	2.7	2.7
Chung-she	36	77.8	8.3	13.9
Hai-shan	882	60.2	29.7	10.1
FEMALES				
1891-1910				
Lung-tu	357	85.7%	4.2%	10.1%
Chung-she	71	46.5	14.1	39.4
Hai-shan	1,491	43.2	41.4	15.4
1911-1920				
Lung-tu	321	94.4	1.9	3.7
Chung-she	52	86.5	1.9	11.5
Hai-shan	797	59.0	29.0	12.0

NOTE: Figures for Chung-she and Hai-shan come from Arthur P. Wolf and Chieh-shan Huang, *Marriage and Adoption in China, 1845-1945* (Stanford, Calif., 1980), pp. 124f, 318. They report the incidence of the three forms of marriage differently for males and females because women generally married earlier, and I follow their procedure. When aggregate percentages for Lung-tu and Hai-shan are standardized by five-year periods within cohorts, the percentages change by less than 1 percent.

were most common along the west-central coastal plain, where Chung-she was located. The best conclusion is that while Chung-she was by no means typical of Taiwan, it was not unique, and may even have been typical of the central coast. The mean frequency of uxorilocal marriages in Chia-yi t'ing, which included Chung-she, for the period 1908-19 (23.04 percent of all marriages) suggests that there were many villages in this area where such marriages were as popular as in Chung-she and probably a few in which they were even more popular. Most villages on this plain shared Chung-she's dependence on rainfall irrigation. The frequency of uxorilocal marriages was clearly lower in Tai-pei t'ing (where Hai-shan was located) and in A-hou t'ing (which included Lung-tu). The northern and southern coastal areas of Taiwan both enjoyed well-developed irrigation canals and ponds.

Clearly the high frequency of uxorilocal marriage in Chung-she and neighboring communities cannot simply be attributed to a cultural predisposition peculiar to Hokkien-speakers. How can we evaluate the suggestion of a connection between the unusual demand for labor associated with rainfall dependence and this form of marriage? If labor need motivated uxorilocal marriages, then we might expect such marriages to be-

TABLE 13.2
Form of First Marriage in Lung-tu by Sex and Birth Cohort

Birth cohort	Form of first marriage			Total
	Major	Minor	Uxorilocal	
MALES				
1886-1890	91	1	1	93
Percent	97.8%	1.1%	1.1%	100%
1891-1895	68	3	5	76
Percent	89.5%	3.9%	6.6%	100%
1896-1900	87	3	8	98
Percent	88.8%	3.1%	8.2%	100%
1901-1905	81	0	8	89
Percent	91.0%	0.0%	9.0%	100%
1906-1910	108	6	6	120
Percent	90.0%	5.0%	5.0%	100%
1911-1915	170	2	2	174
Percent	97.7%	1.1%	1.1%	100%
1916-1920	139	1	2	142
Percent	97.9%	0.7%	1.4%	100%
1921-1925	103	4	0	107
Percent	96.3%	3.7%	0.0%	100%
1926-1930	23	0	0	23
Percent	100.0%	0.0%	0.0%	100%
TOTAL	870	20	32	922
Percent	94.4%	2.2%	3.5%	100%
FEMALES				
1891-1895	46	6	7	59
Percent	78.0%	10.2%	11.9%	100%
1896-1900	68	3	9	80
Percent	85.0%	3.8%	11.3%	100%
1901-1905	73	1	10	84
Percent	86.9%	1.2%	11.9%	100%
1906-1910	119	5	10	134
Percent	88.8%	3.7%	7.5%	100%
1911-1915	145	2	8	155
Percent	93.5%	1.3%	5.2%	100%
1916-1920	158	4	4	166
Percent	95.2%	2.4%	2.4%	100%
1921-1925	154	4	2	160
Percent	96.3%	2.5%	1.3%	100%
1926-1930	26	0	0	26
Percent	100.0%	0.0%	0.0%	100%
TOTAL	789	25	50	864
Percent	91.3%	2.9%	5.8%	100%

TABLE 13.3

Uxorilocal Marriages as Mean Percent of All Marriages
in Three Regions of Taiwan, 1908-1919

Administrative unit (*t'ing*)	Mean percent of all marriages uxorilocal
Northwest Coast	
Tai-pei	18.44%
Hsin-chu	13.94
Tao-yüan	11.16
Central-west Coast	
Tai-chung	20.11
Nan-tou	22.76
Chia-yi[a]	23.04
Southwest Coast	
Tai-nan	15.38
A-hou	14.67

SOURCE: *Taiwan jinko dotai tokei.*
NOTE: The calculation of the means excludes the years 1911, 1915, and 1916.
[a]Includes Chung-she.

come less common after completion of the Chia-nan irrigation system. With data from Chung-she's household registers, I can now demonstrate that this was indeed what happened; Table 13.4 shows that the proportion of uxorilocal marriages was high until about 1930 or 1935, after which it precipitously declined.[11] Figure 13.1 suggests that the uxorilocal proportion of all marriages may have modulated around a mean of about 30 percent until 1935, after which this form of marriage lost its appeal. The data from Hai-shan and Lung-tu reflect no comparable change. Wolf's analysis of Hai-shan's registers indicates that the proportion of uxorilocal marriages remained within the 10-13-percent range for males and declined only gradually for females from about 18 to 11 percent;[12] the figures for Lung-tu in Table 13.2 show even greater constancy there.

When we examine family composition at the time of marriage, we find additional support for the view that the high level of uxorilocality in Chung-she was motivated by practical concerns. Comparing families that called in husbands with those that married daughters in the major fashion, we would expect to find fewer adult males but not necessarily fewer subadult males before the Chia-nan irrigation system was in place. In other words, we would expect to find a shortage of labor but not of heirs, and this is precisely what Tables 13.5 and 13.6 indicate. While there were somewhat fewer subadult males in families that called in husbands before the introduction of canals, the difference between these families and those contracting major marriages was not statistically significant. There were, however,

TABLE 13.4

Form of First Marriage by Sex and Marriage Cohort
of Persons Born 1886-1930 and Raised in Chung-she

Date of first marriage	Number of marriages	Form of first marriage					
		Major		Minor		Uxorilocal	
		Number	Percent	Number	Percent	Number	Percent
MALES							
1906-1910	7	6	85.7%	0	0.0%	1	14.3%
1911-1915	29	20	69.0	2	6.9	7	24.1
1916-1920	13	9	69.2	1	7.7	3	23.1
1921-1925	14	7	50.0	2	14.3	5	35.7
1926-1930	20	12	60.0	2	10.0	6	30.0
1931-1935	26	18	69.2	1	3.8	7	26.9
1936-1940	17	15	88.2	0	0.0	2	11.8
1941-1945	19	17	89.5	2	10.5	0	0.0
TOTAL	148	107	72.3%	10	6.8%	31	20.9%
FEMALES							
1906-1910	18	12	66.7%	0	0.0%	6	33.3%
1911-1915	11	6	54.5	2	18.2	3	27.3
1916-1920	15	7	46.7	1	6.7	7	46.7
1921-1925	18	7	38.9	2	11.1	9	50.0
1926-1930	25	17	68.0	2	8.0	6	24.0
1931-1935	20	13	65.0	1	5.0	6	30.0
1936-1940	25	22	88.0	0	0.0	3	12.0
1941-1945	34	30	88.2	2	5.9	2	5.9
TOTAL	168	114	67.9%	10	6.0%	44	26.2%

fewer adult males and more adult females in families opting for the uxorilocal form of marriage.

The preservative concerns that apparently increased in importance as a
motive for uxorilocality in Chung-she after 1930 were probably always
more important in Hai-shan. Extrapolating from several sets of figures
provided by Wolf, I found that 44 percent of the women born 1891-1920
and raised in Hai-shan who married uxorilocally had no brothers when
they were 15. This suggests that a substantial number of families used uxorilocal marriage to ensure family continuity. On the other hand, the fact
that 56 percent (128 out of 230) of these women did have brothers, and
that in most cases these were younger brothers, suggests that in Hai-shan,
too, uxorilocality may to some extent have constituted a response to need
for labor.

We have been discussing a composition of families that called in husbands. What kind of families provided such husbands? Traditional wis-

Fig. 13.1. First uxorilocal marriages as percent of all first marriages of persons born 1886 and later and brought up in Chung-she, by year of marriage

dom holds that only poor families with many sons are likely to submit their children to such a marriage. Yet of all the Chung-she men who married uxorilocally, 71 percent (22 of 31) had no other males present in their families when they married. Only 13 percent came from households with two or more males (including parents, grandparents, and siblings). In most cases their families also lacked females; in 71 percent there were no women, and in only 16 percent was there more than one. Indeed, 21 of the 31 uxorilocally married husbands were living with no relatives when they married. They resided with other village families and were employed as laborers or tenant farmers.

Thus it may not have been the pressure of many sons on limited family resources that prompted uxorilocal marriage in Chung-she as much as absolute poverty and the absence of a family unit upon which to build. Although comparable data are not yet available for Lung-tu, we have evidence from Hai-shan. Wolf's calculations indicate that only 28 percent of all uxorilocally marrying men (born 1891-1920) had no older brothers at age 15. Since some of these men had younger brothers, the percentage with no brothers was lower. Fully 36 percent had two or more older brothers, and a higher percentage still had younger brothers. Compared to Chung-she, then, a higher proportion of uxorilocal husbands came from families with male siblings, which suggests that size of family in relation to resources played a greater role in motivating uxorilocality in Hai-shan.

If the high frequency of uxorilocal marriages in Chung-she was stimu-

TABLE 13.5

First Marriages by Composition of Receiving Family at Time of Marriage and Form of Marriage of Persons Born 1886-1930 and Raised in Chung-she

Date and form of first marriage	Number of cases	Composition of receiving family			
		Mean no. of adult males (15-60)	Mean no. of subadult males	Mean no. of adult females (15-60)	Mean no. of subadult females
Before canals (1901-1915)					
Major	29	2.03	0.79	0.90	0.62
Minor	4	2.00	0.00	1.00	0.00
Uxorilocal	11	1.00	0.27	1.45	0.64
Before canals (1916-1930)					
Major	29	2.07	0.69	1.24	0.83
Minor	10	3.20	0.60	2.80	2.10
Uxorilocal	22	0.64	0.50	2.00	1.00
After canals (1931-1945)					
Major	50	2.38	1.24	1.72	1.56
Minor	6	1.67	0.67	3.00	1.00
Uxorilocal	10	0.60	0.40	2.50	1.10

TABLE 13.6

Comparison of Family at Marriage for Major and Uxorilocal First Marriages of Persons Born 1886-1930 and Raised in Chung-she

Date of marriage and composition of receiving family	t	df	Significance
1901-1915			
Adult males	3.152	38	$.01 > p > .001$
Subadult males	1.908	38	not significant
Adult females	2.113	38	$.05 > p > .02$
Subadult females	0.051	38	not significant
1916-1930			
Adult males	7.194	49	$p < .001$
Subadult males	0.621	49	not significant
Adult females	3.023	49	$.01 > p > .001$
Subadult females	0.481	49	not significant
1931-1945			
Adult males	5.779	58	$p < .001$
Subadult males	2.024	58	$.05 > p > .02$
Adult females	1.748	58	not significant
Subadult females	0.912	58	not significant

lated by the need to maintain an assured labor force, one might expect families to have been highly motivated to replace men who died despite the traditional ideology opposing remarriage. We might therefore expect to discover an unusual propensity for widows to remarry in Chung-she, and if widows often remarried to replace lost labor, then widowers, too, would have been more likely to remarry if only because they had more opportunity to remarry than in other communities. Table 13.7 indicates that younger women (29 or under) were indeed significantly more likely to remarry in Chung-she than in Hai-shan or Lung-tu. The difference for older women was less striking probably because many had adult sons upon whom they could depend and were therefore under less pressure to remarry.[13] If labor needs associated with rainfall dependence provided an inducement for widow remarriage in Chung-she, then widows should have remarried less commonly after 1930. The figures in Table 13.8 confirm this expectation.

Young men everywhere had a strong incentive to replace dead wives, so it is not surprising that Table 13.9 reveals no significant difference in the likelihood of younger widowers' remarrying. Older widowers, however, were significantly more likely to remarry in Chung-she than in either Hai-shan or Lung-tu. These older males would not normally have been considered desirable spouses, but in Chung-she their ability to work a plow made them marriageable.

We know there was a higher rate of widow remarriage in Chung-she than in Hai-shan or Lung-tu, but we have not yet established that these marriages were primarily motivated by the need for adult male workers. If labor needs were the motive, we should expect that widows with no adult males in their families would have been especially likely to remarry. One of my students has found that 90 percent of all remarrying widows in 1900 to 1944 lived in households with no adult males, while 69 percent of those who did not remarry had at least one adult male in their household. The absence of adult males is a significant and strong predictor of remarriage.[14] Although most widows had subadult children, the presence or absence of children was a less crucial determinant of remarriage than the presence or absence of adult males. For women with children, too, there was a strong likelihood of remarriage if adult males were absent and a disinclination to remarry if they were present.

Since families with larger holdings presumably needed more labor than those with small holdings we might expect to find that, contrary to conventional wisdom, the wealthy were more likely to call in sons-in-law than the poor. When I tested this expectation, however, the data indicated just the opposite. Table 13.10 shows that uxorilocally married men and women

TABLE 13.7

TABLE 13.7

Frequency of Widow Remarriage in Chung-she, Hai-shan, and Lung-tu among Women Born 1856-1920 Whose Husbands Died Before 1940

Age at husband's death and locality	Number of widows	Percent remarried
Under 30		
Chung-she	31	77.4%
Hai-shan	230	53.9
Lung-tu	55	49.1
30-44		
Chung-she	37	27.0
Hai-shan	347	17.0
Lung-tu	124	11.3

TABLE 13.8

Likelihood of Widow Remarriage in Chung-she, 1901-1920 and 1921-1940, for Women Born 1856-1920 Whose Husbands Died Before 1940 and Who Lived at Least Three Years After Husband's Death

Year widowed	Number of widows	Number remarried	Number not remarrying
1901-1920	69	34	35
1921-1940	33	6	27

NOTE: A three-year duration from widowhood was used because during both periods the sum of the mean interval before remarriage and the standard deviation did not exceed three years. Chi-square for this comparison is 9.05; $p < .01$. If we compare 1901-30 with 1931-45 (canals completed 1930), the Chi-square is 10.39; $p < .01$.

TABLE 13.9

Frequency of Widower Remarriages in Chung-she and Hai-shan among Men Born 1856-1920 Whose Wives Died Before 1940

Age at wife's death and locality	Number of widowers	Percent remarried
Under 35		
Chung-she	29	72.4%
Hai-shan	159	60.4
Lung-tu	50	68.0
35-49		
Chung-she	20	70.0
Hai-shan	178	27.0
Lung-tu	49	42.9

TABLE 13.10

Form of Marriage by Amount of Land Owned
for Chung-she Villagers Born 1886-1930

Amount of land owned by groom's or bride's family	Form of marriage		
	Major	Minor	Uxorilocal
Males			
Family owns under 2 hectares	80	9	33
Family owns 2 or more hectares	31	1	0
Female			
Family owns under 2 hectares	78	9	42
Family owns 2 or more hectares	39	1	3

were both more likely to come from families with below-average landholdings (i.e., under two hectares) than people married in other ways.[15] In
short, uxorilocality does seem to have been an option most commonly exercised by the relatively poor.

But if labor need was behind the high proportion of uxorilocal marriages in Chung-she, why should it have been families with minimal resources that most often married daughters this way? Most poor families in
Chung-she worked for a few wealthy families, as tenants or hired hands.
Although the labor needs of the wealthy landowners were considerable,
they rarely had to satisfy them by resorting to a low-status form of marriage. Indeed, they may have been particularly inclined to avoid marriages
that were considered unstable and therefore a potential threat to family
property. Instead, they met their requirements another way—by attracting
tenants and wage laborers.

Uxorilocal marriages may have been more attractive to the poor for several reasons. As mentioned earlier, they were relatively inexpensive. In addition poor farmers could not afford to hire workers to help them with
their own holdings; indeed the meagerness of their resources made many
of them heavily dependent on wages, and thus more in need of assistance
from other males in the household. The wealthy, by contrast, could always
count on a regular pool of labor. This suggests that we might usefully re-
fine our original hypothesis. Rainfall dependence did not uniformly mod-
ify marital behavior, but affected the poor more than the relatively well off.
The need for labor, increased by rainfall dependence, attracted poor labor-
ing families to Chung-she and made it especially important for them to
assure their livelihood by having a sufficiency of adult male workers
on hand.

We turn now to the demographic consequences of Chung-she's unusual
commitment to uxorilocality. I have been arguing that we should think of
uxorilocal marriage as a flexible institution that occurred in varying fre-

quencies and served varying functions. If that was so, then the effects of uxorilocal marriage would also have varied. It is often assumed, for example, that uxorilocal marriage is likely not only to be disdained in patrilineal societies but also to be relatively unstable and even less fertile than other forms of marriage. Certainly the Chinese had this impression. Because uxorilocal marriages are expected to be unstable, the terms of the marriage contract had to be clearly settled in advance: which and how many children will take the maternal surname, how long will the husband remain with his wife's family, etc. But even with scrupulously drawn contracts, people felt that uxorilocal husbands would eventually become discontented and demanding. By common agreement, male adoption was a better way to solve the problem of family continuity if one could find a son to adopt.

There are other dangers. One corollary of the husband's assuming characteristics of the bride is that his wife takes on attributes more appropriate to a husband. The parent-daughter bond rather than the parent-son bond is primary in a uxorilocal marriage, and the bride's parents must make a special effort to ensure that her loyalty will be to them rather than to her husband and his family. In the uxorilocal marriage the groom rather than the bride is the threatening outsider. Under such circumstances it seems inevitable that the conjugal bond will eventually be strained. It might even be in the interests of the bride's parents to foster such tensions. We might, then, expect uxorilocal marriages to be especially prone to divorce and also to be less fertile than major marriages.

Wolf has shown that uxorilocal marriages were indeed less stable than major marriages in Hai-shan,[16] but since the frequency and function of this form of marriage was different in Chung-she we cannot take his observation as predictive of the situation there. The need for labor in Chung-she provided a special inducement to prevent any disruptions that would remove rather than add adult males, and uxorilocal marriages might even have been arranged in a way that reduced the likelihood of divorce. Table 13.11 indicates that the proportion of major marriages ending in divorce in Chung-she, Hai-shan, and Lung-tu did not differ significantly. While uxorilocal marriages were significantly more likely than major marriages to end in divorce in Hai-shan and Lung-tu, this was not true of Chung-she. In short, uxorilocal unions were less fragile in Chung-she than in Hai-shan and Lung-tu; they were no less stable than major marriages in Chung-she.

Were uxorilocal marriages in Chung-she arranged in a way that minimized the likelihood of conjugal conflict? One way to increase the strength of the conjugal tie would be to tolerate or even encourage unions based on some degree of premarital familiarity. Indeed, Table 13.12 indicates that uxorilocally married women were more likely to marry men from their

TABLE 13.11

Percent of First Marriages Contracted 1901-1940 Ending in Divorce, by Form of Marriage, in Chung-she, Hai-shan, and Lung-tu

Locality	Number of first marriages	Form of first marriage		
		Major	Minor	Uxorilocal
Chung-she	185	7.7%	21.4%	7.3%
Hai-shan	3,179	5.9	15.5	16.1
Lung-tu	944	7.2	23.5	15.8

TABLE 13.12

Frequency of Major and Uxorilocal Intravillage Marriage among Chung-she Women, All Marriages Initiated 1877-1945

Form of marriage	Number of marriages	Number of intravillage marriages	Number of extravillage marriages	Percent of intravillage marriages
Uxorilocal	40	23	17	57.5%
Major	171	22	149	12.9%

NOTE: Chi-square = 38.5; $p < .001$.

own village than were women who married in the major fashion. Fully 87 percent of the women who married Chung-she men in the major way came from other communities, while 58 percent of those who married uxorilocally married Chung-she residents. This element of premarital familiarity was apparently less common in Hai-shan. According to Wolf, only 15.7 percent of the uxorilocally married women there took husbands from their own village. There is another fact that suggests considerable familiarity between uxorilocal partners in Chung-she. While none of the women aged 15-19 who married in the major fashion from 1906 to 1946 were pregnant at marriage, 13 percent of their uxorilocal counterparts were. If we expand the number of cases by considering all women born in Chung-she 1891-1920, we again find a significantly greater tendency to premarital conception among those who married uxorilocally (see Table 13.13).

Whether uxorilocal marriage was motivated by practical or preservative concerns, they provided strong motivation to consummate such a marriage as soon as possible. We should therefore expect that women who married in this fashion to have been younger than those who married in the major mode. If we compare ages at marriage in Chung-she, Hai-shan, and Lung-tu, we find differences when the data are analyzed by form of marriage (see Table 13.14). As expected, uxorilocal wives married earlier. Uxorilocal husbands were older than their major counterparts in all three localities,

TABLE 13.13

Frequency of Premarital Conception in Major and Uxorilocal First Marriages of
Women Born in Chung-she 1891-1920

Date of conception of first child	Number of major and uxorilocal marriages	Major marriages		Uxorilocal marriages	
		Number	Percent	Number	Percent
Premarital[a]	15	6	7.1%	9	22.0%
Postmarital	111	79	92.9	32	78.0
TOTAL	126	85	100.0%	41	100.0%

NOTE: Chi-square = 5.85; $p < .01$.
[a]A conception is considered premarital if the child was born eight months or less after the registered date of the marriage.

TABLE 13.14

Median Age at First Marriage by Form of Marriage in
Chung-she, Hai-shan, and Lung-tu

Form of marriage and locality	Women born 1891-1920		Men born 1886-1915	
	Number of first marriages	Median age at first marriage	Number of first marriages	Median age at first marriage
Major				
Chung-she	79	19.6	74	21.7
Hai-shan	1,114	19.3	1,244	23.4
Lung-tu	609	18.5	605	21.0
Minor				
Chung-she	9	19.2	10	23.0
Hai-shan	848	17.1	857	20.7
Lung-tu	20	18.6	15	19.6
Uxorilocal				
Chung-she	32	17.3	27	22.9
Hai-shan	326	18.0	249	25.0
Lung-tu	48	18.5	29	25.4

probably because, from the man's point of view, uxorilocal marriage was usually a last resort.

Perhaps the most surprising result of my comparison of household registers is the relative fertility of uxorilocal marriages. If conjugal tension is characteristic of uxorilocal marriages, we would expect such unions to be less fertile than major marriages. Tables 13.15 and 13.16 provide figures on fertility for Chung-she, Lung-tu, and Hai-shan, and Figure 13.2 presents these data graphically. The tables tell us that first marriages were generally more fertile in Lung-tu and Chung-she than in Hai-shan. They say that while fertility is affected by the way people marry, the relationship is not a simple one. For example, minor marriages were less fertile than major and uxorilocal marriages in Lung-tu and Hai-shan; they were as fertile as ma-

TABLE 13.15

Age-Specific Fertility by Form of First Marriage in Lung-tu, Chung-she, and Hai-shan, ca. 1900-1945

| | Form of first marriage | | | | | | |
| | Major | | Minor | | Uxorilocal | | |
Age group	Births per 1,000 woman-yrs.	No. of woman-yrs.	Births per 1,000 woman-yrs.	No. of woman-yrs.	Births per 1,000 woman-yrs.	No. of woman-yrs.	General fertility, three forms combined
		LUNG-TU, 1906-1945					
15-19	320	964	133	105	326	86	
20-24	393	3,474	306	85	369	203	
25-29	349	3,397	315	54	320	181	
30-34	303	2,670	150	40	294	153	
35-39	244	2,006	77	26	306	108	
40-44	104	1,541	0	19	101	79	
All ages							305
		CHUNG-SHE, 1906-1945					
15-19	303	142	214	14	453	88	
20-24	345	432	303	33	319	166	
25-29	296	419	387	31	340	147	
30-34	250	336	346	26	308	104	
35-39	223	242	276	29	308	52	
40-44	148	149	56	18	238	21	
All ages							292
		HAI-SHAN, WOMEN BORN 1881-1915					
15-19	286	1,919	227	2,694	368	484	
20-24	336	4,910	238	4,332	300	1,189	
25-29	305	5,355	235	3,997	288	1,252	
30-34	262	4,881	207	3,374	257	1,093	
35-39	206	3,586	154	2,558	179	801	
40-44	108	2,424	76	1,831	120	576	
All ages							239

NOTE: Figures for Hai-shan are from Wolf & Huang, *Marriage and Adoption in China*, p. 169.

jor marriages in Chung-she, where uxorilocal marriages were most fertile. The relationship between form of marriage and fertility in general, and the high fertility of Lung-tu women in particular, must be discussed elsewhere. For the present, let me simply point out that Figure 13.2 indicates a fertility advantage for uxorilocally married women aged 15-19 in Chung-she, and a reversal in favor of major marriage in the 20-24 age category. What is notable about the display, however, is the fertility advantage of uxorilocal unions vis-à-vis major marriages in all subsequent age groups. Is this overall fertility advantage a general characteristic of uxorilocality, or was it peculiar to Chung-she? As Figure 13.2 shows, uxorilocal marriages were uniformly more fertile in Chung-she than in Hai-shan. Lung-tu seems to have

TABLE 13.16

General and Total First Marital Fertility Rates by Form
of First Marriage in Lung-tu, Chung-she, and
Hai-shan, ca. 1900-1945

Locality and form of marriage	General first marital fertility rate	Total first marital fertility rate
Lung-tu		
Major	307	8.57
Minor	198	4.90
Uxorilocal	305	8.58
Chung-she		
Major	277	7.83
Minor	285	7.91
Uxorilocal	339	9.84
Hai-shan		
Major	265	7.52
Minor	203	5.69
Uxorilocal	261	7.63

occupied a middle position. Uxorilocal unions were more fertile than major marriages in Hai-shan only during the earliest years of marriage. We observe no remarkable difference between the curves for major and uxorilocal marriage in Lung-tu. Chung-she's fertility advantage over Hai-shan did not extend to major marriages; the figure reveals no difference between the localities in this regard. Taken together, all this evidence suggests that the differences in frequency and function in uxorilocal marriage that resulted from Chung-she's unusual labor requirements affected the fertility of these unions as well as their stability.

Minor marriages were unusually common in Hai-shan, and Wolf's analysis of Hai-shan's registers, and my own of Lung-tu's registers, indicate that they were less fertile than other marriages. Wolf attributes their poorer fertility performance to the sexual aversion that developed between partners during their early common socialization.[17] Although minor marriages were rare in Chung-she, my findings suggest that these marriages may actually have been somewhat more fertile than major marriages. Before we discard Wolf's explanation, we should recall that it requires the partners to have been raised together from infancy. In Chung-she only one of the ten relatively fertile adopted wives (born 1886-ca. 1925) had been adopted before age 1; the others had all been adopted after age 9. When I expanded the number of females married in minor fashion to include all cases in the registry (regardless of year of birth), I discovered that only five of the twenty girls had been adopted during the first year of their lives. The rest had been adopted at widely varying ages ranging from 3 to 20.

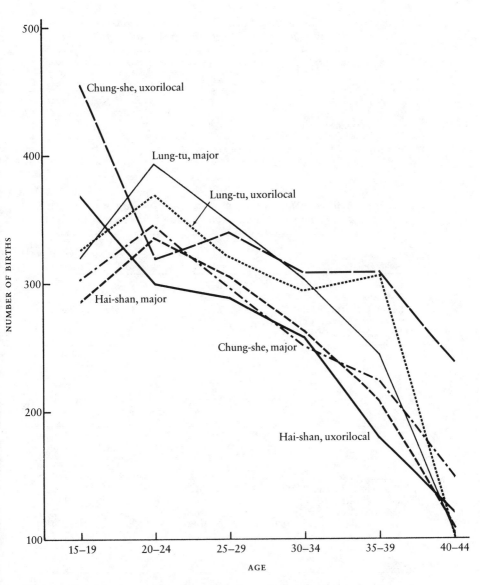

Fig. 13.2. Births per thousand woman years, by form of marriage, Lung-tu (1906-1945), Chung-she (1906-1945), and Hai-shan (women born 1881-1915)

TABLE 13.17

Frequency of Families with at Least One Adopted Daughter in Selected Communities in Taiwan and South China in the 1930's

Locality	Number of families	No. of families with an adopted daughter	Pct. of families with an adopted daughter
Hai-shan (Taiwan, 1935)	1,426	517	36.3%
Chung-she (Taiwan, 1935)	100	10	10.0
Lan-hsi (Chekiang, 1934)	538	97	18.0

NOTE: I am indebted to Arthur Wolf for this and the next two tables.

TABLE 13.18

Percent of Population in Status of Adopted Daughter of Head of Household in Selected Communities in Taiwan and South China in the 1930's

Locality	Total population	No. of adopted daughters	Pct. of population in status of adopted daughter
Hai-shan (Taiwan, 1935)	11,663	645	5.5
Tai-pei chou (Taiwan, 1935)	6,335	373	5.9
Shih-lin (Taiwan, 1934)	1,563	53	3.4
Chung-she (Taiwan, 1935)	592	13	2.2
Lung-ki (Fukien, 1930-31)			3.7

TABLE 13.19

Number of Adopted Daughters per 100 Unmarried Daughters in Selected Communities in Taiwan and South China

Locality	No. of unmarried daughters	No. of adopted daughters	No. of adopted daughters per 100 daughters
Hai-shan (Taiwan, 1935)	568	645	114
Tai-pei chou (Taiwan, 1935)	313	373	119
Shih-lin (Taiwan, 1934)	48	53	110
Chung-she (Taiwan, 1935)	106	13	12
Kai-hsien-kung (Kiangsu, 1934)	149	95	64
Chia-hsing (Chekiang, 193?)	2,808	196	7
Wu hsien and Kun-shan hsien (Kiangsu, 1940-41)	455	7	2

While the evidence from Chung-she does not seriously challenge Wolf's interpretation, it does suggest that minor marriage, like uxorilocal marriage, may provide a solution to a variety of problems and may therefore take different forms at different times and places and have different attributes. Minor marriage in Chung-she may primarily have served the purpose normally attributed to it—providing a relatively inexpensive way to contract a marriage. Nine of the ten families in my first sample that contracted minor marriages all owned minuscule amounts of land. Only one owned as much as one hectare, and three owned no land at all.

Minor marriages may have been uncommon in Chung-she because they presuppose a supply of girls for adoption, a supply probably lacking in this part of Taiwan. Given the heavy demand for males and the frequent recourse to uxorilocal marriage to meet that need, one expects a disinclination to give daughters away in adoption. Families would have held on to one or more daughters until they were certain they had enough healthy sons to rely upon; failing that, a daughter could be used to bring in a son-in-law. Compared to most communities for which data are available, Chung-she villagers rarely adopted daughters (see Tables 13.17-13.19). The number of families with an adopted daughter was significantly lower in Chung-she than in Hai-shan.[18] Chung-she had fewer adopted daughters relative to total population and fewer relative to other unmarried daughters.[19] Table 13.20 indicates that while males were not commonly adopted in either Chung-she or Hai-shan, females were very commonly given in adoption in Hai-shan and rarely in Chung-she.

If Chung-she villagers anticipated that daughters might eventually prove essential in assuring the family's livelihood, then daughters might have been less likely to die young in Chung-she than elsewhere. Wolf has shown that adopted daughters were at much greater risk of early death than daughters raised by their natural parents.[20] Although it is not clear if adopted daughters were disadvantaged by early weaning, less effective wet nursing, or general ill-treatment, the difference is striking. Since daughters were rarely adopted in Chung-she, girls there may have had greater survival potential relative to boys in Chung-she and relative to girls in Hai-shan. The numbers are too small to permit a satisfactory test of this notion with data from Chung-she alone, but we can compare Tainan *chou* (where Chung-she was located) with Taipei *chou* (which contained Hai-shan) on the basis of published vital statistics and census data. Table 13.21 indicates that death rates for children aged 0-4 in 1921 were lower in Tainan than in Taipei *chou*. Females had a higher death rate than males in Taipei, but a lower death rate than males in Tainan. The difference between the male death rates in the two localities is considerably less striking than the difference for females. Females in Tainan chou clearly did better than their Taipei counterparts, a finding consistent with our expectations.

TABLE 13.20

Probability of Adoption by Sex of Legitimate Children Born in Chung-she and Hai-shan, 1906-1935

Year of birth	Hai-shan		Chung-she	
	Number born	Probability of adoption	Number born	Probability of adoption
BOYS				
1906-1910	666	.058 ⎫		
1911-1915	758	.072 ⎬	129	.071
1916-1920	750	.056 ⎭		
1921-1925	819	.059 ⎫		
1926-1930	968	.045 ⎬	180	.055
1931-1935	1,070	.031 ⎭		
GIRLS				
1906-1910	657	.738 ⎫		
1911-1915	674	.694 ⎬	130	.225
1916-1920	645	.645 ⎭		
1921-1925	783	.594 ⎫		
1926-1930	874	.566 ⎬	192	.072
1931-1935	983	.471 ⎭		

NOTE: This table is constructed from data provided by Arthur Wolf.

TABLE 13.21

Death Rates of Children Aged 0-4 in Tai-pei Chou and Tai-nan Chou, 1921

Locality and sex	Death rate per 1,000
Tai-pei chou	
Males	88.92
Females	92.16
Tai-nan chou	
Males	80.83
Females	75.41

NOTE: Rates were calculated using deaths in 1921 and census population for 1920 (rather than the more conventional population as of mid-year 1921, which was not available). Since the same census was used for both administrative units, this departure from convention should not affect our comparison.

We observed earlier that the frequency of uxorilocal marriage in Chung-she may have modulated around a mean of about 30 percent before 1935. Since the time covered by the registers is short, we cannot be certain this was the case. Nonetheless, I would hazard a guess as to why such a modulation might have occurred. Note that the interval between peak frequencies in Figure 13.2 is about twenty years, sufficient time for sons to approach maturity. If uxorilocally married Chung-she women were more fertile than women married in the major fashion, the result of a rising frequency of such unions would be a larger number of sons and, in time, a reduced need both for adult males and for uxorilocal marriages. But as the frequency of these marriages declined, the associated drop in fertility would intensify the need for male laborers. In short, there may have been a modulation that reflected a regulatory feedback between frequency of uxorilocal marriage and changing labor supply.

Perhaps the initial fertility advantage of uxorilocal marriage in Chung-she was more apparent than real. Perhaps unions intended to ensure family continuity were not officially registered until a pregnancy was evident. To evaluate this possibility I removed all women who had given birth up to eight months from their marriage date to see if the initial fertility advantage of uxorilocality would vanish. It persisted; the fertility rate for women married in the major fashion was 302 per 1,000 woman years compared to 440 for uxorilocally married women aged 15-19.

Could the higher fertility of uxorilocally married women aged 15-19 be simply the result of their earlier age at marriage? That women 20-24 married in major fashion appear to have been more fertile than their uxorilocal counterparts in Chung-she, Lung-tu, and Hai-shan suggests that given their higher age at marriage, a greater proportion of them may have conceived their first child while they were 19 but delivered them after they turned 20. This would contribute to the fertility reversal in the 20-24 age group. I have compared the fertility of Chung-she women controlling on this possibility, by removing all 15-19-year-old women who give birth when married less than 270 days. Comparison of the remaining women still indicates a fertility advantage for uxorilocal marriage; the fertility rate per 1,000 woman years was 412 for women married in the major fashion but 456 for uxorilocally married women. In sum, while uxorilocal marriages may have been inspired in part by concern for family continuity, and while the fertility of some uxorilocally married women may reflect their earlier age at marriage or premarital sexual relations, the high fertility of these women cannot be attributed entirely to such factors.

The greater fertility of young uxorilocally married women could result from their being spared the anxieties associated with having to shift residence when first married and adapting to an unfamiliar husband, family, and community. They do not find themselves surrounded by curious, even hostile, in-laws at marriage, nor do they have to contend with the demands of a competitive mother-in-law. In short, uxorilocal marriage probably generates far less anxiety among new brides than major marriage, and if anxiety undercuts fertility, we might expect women who marry in the major fashion to be less fertile during the early years of their marriage.

The relative stability of uxorilocal unions and the higher overall fertility of uxorilocally married women in Chung-she could have prevailed because the primary function of these marriages was to provide labor rather than to ensure continuity of the family. There was undoubtedly less controversy over the assignment of children to lines of descent in Chung-she; indeed, there are numerous instances on record in which none of the offspring of uxorilocal couples took the maternal surname. And since the families on both sides were usually poor, disparities in the spouses' status were a less likely source of conflict than elsewhere. Uxorilocally married couples who in many cases knew each other before marriage, and who managed to endure the difficult initial period of adjustment, may have been particularly well-adjusted spouses.

Uxorilocal marriages, then, were unusually common in Chung-she, and they did not serve the same purposes there that they did in other Chinese localities, including Hai-shan and, by the account cited at the beginning of this paper, in Shang-nan. The special frequency and function of uxorilocal marriage in Chung-she had distinctive demographic consequences. In particular, uxorilocal marriages were unusually stable and fertile in Chung-she, although the responsible mechanisms remain to be identified. It is clear, however, that uxorilocality in Chung-she was different from uxorilocality elsewhere, and that this difference had demographic correlates. That may be the most important contribution of this essay: it underlines the need to look beyond the formal characteristics of Chinese institutions if we are to understand regional variation in demographic trends.

Notes

Notes

1. Wolf and Hanley: Introduction

1. J. Hajnal, "European Marriage Patterns in Perspective," in D. V. Glass and D. E. C. Eversley, eds., *Population in History* (London, 1965), p. 101.

2. Thomas Robert Malthus, *On Population* (New York, 1960), p. 219.

3. Hajnal, "European Marriage," p. 133.

4. *Ibid.*, p. 103.

5. See R. M. Smith, "The People of Tuscany and Their Families," *Journal of Family History*, 6 (Spring 1981): 111.

6. Michael W. Flinn, *The European Demographic System, 1500-1820* (Baltimore, 1981), Table 7, pp. 124-29.

7. Peter Czap, Jr., "The Perennial Multiple Family Household, Mishino, Russia 1782-1858," *Journal of Family History*, 7 (Spring 1982): Table 1, p. 10.

8. Lutz K. Berkner, "Inheritance, Land Tenure and Peasant Family Structure: A German Regional Comparison," in Jack Goody, Joan Thirsk, and E. P. Thompson, eds., *Family and Inheritance* (London, 1976), pp. 71-95.

9. Lutz K. Berkner and John W. Shaffer, "The Joint Family in the Nivernais," *Journal of Family History*, 3 (Summer 1978): 150-62.

10. See Lutz K. Berkner, "The Stem Family and the Developmental Cycle of the Peasant Household: An Eighteenth-Century Austrian Example," *American Historical Review*, 77 (1972), 398-418.

11. See E. A. Hammel, "The Zadruga as Process," in Peter Laslett and Richard Wall, eds., *Household and Family in Past Time* (London, 1972), pp. 335-73; E. A. Hammel, "Household Structure in Fourteenth-Century Macedonia," *Journal of Family History*, 5 (Fall 1980): 242-73; and Michael Mitterauer and Alexander Kagan, "Russian and Central European Family Structures: A Comparative View," *Journal of Family History*, 7 (Spring 1982): 103-31.

12. Czap, p. 22.

13. Hajnal, p. 102.

14. Robert J. Smith, "The Domestic Cycle in Japan," *Journal of Family History*, 3 (Fall 1978): 226.

15. See Marion J. Levy, Jr., "Aspects of the Analysis of Family Structure," in Ansley J. Coale, Lloyd A. Fallers, Marion J. Levy, Jr., David M. Schneider, and Silvan S. Tompkins, eds., *Aspects of the Analysis of Family Structure* (Princeton, N.J., 1965), pp. 1-65.

16. Czap, Table 7, p. 20.

17. Okada Yuzuru, *Kiso Shakai* (Elementary groups of society; Tokyo, 1949), Table 3, p. 8.

18. George W. Barclay, Ansley J. Coale, Michael A. Stoto, and T. James Trussell, "A Reassessment of the Demography of Traditional Rural China," *Population Index*, 42 (1976): 606-35.

19. Hajnal, p. 106.

20. *Ibid.*, p. 108.

21. Thomas C. Smith, *Nakahara* (Stanford, Calif., 1977), p. 85.

22. See, for example, *ibid.*, pp. 84-85, 156.

23. See Ruth B. Dixon, "Explaining Cross-Cultural Variations in Age at Marriage and Proportions Never Marrying," *Population Studies*, 25 (July 1971): Table 2, p. 220.

24. Akira Hayami has analyzed how many children were averted by raising the age of marriage in several villages during the Tokugawa period. For a summary of his conclusions (originally published in Japanese), see Susan B. Hanley and Kozo Yamamura, *Economic and Demographic Change in Preindustrial Japan, 1600-1968* (Princeton, N.J., 1977), pp. 296-300.

25. See Susan B. Hanley, "The Influence of Economic and Social Variables on Marriage and Fertility in Eighteenth- and Nineteenth-Century Japanese Villages," in Ronald Lee et al., eds., *Population Patterns in the Past* (New York, 1976).

26. Barclay et al., p. 626.

27. See also Ts'ui-jung Liu, "Chinese Genealogies as a Source for the Study of Historical Demography," in *Studies and Essays in Commemoration of the Golden Jubilee of Academic Sinica* (Taipei, 1978), and "The Demographic Dynamics of Some Clans in the Lower Yangtze Area, ca. 1400-1900," *Academia Economic Papers*, 9 (March 1981): 115-60.

28. See Maurice Freedman, *Chinese Lineage and Society* (London, 1966), pp. 44-45.

29. Arthur P. Wolf, "Chinese Family Size: A Myth Revitalized," in Hsieh Jih-chang and Chuang Yin-chuang, eds., *The Chinese Family and Its Ritual Behavior* (forthcoming).

30. Louis Henry, *Anciennes familles genevoises* (Paris, 1956).

31. For a summary of this literature and references, see Herbert D. Lampson, "Differential Reproduction in China," *Quarterly Review in Biology*, 10 (Sept. 1935): 308-21.

32. Kingsley Davis, "Cities and Mortality," in *Papers Delivered at the International Population Conference, Liége, 1973* (International Union for the Scientific Study of Population), p. 260.

33. It should also be noted that this hypothesis was first suggested by E. A. Wrigley on the basis of European data. See E. A. Wrigley, *Population and History* (New York, 1969), chs. 3 and 4.

34. Marcel Granet, *The Religion of the Chinese People*, trans. Maurice Freedman (Oxford, Eng.), p. 64.

35. Hajnal, p. 132.

2. Liu: Two Chekiang Clans

1. Ts'ui-jung Liu, "Chinese Genealogies as a Source for the Study of Historical Demography," *Studies and Essays in Commemoration of the Golden Jubilee of Academia Sinica* (June 1978), pp. 849-70.

2. George W. Barclay, Ansley J. Coale, Michael A. Stoto, and T. James Trussell, "A Reassessment of the Demography of Traditional Rural China," *Population Index*, 42, 4 (1976): 625.

3. *Hsiao-shan Ch'ang-hsiang Shen-shih tsung-p'u* (The genealogy of the Shen clan in Hsiao-shan), 1893 ed., ch. 40; *Hsiao-shan T'ang-wan Ching-t'ing Hsü-shih tsung-p'u* (The genealogy of the Hsü clan in Hsiao-shan), 1911 ed., ch. 1. Hereafter cited as *Shen-shih* and *Hsü-shih*.

4. Though clan rules urged members to adopt children from within the clan, exceptions did occur. Boys adopted from outside (*ming-ling*) were not listed individually in the genealogies, but their names were noted under the adopting father's name. One way to avoid adopting from outside the clan was to allow one boy to carry two lines of descent (*chien-t'ao*). Instances of both practices are to be found in the Shen and Hsü genealogies; I have not tabulated the frequency.

5. *Shen-shih*, ch. 32.

6. *Hsü-shih*, ch. 1, 3.

7. T. H. Hollingsworth, *The Demography of the British Peerage*, supplement to *Population Studies*, 18, 2 (1964).

8. In 24 cases the Shen genealogy indicates that the birth of a second or third wife's first son occurred before her predecessor's death. Though these anomalies could be the result of recording errors, it is more likely that a concubine was elevated to the status of wife after the wife's death. In every case the wife who died had failed to produce a male heir.

9. The mourning period prescribed for a husband was one year (in practice, nine months), but a man was free to ignore this obligation if his parents were alive. See *Ch'ing-hui-t'ien* (Statutes of the Ch'ing), 1818 ed., 30: 30a.

10. John Hajnal, "Age at Marriage and Proportions Marrying," *Population Studies*, 7, 2 (1953): 111-36. SMAM = $(15 + S_i - 50S_{50}) / (1 - S_{50})$, where S_i denotes the proportion single at each age group and S_{50} the proportion single at age 50. S_{50} is calculated as the average of S_{45-49} and S_{50-54}.

11. Barclay et al., p. 609.

12. This difference in the age of husband and wife is confirmed by calculating their ages at the birth of their eldest son. The average for the Shen clan was 25.17 for wives and 30.51 for husbands; for the Hsü clan the averages were 24.64 and 29.81. One of the Taiwan genealogies I studied yielded averages of 21.18 and 26.65; the other, 22.07 and 27.06. Taken together with the statistics showing that the ages of all husbands and wives in Taiwan in 1910 and 1915 differed by 5.3 years and 5 years (see Bank of Taiwan, ed., *The Population in Taiwan*, 1949, p. 10), this evidence says that a difference of five years was the rule in late traditional China.

13. Barclay et al., p. 609.

14. See Michel Cartier, "Nouvelles données sur la demographie chinoise à l'époque des Ming (1384-1644)," *Annales*, 6 (Nov.-Dec. 1973): 1344-45.

15. *Hsiao-shan hsien-chih kao* (Draft gazetteer of Hsiao-shan), 1935, ch. 22-24. The age distribution of the women by sui is as follows:

Sui	14	15	16	17	18	19	20	21	22	23	24	25
Number	1	11	15	15	16	19	12	2	0	2	0	1

16. "Chinese Genealogies," pp. 858-59.

17. Because the number of cases is not very large, this procedure is not entirely

Table for Note 20

Age	Known	Unknown	Low	High
15-19	0	1	0	1
20-24	3	0	3	3
25-29	3	3	3	4
30-34	4	3	4	5
35-39	4	1	4	5
40-44	3	2	3	4
45-49	3		3	4
50-54	7		7	10
55-59	2		2	3
60-64	10		12	10
65-69	12		15	12
70-74	13		16	13
75-79	3		4	3
80+	6		7	6

satisfactory. Some of the remaining irregularities could be smoothed by applying techniques developed by William Brass (see "The Graduation of Fertility Distribution by Polynomial Functions," *Population Studies*, 14, 2 [1930]: 148-62).

18. See William Brass et al., *The Demography of Tropical Africa* (Princeton, N.J., 1968), pp. 92-93.

19. Barclay et al., p. 614, Table 5.

20. For a description of the method, see Louis Henry, *Manuel de demographie historique* (Genève-Paris, 1970), pp. 113-15; E. A. Wrigley, "Mortality in Pre-Industrial England: The Example of Colyton, Devon, Over Three Centuries," *Daedalus* (Spring 1968), pp. 553-55. The results obtained for the Shen wives born in the years 1760-64 are given in the accompanying table.

21. The method employed is described in Henry, p. 108.

22. I use this equation because it was employed in another study of Chinese genealogies. See I-chin Yüan, "Life Tables for a Southern Chinese Family from 1365 to 1849," *Human Biology*, 3, 2 (1931): 157-79.

23. Ansley J. Coale and Paul Demeny, *Regional Model Life Tables and Stable Populations* (Princeton, N.J., 1968).

24. For discussions of food supply during this period, see Ping-ti Ho, *Studies on the Population of China, 1368-1953* (Cambridge, Mass., 1959), pp. 169-95, and Dwight H. Perkins, *Agricultural Development in China, 1368-1968* (Cambridge, Mass., 1969), pp. 13-19.

25. Suffice it to note here that Taiwan life tables show a sharp rise in mortality after age 45. See Department of Statistics of the Provincial Government of Taiwan, *Life Tables of Taiwan, 1936-1949*, p. 30.

26. The flood is mentioned in *Hsiao-shen hsien-chih kao*, 5: 27b.

27. Barclay et al., p. 620, Table 13.

28. I-chin Yüan, pp. 168-69.

29. See Henry Shryock et al., *The Methods and Materials of Demography* (Washington, D.C., 1971), p. 528, for the method of calculating the intrinsic rate of increase.

3. Yamamura: Tokugawa Bannermen

An earlier version of this paper was published in my book *A Study of Samurai Income and Entrepreneurship: Quantitative Analysis of Economic and Social Aspects of the Samurai in Tokugawa and Meiji Japan* (Cambridge, Mass., 1974), © 1974 by Harvard University Press. I am grateful to Susan B. Hanley for help in preparing this paper.

1. These volumes were published by Taibōsha Publishing Co., Tokyo.

2. Even in Japanese, useful sources on the bannermen are limited. The standard definition in the text and much of the information needed for this essay were obtained from Sasama Yoshihiko, *Edo bakufu yakushoku shūsei* (Tokyo, 1967), and Kitajima Masamoto, *Edo bakufu no kenryoku kōzō* (Tokyo, 1964). In English, the following two books were useful: John W. Hall, *Tanuma Okitsugu* (Cambridge, Mass., 1955), and Conrad Totman, *Politics in the Tokugawa Bakufu, 1600-1843* (Cambridge, Mass., 1967).

3. Totman, pp. 131-32.

4. A discussion of this point is found in Shinmi Kichiji, *Hatamoto* (Tokyo, 1967).

5. This source, written in 1705 in 17 folios, is closely examined in Suzuki Hisashi, "Tokugawa Bakushindan no chigyō ketai," *Shigaku zasshi,* 71, 2 (Feb. 1962): 144-84.

6. *Ibid.,* p. 153.

7. Suzuki Hisashi, "Bakushindan no chigyō keitai," pp. 181-84; and the same author's "Hatamoto-ryō no kōzō," *Rekishigaku kenkyū,* 208 (1957): 13-30. As far as I know, no reliable source exists for the exact number of housemen, let alone for the hundreds of thousands of daimyo retainers of samurai status.

8. Fujino Tamotsu, *Bakuhan taiseishi no kenkyū* (Tokyo, 1961), p. 321. The *bakuhan* system is a term used in Japanese history to denote the Bakufu and *han* complex of the Tokugawa political system.

9. The internal consistency of the information on male children has also been examined by tracing the information for all yōshi (adopted sons) available in the genealogies.

10. For cohort groups I and II, the relative frequency of three-person households shown in the table may well be larger than it was in reality, since for an undetermined number of entries only the bannerman and his wife and eldest son (or only the bannerman and two children) may have been listed instead of all members of the family. However, as the improving sex ratio makes clear, this bias is not likely to have significantly affected cohort group III.

11. Though the relationship is evident at a glance, the rank correlation coefficient between the proportion unmarried and the stipend level is $-.73$. This calculation does not include the 7,000- and 8,000-koku-stipend classes.

12. The data clearly show that the proportion of bannermen with two or more wives in each stipend class rose with the amount of stipend. Although only 7 percent of bannermen with less than 100 koku in stipend had two or more wives either consecutively or concurrently, the percentage steadily rose to 65.1 percent for bannermen with 9,000-9,999 koku.

13. In another 41 cases all sons, ranging in number from two to six, died; in two cases the only son "went mad"; and in one case the only son's whereabouts were unknown. In the remaining 18 cases descriptions were either incomplete or lacking. Shinji's collection of about thirty jingles included one that went: "Even a real

son [should be denied the succession] if he is of ill repute and useless; replace him with a yōshi, reporting the son is in ill health." Shinji Yoshimoto, *Edo jidai no buke no seikatsu* (Tokyo, 1966).

14. The remainder, 39 cases, consisted of "unknown" and death at an early age.

15. For the literature on this subject and a good related study on the yōshi of samurai in four han, see Ray A. Moore, "Adoption and Samurai Mobility in Tokugawa Japan," *Journal of Asian Studies*, 29, 3 (1970): 617-32.

16. For the purpose of tracing intergenerational changes in stipends and positions, my random sampling of the bannermen was done by genealogy. To obtain approximately 5,000 bannermen, I selected a random sample of 1,000 genealogies. Two genealogies were discarded because they each contained only one bannerman for whom no usable information was available, thus yielding the final figure of 998.

17. This is the case of Hineno Yoshiakira, found in the *Kansei chōshū shokafu*, 15: 334. He was a son of a daimyo who distinguished himself militarily in the service of Oda Nobunaga. He was given 20,000 koku for his services in the Battles of Osaka, but the Bakufu chose to discontinue his line by refusing to accept his nephew as his heir.

18. This happens to be the house of Asano of Chushingura fame. *Kansei chōshū shokafu*, 5: 349.

19. This is the only case in the sample in which homosexual involvement was explicitly stated. *Ibid.*, 10: 206.

20. Hall, *Tanuma*, and Kitajima, *Kenryoku kōzō*, provide good descriptions and analyses of the political and social changes of the period. See especially Kitajima, pp. 417-28.

21. Fujino, p. 321.

22. One of the best descriptions of Edo markets and Edo life is found in Kitajima Masamoto, *Edo jidai* (Tokyo, 1958), pp. 101-24.

23. Kaga Jushirō, *Genroku kakyū bushi no seikatsu* (Tokyo, 1970), pp. 80, 171, 231, 237, and 245. See, for example, Tamura Eitarō, *Edo jidai chōnin no seikatsu* (Tokyo, 1966), for the changing consumption patterns of merchants in food, clothing, hair styles, and household goods during the Tokugawa period and especially during the Genroku years.

24. Younger sons who were fortunate enough to become yōshi of bannermen or to receive a part of their father's stipend were a small minority. Some younger sons became yōshi of the retainers of daimyo, and some found minor posts within the Tokugawa hierarchy in lesser capacities than those usually enjoyed by bannermen, i.e., as housemen. A few chose to become Buddhist monks or Confucian scholars. We do not know exactly what happened to a large number of younger sons of bannermen. Since the fate of younger sons was important in terms of the stability of Tokugawa social classes and the Tokugawa regime itself, an in-depth examination of this group would be welcome. In any event, most younger sons were not attractive marriage prospects.

25. The economic status of the retainers of daimyo was significantly lower than that of bannermen. Bannermen also enjoyed high prestige as direct retainers of the shogun. Here we should recall that the mean stipend of daimyo was only about 50,000 koku.

26. My source does not allow me to discriminate between successive and concurrent multiple wives. This means that some proportion of bannermen with multiple wives had wives consecutively, not concurrently. Since successors, whether eldest sons, younger sons, or yōshi, were selected in part on the grounds of health, demographically bannermen formed a select group that would have had a higher

mean age at death than their wives. Since, in addition, divorces were not uncommon (my source shows that 5 or 6 percent of bannermen's wives were divorced by their husbands, a higher incidence than in prewar Japan), it is probable that many second and third wives were sole wives and not concubines. Why the data indicate an increase over time in the proportion of bannermen with multiple wives cannot yet be explained.

27. Shinji, pp. 167-74.

28. This would be a consensus of Japanese scholars. See, for example, Kitajima, *Kenryoku kōzō*, p. 482. For a good description and examples, see Naramoto Tatsuya, *Chōnin no jitsuryoku* (Vol. 17 of *Nihon no rekishi*; Tokyo, 1966), pp. 294-99.

29. See my *Study of Samurai Income and Entrepreneurship*, ch. 7.

30. For example, Takimoto Seiichi, *Nihon hōken keizaishi* (Tokyo, 1930), pp. 350-51.

31. Two good studies are Sasaki Junnosuke, "Han kashindan no tenkaikatei; Suwa han o sozai ni," *Shakai keizai shigaku*, 28, 1 (1962); and Fujino, *Bakuhan taiseishi no kenkyū*, pp. 499-690. There are about twenty case studies covering nearly 55 *han*. Because of a lack of suitable data sources, the demographic characteristics of lower-class samurai have not been investigated. Unless usable data can be found for this class, we can only surmise their demographic patterns from our knowledge of other classes.

32. Sekiyama Naotarō, *Kinsei Nihon no jinkō kōzō* (Tokyo, 1958), p. 301.

33. Nishijima Minoru, *Edo jidai no seiseikatsu* (Tokyo, 1969), p. 236.

34. Kaga, pp. 41, 168-69, 186. Abortion must have been routine by this time as a means of terminating unwanted pregnancies. The tatami bugyō wrote on January 16, 1703, that "Ren [the maid] began to induce abortion" and noted that on the following day, "Ren had pains in the abdomen, but they ceased after the passing of the infant. The abortion was completed easily." *Ibid.*, p. 169. By the beginning of the eighteenth century a variety of medical "lines" had developed, each line using its own secret medicine and tools to induce abortions. The best known among them was the Chūjō line, which used a surgical scoop along with its own medicine, taken internally. Some abortionists used "poisoned needles" to induce abortions. In cities little effort was required to find an abortionist during most of the eighteenth and nineteenth centuries. I have been unable to ascertain the exact content of the "secret" medicine and the "poison" used. See Ishihara Akira, *Nihon no igaku* (Tokyo, 1966), p. 68, and Sekiyama Naotarō, *Kinsei Nihon jinkō no kenkyū* (Tokyo, 1948), pp. 201-2.

35. According to Sekiyama (*Kinsei Nihon no jinkō kōzō*, p. 301), there are demographic data on daimyo's retainers for only two domains. For one domain the data are only for a few years; for the other they are incomplete and for only part of the domain.

36. For good descriptions of the development of medical science in Tokugawa Japan and the influence of foreign knowledge on Tokugawa medical and sanitation practices, see Ishihara, *Nihon no igaku*, and Fujikawa Yū, *Nihon shitsubyōshi* (Tokyo, 1969).

4. Harrell: Three Chekiang Lineages

Some of the work that went into this paper was supported by two grants: from the Ning-Shao Project at Stanford University in the summer of 1971, and from the Graduate School Research Fund of the University of Washington in the summer of 1977. I am grateful for this support. Much of the work of collecting and processing data was done by Ms. (now Dr.) Sun-ming Wong and by Mr. Colin Chan. I wish to thank both of them for their able and patient assistance.

1. The cyclical nature of the process has been demonstrated for the Ho lineage only; lack of time prevented me from doing the careful analysis that would, I think, discover it at least in the Wu and perhaps in the Lin lineage as well. I hope to present a fuller account at some future date.

2. Hsien-Chin Hu, *The Common Descent Group in China and Its Functions* (New York, 1948).

3. Maurice Freedman, *Lineage Organization in Southeastern China* (London, 1958); and *Chinese Lineage and Society: Fukien and Kwangtung* (London, 1966).

4. C. K. Yang, *A Chinese Village in Early Communist Transition* (Cambridge, Mass., 1959); Hugh D. R. Baker, *Sheung Shui, a Chinese Lineage Village* (Stanford, Calif., 1968); Jack M. Potter, *Capitalism and the Chinese Peasant* (Berkeley, Calif., 1968); and Potter, "Land and Lineage in Traditional China," in Maurice Freedman, ed., *Family and Kinship in Chinese Society* (Stanford, Calif., 1970).

5. Freedman, *Chinese Lineage*, pp. 37-39.

6. Potter, "Land and Lineage," pp. 124-27.

7. Ping-ti Ho, *Studies on the Population of China* (Cambridge, Mass., 1959).

8. G. William Skinner, "Regional Urbanization in Nineteenth-Century China," in G. William Skinner, ed., *The City in Late Imperial China* (Stanford, Calif., 1977).

9. Myron L. Cohen, "Developmental Process in the Chinese Domestic Group," in Maurice Freedman, ed., *Family and Kinship in Chinese Society* (Stanford, Calif., 1970); and Cohen, *House United, House Divided* (New York, 1976).

10. Freedman, *Lineage Organization*, p. 28.

11. Whenever anyone is referred to in this paper as an *n*th-generation descendant of X, this refers to the number of generations from the *founder*, with the founder himself as 1, *not* to the number of generations *from* X.

12. There were corporate estates held by segments of the Wu lineage, but none below the level of the fourth generation from the founder. They were all in the second *chih*, and were focused on Yü-hsien and Shih-hsien in the third generation, and on I-sheng and Hsi-sheng, the ancestors of the third and seventh fang, respectively, in the fourth generation.

13. I suspect this loss is due to out-migration: the Wu genealogy sometimes notes that particular men (usually without sons or death-dates listed) migrated to such places as Peking, Mukden, Soochow, Huchow, Kwangtung, and Hangchow. Only a small number of such migrants are clearly noted, however; there is no way to test my hypothesis that there were many more emigrants whose migration is not specifically noted in the genealogy. Some of the migrants ran shops, and they may well have provided local connections for other migrants from their home lineages.

14. Chang Chung-li, *Chinese Gentry: Studies of Their Role in Nineteenth-Century Chinese Society* (Seattle, Wash., 1955), p. 164.

15. Freedman, *Lineage Organization*.

5. Hayami: The Village of Nishijo

I express my deepest gratitude to Susan B. Hanley and Laurel Cornell, who not only translated my work but gave me much useful advice. The basic data in this paper were published in English in my article "Labor Migration in a Pre-Industrial Society: A Study Tracing the Life Histories of the Inhabitants of a Village," *Keio Economic Studies*, 10, 2 (1973): 1-17.

1. These may be literally translated "faith investigation registers." They are de-

scribed in great detail in Robert J. Smith, "Small Families, Small Households and Residential Instability: Town and City in 'Pre-Modern' Japan," in Peter Laslett, ed., *Household and Family in Past Time* (Cambridge, Eng., 1972), pp. 431-36.

2. These documents are in St. Paul's University Library, Tokyo. The author is very thankful to Professor Hideo Hayashi for having kindly given him the opportunity to use them.

3. Special attention must be given to the following points regarding the births and deaths obtained from the shūmon-aratame-chō: These records were compiled once a year, with the people living at the time of compilation being the subject of the investigation. In consequence, those who died before a year's documents were compiled or were born afterward are not included in that year's data. The birth and death rates used here are therefore understated. For accurate rates, the figures given should be multiplied by 1.25.

4. Minami Kazuo, *Edo no shakai kōzō* (Tokyo, 1969), p. 196.

5. Hayami Akira, "Demografia e economia no Japão pré-Industrial," *Anais de História*, No. 4 (Brazil), 1972.

6. For observations concerning Suwa county, Shinano province, see Chapter 2 of Hayami Akira, *Kinsei nōson no rekishi jinkōgakuteki kenkyū* (Tokyo, 1973).

7. In the traditional Japanese method of calculating age, a person is one year old at birth. When the new year arrives, the child will have another year added to his age, irrespective of his chronological age calculated in the Western way. In this paper the traditional Japanese method is used.

8. Households of the landlord class constituted 5-15 percent of the total number of households, the owner-cultivators 5-20 percent, the owner-tenant cultivators 0-20 percent, and the tenants 60-70 percent. The fluctuations are due to administrative changes in the evaluation of households in 1810.

9. This classification is for the sake of convenience and is only nominal. Cities here have populations above 10,000, while towns have the suffixes *-machi* and *-shuku* and populations below 10,000.

10. Takehana of Mino province and Ichinomiya and Okoshi of Owari province are its centers. Hayashi Hideo, *Kinsei nōson kōgyō no kiso katei* (Tokyo, 1960).

11. Families where wives remained married to age 50 and beyond.

12. Hayami, *Kinsei nōson no rekishi*, pp. 166-67.

13. Thomas C. Smith, *Nakahara: Family Farming and Population in a Japanese Village, 1717-1830* (Stanford, Calif., 1977).

14. Susan B. Hanley, "Migration and Economic Change in Okayama during the Tokugawa Period," *Keio Economic Studies*, 10, 2 (1973): esp. Table II.

15. W. Mark Fruin, "Farm Family Migration: The Case of Echizen in the Nineteenth Century," *Keio Economic Studies*, 10, 2 (1973): 37-46.

16. Hayami Akira, *Kinsei nōson no rekishi*, Figs. 2-6, pp. 54-55.

17. Akira Hayami, "Demographic Aspects of a Village in Tokugawa Japan," in P. Deprez, ed., *Population and Economics* (Winnipeg, 1970), Fig. 3, pp. 115-16.

18. Hayami Akira, *Kinsei nōson no rekishi*, Figs. 8.8, 8.9, and 8.10, p. 166.

19. Thomas C. Smith, "Pre-Modern Economic Growth: Japan and the West," *Past and Present*, 60 (1973).

20. Susan B. Hanley and Kozo Yamamura, *Economic and Demographic Change in Preindustrial Japan, 1600-1868* (Princeton, N.J., 1977), ch. 3; Hayami Akira, "Mouvements de longue durée et structures japonaises de la population à l'époque de Tokugawa," *Annales de démographie historique*, 1971, pp. 247-63.

21. E. A. Wrigley, *Population and History* (London, 1969), chs. 3, 4.

6. Sasaki: The City of Takayama

1. In addition to the *ninbetsu-chō* for Takayama, those for Nagasaki Okeya-machi and several *machi* in Kōfu are currently being examined, and work is to start shortly on those for Kōriyama.

2. For example, one reason for problems with several population indicators, such as birth rates, death rates, proportions married, fertility rates, and survival rates, must be differences in income levels. We note, however, that the income distribution was almost identical in all three sections.

3. For those immigrants whose origin can be determined, 89.1 percent came from surrounding farming villages, areas thought to have been in the process of being urbanized.

4. It should be noted that since our analysis is based on the shūmon-ninbetsu-chō, we do not take into account people unrecorded in the registers, which may be a considerable number, especially in times of famine.

5. Suda Keizō's "Jidai betsu eisei tōkei sōkatsu ichiran hyō" was compiled using the *kako chō* (burial records) of a temple in Takayama, and the population covered is comparable to Ni-no-machi's.

6. The data for Kandō-shinden have been taken from Hayami Akira, "Toku-gawa kōki Owari ichi nōson no jinkō tōkei zokuhen," *Management and Labor Study Series*, No. 213 (Tokyo, 1967-68), and those for Nishijō-mura from Ha-yami, "Jinkō gakuteki shihyō ni okeru kaisōkan no kakusa—Nishijō-mura no nōmin," *Kenkyū kiyō* (Tokyo, 1973).

7. The proportion married in Takayama could not be explained satisfactor-ily within the present limited data. Furthermore, the "proportion ever married" method developed by Ansley Coale, which might seem promising, is inapplicable, since, as we shall see, some of the immigrant women from rural areas were coming to the city for remarriage.

8. The figures for Kandō-shinden are from Hayami Akira, "Tokugawa kōki Owari ichi nōson no jinkō tōkei," *Mita Gakkai Zasshi*, 59, 1 (1966), and those for Nishijō-mura from Hayami, "Nōshū Nishijō-mura no jinkō shiryō—An'ei 2—Meiji 2," *Kenkyū kiyō* (Tokyo, 1972).

9. Hayami Akira, *Kinsei nōson no rekishi jinkōgakuteki kenkyū* (Tokyo, 1973).

10. A. J. Coale and T. J. Trussell, "Model Fertility Schedules: Variations of Childbearing in Human Population," *Population Index*, 40 (1974).

11. From 1773 to 1812, the average number of years each woman was listed in the register was 16.2; for women who immigrated into the city, it was 12.8.

12. These figures are calculated ignoring the death rate at age zero. Because the death rates of native-born and immigrants cannot be separated from Suda's data, we have had to calculate the life expectancy at age 1.

13. Sasaki Yōichirō, "Edo jidai toshi jinkō iji nōryoku ni tsuite—Hida Taka-yama no keikenchi ni motozuku ichi jikken no kekka," in Shakai Keizai Shigakkai, ed., *Atarashii Edo jidai shizō o motomete* (Tokyo, 1977).

14. See Henry S. Shryack, Jacob S. Siegel, et al., *The Methods and Materials of Demography* (New York, 1976), ch. 18, "Reproductivity."

15. Hayami Akira, "Kinsei kōki chiiki-betsu jinkō hendō to toshi jinkō hiritsu no kanren," *Kenkyū kiyō* (Tokyo, 1974).

7. Wolf: Fertility in Rural China

In presenting this critique of the work of what I call the Princeton group, I want it to be known that the acknowledged leader of that group, Ansley J. Coale, has kindly read the paper and taken the time to correct misunderstandings and to help clarify critical issues. My argument may still be wrong, but it is a stronger argument than it would have been without Coale's assistance. My research on the China mainland was conducted under the auspices of the Committee on Scholarly Communications with the People's Republic of China, and the analysis of data I collected there was supported by a grant from the Population Council (Subordinate Agreement CP82.28A).

1. Thomas Robert Malthus, *On Population* (New York, 1960), p. 206.
2. Walter H. Mallory, *China: Land of Famine* (New York, 1926), p. 87.
3. R. H. Tawney, *Land and Labour in China* (New York, 1932), p. 104.
4. Mallory, p. 17.
5. E. F. Penrose, *Population Theories and Their Application* (Stanford, Calif., 1934), p. 107.
6. *Ibid.*, p. 108.
7. John Lossing Buck, *Land Utilization in China* (Nanking, China, 1937).
8. Penrose, p. 109.
9. Frank W. Notestein and Chiao Chi-ming, "Population," in Buck ed., *Land Utilization*, 1: 358-99.
10. George W. Barclay, Ansley J. Coale, Michael A. Stoto, and T. James Trussell, "A Reassessment of the Demography of Traditional Rural China," *Population Index*, 42 (Oct. 1976): 606-35.

11. *Ibid.*, p. 613.	12. *Ibid.*, p. 625.
13. *Ibid.*	14. *Ibid.*

15. *Ibid.*, p. 626.
16. The data are taken from tabulations prepared by Frank Notestein, who kindly retrieved them from his attic and allowed me to make copies.
17. There are also slight differences deriving from an age adjustment made by the Princeton group.

18. Barclay et al., p. 617.	19. *Ibid.*, p. 609.
20. *Ibid.*, p. 609.	21. *Ibid.*

22. Buck, p. viii.
23. Notestein and Chiao, "Population."

24. *Ibid.*	25. *Ibid.*
26. Barclay et al., p. 620.	27. *Ibid.*, pp. 612-13.
28. *Ibid.*, p. 612.	29. *Ibid.*, p. 613.

30. *Ibid.*, p. 617.
31. Arthur P. Wolf and Chieh-shan Huang, *Marriage and Adoption in China, 1845-1945* (Stanford, Calif., 1980).
32. See *ibid.*, Appendix B ("Social Science Research in Hai-shan: A Bibliographical Listing"), pp. 381-86.
33. Wolf & Huang, ch. 2.
34. For detailed descriptions of these marriage forms, see *ibid.*, chs. 5-7.
35. See *ibid.*, chs. 9, 26.
36. I asked to interview all women aged 55 and over, but in translation this became all women aged 55 *sui* and over, which meant that I interviewed a number of women aged 54 and a few aged 53.
37. C. M. Chiao, Warren S. Thompson, and D. T. Chen, *An Experiment in the Registration of Vital Statistics in China* (Oxford, Ohio, 1938).
38. *Ibid.*, pp. 10-11.
39. *Ibid.*, p. 41.

40. See Louis Henry, "Some Data on Natural Fertility," *Eugenics Quarterly*, 8 (1961): 81-91.

41. National Coordinating Group on Male Antifertility Agents, "Gossypol—A New Antifertility Agent for Males," *Chinese Medical Journal*, 4, 6 (1978): 417-28.

42. Buck, pp. 385-86.

43. This literature is reviewed in Herbert D. Lamson, "Differential Reproduction in China," *Quarterly Review in Biology*, 10 (Sept. 1935): 308-21.

44. For the evidence on this point see Wolf & Huang, chs. 11-13.

8. Coale: The Barclay Reassessment

1. Techniques for correcting inaccurate data or extracting information from incomplete data have become a well-worked subfield in demography, with a voluminous literature, summarized in two manuals published by the Population Division of the Department of International Economic and Social Affairs of the United Nations. The first of these manuals (Manual IV) was published in 1967; the second one (prepared by the Committee on Population and Demography of the U.S. National Academy of Sciences) was published in 1983 as Manual X.

2. Francene van de Walle, "Migration and Fertility in Ticino," *Population Studies*, 29, 3 (1975): 447-62. See also Jane Menken, "Seasonal Migration and Seasonal Variation in Fecundability: Effects on Birth Rates and Birth Intervals," *Demography*, 16, 1 (1979): 103-19.

3. Melvin Konner and Carol Worthman, "Nursing Frequency, Gonadal Function, and Birth Spacing among !Kung Hunter-Gatherers," *Science*, 207 (1980): 788-91.

4. Ansley J. Coale, "The Decline of Fertility in Europe since the 18th Century as a Chapter in Demographic History," in Ansley J. Coale and Susan Watkins, eds., *Proceedings of a Conference on the European Fertility Project* (forthcoming).

5. E. A. Wrigley, "Fertility Strategy for the Individual and the Group," in Charles Tilly, ed., *Historical Studies of Changing Fertility* (Princeton, N.J., 1978).

6. R. M. May and D. Rubinstein, "Reproductive Strategies," in C. R. Austira and R. V. Short, eds., *Reproductive Fitness* (Cambridge, Eng., forthcoming).

7. Jacques Dupâquier, "De l'animal à l'homme: le mécanisme autorégulateur des populations traditionelles," *Revue de l'Institut de Sociologie* (Brussels), 2 (1972): 177-211.

9. Hanley: Four Tokugawa Villages

The author is grateful to Gary S. Shea not only for the computer programming he undertook for this paper, but for the hours he spent unraveling the code to the tapes containing the data. She is indebted to Daniel Scott Smith and Arthur P. Wolf for suggestions for revising the original conference paper, and to all the conference participants for their insightful comments.

I have discussed the importance of the household and the significance of various social factors for fertility in "The Influence of Economic and Social Variables on Marriage and Fertility in Eighteenth and Nineteenth Century Japanese Villages," in Ronald Lee, ed., *Population Patterns in the Past* (New York, 1976), and in *Economic and Demographic Change in Preindustrial Japan, 1600-1868* (Princeton, N.J., 1977), co-authored by Kozo Yamamura. I have drawn on data from these studies for the present paper.

1. See Lawrence Stone, "The Rise of the Nuclear Family in Early Modern England," in Charles E. Rosenberg, *The Family in History* (Philadelphia, 1975), pp. 13-57.

2. Robert J. Smith, *Ancestor Worship in Contemporary Japan* (Stanford, Calif., 1974), p. 33.

3. The first regulation in Okayama against the parceling of land was issued in 1656. Subdividing land was prohibited except where land was acquired through the ending of a family line or where large tracts of land were being given out to a number of people. The prohibitions against the alienation of land were gradually relaxed, however, as they proved unworkable in the long run, and by 1715 it was legal to pawn land for ten years. But the regulations against willing land to more than one heir were maintained; in 1798 it was ruled that a family had to have at least 3 *tan* (.75 acre) to establish a branch line. See the following works for discussions of this subject: Taniguchi Sumio, *Okayama han* (Tokyo, 1964), pp. 131*ff*, 200*ff*; Taniguchi Sumio and Shibata Hajime, "Kinsei ni okeru kazoku kōsei no henshitsu katei," *Bulletin of the School of Education*, Okayama University, 1 (1955); and Otake Hideo, *Hoken shakai no nomin kazoku* (Tokyo, 1962), p. 155.

4. For a fuller explanation of this model, see Hanley and Yamamura, *Economic and Demographic Change*, pp. 188–89. The model comes from Naitō Jirō, *Honbyakushō taisei no kenkyū* (Tokyo, 1968), p. 168.

5. For a discussion of *kakaku* and its determination, see Kodama Kōta, *Kinsei nōmin seikatsu-shi* (Tokyo, 1957), pp. 227–28.

6. See Andō Seiichi, *Kinsei zaikata shōgyō no kenkyū* (Tokyo, 1958), pp. 95, 125.

7. The term household is here used to denote all persons included in one listing in the shūmon-aratame-chō. The term family is used to denote all persons related to the head of the household. For practical purposes, the family equals all the persons in a household except servants. Since the number of servants fluctuated from year to year and since there tended to be more of them in the earlier years, the calculations throughout this paper have been based on family size rather than on household size.

8. Although the percentage of persons classified as members of the head's nuclear family remained nearly constant over time, the variety of such classifications greatly increased over time. For example, in Fukiage, villagers were related to the head of the household in which they lived in 16 different ways in 1683. This had increased to 32 in 1712, to 44 in 1781, and to 52 by 1860. I am not sure whether the kinds of relationships had actually increased or whether people were being more explicit. In Fujito, for example, by the end of the Tokugawa period there were fourth cousins, children of wives by former marriages, etc., none of which is mentioned a century earlier.

Moreover, variations in the percentage of people in various relationships from year to year partly reflect the age of the household heads. The variation in Fujito is actually very small, but a sample of the mean age of household heads for various years is as follows: 1775, 50.1; 1794, 46.5; 1810, 49.3; 1825, 46.6; 1835, 48.2; 1845, 46.1; 1863, 48.5.

9. See Tsuge Takeshi, "Nōson mondai no ichi to shite no mabiki ni tsuite," *Keizai-shi kenkyū*, 15, 2 (Feb. 1936): 15–32.

10. See the discussion in Kozo Yamamura and Susan B. Hanley, "*Ichi hime, ni taro*: Educational Aspirations and the Decline in Fertility in Postwar Japan," *The Journal of Japanese Studies*, 2, 1 (Autumn 1975): 83–125.

11. See the studies by the author cited in the first note above and the numerous works of Hayami Akira and Thomas C. Smith.

12. See Kozo Yamamura, *A Study of Samurai Income and Entrepreneurship* (Cambridge, Mass., 1974), pp. 79–83.

13. See Robert J. Smith, *Ancestor Worship*, pp. 164*ff*.

14. The *Nengumai toritate sanyō-chō* for Fujito, held by the Okayama University Library, are available for the years 1804, 1809, 1828, 1851, 1857, and 1863.

10. Morris and Smith: A Japanese Outcaste Village

1. Documents relating to Minami Ōji have been published by Ōsaka Furitsu Toshokan as *Okuda-ke monjo*, 13 vols., 1969-75. References to this set are noted in parentheses by volume and page number.

2. There is some disagreement over how the *eta* class of Tokugawa Japan evolved from earlier outcaste segments of society. Their official position in the Tokugawa social hierarchy, however, was that of the "outcaste" in the most literal sense, for they ranked outside of, and below, the four officially recognized classes of warrior, peasant, artisan, and merchant. Found primarily in central and western Japan, eta lived segregated from the general population and were associated with jobs involving blood and death, which were viewed as despicable by society at large. They were responsible for disposing of dead animals and processing products derived from their carcasses, including leather. From their position as executioners of public criminals, they also came to perform many other police or criminal justice functions, including administering other punishments and serving as all-purpose spies for the government.

3. This document, whose data can be inferred from the village population given, presents net income figures from various sources, both in kind and in monetary equivalents. These figures were obtained by subtracting expenses and taxes from initial gross income figures, which the document does not give. Since nearly all taxes borne by the village were applied to agriculture, income from farming must have represented a higher percentage of total gross income than of total net income. The wage-income figures are not actual, but estimates based on an assumed number of man-days worked and average wages paid.

4. As they operated work areas in other villages for the preliminary processing of dead animals, villagers were also charged by the government with keeping an eye out for illegal activity by inhabitants of villages in which they were working (6: 225).

5. The 1870 register also lacks this information.

6. Since registers were compiled in the third lunar month of each year, the conversion of Japanese to standard age requires the subtraction of one and one-quarter from the Japanese age at the time of compilation of a register, or of one and three-quarters years to determine the age at the time of an undated event occurring between registrations (which may be presumed to have occurred on average six months prior to the register first recording them). For the logic of this, see Thomas C. Smith, *Nakahara: Family Farms and Population in a Japanese Village, 1717-1830* (Stanford, Calif., 1977), pp. 18-21.

7. Consecutive annual records survive for 1784-86, 1828-32, and 1836-37.

8. Between 1721 and 1843 the population of Izumi province fell from 218,405 to 197,656, a drop of 9.5 percent. Sekiyama Naotarō, *Kinsei Nihon no jinkō kōzō* (Tokyo, 1958), p. 137.

9. See Smith, *Nakahara*, p. 50.

10. *Ibid.*, pp. 45-58.

11. From 1830 to 1869 some 3.3 percent of recorded births appear to have been illegitimate.

12. Gap-year marriages can be surmised from the registers following the gap, except for any marriage commenced and terminated entirely between the dates of successive registers. The presence of three-year gaps in the record, however, poses

more serious problems. Confining the sample only to cases not crossing over any three-year gaps between a reasonable minimum age of marriage (taken as 13 for women, 15 for men) and first recorded marriage yields a mean age at first marriage of 17.0 for women and 20.2 for men. This, however, favors early over late marriages, since the latter are far more likely to pass over a three-year gap before marriage. Including all conceivable first marriages, no matter how many three-year gaps are passed over between the minimum age and the recorded age, yields maximum ages of 18.8 for women and 21.9 for men. The figures given in the text are averages of these minimum and maximum figures.

11. Smith: Commoners in Tennōji-mura

I wish to thank William B. Hauser of the University of Rochester for calling my attention to the local histories relating to Tennōji-mura, and Laurel Cornell of Cornell University for her penetrating discussion of the analysis at earlier stages of the research. The Tennōji registers are located in the *Monbushō shiryō kan* in Tokyo. My thanks go to the staff of the institute for their cooperation in making it possible for me to copy the materials.

1. Inoue Masao, ed., *Ōsaka fu zenshi* (Ōsaka, 1922 [reprinted 1975]), 3: 220-21.

2. *Tennōji son shi* (Ōsaka, 1925 [reprinted 1976]), p. 86.

3. Higashinari gun yakusho, ed., *Higashinari gun shi* (Tokyo, 1922 [reprinted 1972]), p. 370.

4. *Ibid.*, p. 411.

5. *Tennōji son shi*, p. 15.

6. Sasaki Yōichirō, "Tokugawa jidai kōki toshi jinkō no kenkyū: Settsu no kuni, Nishinari no kōri, Tennōji mura," *Shikai*, 14 (1967): 31-44.

7. *Ibid.*, p. 32.

8. *Ibid.*, p. 34.

9. *Ibid.*, p. 37.

10. Akira Hayami and Nobuko Uchida, "Size of Household in a Japanese County Throughout the Tokugawa Era," in Peter Laslett and Richard Wall, eds., *Household and Family in Past Time* (Cambridge, Eng., 1972), pp. 473-516.

11. In an earlier publication I gave slightly different totals for the number of occurrences, but the number of households is the same. The present count is the more accurate of the two. See Robert J. Smith, "Small Families, Small Households, and Residential Instability: Town and City in 'Pre-Modern' Japan," in Laslett and Wall, eds., *Household and Family in Past Time*, pp. 429-72.

12. Sa: Marriage in Taipei

1. Arthur P. Wolf, "Childhood Association and Sexual Attraction: A Further Test of the Westermarck Hypothesis," *American Anthropologist*, 72, 3 (June 1970): 503-15.

2. *Ibid.*; also Arthur P. Wolf, "Adopt a Daughter-in-Law, Marry a Sister: A Chinese Solution to the Problem of the Incest Taboo," *American Anthropologist*, 70, 5 (Oct. 1968): 864-74, and Tai Akiyo (Tai Yen-hui), "*Simpua* zakkō" (Miscellaneous thoughts on *simpua*), *Minzoku Taiwan*, 3, 11 (Nov. 1943): 2-4.

3. For the history of the Taipei area, the periodical *T'ai-pei wen wu*, published by the T'ai-pei Shih Wen-hsien Wei-yuan-hui, is of great interest. The first issue was published in December 1952. The name of the publication was changed in 1963 to *T'ai-pei wen-hsien*. *T'ai-pei wen wu*, 2, 1 (April 1953), is a special issue on Bankha; 2, 3 (Nov. 1953), is a special issue on Toatotia:.

4. Liao Han-ch'eng, "Meng-chia yen-ko chih" (Records of Meng-chia's development), *T'ai-pei wen wu*, 2, 1 (April 1953): 12-13; Huang Te-shih, *T'ai-pei shih yen-ko chih kao* (Draft records of the development of Taipei City; 1961), pp. 31-32.

5. Lien Hsiao-ch'ing, "Meng-chia ta-shih chi" (Record of major events of Meng-chia), *T'ai-pei wen wu*, 2, 1 (April 1953): 65-68.

6. Liao Han-ch'eng, "Meng-chia yen-ko chih," pp. 12-17. Huang Te-shih, *T'ai-pei shih yen-ko chih kao*, pp. 31-33.

7. Lien Hsiao-ch'ing, "Meng-chia ta-shih chi," pp. 65-68.

8. Lien Wen-ch'ing, "Ta-tao-ch'eng ti ching-chi fa-chan" (Economic development of Ta-tao-ch'eng), *T'ai-pei wen wu*, 2, 3 (Nov. 1953): 16.

9. *Ibid.*, pp. 18-20.

10. Huang Te-shih, "Ta-tao-ch'eng fa-chan shih" (Developmental history of Ta-tao-ch'eng), *T'ai-pei wen wu*, 2, 1 (April 1953): 88-89.

11. Ch'en Kuang-hui, "T'ai-pei shih she-hui pien-ch'ien yin-su chih yen-chiu" (Research on the causes of social change in Taipei), *T'ai-pei wen hsien*, vols. 13-16 (combined) (Dec. 1966): 34*ff*.

12. Department of Sociology, National University of Taiwan, ed., *Social Base Maps of Taipei City* (Taipei, 1965), pp. 25-26, puts the native population of Lung-shan district at 80.1 percent, and that of Yenping at 84.3 percent, in 1963.

13. These include articles in *T'ai-pei wen wu* and *T'ai-pei wen-hsien*, plus compilations made by both Japanese colonial government sources and post-Japanese sources that deal with famous personages.

14. Some of the original 200 of each of these two lower-status groups selected for analysis were discarded because of internally contradictory and thus obviously faulty data.

15. Wang I-kang, "Lung-t'ang Wang-shih chia-p'u," (Genealogy of the Wangs of Lung-t'ang), *T'ai-pei wen wu*, 8, 3 (Oct. 1959): 84-94; Wu I-sheng, "Meng-chia san chü-fu ch'i-chia t'an" (On the beginnings of Meng-chia's three families of great wealth), *T'ai-pei wen wu*, 8, 1 (April 1959): 90-93; Lü Ling-shih, *Taiwan jinshi kan* (Mirror of Taiwanese people; Taipei, 1937), p. 38.

16. Wu I-sheng, "Meng-chia ku hang-hao kai-shu" (Sketches of Meng-chia's old commercial houses), *T'ai-pei wen wu*, 9, 1 (March 1960): 1-11; "Meng-chia i-wen-chi" (Collected anecdotes of Meng-chia) *T'ai-pei wen wu*, 9, 1 (March 1960): 48-52. Wang I-kang, "Meng-chia Li-shih chia-pu" (Genealogy of the Li family of Meng-chia), *T'ai-pei wen wu*, 8, 4 (Feb. 1960): 89-94.

17. At one time, Li was reputed to be the second wealthiest man in northern Taiwan, surpassed only by the Lins of Pan-ch'iao, whose family compound, styled after the model for the compound in the *Dream of the Red Chamber*, remains a major tourist attraction today.

18. Liu Lung-kang, "Tao-chiang jen-wu hsiao-chih" (Brief accounts of Ta-tao-ch'eng's notables), *T'ai-pei wen wu*, 2, 3 (Nov. 1953): 103-4. Lü Ling-shih, *Taiwan jinshi kan*, pp. 401-2.

19. See Meng-chia Lung-shan shih ch'üan-chih pien-chi wei-yuan-hui, compilers, *Meng-chia Lung-shan shih ch'üan-chih* (Complete annals of the Lungshan temple of Meng-chia; Taipei, 1951). Lü Ling-shih, *Taiwan jinshi kan*, pp. 267-68, 272, gives biographies of members of Ch'en T'ien-lai's family. Also see Liu Lung-kang, "Tao-chiang jen-wu hsiao-chih," pp. 103-6.

20. Liu Huang-ch'un, "Meng-chia jen-wu chih" (Records of Meng-chia's notables), *T'ai-pei wen wu*, 2, 1 (April 1953): 28-34.

21. Wu Ch'un-hui, "Wu Yin-huai ch'i jen ch'i shih" (Wu Yin-huai, the man and his deeds), *T'ai-pei wen wu*, 8, 1 (April 1959): 39-41; Lü Ling-shih, *Taiwan jinshi kan*, pp. 97, 102.

22. Wu Ch'un-hui, "Wu Yin-huai," pp. 39-41.

23. Lü Ling-shih, *Taiwan jinshi kan*, pp. 267-68, 272; Liu Lung-kang, "Tao-chiang jen-wu hsiao-chih," pp. 103-6.

24. Lü Ling-shih, *Taiwan jinshi kan*, p. 96; Liu Lung-kang, "Tao-chiang jen-shih hsiao-chih"; Wu I-sheng, "Jen-wu suo-t'an: Meng-chia i-wen-chi chih erh" (Miscellanea on notables: collection of Meng-chia anecdotes, part 2), *T'ai-pei wen wu*, 8, 2 (June 1959): 91-92.

25. George W. Barclay, *Colonial Development and Population in Taiwan* (Princeton, N.J., 1954), p. 212.

26. Suzuki Seiichirō, *Taiwan kyūkan: kankonsōsai to nenjū gyōji* (Taiwanese customs: Coming-of-age, marriage, funerals, and annual rites; Taipei, 1934), pp. 138-96; Maurice Freedman, "Ritual Aspects of Chinese Kinship and Marriage," in Freedman, ed., *Family and Kinship in Chinese Society* (Stanford, Calif., 1970).

27. *Taihoku-shi shi* (History of Taipei City; n.p., 1930?).

28. Suzuki Seiichirō, *Taiwan kyūkan*, pp. 174-75.

29. Ikeda Toshio, *Taiwan no katei seikatsu* (Family life in Taiwan; Taipei, 1944), pp. 150-58.

30. Suzuki Seiichirō, *Taiwan kyūkan*, pp. 137-39.

31. Arthur P. Wolf and Chieh-shan Huang, *Marriage and Adoption in China: 1845-1945* (Stanford, Calif., 1980), p. 238.

32. See works cited in notes 1 and 2 above and Arthur P. Wolf, "Childhood Association, Sexual Attraction, and the Incest Taboo: A Chinese Case," *American Anthropologist*, 68, 4 (Aug. 1966): 883-98.

33. Wolf & Huang, p. 158.

34. Suzuki Seiichirō, *Taiwan kyūkan*, pp. 202ff; T'ien Ta-hsiung, "Hontōjin mukoiri kon-in no fūshū" (Uxorilocal marriage customs of the Taiwanese), *Minzoku Taiwan*, 1, 2 (August 1941): 6-7.

35. Suzuki Seiichirō, *Taiwan kyūkan*, pp. 202ff.

36. See, for example, Ts'ao Chia-i, "T'ai-wan chiu-shih ti hun-yin hsi-su" (Marriage customs in early Taiwan), *T'ai-pei wen-hsien*, 9/10 (Dec. 1969): 190-214.

37. *Ibid.* See also William J. Goode, *World Revolution and Family Patterns* (New York, 1963), pp. 285-91; Suzuki Seiichirō, *Taiwan kyūkan*, p. 131.

38. Wolf & Huang, p. 183.

39. *Ibid.*, p. 252.

40. For a discussion of this issue and of the reciprocal interaction between family and society in the application and transmission of cultural values, see Leonard Pearlin, *Class Context and Family Relations: A Cross-National Study* (Boston, 1971).

13. Pasternak: Uxorilocal Marriage in China

I am grateful to the National Science Foundation, the National Institute of Child Health and Human Development, and the Research Foundation of the City University of New York for supporting the fieldwork and data analysis that led to this paper. I am also indebted to Arthur Wolf for his valuable suggestions and criticisms, and for his generous consent to my use of his tables.

1. Eduard J. M. Kroker, trans., *Die amtliche Sammlung chinesischer Rechtsgewohnheiten* (a translation of *Min-shang-shih hsi-kuan tiao-ch'a pao-kao lu*, The

official collection of Chinese customary law; Bergen-Enkheim, 1965), ch. 15, para. 54.

2. For a general discussion of uxorilocal marriage in China, see Arthur P. Wolf and Chieh-shan Huang, *Marriage and Adoption in China, 1845-1945* (Stanford, Calif., 1980), pp. 11-14, 88-101.

3. Burton Pasternak, *Kinship and Community in Two Chinese Villages* (Stanford, Calif., 1972), p. 85.

4. Hai-shan's registers were made available by Arthur Wolf. The Lung-tu registers were obtained by Myron Cohen and me in the course of fieldwork in Mei-nung township, of which Lung-tu is a part. For the ethnography of Hai-shan, readers should consult Emily M. Ahern, *The Cult of the Dead in a Chinese Village* (Stanford, Calif., 1973); Margery Wolf, *The House of Lim* (New York, 1968) and *Women and the Family in Rural Taiwan* (Stanford, Calif., 1972); and Wolf & Huang. Chung-she is described in my own work (1972), and a number of sources provide information about Lung-tu, notably Myron L. Cohen, *House United, House Divided* (New York, 1976), and Burton Pasternak, "Chinese Tale-Telling Tombs," *Ethnology*, 12 (1973): 259-73, and "Seasons of Birth and Marriage in Two Chinese Localities," *Human Ecology*, 6 (1976): 299-323.

5. *Kokusei chosā kekka hyō* (Taipei, 1937).

6. Ahern, p. 12.

7. Chen Cheng-siang, *Taiwan: An Economic and Social Geography* (Taipei, 1963), 1: 105.

8. A number of statistical tests in this paper involve a comparison of proportions. When the total number of cases was small enough (30 or fewer cases), I used Fischer's Exact Tables. For larger numbers I used the formula

$$\frac{P_1 - P_2}{\sqrt{\dfrac{p_1 q_1}{N_1} + \dfrac{p_2 q_2}{N_2}}}$$

See Richard D. Remington and M. A. Schork, *Statistics with Applications to the Biological and Health Sciences* (New York, 1970), p. 218. Wherever I assert that a difference is significant, appropriate tests have indicated significance at the 5 percent confidence level or better (1 tail).

9. The differences between Lung-tu and Hai-shan were in all cases significant. Those between Lung-tu and Chung-she were significant only for males and females born 1886-1905.

10. The differences in proportion are significant in all cases but one: the contrast between Lung-tu and Chung-she females born 1911-20 was only marginally significant ($p < .10$), but in the same direction—the proportion of major marriages being higher in Lung-tu.

11. If we compare 1916-35 with 1936-45, chi-square = 7.81 ($p < .001$) for men and 13.80 ($p < .001$) for women (two tails).

12. Wolf & Huang, pp. 124-25.

13. For older widows the difference between proportions remarrying in Chung-she and Lung-tu was significant; between those for Chung-she and Hai-shan it was only marginally so ($p < .10$). Note, however, that the direction of the difference was the same for younger widows.

14. A two-by-two contrast between adult women who remarried and those who did not, controlling on the presence of one or more adult males, yielded a chi-square of 38.63 ($p < .001$; phi = .57). This result is reported with the permission of M. Numeroff.

15. Chi-square for men, 11.02 ($p < .001$); for women, 10.93 ($p < .001$).

16. Wolf & Huang, pp. 182-83.

17. Arthur P. Wolf, "Childhood Association, Sexual Attraction, and the Incest Taboo," *American Anthropologist*, 68 (1968): 883-98, and "Marriage and Adoption in Northern Taiwan," in R. J. Smith, ed., *Social Organization and the Application of Anthropology* (Ithaca, N.Y., 1974), pp. 128-60; Wolf & Huang, *Marriage and Adoption*.

18. Chi-square = 28.5 ($p < .001$).

19. Chi-square is 12.33 ($p < .001$) relative to total population, and 77.38 ($p < .001$) relative to unmarried daughters.

20. Wolf & Huang, p. 265.

Index

A-hou t'ing, Taiwan, 315, 317
Abortion, Japan, 78, 217f, 225, 227
Adoption, China, 339; frequency of, 277, 308, 330–31; and mortality, 293, 305–6, 331; and marriage, 301–3, 324, 328; and social stratification, 306–8
Adoption, Japan, 219–23, 226f; of bannermen, 72–73, 220; revocation of, 222f
Age at marriage, China, 22–28, 340; compared with Japan and Europe, 4f; and social stratification, 101–3, 297–98; by form of marriage, 325–26
Age at marriage, Europe, 1–2; compared with China and Japan, 5, 229
Age at marriage, Japan, 214–17, 227; compared with China and Europe, 4, 229; and social stratification, 125, 141–42, 223, 240–42
Ahern, Emily, 313
An-ch'iu hsien, Shantung, 171
Ario-shinden, 127–30

Baker, H. D. R., 81
Bankha, see Lungshan
Bannermen: definition of, 64–65; income of, 66, 76; family size of, 67–71, 77; proportion unmarried, 69; succession by yōshi, 72–73; adoption, 72–73, 220; lineage termination of, 73–75; mortality of, 78–79; mean age, 79–80
Barclay, George W., 155, 186, 189, 290
Birth control: China, 5, 7, 177–79, 181, 186; Japan, 217
Breast feeding, China, 7, 155, 192, 293
Bridewealth, China, 291–93, 310
Buck, John Lossing, 4, 7, 13, 61, 154–65 passim, 171, 176f, 186–89 passim

Cartier, Michel, 23
Chang, Hsin-yi, 162–63, 164
Chekiang, 15, 58, 81–83 passim, 97, 160, 162, 171, 173f
Chen, D. T., 175ff
Chia-yi t'ing, Taiwan, 315, 317
Chiang-yin hsien, Kiangsu, 175–77, 179
Chiao, Chi-ming, 155
Chinese Farm Survey: accuracy and interpretation of, 7, 13, 23, 31, 61, 155, 162–64, 177, 186–87, 195; demographic techniques, 13, 164–65, 186–89; unadjusted data, 157–59, 164; representativeness of, 160–62; data as adjusted by Princeton group, 165
Chungshe, Taiwan, 309–34 passim
Ch'üan-chou, Fukien, 282, 286
Coale, Ansley J., 7–8, 49, 143f, 155
Concubinage, see Polygyny
Czap, Peter, 3f

Dekasegi, see Migration, Japan
Demeny, Paul, 49
Divorce: Japan, 142–43, 230, 232, 240–42; China, 277, 324–25
Dixon, Ruth, 6
Dodd, John, 279, 286f
Dowry, China, 292–93, 310

Eta, see Minami Ōji

Family size and structure, China, 4; and social stratification, 8–9, 82, 288–89; and uxorilocal marriage, 317–21
Family size and structure, Europe, 2–5
Family size and structure, Japan, 196–97, 202–10; of bannermen, 67–71, 77; trans-

formation of, 126, 268–76; regulation of, 213–19, 227; and adoption, 221–22, 227; and social stratification, 253–55, 261–65 *passim*, 269–75 *passim*; and headship, 255–62

Famine, Japan, 200f, 231

Fertility: and marriage, 7, 156, 193–94, 216; and breast feeding, 192; and health, 192; and poverty, 192–93; advantages of moderate rate of, 194

—China, 7–8; and social stratification, 7, 11, 106–8, 181–84, 192–93; and nutrition and health, 7, 155–56, 185, 192; as estimated from genealogies, 28–45; gross reproduction rate, 59–60; and family organization, 154; Malthus, Montesquieu, and others on, 154–55; and breast feeding, 155, 192; Chinese Farm Survey on, 155–65, 177, 186–95; compared to European fertility, 156, 177, 190–91; Taiwan household registers on, 167–70, 189–91; and form of marriage, 169–70, 181, 184–85, 192, 326–28, 333–34; as reconstructed from 1980–81 interviews, 171–74, 191; and natural disasters, 175, 181; and 1931–35 Chiang-yin study, 175–77; and natural fertility rates, 179–80, 186, 188–89; traditional attitude toward, 185; various estimated rates, 189–93

—Japan: and social stratification, 123, 125, 144–47, 223–26, 242–43, 245–46; gross reproduction rate, 126, 150–51; in cities, 138–39, 150–52, 249; in villages, 210–12 *passim*, 223–26, 236f, 242–43; and span of childbearing, 217–19, 221; compared with Europe, 229, 243

Foot-binding, China, 167, 314

Freedman, Maurice, 81f, 108, 160

Frisch, Rose, 193

Fruin, Mark, 131

Fujito, 198–228 *passim*

Fukiage, 198–228 *passim*

Fukien, 90, 160, 171, 173f, 279

Genealogies, China: rules on composition of, 13–16, 28, 83–84, 339; demographic analysis of, 16–17, 28–30, 45–49, 58–61, 84–86

Genealogies, Japan: demographic analysis of, 63–65

Granet, Marcel, 11

Griffing, J. B., 181

Gross reproduction rate: China, 59–60; Japan, 126, 150–51

Hai-shan, Taiwan, 9, 166, 168–70, 178, 182–84, 189–92, 194, 308, 313–34 *passim*

Hajnal, John, 1–6 *passim*, 12, 22f

Hakka, 167, 313f

Hangchow, 11, 17, 83

Hanley, Susan, 3, 6, 131

Harrell, Stevan, 7

Hatamoto, see Bannermen

Hayami, Akira, 6, 9, 152–53, 198

Henry, Louis, 10, 179

Hokkien, 167, 308, 313f, 315

Hollingsworth, T. H., 18

Horikoshi, 274–76

Household registers, China, 167–68, 277–78, 281, 313

Household registers, Japan, 110ff, 115, 132–46 *passim*, 198, 229, 247; analysis of, 232–34, 250–53

Household size and structure, *see* Family size and structure

Hsiao-shan *hsien*, Chekiang, 15, 17, 23, 58, 81, 83, 90, 92

Hu, Hsien-chin, 81

Huang, Chieh-shan, 307

Ie, *see* Family size and structure, Japan

Ikeda, Toshio, 292

Infanticide: China, 5, 178f; Japan, 78, 126, 217f, 225, 227

Infant mortality, *see* Mortality

Kando-shinden, 138–44 *passim*, 146–50 *passim*, 242f

Kansu, 160, 162

Kiangsu, 171, 173–76 *passim*

Kubo, 247–76

Kwangtung, 58, 160

Lamson, Herbert D., 181

Li, Ching-han, 175

Li-ch'üan *hsien*, 171

Life expectancy: China, 58; Japan, 150, 238–40

Lineage organization, China, 18, 81–83, 86–92, 108–9

Liu, Ming-ch'uan, 279

Liu, Wen-tsai, 172

Lung-hai *hsien*, Fukien, 171

Lungshan, Taiwan, 278–92 *passim*

Lungtu, Taiwan, 313–34 *passim*

Major marriage, China: and fertility, 8, 169–70, 178–79, 314–15, 326–28; preference for, 290, 298–99; ritual enactment of, 291–92; and social stratification, 298–301, 323; frequency of by daughters vs. adopted daughters, 301–2; and divorce, 324–25; and intravillage unions, 325; and age of marriage, 325–26

Mallory, Walter H., 154f, 185

Malthus, Thomas, 1, 154, 156

Marriage, China: singulate mean age at, 4, 22–23; relative ages of partners, 23, 297–98, 340. *See also specific forms*: Major marriage; Minor marriage; Polygyny; Uxorilocal marriage

Marriage, Japan: regulation of, 213, 227

Migration, China, 17, 344

Migration, Japan, 16, 112–14; rural, 114–19, 127–31, 200–201, 249–50; destination of, 116, 118–19, 130; and social stratification, 116f; and mortality, 121–22; impact on population, 121–22, 132, 133–37; and age of marriage, 122–24; and fertility, 122–26; urban, 133–37, 249–50

Minami Ōji, 229–46; mortality rate, 235–40, 244f; life expectancy, 238–40; age of marriage, 240–42; divorce rate, 240–42; and fertility, 242–43, 245–46

Minor marriage, China, 290; frequency of, 169, 277, 314–15; and fertility, 169–70, 178–79, 181, 184–85, 192, 277, 326–28; ritual enactment of, 292–93; sexual attraction in, 293, 328; advantages and disadvantages of, 293, 331; and social stratification, 298–301, 306–8, 323; consummation of among planned unions, 304–5; and divorce, 324–25; and intravillage unions, 325; and age of marriage, 325–26

Montesquieu, 154f, 177

Morris, Dana, 5f

Mortality, China, 7, 340; in cities, 11; among married women, 28; male and female rates, 49; among children, 49, 189, 195, 331–32; temporal trend of, 49–58; effect of social disorder and natural disasters, 58; underreporting of, 188–89; among adopted daughters, 293, 305–6, 331

Mortality, Japan: among bannermen, 78–79; among children, 138, 225, 238; in cities, 150–52; in villages, 210–12 *passim*, 235–40, 244f; compared with Europe, 229, 240

Nakahara, 126f, 237–46 *passim*

Neolocal marriage, China, 289–90

Niremata, 127–30

Nishijima Minoru, 78

Nishijo, 110–32, 138–50 *passim*

Nishikata, 199–228 *passim*

Notestein, Frank W., 155, 157ff, 163–65, 176f, 187, 193

Numa, 199–228 *passim*

Okada, Yuzuru, 4

Parental authority, China, 6, 11–12

Pasternak, Burton, 8

Peking, 171–74 *passim*

Penrose, E. F., 154–55

Polygyny, China, 16, 20, 103–6, 339

Population growth, China, 7, 58–61, 82, 92–96, 195, 280; and social stratification, 82–83, 96–109

Population growth, Japan, 243–44; and migration, 121–22, 133–37, 235; urban, 133–37, 152–53, 248–49; rural, 198–99, 234–37; effect of famine, 200f, 234

Potter, Jack, 81

Premarital pregnancy, China, 293–94

Proportions marrying: Europe, 1–2; China, 7, 21–22, 296–97; Japan, 139–41, 145, 149–50, 214–16

Remarriage: China, 20–21, 319–21; Japan, 142f, 150, 240–41

Reproduction rate, *see* Gross reproduction rate

Sa, Sophie, 8–9

Samurai, *see* Bannermen

Sasaki, Yōichirō, 6, 9, 11

Sekiyama Naotaro, 78

Senglai, Taiwan, 280, 290f

Sex ratio: China, 173, 176, 290–91; Japan, 217, 220, 223–25

Shanghai, 4, 162, 172

Shansi, 4, 160

Shantung, 171–74 *passim*, 181

Shensi, 4, 160, 171–74 *passim*, 181

Shūmon-aratame-chō, Shūmon-ninbetsu-chō, see Household registers, Japan

Simpua, see Minor marriage

Singulate mean age at marriage, China, 4, 22–23

Smith, Robert, 4, 10, 196, 198

Smith, Thomas C., 5f, 126, 131, 198, 276

Social stratification, China: and fertility, 7, 11, 106–8, 181–84, 192–93; and marriage choice, 8–9, 280–81, 298–308, 323; and household size and structure, 9,

288–89; and lineage organization, 81–83; and population growth, 82–83, 96–109; and age at marriage, 101–3, 297–98; and age at birth of first son, 101–3; and polygyny, 103–6; and premarital pregnancy, 293–94; and relative age of partners, 297–98; and minor marriages, 304–5; and female adoption, 305–8

Social stratification, Japan: and migration, 116f; and fertility, 123, 125, 144–47, 223–26, 242–43, 245–46; and age at marriage, 125, 141–42, 223, 240–42; and proportion marrying, 145, 150; and divorce, 230; and mortality, 237–40 *passim*; and family size and structure, 253–55, 261–65 *passim*, 269–75 *passim*

Soochow, 11, 17
Staunton, Sir George, 154
Stoto, Michael A., 155
Suda Keizō, 138
Suzuki, Seiichiro, 291f, 295
Szechwan, 160, 171, 173f

Ta-yi *hsien*, Szechwan, 171
Taeuber, Irene B., 155, 161
Tai, Shih-kuang, 175
Tai-pei *t'ing*, Taiwan, 315, 317
Tainan *chou*, Taiwan, 331–32
Taipei *chou*, Taiwan, 331–32
Taipei City, Taiwan, 8–9, 277–308 *passim*
Taiping Rebellion, 58, 82, 172
Taiwan, 4, 9, 165–72, 178–85, 189–92, 277–308 *passim*, 309–34 *passim. See also individual localities by name*
Takayama, 133–53
Tatieh, Taiwan, 310–11
Tawney, H. D., 154, 185

Tennōji-mura, 247–76
Thompson, Warren S., 175ff
Toatotia:, 278–90 *passim*
Trussell, T. James, 143f, 155

Uxorilocal marriage, China, 18, 21, 84, 282, 289f; regional variation of, 8; and social stratification, 21, 298–301, 310, 323; and fertility, 169–70, 179, 184–85, 326–28, 333–34; ritual enactment of, 294; terms of, 294–95, 308; motives for, 295–96, 309–34 *passim*; frequency of by daughters vs. adopted daughters, 301–3; frequency of, 308–11, 314–17, 332–33; and demand for male labor, 311–23; and household composition, 317–21; and remarriage by widows, 319–21; stability of, 324–26; and age of marriage, 325–26, 333–34

Village economy, Japan, 200f, 230–31, 248
Virilocal marriage, China, 289f. *See also* Major marriage; Minor marriage

Westermarck, Edward, 277, 293
Widowhood, *see* Remarriage
Wolf, Arthur P., 5, 7ff, 166, 186–95 *passim*, 277, 293, 307f, 313, 317–32 *passim*
Wrigley, E. A., 132

Yamamura, Kozo, 6, 10
Yang, C. K., 81
Yangchou, 171f
Yenping, Taiwan, 278–90 *passim*
Yokouchi, 131, 242
Yuan, I-chin, 58

Zekke (lineage termination), 73–75